NORTHERN LIGHTS

NORTHERN LIGHTS

Exploring Canada's
Think Tank Landscape

DONALD E. ABELSON

McGill-Queen's University Press
Montreal & Kingston • London • Chicago

ISBN 978-0-7735-4763-6 (cloth)
ISBN 978-0-7735-4764-3 (paper)
ISBN 978-0-7735-9972-7 (ePDF)
ISBN 978-0-7735-9973-4 (ePUB)

Legal deposit third quarter 2016
Bibliothèque nationale du Québec

Printed in Canada on acid-free paper that is 100% ancient forest free
(100% post-consumer recycled), processed chlorine free

This book has been published with the help of a grant from the Canadian Federation
for the Humanities and Social Sciences, through the Awards to Scholarly Publications
Program, using funds provided by the Social Sciences and Humanities Research
Council of Canada. Funding has also been received from the J.B. Smallman
Publication Fund, Faculty of Social Science, University of Western Ontario.

McGill-Queen's University Press acknowledges the support of the Canada Council for
the Arts for our publishing program. We also acknowledge the financial support of the
Government of Canada through the Canada Book Fund for our publishing activities.

Library and Archives Canada Cataloguing in Publication

Abelson, Donald E., author
    Northern lights: exploring Canada's think tank landscape/Donald E. Abelson.

Includes bibliographical references and index.
Issued in print and electronic formats.
ISBN 978-0-7735-4763-6 (cloth). – ISBN 978-0-7735-4764-3 (paper). –
ISBN 978-0-7735-9972-7 (PDF). – ISBN 978-0-7735-9973-4 (ePUB)

    1. Research institutes – Canada. 2. Policy sciences – Canada. I. Title.

H97.A248 2016   320.6   C2016-902980-8
                                                  C2016-902981-6

This book was typeset by Marquis Interscript in 10.5/13 Sabon.

For my father, Alan D. Abelson,
who taught me to always swing for the fences

Contents

Tables and Figures ix

Acknowledgments xiii

Acronyms xvii

Introduction 3

1 What Is (and Is Not) a Think Tank? 14

2 Are All Think Tanks Alike? 37

3 How Has the Role of Think Tanks Changed? 66

4 What Do Think Tanks Do, and How Do They Do It? 82

5 With Whom Do Think Tanks Communicate? 105

6 In What Ways Are Canadian and American Think Tanks Similar? How Are They Different? 121

7 How Do Think Tanks Evaluate Their Impact, and Why Should We Be Skeptical? 140

8 Conclusion: Looking Back and Thinking Ahead: The Future of Canadian Think Tanks 158

9 Profiles of Canadian Think Tanks 166

APPENDICES

1 References to Selected Canadian Think Tanks in the National Media, 2000–2015 275

2   Appearances by Selected Canadian Think Tanks before
    Parliamentary Committees, 1999–2015   290

3   References to Selected Canadian Think Tanks in Parliament,
    1994–2015   306

    Notes   319

    Bibliography   343

    Index   363

Tables and Figures

TABLES

2.1   Profiles of selected Canadian think tanks – overview 46

2.2   Profiles of selected Canadian think tanks – contact information 49

A1.1   References to selected Canadian think tanks in the national media, 2000–2015 275

A1.2   References to selected Canadian think tanks in national newspapers, 2000–2015 279

A1.3   Comparison of annual budget to number of media references for selected Canadian think tanks, 2000–2015 288

A2.1   Appearances by selected Canadian think tanks before parliamentary committees, 1999–2008 290

A2.2   Appearances by selected Canadian think tanks before parliamentary committees, 2008–2015 292

A2.3   Appearances by selected Canadian think tanks before House of Commons committees, 1999–2008 294

A2.4   Appearances by selected Canadian think tanks before House of Commons committees, 2008–2015 297

A2.5   Appearances by selected Canadian think tanks before Senate committees, 1999–2008 300

A2.6   Appearances by selected Canadian think tanks before Senate committees, 2008–2015 303

A3.1   References to selected Canadian think tanks in the House of Commons, 1994–2008 307

A3.2   References to selected Canadian think tanks in the House of Commons, 2008–2015 311

A3.3   References to selected Canadian think tanks in the Senate,
        1994–2008   314

A3.4   References to selected Canadian think tanks in the Senate,
        2008–2015   317

FIGURES

A1.1   References to selected Canadian think tanks in the national
        media, 2000–2015   277

A1.2   References to selected Canadian think tanks in the national
        media (radio and television), 2000–2015   277

A1.3   References to selected Canadian think tanks in the national
        media (newspapers), 2000–2015   278

A1.4   References to selected Canadian think tanks in the *Globe
        and Mail*, 2000–2015   283

A1.5   References to selected Canadian think tanks in the *Toronto
        Star*, 2000–2015   283

A1.6   References to selected Canadian think tanks in the *National
        Post*, 2000–2015   284

A1.7   References to selected Canadian think tanks in the *Toronto
        Sun*, 2000–2015   284

A1.8   References to selected Canadian think tanks in the *Montreal
        Gazette*, 2000–2015   285

A1.9   References to selected Canadian think tanks in the *Vancouver
        Sun*, 2000–2015   285

A1.10   References to selected Canadian think tanks in the *Edmonton
        Journal*, 2000–2015   286

A1.11   References to selected Canadian think tanks in the *Ottawa
        Citizen*, 2000–2015   286

A1.12   References to selected Canadian think tanks in the *Halifax
        Daily News*, 2000–2015   287

A1.13   References to selected Canadian think tanks in the
        Charlottetown Guardian, 2000–2015   287

A1.14   Comparison of annual budget (millions of dollars) to number
        of media references for selected Canadian think tanks,
        2000–2015   289

A2.1   Appearances by selected Canadian think tanks before parlia-
        mentary committees, 1999–2008   291

A2.2   Appearances by selected Canadian think tanks before parlia-
        mentary committees, 2008–2015   293

A 2.3   Appearances by selected Canadian think tanks before House
         of Commons committees, 1999–2008   296

A 2.4   Appearances by selected Canadian think tanks before House
         of Commons committees, 2008–2015   299

A 2.5   Appearances by selected Canadian think tanks before Senate
         committees, 1999–2008   302

A 2.6   Appearances by selected Canadian think tanks before Senate
         committees, 2008–2015   305

A 3.1   References to selected Canadian think tanks in the House
         of Commons, 1994–2008   310

A 3.2   References to selected Canadian think tanks in the House
         of Commons, 2008–2015   313

A 3.3   References to selected Canadian think tanks in the Senate,
         1994–2008   316

A 3.4   References to selected Canadian think tanks in the Senate,
         2008–2015   318

Acknowledgments

Of all the words that fill the pages of this book, none are more important or meaningful to me than the ones penned below. In the course of researching and writing *Northern Lights*, I have benefitted greatly from the support, guidance, and wisdom of many people, and I hope that in the few paragraphs that follow, I can adequately express my gratitude. First and foremost, I would like to thank Philip Cercone, executive director of McGill-Queen's University Press, and his colleagues, for guiding my book through the publication process. Philip has been a strong and committed advocate of my work for many years, and I cannot thank him enough for all he has done to showcase my research. I would also like to thank Gillian Scobie for the superb job she did in copy-editing my manuscript and Anna Zuschlag for being so meticulous in preparing the index. I would also like to thank the anonymous reviewers for their thoughtful and insightful comments. Their efforts on my behalf are greatly appreciated. Any omissions or errors rest entirely with me.

The idea of writing a book on Canadian think tanks had been on my mind for many years, but it was not until the fall of 2014 that I sat down to draft this manuscript. As a visiting professor at Université Aix-Marseilles in Aix-en-Provence, and later at Sciences Po Lyon, I found the ideal environment in which to reflect on this important subject. Greeted every morning with the smell of freshly baked baguettes and piping hot café au lait, my creative juices began to flow. After spending several hours each day reflecting on why writing from France about Canadian think tanks made perfect sense to me, I found myself strolling along ancient cobblestone streets, listening to the beautiful sound and rhythm of church bells, and watching people engage in lively conversation at outdoor cafés. It did not take long for me to understand why so many people begin a new life in this beautiful part of the world. I am forever indebted to my colleagues in the south of France and in Lyon for inviting me to lecture at their welcoming and accommodating institutions and for encouraging me to immerse myself in their culture. I am also indebted to my French teachers at Ottawa's Nepean High School for insisting that I learn to conjugate verbs – a skill that certainly came in handy when I wanted to order dinner! Yet, despite being linguistically challenged, I still dream of the incredible selection of wines I was exposed to, and the heaping platters of fruit and cheese my colleagues insisted I consume. France will always hold a special place for me.

When I returned to Canada in time to embrace our beloved winter, I was able to rely on several talented research assistants at the University of Western Ontario. They include Jeremy Ladd, Michele Muller, Robyn Schwarz-Pimer, and Tom Cooke. Christine Wall of the Centre for American Studies was also tremendously helpful in formatting many of the tables in the appendices.

I would also like to thank Sonia Halpern for helping me gather information for several of the institutional profiles in the book. For years, Sonia, my significant other's twin sister, has asked me repeatedly if think tanks matter, a question inspired by an earlier book I wrote entitled, *Do Think Tanks Matter?* In response to her feeble attempt at humour, I can only say "Yes Sonia!!!! Think tanks matter!"

Over the years, I have been able to solicit the advice and expertise of several friends and colleagues at Western and at other universities in North America and Europe. I would like to thank Dan Abele, David Biette, Stephen Brooks, Mark Garnett, Charles Jones, Evert Lindquist, Inderjeet Parmar, Laura Stephenson, Martin Thunert, Isabelle Vagnoux, Richard Vernon, Kent Weaver, and Bob Young.

I have also been able to count on the love and support of my children, Rebecca and Seth. I must have done something right to deserve them – they are truly special people, and have made their dad so proud. In the course of working on this project, my thoughts often turned to the people who have been with me from the very beginning: my father, Alan, to whom this book is dedicated; my mother, Estelle, who was taken from us far too early; and my sisters, Lynn, Joan, and Karen. They will always play an integral role in my life, as will my closest friends, Susan and Adrian Hoad-Reddick and Mary and Ralph Germaine.

Before this manuscript could be completed, I lost a wonderful friend. A distinguished lawyer, Martin Marcus was among the finest and most decent people I have ever known. I met Martin and his wife Esther when

I first came to London in the early 1990s, and it did not take long for us to strike up a friendship. Along with his brothers Gerry and Terry, also good friends, Martin was a force to be reckoned with. With a shared passion for hockey and politics, we rarely ran out of things to talk about. Even in his final months, he never hesitated to ask how my book was progressing. When he could have been consumed with his health, he preferred to focus on what others were doing. I know he would have enjoyed seeing this book come to fruition and learning more about think tanks. I think of him often.

As I have said on many occasions to family and friends, I am so fortunate to be surrounded by people who are as concerned with my well-being as I am with theirs. But no one has been more invested in my happiness than Monda Halpern, a history professor at Western, and the person with whom I share my life. A gifted scholar, who recently published a fascinating book on a murder trial that took place in Ottawa during the early 1930s, Monda has endured more lectures, and edited more chapters on think tanks, than I can possibly count. And while any devoted and loving partner would request a reprieve from such an obsession, her support for me and for my work has never wavered. She means the world to me. I am truly blessed.

When I began writing about think tanks as a young and ambitious doctoral student at Queen's University in the mid-1980s, a member of the Political Studies Department did his utmost to dissuade me from pursuing this topic. Indeed, after failing to convince me that my time would be better spent conducting research on more traditional subjects such as political parties, interest groups, or the American presidency, he threw up his hands in frustration and proclaimed, "If you insist on writing about institutions that, at best, are of marginal importance to our discipline, I can guarantee two things: one, you will never get published, and two, you will never get hired." It was with these encouraging words that I began my exploration of think tanks, a group of eclectic and diverse organizations that fascinate me as much today as they did on that fateful afternoon when I was urged to follow a different path. It has been a remarkable journey.

Acronyms

AEI	American Enterprise Institute for Public Policy Research
AIMS	Atlantic Institute for Market Studies
APEC	Atlantic Provinces Economic Council
APFC	Asia Pacific Foundation of Canada
CBOC	Conference Board of Canada
CCF	Canadian Constitution Foundation
CCPA	Canadian Centre for Policy Alternatives
CCSD	Canadian Council on Social Development
CDFAI/CGAI	Canadian Defence and Foreign Affairs Institute/ Canadian Global Affairs Institute
CEIP	Carnegie Endowment for International Peace
CFR	Council on Foreign Relations
CIC	Canadian International Council
CIFAR	Canadian Institute for Advanced Research
CIGI	Centre for International Governance Innovation
CIIA	Canadian Institute of International Affairs
CISS	Canadian Institute of Strategic Studies
CPRN	Canadian Policy Research Networks, Inc.
CSE	Citizens for a Sound Economy Foundation
CSIS	Center for Strategic and International Studies
CSLS	Centre for the Study of Living Standards
CTF	Canadian Tax Foundation
CUI	Canadian Urban Institute
CWF	Canada West Foundation
ECC	Economic Council of Canada
FCPP	Frontier Centre for Public Policy

FPI	Foreign Policy Initiative
GDN	Global Development Network
IISD	International Institute for Sustainable Development
IOG	Institute on Governance
IPS	Institute for Policy Studies
IRPP	Institute for Research on Public Policy
MEI	Montreal Economic Institute
NPA	National Planning Association
NRA	National Rifle Association
NSI	North-South Institute
PNAC	Project for the New American Century
PPAC	Private Planning Association of Canada
PPF	Public Policy Forum
PRI	Policy Research Initiative
RIIA	Royal Institute of International Affairs
SCC	Science Council of Canada

NORTHERN LIGHTS

Introduction

The world of think tanks is, as I have discovered over the course of twenty-five years, complex, intriguing and, in many ways, perplexing. It is a world that continues to fascinate me. As a doctoral student in the Department of Political Studies at Queen's University in the mid-1980s, I stumbled across an article (later expanded into a book) on the rise of American think tanks, by cultural and social historian James A. Smith,[1] who would go on to write histories of the Brookings Institution and the Center for Strategic and International Studies (CSIS).[2] By the time I finished reading Smith's account of the evolution of American think tanks, I was hooked. Not only did the study of think tanks become the focus of my PhD thesis, but my heightened interest in these organizations would fuel my research program for the next several decades. Over the years, my preoccupation with understanding how think tanks generate and market ideas to shape public opinion and public policy has intensified. I have become equally consumed by the lengths to which they go to enhance their visibility in the political arena. The premium that several think tanks place on projecting and protecting a carefully constructed image of themselves to, among other things, secure more financial support, compels me to ask whether these organizations are more concerned about self-promotion than they are about helping policy-makers find solutions to complex policy problems.[3] At times, the answer seems obvious, but as is often the case with institutions that are competing for power and influence, the storyline is far more complicated.

Fortunately, others share my passion for making sense of these eclectic and incredibly diverse organizations. Recently, think tanks in Canada, the United States, and many other countries have become the focus of more intense media scrutiny. Much of this attention has been devoted to the sudden closure in 2014 of the North-South Institute (NSI),[4] Canada's premier international development policy shop which, over the years, had become highly respected in the global think tank community. Attention was also focused on Revenue Canada's audits of the Canadian Centre for Policy Alternatives (CCPA) and dozens of other not-for-profit organizations.[5] Other factors have also propelled think tanks into the spotlight: revelations about the intimate ties between the former Harper government and a cadre of conservative policy institutes;[6] and a fascinating exposé on the extent to which foreign governments fund several high-profile American think tanks,[7] including the Brookings Institution, the Center for Global Development, and the Center for Strategic and International Studies (CSIS).

Many journalists and scholars chronicle the behaviour of think tanks in North America, Europe, and other parts of the globe. The more they learn about these institutions and the strategies they employ to navigate their way through an increasingly crowded marketplace of ideas, the more they feel compelled to explain why think tanks have emerged as important and, at times, controversial participants in the political arena. The growing body of literature on think tanks in recent years shows that interest in this subject has risen dramatically and shows few signs of waning.[8] The study of think tanks has yet to attract the attention of interest groups, political parties, and political institutions, but, nonetheless, their relevance to how policy decisions are formulated and implemented is widely acknowledged.

What began as an inquiry by a small and dedicated group of investigative reporters, historians, political scientists, and sociologists in the 1970s and early 1980s into the role and function of a handful of think tanks in the United States, the United Kingdom, and other parts of Europe[9] has morphed into a rigorous field of research conducted by scholars around the globe. Although some academics remain convinced that the topic of think tanks is a niche that appeals only to a small target audience, the appetite for more credible and detailed information about these institutions is growing quickly.

Those who monitor think tanks and their ties to key stakeholders periodically feel obliged to justify, often at length, why these organizations warrant closer scrutiny. Yet, given the extent to which think tanks have made their presence felt in virtually every country and region of the world, it no longer seems necessary to construct a convincing argument as to why they should be examined. At the risk of stating the obvious, ideas have consequences. Those that are poorly conceived and carelessly executed can and often do lead to horrific outcomes. As institutions that are in the business of generating ideas and disseminating them to those in positions of power, think tanks – what they do, the interests they represent, from foreign governments to philanthropic foundations and corporate donors, and how they frame the discourse around policy issues – matter.

One of the main questions driving this study is not whether think tanks are relevant to the study of public policy, but, more pressingly, why think tanks have become increasingly visible and active players in the policy-making process, and under what conditions they have been able to affect policy change. Notwithstanding the musings and protestations of some conspiracy theorists that small groups of think tanks rule the universe, it is important to keep in mind, however, that think tanks do not make public policy – elected officials do. Although those who labour at think tanks often claim to serve the public interest, they do not represent parliamentary ridings or congressional districts, nor do their names appear on ballots. They are policy experts who interact regularly with policy-makers and the public for the purpose of shaping public opinion and public policy in ways that satisfy their institutional interests and those of their generous benefactors. In these and other ways that will be investigated in the pages to follow, think tanks have made their presence felt. As several scholars have demonstrated in exploring the close ties between a handful of think tanks and the administrations of Margaret Thatcher and Ronald Reagan, key policy recommendations promoted by these institutes not only helped influence the direction of world markets, but, indeed, also inspired historic ideological and political revolutions.[10] Some studies have even gone so far as to suggest that some think tanks have not only provided the rationale for recent military incursions around the globe, they have, in fact, planted the seeds for regional conflicts.

As this study will reveal, think tanks leave more than an indelible mark on domestic and foreign policy; they engage in policy research and political advocacy (which at times appears to spill over into lobbying), by relying on a multiplicity of governmental and non-governmental channels, and by tapping into an extensive and intricate web of policy networks and social movements. Think tanks, like advertising firms that market products and services, have also become adept at convincing potential target audiences of the benefits they can derive by seeking their expertise. By doing so, not only are they able to compete more efficiently in the marketplace of ideas, they are also able to help rewrite the rules that those seeking to shape the political destiny of the nation live by.

Over the past two decades, an impressive array of books, edited collections, and refereed journal articles have examined think tanks and their contributions to policy discussions.[11] This body of work stands in stark contrast to the sparse literature that existed on this topic in the first half of the twentieth century when today's most celebrated think tanks in North America and Europe were in their infancy. As a result of this burgeoning scholarship, and the willingness of scholars to share their research findings with students, courses on how these organizations contribute to, and, at times, undermine, the public interest, are now being offered at universities in North America, Europe, and Asia. But students and other members of the attentive public need not enroll in university lectures and seminars to learn about think tanks, although I would encourage them to do so. In addition to the scholarly literature, they can find information about the activities of these institutions in directories, electronic newsletters, bulletins, and countless blogs. A plethora of material is also available on the websites of thousands of think tanks which, understandably, rely increasingly on social media such as Twitter and Facebook to reach some of their followers. Rest assured, on any given day, print, broadcast, and digital media are reporting on the latest developments in the think tank world.

What happens inside the think tank community has not only become a preoccupation of those peering in. Indeed, think tanks and other research organizations and independent scholars who study public policy possess a strong intellectual curiosity about and healthy obsession with the think tank phenomenon. For instance, at the Shanghai Academy of Social Science, the largest think tank in China, an entire research unit has been established to study think tanks. China's Nanjing University, one of the country's most venerable universities, has also developed a keen interest in think tanks. It is home to the Center for Chinese Think Tank Studies and Evaluation, and is in the process of translating several North American studies of think tanks. And in Paris, the activities of dozens of think tanks are monitored by L'Observatoire des think tanks (OTT), an organization founded in 2006 primarily to study the development of think tanks in Europe. Under the guidance of its founder, Sélim Allili, OTT sponsors conferences and workshops, and undertakes comparative research on these organizations. Interest in the global reach of think tanks does not end there. For over fifteen years, the Global Development Network (GDN),[12] a program launched by the World Bank, has fostered strong ties among think tanks throughout the international community. Along similar lines, the Ottawa-based International

Development Research Centre (IDRC), supported by the Canadian government and several private donors, including the Bill and Melinda Gates Foundation, has committed over US$100 million to the Think Tank Initiative (TTI), a project established in 2008 to augment the work of think tanks in developing countries.

To provide even more coverage of think tank activities, the Canadian embassy in Washington, DC distributes *Think Tank Watch*, a newsletter that tracks research projects, lectures, seminars, and other events taking place in the US think tank community. Additional information about think tanks in the US and beyond is meticulously gathered and circulated by Transparify, an organization created in January 2014 to encourage think tanks to be more transparent about the corporations, philanthropic foundations, and private individuals who support their work. Transparify founders Hans Gutbrod and Till Bruckner, two scholars with considerable experience in the NGO community, recognized, as did many of their colleagues, how reluctant think tanks were to share data about funding. To encourage think tanks to be more forthcoming, Gutbrod, Bruckner, and their dedicated team of researchers established a rating system for over 150 think tank websites. Think tanks that posted this information in an easily accessible and comprehensive manner could be assigned a score of 5, the highest rating possible. Not surprisingly, institutions that were less willing to publicize this information received a much lower score. For the most part, think tanks have responded favourably to Transparify's rating project and their funding has become more transparent. Other enterprising scholars, including Enrique Mendizabal, have taken it upon themselves to further educate the attentive public about think tanks. Mendizabal's website, *On Think Tanks*, is a virtual smorgasbord of information on the international think tank scene.

Recognizing the importance of tracking the emergence of think tanks worldwide, James McGann, a recognized expert on the subject, began publishing *The Global Go To Think Tanks Index Report* in 2006.[13] Released with much fanfare, the report, published under the auspices of the Think Tanks and Civil Societies Program at the University of Pennsylvania, has created a database of close to 7,000 think tanks. According to its 2014 findings, while there has been tremendous growth in the global think tank population over the past two decades, about half of these institutes can be found in North America and in Europe. With an estimated 1,830 think tanks, the United States boasts the largest number of these organizations. Canada is credited with having a roster of close to 100 think tanks, a figure that, when subjected to closer scrutiny, might be inflated.[14] Nonetheless, as in the United States and in much of the advanced and developing world, the number of Canada's think tanks, particularly those that concentrate on domestic policy, is increasing. However, in light of the recent closure of the North-South Institute (2014), the Pearson Peacekeeping Centre (2013), and other NGOs with expertise in international affairs, a much less optimistic picture has been painted by some of the country's foreign policy and international development think tanks. Although the foreign policy think tank community in Canada has indeed suffered significant losses,[15] it has not disappeared or been rendered irrelevant. The research conducted on various aspects of world affairs at the Centre for International Governance Innovation (CIGI), the Canadian International Council (CIC) (formerly the Canadian Institute of International Affairs), and the Canadian Global Affairs Institute (formerly the Canadian Defence and Foreign Affairs Institute [CDFAI]) plays an important role in informing and educating policy-makers and the public about key foreign policy issues. There are also plenty of research centres at some of the country's most distinguished universities that are engaged in important international affairs projects. In short, while it is entirely understandable why scholars mourn the loss of several think tanks that made invaluable contributions to the study of Canada's role in world affairs, we can ill afford to overlook those institutions that continue to make their voices heard.

Even with the monumental changes that have taken place in the Canadian think tank community, it is hardly a revelation that top-tier think tanks in the United States continue to attract the lion's share of media and scholarly attention. After all, few countries enjoy the kinds of resources available to scholars and administrators at the RAND Corporation, the Brookings Institution, the Carnegie Endowment for International Peace, the Council on Foreign Relations, the Heritage Foundation, and the American Enterprise Institute. These institutes have both the financial capital and the political connections at their disposal to engage policy-makers at all levels of government.[16] Moreover, in light of the widely held perception and prevailing narrative that elite US think tanks wield enormous influence, a perception that undoubtedly helps to explain why several philanthropic foundations, corporations, and foreign governments bestow millions of dollars on them, it is not surprising that think tanks from Bangladesh to Beijing attempt to emulate the success of their US counterparts. Still, as this study will demonstrate, think tanks do not necessarily require multimillion dollar budgets and dozens of staff to attract the attention and interest of the public, policy-makers, and other key stakeholders. Think tanks with deep pockets can enhance their exposure in ways that less affluent institutions cannot. However, what matters more is how think tanks position themselves in a congested marketplace. When funds are in short supply, institutions engaged in strategic research and analysis must re-evaluate their priorities and determine the most effective ways to affect policy change.

The purpose of this book is not to add to the already substantial body of material on think tanks in the United States, although frequent references to the American think tank experience will be made, but to enrich our understanding of public policy institutes in Canada. I will explain what Canadian think tanks do, the challenges and opportunities they face, the various ways they have distinguished themselves from their counterparts in the United States, the United Kingdom, and European countries, and the channels on which they depend to further entrench themselves in the policy-making process.

The second and perhaps more important reason for writing this book is to help bring the Canadian think tank community to life. Although the Canadian think tank landscape is often referred to in the comparative literature on public policy institutes, it has not received the more detailed treatment it so richly deserves. Canadians may be familiar with the work of the Fraser Institute, the C.D. Howe Institute, and the Centre for International Governance Innovation (CIGI), three organizations that generate considerable media coverage. And depending on the policy question being addressed, Canadians might have had some exposure to the Institute for Research on Public Policy, the Mowat Centre, and the Canada West Foundation. But how many Canadians are aware of the contributions made by the Ottawa-based Caledon Institute to social welfare policy, or the research conducted by the Vanier Institute of the Family on how to address major challenges experienced by middle-class Canadians? From the Atlantic provinces to the shores of British Columbia, think tanks have become an important part of the Canadian policy landscape. Unfortunately, most scholars studying think tanks in North America have become so captivated by the high-profile American policy institutes, they have neglected to consider how, and to what extent, think tanks in Canada have contributed to Canadian policy development. By focusing on Canadian policy institutes, this study is intended to help fill this void.

This study also provides readers with far more than they can learn from skimming the pages of think tank directories and guides. The information contained in these and similar publications, though useful, quickly becomes outdated and, even more troubling, does little to further our understanding of how these organizations participate in policy-making. This is to be expected, given that the purpose of think tank directories and guides is to present institutional data, not to analyze why some organizations are more successful in achieving their goals. After flipping through these volumes, we might be better informed about when particular think tanks were established and about some of the resources on which they can draw, but that is usually where the story begins and ends.

In this study, readers will learn both about the world of think tanks, and how the Canadian think tank community has evolved since the first decades of the twentieth century. By becoming acquainted with two dozen of the most significant think tanks in the country, we will acquire a far greater appreciation for what these institutions do, the areas of research in which they have developed expertise, and the various ways they become involved in the policy-making process. We will then be able to engage in a more thoughtful and nuanced discussion about think tanks and their contribution to public policy.

The question of how much or how little impact think tanks have on public opinion and public policy continues to generate intense discussion and debate in the academic and policy-making worlds, and it should. If policy experts at various think tanks are equipped and positioned to influence the direction of public policy, as I and others have claimed, then it is important to understand how these organizations participate in policy discussions with the public, with policy-makers, and with other key stakeholders. As noted, it is equally important to understand what motivates think tanks to become more entrenched in the policy-making process: is it a desire to help government think its way through complex policy issues by providing elected officials and public servants with sound and impartial policy expertise? Or do think tanks, like interest groups, lobbyists, and social movements, place a higher premium on influencing policy decisions by embracing various forms of political advocacy? In other words, are think tanks genuinely committed to advancing the public interest, as directors of several leading institutes proclaim, or are they and the individuals who guide them preoccupied with pursuing narrowly defined self-interests?

It would be refreshing for think tanks to acknowledge that they have several priorities, which include helping policy-makers and leaders of industry navigate their way around the complex world of policy-making. But directors of think tanks usually steer clear of discussions about what motivates their organizations' behaviour. When they do outline their goals, they usually present them in the most altruistic light. Flip through any of the countless annual reports and promotional materials prepared by think tanks and they all convey a similar message: our goal is to encourage discussion and debate on key domestic and foreign policy issues – to enlighten, inform, and educate. Ironically, while these and other familiar messages are usually couched within the context of the public interest, think tanks also do not hesitate to highlight their accomplishments.

Accountable to multiple masters who keep a close watch on how the policy institutes they support perform compared with their competitors, think tanks have a vested interest in showcasing the nature and extent of their influence. For those entrusted with overseeing think tanks, the question of how and when their institutes have left their fingerprints on public policy is rather simple, though it requires two vastly different responses. Indeed, think tank directors and presidents have become increasingly adept at both answering and sidestepping questions about how much influence their organizations have to affect policy change. In a sense, those representing think tanks wear different faces for the faces they meet. When speaking to scholars and journalists familiar with the work of their organization, think tank leaders can be rather circumspect. "Measuring or assessing the influence of think tanks is notoriously difficult," a president of one of Canada's leading think tanks conceded recently. However, when addressing potential donors about the activities of their organization, or presenting annual reports to their board of trustees, those at the helm can ill afford to be modest. This is why think tanks pay close attention to various performance indicators (a euphemism for indicators of influence) such as media exposure, followers on social media, number of publications downloaded from their institute's website, and the frequency with which their staff testifies before parliamentary committees, indicators that are often highlighted and summarized in organizational reports.

The narrative that think tank directors construct around the work of their institute is clear. Visibility means influence and influence means dollars. But does it? As we will discuss, there are think tanks in Canada, such as the Ottawa-based Caledon Institute, that maintain a modest public profile but still manage to convey their ideas effectively to their target audiences. Conversely, there are think tanks that regularly find themselves in the spotlight, but are barely noticeable when the details of important legislation are being crafted. The reality is that how much or how little influence these organizations wield over the direction and content of public policy is buried somewhere in these conflicting messages, an observation often lost in the several annual rankings of think tanks. Our challenge is to discover where the truth lies.

Studying think tanks in Canada, or, for that matter, in any country, can be a frustrating undertaking, in large part because the think tank community, as has been noted, is incredibly diverse. Think tanks have vastly different resources at their disposal, pursue a range of mandates, concentrate on either narrow or broad fields of interest, and do not necessarily assign the same priority to engaging in research, advocacy, and other activities. This helps to explain why scholars have had so much difficulty agreeing on how to define and classify these organizations. Strangely enough, it is because think tanks are very different in some ways and so similar in others that make them such interesting subjects to explore.

At its core, then, this book is a primer to introduce readers to the world of Canadian think tanks. You don't need a degree in history, political science, and/or sociology to discern why it is important to understand what think tanks do and how they do it. Although much of the material contained in this book is drawn from the academic literature on non-governmental organizations (NGOs), my aim is not to create more clutter and confusion about think tanks. Nor is it to construct a grand theory that will explain how all think tanks behave in every imaginable political system. My goal is more modest – to clarify and illuminate the nature of these organizations, and how they both seek to shape and are shaped by the political environment they inhabit.

To be clear, I am neither an admirer nor an ardent critic of think tanks, and it is not my intention to condone or condemn their behaviour. What I strive to be is an honest, astute, and, I hope, enlightened observer. For more than two decades, I have tracked the activities of think tanks in the United States and Canada, and have tried to provide a fair and accurate assessment of the contribution these organizations make to public policy. In the process, I have come to the realization that while think tanks can and often do exercise considerable influence during different stages of the policy cycle, in many instances their presence in the court of public opinion and in the corridors of political power is barely noticeable, an observation also shared by some think tank insiders. In the words of Leslie Gelb, former president of the New York–based Council on Foreign Relations, it is difficult to make bold claims about the impact of think tanks since their "influence is highly episodic, arbitrary and difficult to predict."[17] Although think tanks might not wield as much influence as they pretend or hope to, the unique position they occupy at the intersection of the academic and policy-making worlds has given them many opportunities to extend their reach into government, into civil society, and into public debates that shape what and how the public think about issues ranging from retirement savings to ways to increase the Canadian military.

Over the course of my career, I have devoted the bulk of my time and energy to studying the American think tank experience, a topic that continues to have a hold over me. However, when I speak about American think tanks to predominantly Canadian audiences, someone invariably raises their hand to ask, "What about think tanks in Canada? What do they do?" After years of responding to these and similar questions about Canadian think tanks, I decided it was time to put my thoughts down on paper.

This book is divided into two main parts. The first consists of eight chapters that address the most commonly asked questions I have fielded, about think tanks more generally, and about Canadian think tanks more specifically. We will then turn our attention to profiling two dozen of Canada's leading public policy institutes. In this section, readers will learn about the wide-ranging expertise available in the Canadian think tank community, and will acquire a better understanding of the history, activities, and research programs underway at think tanks such as the Fraser Institute, the Centre for International Governance Innovation (CIGI), the Canada West Foundation, and the Institute for Research on Public Policy.

As you will discover in the pages that follow, Canada is home to a diverse and burgeoning think tank population that deserves to be recognized. While think tanks with expertise in defence and foreign policy are, regrettably, in short supply, those with a focus on domestic policy are becoming plentiful, and, might I add, scrutinized. The history of think tanks in Canada is an important one which, until recently, has been largely neglected. By delving into the role of think tanks, and the position they have forged on the Canadian political landscape, we will gain far more insight into a group of organizations that can and often do compel the public and policy-makers to reconsider how they think about key policy issues. Such an inquiry will also contribute to our understanding of who shapes public policy, a conversation that the public rarely requires encouragement to join.

1

What Is (and Is Not) a Think Tank?

KATE: Put the kids on, let me talk to someone.

TOM: Oh, well, they're studying, and it's the tri, trigo, trig stuff we aren't all that good at, and they've formed a study group. It's like a little *Think Tank* thing (Italics added) ... I ... I'd just hate to break that up.

(Dialogue from the 2003 film *Cheaper by the Dozen,*
starring Steve Martin [Tom] and Bonnie Hunt [Kate].)

Type "think tank" into Google, Yahoo, or any one of the other search engines, and within a matter of seconds, you can access upwards of 100 million hits, in no particular order of importance or relevance. Given the frequency with which these two words appear together in print, broadcast, and electronic media, it would be reasonable to conclude that the journalists, scholars, pundits, and bloggers who refer to think tanks with great regularity usually agree on what these organizations are, and have a shared understanding of the various functions they perform. However, after skimming through dozens of articles and blogs in which references to these entities are made, it becomes abundantly clear that there is no consensus on the meaning of this ambiguous and elusive term.

According to the *Compact Oxford English Dictionary,* a think tank is defined simply as "a group of experts providing advice and ideas on specific political or economic problems."[1] *Webster's New World Dictionary* provides slightly more detail, noting that a think tank is "a group or center organized, as by a government or business, to do intensive research and problem solving."[2] Unfortunately, these definitions are both too broad and too narrow to advance our understanding of what criteria organizations need to satisfy to qualify as a think tank, and raise more questions than answers: Is there a minimum number of experts required to constitute a think tank? In some cases, it takes only one person to operate a small business. Could an enterprising individual conceivably run a think tank? If not, could two or three experts collaborating on a project legitimately claim to have formed one? In fact, do people even have to be recognized as certified experts in their field to be part of a think tank? To put it another way, we know that most university professors holding tenure or tenure-track positions have a PhD, but what kinds of credentials do policy experts require to work at a think tank? Considering that many former policy-makers without advanced degrees take up residence at these institutions, it is not entirely clear what kind of background is best suited for this kind of work. Can people interested in providing policy solutions to domestic and international problems simply declare themselves to be think tankers and hang up a shingle outside their office, as many so-called "therapists" with questionable credentials have done? And even if a regulatory body, akin to the Royal College of Physicians and Surgeons or the Law Society of Upper Canada, were established to develop and administer guidelines about which organizations qualify as think tanks, and what kind of educational and/or professional experience their employees require, another question remains: Is a physical structure required to house such a body, or can a think tank exist in cyberspace? What about an administrative hierarchy, staff, budget, and research program? Are they necessary to form a think tank? Do think tanks require donors? If they do, what, if any, role should they play in shaping an institution's research agenda? At a time when many think tanks are competing for limited resources, which often come with strings attached, can they ever really claim to be independent? How should experts at think tanks share their advice? Is advocacy an appropriate way to convey information and ideas, or should think tanks rely solely on their publications and other research outlets to make their views known? And to whom should ideas about political, economic, or other national and international problems be communicated? Must think tanks be created by government or business, or can they also be established by universities and policy entrepreneurs? And so the endless questions about "what is a think tank" begin.

Although considerably more information about these and other issues have been addressed in several recent encyclopaedic entries,[3] confusion over how to identify and classify these organizations persists. On 20 September 2014, the *National Post* published an article by Jen Gerson in which she profiled five "think tanks" that apparently "hold so much sway over policy."[4] Included on the *Post's* think-tank lineup card is the Manning Centre for Building Democracy, an organization founded by Preston Manning to help educate and train future leaders of the conservative movement. The Calgary-based centre does this by offering internships and sponsoring various educational programs, seminars, and workshops. It also participates in several partisan-related activities and events which are listed on the centre's website. What it doesn't do is conduct research and analysis, a function performed by the Manning Foundation. As we will discuss, the Manning Foundation is a registered charity that more closely resembles a think tank, and as such, it, rather than the Manning Centre, should have appeared on Gerson's list. But in all fairness, in the absence of an agreed-upon definition, it is surprising these mistakes don't happen more often. Nonetheless, Gerson is correct in her general description of these organizations. A think tank can refer to a place and a thing, or both at times. It may invoke images of scholars working at traditional research institutions such as the Conference Board of Canada, the Brookings Institution, and the RAND Corporation, or to an experiment that exists in virtual reality. As we will discover in this chapter, determining what a think tank is and is not is far more difficult than meets the eye.

After years of tinkering with a definition that could conceivably account for the entire range and diversity of the think tank population, many scholars have simply thrown up their hands in frustration. Others, including James McGann, a long-time student of think tanks, have sidestepped academic exchanges about which organizations deserve to be labelled as such, conceding, "I know one when I see one."[5] But without pointing to certain attributes that think tanks are expected to possess, even the most discerning observers can lose sight of whether some organizations qualify as think tanks. Nowhere is this more evident than in the *Global Go To Think Tanks Index Report*,[6] an annual study published by McGann and his team of associates in the Think Tanks and Civil Societies Program at the University of Pennsylvania. For example, in the 2012 edition of the report, several academic associations, including the Canadian Economics Association, and more than a handful of university-based teaching and training centres and institutes, are included in their database of close to 7,000 think tanks. If the generation and dissemination of research are among the defining characteristics of think tanks, as several scholars who study these institutions maintain,[7] then the types of organizations mentioned above should not be classified as think tanks. After all, academic associations, and centres and institutes devoted to overseeing undergraduate and graduate programs, by their very nature, do not usually place a premium on research. It is simply not part of their mandate, nor do they necessarily have the resources to support this function. To avoid what has become an ad hoc, arbitrary, and impressionistic approach to identifying think tanks, it is important to understand what makes these institutions unique. Doing so will allow us to distinguish between think tanks and other actors, such as the interest and pressure groups, advocacy organizations, government relations firms, and lobbyists that grace the political landscape.

A useful place to begin this inquiry is by understanding the origins of the term "think tank." When the term "think tank" was coined in the United States during the Second World War, it was not intended to describe institutions that were created for policy experts to reflect on, and to write about, domestic and foreign policy. Nor, for that matter, was it meant to single out organizations engaged in marketing and promoting ideas. The term actually signified a location – a secure room or environment – where military planners could meet to discuss wartime strategy.[8] However, the meaning of think tanks, and what they could offer, would soon change. For example, in the immediate postwar years, journalists periodically described the Santa Monica, California–based RAND Corporation, a research institution that began its life as a project to assist the US Air Force, as one of America's leading defence and security affairs think tanks.[9] Think tanks attracted attention at this time, not because they provided a venue where policy experts could exchange ideas in secrecy but because they were institutions ostensibly committed to helping government think its way through complex policy problems. By making policy recommendations to members of the Executive, Congress, and the bureaucracy, think tanks suddenly assumed a new role.

The RAND Corporation may have helped to popularize the term "think tank," but it was certainly not the first research institution to emerge in the United States or abroad. Some scholars think that London's Fabian Society (1884), home to several prominent intellectuals, including Sidney and Beatrice Webb, co-founders of the London School of Economics, deserves to be recognized as one of the oldest think tanks in the Western world. But the roots of modern-day think tanks go back even further. A half-century before the Fabian Society opened its doors, the first Duke of Wellington established the Royal United Services Institute for Defence and Security Studies (1831). Moreover, in the latter half of the nineteenth century, settlement houses like London's Toynbee Hall (1884) and Chicago's Hull House (1889) carried out many of the functions of contemporary think tanks.[10] Several other think tanks in the United States and in Canada predate RAND. These include the Russell Sage Foundation

(1907), the Carnegie Endowment for International Peace (1910), the Institute for Government Research (1916; which became the Brookings Institution in 1927), the Hoover Institution (1919), the Canadian Council on Social Development (1920), the Council on Foreign Relations (1921); the Institute of Pacific Relations (1925), the Canadian Institute of International Affairs (1928, now known as the Canadian International Council), and the American Enterprise Institute (1943).[11]

But it is important to return to the issue at hand: What is and is not a think tank? To explain what a think tank is, we need to focus on five defining characteristics that differentiate them. We will then be able to more effectively distinguish between think tanks and other organizations – lobbyists, interest groups, government relations firms – that compete for visibility and influence in the policy-making community.

FIVE WAYS TO IDENTIFY A THINK TANK

1. Registered Charity vs Non-profit Organization

Most think tanks in Canada and in the United States qualify as non-profit organizations, a broad category that includes thousands of groups, ranging from minor hockey associations to alcohol and drug rehabilitation centres. But in most cases, stand-alone (as opposed to university-based) think tanks, such as the Fraser Institute[12] and the C.D. Howe Institute, are also registered as charities under the Income Tax Act (ITA).[13] Two notable exceptions are the Manning Centre for Building Democracy, founded in Calgary in 2005 by Preston Manning, former leader of the Reform Party of Canada, and the Broadbent Institute, established in Ottawa in 2011 by Ed Broadbent, the former long-time leader of the federal NDP. Both decided not to apply for charitable status so they could have the freedom to engage in a wide range of political activities, a subject that we will return to shortly.

A charitable organization designation is reserved for religious institutions, and for organizations committed to education, to the alleviation of poverty, and/or to improving conditions in local communities (by providing animal shelters, libraries, volunteer fire departments, etc.) According to the Canada Revenue Agency (CRA), think tanks are eligible for charitable status because they are committed to education through policy research. Along with universities, colleges, and other educational institutions, think tanks are tax-exempt (as are non-profit organizations that are not registered as charities) and are permitted to issue official donation receipts, a critically important benefit that allows them to attract and retain donor support.[14] Similar benefits are available to think tanks in the United States that are registered as charitable organizations under section 501(c)(3) of the Internal Revenue Code.[15]

Despite the many advantages afforded to think tanks as charities, not all institutions engaged in research and analysis desire this status. Indeed, several think tanks in North America, Europe, and in many other regions of the globe have been established as profit-seeking enterprises, providing strategic advice, risk assessment, and a host of other services to clients. One example is the Kansas-based Profit Think Tank, which, as its name suggests, is a for-profit corporation that advises businesses on how to strengthen profit margins. However, these and similar private-sector-based organizations represent only a fraction of the think tank population across the globe.[16] In addition to the obvious perks of running a successful operation, the decision not to assume charitable status can be motivated by other, more practical, concerns. As will be discussed shortly, charities in Canada are prohibited from engaging in certain types of political activities – they cannot, for instance, "openly [support] one political party over another," and can only devote up to 10 per cent of their resources to what the CRA considers political activities, a concession some non-profit organizations are not prepared to make.[17] The statutory authority of the CRA to determine what constitutes "political activities," along with allegations that the Harper government pressured the agency to place a chokehold around left-leaning think tanks, has fuelled controversy over the audits of these charities. Growing concern among think tanks in the United States over IRS audits may also explain why, in recent years, several US think tanks, including the Heritage Foundation and the Center for American Progress, have established 501(c)(4) sister organizations. Unlike 501(c)(3), think tanks that must avoid participating in certain partisan activities, those with a 501(c)(4) designation have the freedom to participate in more political advocacy,[18] a subject we will return to in the next section. Nonetheless, most think tanks have decided to join the thousands of other tax-exempt, non-profit, and charitable organizations competing for space in what has become an increasingly crowded marketplace of ideas.

When the think tank community in the United States and other Western countries was in its infancy in the early decades of the twentieth century, the main goal of the directors and scholars of policy institutes seemed to be to produce high-quality research that would attract the attention of policy-makers. As long as think tanks generated solid work, they appeared confident that they could help elected officials make more informed decisions about key domestic and foreign policies. The needs of government, not upstaging their competitors, was their priority. However, as the think tank community began to grow in the postwar era, and as hundreds of interest groups, unions, and other organizations with their own political agendas began to surface, think tanks had to decide what role they would embrace, and what strategies they would employ to enhance their stature in the policy-making community. Some think tanks saw their role as unambiguous: to produce scientifically sound and rigorous research. If they did this, there appeared little need to develop a multifaceted strategy to capture the attention of policy-makers. After all, if the research was credible, why would policy-makers not listen? However, as we will discuss in more detail in later chapters, by the early 1970s, when the Heritage Foundation opened its doors, the roles and strategies of think tanks began to change. Rather than simply producing a steady stream of studies that might or might not capture the interest of members of Congress and the Executive, think tanks became more proactive. Indeed, recognizing that a larger number of think tanks and interest groups were competing to be heard in the aftermath of the civil rights era and the Vietnam War, think tanks no longer felt they could remain disinterested observers of the political process. Instead, they began to employ several of the marketing strategies popularized by corporate America to become more active participants in the ideas industry.

2. Non-partisan or Non-ideological?

When think tanks apply for charitable status under the detailed guidelines of the Canada Revenue Agency, they are well aware that if their application is successful, they will be bound by a legal obligation to remain non-partisan.[19] This does not mean that, as a registered charity, think tanks must refrain from expressing their views or opinions on policy issues. After all, this is one of the main reasons why think tanks are established – to engage in research and analysis, and to share their findings with multiple audiences. Moreover, adhering to the strictures of non-partisanship does not prevent think tanks from embracing a particular ideology.[20] Even the most casual observers of Canadian politics would have little difficulty distinguishing between the conservative leanings of the Fraser Institute and the more liberal/progressive policy views espoused by the Canadian Centre for Policy Alternatives. To be clear, as charitable, non-partisan institutions, think tanks do not forfeit their democratic right to free expression. Regardless of where they situate themselves along the ideological spectrum, think tanks can and do analyze policy problems through particular political lenses, and rely on various channels to convey their ideas. Some scholars may question whether the research produced by some think tanks adheres to rigorous scientific standards, but one thing is certain. When it comes to commenting on important policy issues, think tanks rarely strive for neutrality. Indeed, as we will reveal later in this study, both think tanks and the policy research they generate have become increasingly politicized in recent years.

What then does non-partisanship actually entail? In theory, satisfying the CRA's conditions of non-partisanship may not seem onerous. They simply mean that think tanks are prohibited from engaging in specific kinds of political activities – activities that could allow these organizations to advance their interests and those of their benefactors at the expense of the public interest. If think tanks were permitted to engage in direct political activity, their very purpose as research organizations would be significantly transformed, and they would join the ranks of other interest groups and advocacy bodies in short order. From the government's standpoint, charities should be established to promote the public good, not private interests. Therefore, to CRA officials, it stands to reason that in exchange for charitable status, think tanks are expected to assign a much higher priority to thinking about what is good for the nation, rather than concentrating on how their ties to elected officials and political parties could be used to exercise influence over policy.[21] However, as noted, the CRA's authority to determine what constitutes political activity, and whether charitable organizations have devoted more than 10 per cent of their resources to such endeavours, has generated considerable concern, confusion, and resentment among think tanks and other charitable organizations, including Oxfam, that have found themselves under the agency's microscope. What might work in theory has, for all intents and purposes, hit several practical and formidable roadblocks. Recognizing this, think tanks have to weigh the costs and benefits of registering as a charitable organization against the potential advantages of participating as full-fledged partisan institutions in the policy-making process. In most cases, think tanks choose the former. In an ideal world, the limited restrictions placed by the Canadian government on the political activities of think tanks would do little, if anything, to prevent these institutions from pursuing their core mission to shape public opinion and public policy. They could still devote unlimited resources to research, spend countless hours building coalitions and networks, expand their fundraising activities,[22] and, in the process, market themselves as effective policy advocates. To be blunt, think tanks in Canada should not have to engage in partisan activities to advance their agenda, nor should they require preferential treatment by elected officials to find their voice in the marketplace of ideas. As long as they are generating thoughtful, rigorous, and well-reasoned research, and are not being subjected to political pressure by government agencies to censure themselves, think tanks should be able to establish themselves as important players in the policy-making process. But is this too much to ask? If the CRA sticks to its stated policy on charitable organizations, think tanks could have their cake and eat it too.

According to CRA's Policy Statement CPS-022,[23] a document that, among other things, outlines what constitutes acceptable and unacceptable political activities for charities: "A charity cannot be established with the aim of furthering or opposing the interests of a political party, elected representative, or candidate for public office. Also, a charity cannot be formed to retain, oppose, or change the law, policy, or decision of any level of government in Canada or a foreign country."

As charitable organizations, think tanks are not permitted to publicly support or oppose candidates running for office; however, they are still entitled to allocate "a small amount of resources for political activity."[24] Moreover, while think tanks are prohibited from engaging in partisan political activity, they are allowed

> to make the public aware of [their] position on an issue, provided:
> 1 [they do] explicitly connect [their] views to any political party or candidate for public office;
> 2 the issue is connected to its purposes;
> 3 its views are based on a well-reasoned position;
> 4 public awareness campaigns do not become the charity's primary activity.[25]

In its policy statement, CRA provides more information on *prohibited* political activities. These include:

- supporting an election candidate in the charity's newsletter,
- distributing leaflets highlighting the lack of government support for charity goals,

- arranging and sponsoring meals for campaign organizers of a political party, and
- inviting select election candidates to speak at separate events.

Despite these and other restrictions on political activities, "a charity that devotes substantially all of its resources to charitable activities may carry on political activities within the allowable limits."[26] Assuming that charities adhere to the spending guidelines set out by CRA, the following political activities are deemed *permissible*:

- buying a newspaper advertisement to pressure government;
- organizing a march to, or a rally on, Parliament Hill;
- organizing a conference to support the charity's opinion;
- hiring a communications specialist to arrange a media campaign; and
- using a mail campaign to urge supporters to contact the government.

The problem is that CRA's list of prohibited and permissible political activities can either be broadly interpreted or narrowly defined. However, what is apparent is that the federal government is trying, albeit not always successfully, to differentiate between partisan involvement and policy engagement. In the case of think tanks, the message contained in this policy document is clear. As research institutions, think tanks are expected to generate and disseminate ideas on a range of policy issues to various target audiences, including policy-makers. They can invite elected officials and their staff to conferences, workshops, and seminars, provide them with their publications, and even offer solicited and unsolicited policy advice. Nothing in the CRA guidelines prevents think tanks from communicating to members of Parliament, Cabinet, or the bureaucracy, but they can't support or oppose candidates running for office, contribute funds to political parties, or devote a disproportionate amount of institutional resources to changing a law, policy, or decision made by the Canadian government or a foreign state. Unlike Germany, where a select group of think tanks is funded by the state to serve the research needs of political parties,[27] in Canada efforts have, ostensibly, been undertaken by the government to establish boundaries between members of political parties and think tanks. While some Canadian political parties might prefer to have stronger ties with particular think tanks, there is not always an incentive for policy institutes to compromise their "independence" by tying their political fortunes to the government, the official opposition, or other parties represented in Parliament.

In the United States, even stronger and more precise language has been incorporated in the Internal Revenue Code to restrict the partisan or political activities of think tanks. According to Section 501(c)(3), all tax-exempt organizations, which include most American think tanks, must adhere to the following:

> All section 501(c)(3) organizations are absolutely prohibited from directly or indirectly participating in, or intervening in, any political campaign on behalf of (or in opposition to) any candidate for elective public office. Contributions to political campaign funds or public statements of position (verbal or written) made on behalf of the organization in favor of or in opposition to any candidate for public office clearly violate the prohibition against political campaign activity. Violating this prohibition may result in denial or revocation of tax-exempt status and the imposition of certain excise taxes.[28]

Under section 501(c)(3), US think tanks are also subject to restrictions on the kinds of legislative activities in which they can take part, activities euphemistically referred to as lobbying. However, unlike the IRS's unambiguous stance on partisanship, its position on lobbying leaves plenty of room for interpretation. Rather than declaring, for example, that lobbying members of Congress is prohibited, the IRS simply states that think tanks cannot devote "a substantial part of [their] activities [to] influencing legislation."[29] Think tanks can participate in some lobbying efforts on Capitol Hill, in state legislatures, and in other legislative bodies, but, in the words of the IRS, must be careful not to become involved in "too much lobbying activity."[30] But, when it comes to engaging members of the executive, judicial, and administrative arms of government in discussions about public policy – institutions that do not have the power to make laws – think tanks are granted far more latitude. In sum, the IRS appears more concerned about restricting the activities of think tanks during campaigns than with the actions they undertake once officials have assumed office. After all, when elections have been decided, think tanks must distinguish themselves from thousands of other organizations attempting to shape public opinion and public policy. Placing greater limits on the partisan activities of think tanks may allow the US government to establish a more level playing field for non-profit organizations, but even these restrictions have not discouraged think tanks from trying to make their presence felt.

Think tanks in the United States and Canada[31] understand the implications of having their charitable status revoked (they would no longer be authorized to issue donation receipts), but they also appreciate the importance of maintaining and strengthening ties to policy-makers at all levels of government. In the United States, think tanks have found a creative and innovative solution to avoid the heavy hand of the IRS. When members of their staff are invited to participate in presidential and congressional campaigns, they simply request a leave of absence. This way, policy experts from some of the nation's top think tanks can exchange ideas with candidates without their employer having to fear reprisals from the IRS. No official position is taken by a think tank on any candidate, thus satisfying the conditions set out in section 501(c)(3). However, at the same time, their employees are able to help shape the political platforms of candidates running for public office. Moreover, even if a think tank does not endorse or oppose a candidate, researchers in their organizations are still encouraged to write position papers and policy blueprints that make recommendations on how the US government should address key domestic and foreign policy issues. Some of these documents, including the Heritage Foundation's tome, *Mandate for Leadership*, in 1980, played a critical role in helping future administrations chart a course for America.[32]

American think tanks have thought of other ways to insulate themselves, and the political and legislative activities in which they participate, from the IRS. In 2005, the Center for American Progress (CAP) established its sister organization, the Center for American Progress Action Fund, to engage in more lobbying. Since then, other think tanks, including the Heritage Foundation, have followed suit. In 2010, Heritage founded Heritage Action for America, also known as Heritage Action, so that it could expand its legislative activities. Considered social welfare organizations under section 501(c)(4) of the Internal Revenue Code, these non-profit, tax-exempt entities are able to treat lobbying as their primary activity. Among other things, this designation provides them with far more opportunities to participate in legislative matters than those afforded to their 501(c)(3) counterparts.

It bears repeating that non-partisanship should not be confused with ideological neutrality – the two are not synonymous. All think tanks, regardless of their mission and mandate, produce policy papers that, in some way, reflect a particular ideology. That some think tanks are more liberal or conservative than others does not cause alarm in policy-making circles in Canada and in the United States, as long as these institutions respect the limits imposed on partisan activities. However, interestingly enough, although policy-makers do not appear overly concerned about the increased politicization of think tanks, scholars who study think tanks have serious reservations about the desire of these organizations to assign a higher priority to political advocacy than to policy research. Whether this has resulted in a fundamental transformation, or simply a reorientation in the traditional role of think tanks has yet to be determined. What is clear, though, is that in recent years, think tanks have given considerable thought, and devoted extra resources, to marketing their ideas.[33]

3. Policy Research vs Political Advocacy

Nothing is more salient for think tanks than the emphasis they place on generating and disseminating timely and relevant policy research. Indeed, without a *sustained* commitment to analyzing and dissecting various domestic and/or foreign policies, organizations cannot legitimately claim to be think tanks, nor should they be regarded as such. After all, conducting research is at the very heart of what think tanks do. Or is it?

When Andrew Carnegie, Robert Brookings, Herbert Hoover, and other leading philanthropists of the progressive era established the American think tanks that bear their names, their intention was to fund institutions where the best and brightest minds in the country could congregate to help government think its way through complex policy problems.[34] In return, think tanks created conditions that made it possible for experts to engage in long-term strategic thinking, a luxury rarely afforded to policy analysts in government consumed by the daily machinations of politics. Attracting accomplished scholars from various academic disciplines provided early-twentieth-century think tanks with credibility and legitimacy, but it was the quality of research these institutions produced that made policy-makers take notice.[35] Research that adhered to rigorous scientific standards became the hallmark of these early-twentieth-century think tanks, such as the Brookings Institution and the Carnegie Endowment for International Peace. Think tanks were committed to developing well-reasoned ideas and policy options deeply rooted in the social sciences and humanities. In time, that allowed them to influence policy. Although research remains a priority for most think tanks in Canada, the United States, and beyond, it is not necessarily *the* priority. Indeed, for think tank directors, the resources devoted to research must be weighed against the benefits of pursuing other institutional activities, including marketing, networking, and promotion.

By portraying themselves as policy research institutes dedicated to producing independent and scientific research, think tanks hope to strike a responsive chord with the public and with policy-makers looking for new and creative solutions to pressing policy problems. However, unlike many think tanks established during the early decades of the twentieth century, contemporary public policy institutes typically regard research as a means to an end, not as an end in itself. Producing high-quality research may create opportunities for think tanks to generate more exposure and notoriety, but to achieve long-term policy influence they can ill afford to place all of their eggs in one basket. Instead, think tanks prefer to rely on diverse channels to realize their goals. Put simply, maintaining a steady stream of publications may help think tanks create the impression that they are relying on their expertise and knowledge to serve the public interest, but what matters even more to them is determining how to most effectively market their ideas. We will return to this subject shortly.

Along with gauging how important research is compared with other institutional priorities, several other factors influence the type of research programs think tanks elect to undertake. Of course, the size of an institute's budget will dictate the number of researchers that can be employed and the kind of research that is produced. For example, given the high cost of conducting surveys, particularly for studies requiring the assistance of prominent polling companies, think tanks may shy away from some quantitative research projects. Even Statistics Canada, which has far more resources at its disposal than any domestic-policy think tank in the country, has had to scale back its research due to budget cutbacks. Still, most think tanks in Canada publish policy briefs, position papers, technical reports, and newsletters, all of which are available electronically and in print. Some think tanks, including the Montreal-based Institute for Research on Public Policy, also publish opinion magazines and monographs.

Funding plays an important role as well when it comes to determining geographic areas of specialization. For instance, with limited funding, some think tanks may decide to focus primarily on local and national issues, rather than on international concerns. Despite the ease with which information about global events can be accessed through digital technology, it is not a substitute for having people on the ground observing first-hand what is taking place. Lack of funding may help to explain why there are so few think tanks in Canada with expertise in defence and security matters.[36]

But for most think tanks, these issues are only half the battle. What keeps think tank directors up at night is figuring out how best to communicate their research findings to key stakeholders. As the marketplace of ideas becomes increasingly crowded, think tanks have devoted more of their time, energy, and resources to thinking about political advocacy. Although they generally view advocacy as an important and necessary component of their work, to some observers[37] advocacy has evolved into an unhealthy obsession that has undermined the integrity and quality of the research produced by policy institutes. If this is indeed the case, how do think tanks strike a balance between policy research and political advocacy, assuming they are interested in doing so, and why do they regard both functions as critical to their success?

A detailed response to these and other questions about the emergence of advocacy think tanks will be provided in the following chapters, but for now it is sufficient to briefly discuss the concept of political advocacy. The term *political advocacy* is neither new, nor unique to think tanks. In fact, for years, political scientists have investigated advocacy groups, advocacy coalitions, and advocacy networks to better understand how individuals and organizations mobilize resources to support or oppose various public policies. But in the context of how think tanks set their priorities, this concept has taken on a slightly different meaning. Although it can and often does refer to efforts by think tanks to stake out and defend positions on particular issues, it can also be understood as a strategy, orientation, or posture. The desire of think tanks to become more advocacy-oriented is closely linked to the success of the conservative Heritage Foundation, based in Washington, DC, and the generations of policy institutes it has influenced.

When congressional aides Paul Weyrich and Edwin Feulner established Heritage in 1973 to counter the influence of the more liberal Brookings Institution, they realized how important it was for think tanks to combine policy research with aggressive marketing, the hallmark of advocacy think tanks.[38] Armed with a PhD from the University of Edinburgh and an MBA from the Wharton School of Business, Feulner, with his colleagues, transformed political advocacy into a fine art. By the time Ronald Reagan was elected president in November 1980, Heritage had made great strides in changing the complexion of the think tank community by developing a range of strategies to convey ideas to policy-makers and to other stakeholders clearly and accessibly. Feulner's focus on providing "quick response policy research" – research that was concise, timely, and relevant – became a winning formula at Heritage, an organization that President-elect Reagan affectionately referred to as "the feisty new kid on the block."[39]

It did not take long for other think tanks in the United States to take notice of Heritage's recipe for success, and within a matter of years, several, including the Center for American Progress, had embraced the "Heritage model."[40] Heritage's impact on changing the orientation of think tanks has extended far beyond America's shores. Both the Fraser Institute in Vancouver, which opened its doors less than a year after Heritage, and the Adam Smith Institute in London, were among the first non-US-based think tanks to realize that the key to achieving policy influence could be found in Heritage's playbook.[41] Heritage's institutional priorities, based largely on the organization's commitment to political advocacy, has been contagious. In virtually every region of the globe, think tanks have tried to emulate the strategies employed by Heritage. Not surprisingly, as advocacy think tanks have increased in popularity in recent decades, and as policy-makers and their staff have begun to rely more heavily on the kinds of concise analyses of domestic and foreign policy issues these think tanks produce, scholars have expressed concern about how this has marginalized social science research at leading universities.[42] Their misgivings are warranted, particularly since policy-makers are more inclined to base their decisions on publications that provide little more than an overview of key policy issues instead of on detailed studies being generated by the professoriate. While this realization may cause further anxiety in academic circles, it is welcome news to think tanks that have clearly decided to become more advocacy-oriented.

In viewing the annual reports of think tanks, it is easy to discern how much of an investment policy institutes have made in policy research and political advocacy – pie charts disclose these and other kinds of expenditures. And, in some instances, think tanks devote as much, if not more, funds to advocacy-related activities as they do to producing research.[43] But before we draw any conclusions from how think tanks allocate their resources, it is important to keep a few things in mind.

While there is no doubt that think tanks continue to spend considerable time, energy, and money on political advocacy, this does not necessarily mean that they have abdicated their core mission. In fact, it could be argued that by aggressively marketing their research findings, think tanks have simply tried to bring their ideas to life. Advocacy takes different forms, and is played out on different stages, and although often cloaked in mystery, it simply involves promoting a particular vision or set of beliefs to various audiences. By participating in advocacy-related activities, think tanks are no less noble or virtuous than their competitors who assign a higher priority to research. Indeed, all think tanks immerse themselves in research and advocacy; what distinguishes them is how much emphasis they place on each. Advocacy think tanks are often portrayed as sinister and self-interested organizations determined to leave an indelible mark on public policy. While they readily admit that they are committed to promoting a particular agenda, there is nothing nefarious about sharing and promoting ideas, even those that could conceivably undermine the public interest. After all, it is the responsibility of policy-makers and the public to decide if there is any merit to the recommendations presented by think tanks and other organizations seeking to effect policy change. Ultimately, the fate of think tanks rests in the hands of those responsible for drafting, approving, and implementing public policy. Even though think tanks might do everything possible to educate, inform, and advocate for a particular policy initiative, they do not, as noted in the introduction, make public policy; rather, they try to shape it in ways that satisfy their principles and beliefs. In the process, they must weigh ideas against interests, an all too familiar tension that shadows think tanks as they tiptoe through ideological and political battlefields.

4. *Ideas and Interests*

By now, readers will have gathered that when scholars study think tanks, they often focus on the ideas these organizations generate. Without ideas to share and exchange with policy-makers and other stakeholders, think tanks would cease to exist. Ideas are their stock in trade, defining who they are and what they do. This is why think tanks are often described as idea brokers or peddlers that compete in the marketplace of ideas.[44] But, over time, as think tanks cultivate a set of ideas, they also attract various target audiences interested in their policy prescriptions. The result is a confluence of ideas and interests – the fourth identifiable characteristic of think tanks. What does this mean? At the risk of getting ahead of ourselves, it means that the ideas think tanks propose, ranging from how to reduce spending in our health care system to how to reform the Canadian military, will naturally find either support or opposition among different constituencies. The question then becomes, what is more important to think tanks, ideas or interests? The short answer is both.

For think tanks to achieve even a modicum of policy influence, their ideas must gain traction. Although they do not claim to speak on behalf of any particular constituency, think tanks do require the support of key stakeholders. In addition to satisfying the concerns of their principal benefactors, think tanks need to consider how the public, policy-makers, journalists, business leaders, and other opinion-makers will react to their policy prescriptions. Ideally, the ideas think tanks propose will align perfectly with the interests they are targeting. However, in most cases, this does not happen. As a result, directors of think tanks must strike a balance between promoting ideas that advance the core mission of their institute without alienating the very individuals and organizations upon which they have come to depend.

As with political parties that constantly soften or harden their platform to broaden their base of support, think tanks often find themselves massaging their message about various domestic and foreign policies to generate greater visibility and influence. Granted, unlike those seeking public office, think tanks do not have to concern themselves with appeasing voters in a particular riding. Still, in order to attract and retain the support of donors, and to establish strong ties to those in positions of power, think tanks must be engaged in the political process. Among other things, this requires careful planning, a strategic allocation of resources, a talented stable of experts, and a sophisticated and nuanced understanding of the policy-making process.[45] Unlike some non-profit organizations that are content to achieve short-term political success, think tanks, and the individuals and foundations that support them, are not consumed with winning particular battles but with declaring victory in the war of ideas. Influencing how the public and policy-makers approach key policy issues is a long-term investment that think tanks and their backers are only too willing to make.

There is no magic formula for achieving a balance between ideas and interests, but there is no doubt that both figure prominently in determining how think tanks position themselves on the political landscape. They are the key ingredients that think tanks have to work with in producing what for them is their raison d'être – influencing public opinion and public policy.

5. Shaping Public Opinion and Public Policy

Interest groups, political parties, advocacy coalitions, and a host of other non-governmental, governmental, and for-profit organizations are committed to shaping public opinion and public policy, but few have the capacity to engage the public and policy-makers as effectively and systematically as think tanks. By bridging the academic and policy-making worlds, think tanks, and the experts who populate them, occupy a unique space from which to share and exchange ideas on a host of pressing policy matters, drawing on their expertise and political connections to become entrenched in the policy-making process.

The importance think tanks assign to marketing themselves as research institutions with established expertise in various policy fields cannot be emphasized enough. With expertise comes credibility, or so think tanks claim, a currency they can and have used to earn the trust of the public, policy-makers, and other stakeholders. However, it is an intangible factor – their ability to predict what domestic and foreign policies will dominate the political agenda in the weeks, months, and years to come, and their capacity to provide timely and relevant advice that is ultimately responsible for allowing think tanks to distinguish themselves from other players in the political arena. While think tanks vary enormously in size, resources, areas of specialization, and ideological orientation, they share a common desire to leave a significant mark on public policy. To do this, they rely on multiple channels to shape the public discourse around policy issues, and to extend their reach into important policy circles, a subject that will be explored in considerable detail in chapter 4.

Scholars have yet to resolve the question of how much of an impact think tanks have in influencing public opinion and the policy decisions of elected officials. But before we can tackle this and other related issues, it is important to bring this discussion to a close by explaining what a think tank is not. Having outlined, in some detail, what can be considered the five identifiable or defining characteristics of think tanks, we will now differentiate think tanks and other organizations that seek to influence public policy. As think tanks have become more invested in political advocacy, it is not surprising that they are frequently mistaken for interest groups and lobbyists. Yet, as noted throughout this chapter, there are some fundamental differences.

WHAT IS NOT A THINK TANK?

Think tanks are in the business of generating and disseminating ideas; interest groups are formed to pressure government to adopt legislation that supports their mandate, and/or to oppose initiatives that undermine it; and lobbyists and lobbying firms seek to influence elected officials in ways that satisfy the interests of their clients. On the surface, the key differences between these organizations are clear, but in reality, the lines between them have become increasingly blurred.

Some of the confusion around what is and is not a think tank stems from the various ways in which these institutions immerse themselves in the policy-making process. Think tanks, like interest groups, rely on both public and private channels to convey their ideas to policy-makers and to the public. They

- organize speakers' series, conferences, seminars, and workshops;
- use social media to keep followers up to date on their most recent projects;
- give interviews to the print, broadcast, and electronic media;
- encourage their researchers to testify before legislative committees; and
- circulate newsletters, policy briefs, blogs, and other publications that are accessible to diverse audiences.

In short, much of what think tanks do resembles the types of activities undertaken by interest groups. Still, there are some notable differences.

First, while policy experts at think tanks conduct research on issues that are often directly relevant to the work of some interest groups, their objective is not to represent the concerns of any particular constituency. Think tanks do not claim to speak for victims of drunk driving, as Mothers Against Drunk Driving (MADD), a highly vocal and organized interest group, does, nor do they launch aggressive lobbying campaigns in the halls and offices of Parliament to convince MPs to listen to their concerns about international trade agreements, as the Alliance of Manufacturers & Exporters Canada does with great regularity. Morever, as noted, unlike interest groups and the political action committees (PACs), and the super PACs with whom they interact, think tanks do not publicly support or oppose candidates running for office, or donate funds to political campaigns and/or to the war chests of political parties. As discussed, in exchange for charitable status, they are prohibited from participating in these and related activities. Neither do think tanks become involved in mass demonstrations and protests, circulate petitions, engage in letter writing campaigns that target members of the executive and the legislature, monitor and publicize the voting records of legislators, or publicly align themselves with other organized interests. These are tactics commonly employed by interest groups.

However, to establish greater credibility and legitimacy, interest groups have followed the lead of think tanks by expanding their research activities. For instance, several environmental interest groups in Canada and in the United States, including the Sierra Club, Greenpeace, and Friends of the Earth, have developed expertise in environmental law, a subject that attracted considerable interest during the North American Free Trade Agreement (NAFTA) negotiations.[46] As interest groups devote more resources to strengthening their research profile, and as think tanks become increasingly invested in political advocacy, the likelihood that the latter will be mistaken for the former will undoubtedly increase.

The confusion over what is and is not a think tank becomes murkier when we introduce lobbyists and lobbying firms into the equation. If scholars agreed that think tanks simply think and lobbyists lobby, there would be little need to engage in further discussion. But the reality is that think tanks do more than think; they rely on various strategies to convey their ideas to policy-makers. As part of their ongoing efforts to shape public opinion and public policy, experts from think tanks meet regularly with elected and appointed officials and their staff at all levels and in all branches of government. Some American think tanks also maintain liaison offices with the US Senate and the US House of Representatives so they can monitor the daily workings of Congress more closely.[47] Staff from think tanks discuss various policy issues with government officials over drinks; invite them to participate in think-tank-sponsored conferences, workshops, and seminars, including sessions organized to educate incoming members of Congress about pressing domestic and foreign policy concerns; and provide officials with the expertise they need to navigate their way through complex policy problems. In exchange for large donations, some American think tanks, including the Atlantic Council, the Center for Global Development, the Brookings Institution, and the Heritage Foundation will also make arrangements for individuals representing foreign governments and private sector interests at home and abroad to meet and interact with top US government officials. In these and other ways, think tanks help to facilitate the access of donors to government officials.

If lobbying, as defined by the Lobbying Act in Canada,[48] and by the Lobbying Disclosure Act in the United States,[49] refers to actions taken by lobbyists on behalf of their clients to influence the decisions of elected officials, is it reasonable to conclude from our brief discussion above that think tanks engage in lobbying? Although think tanks were ostensibly created to advance a set of guiding principles enshrined in their mandate or mission statement, increasingly they are being portrayed as hired guns for various domestic and foreign clients who are looking to them to achieve particular policy outcomes. Put simply, many of the activities in which think tanks take part are very similar, if not identical, to those pursued by lobbyists. The difference is that, as charitable organizations, think tanks may only devote a limited amount of time and resources to lobbying. Unlike professional lobbyists, who are paid handsomely to influence policy-makers, lobbying constitutes only one of the many functions think tanks perform. Yet, by some accounts, think tanks are beginning to pay far more attention to this lucrative aspect of their work. At the very least, the relationship between think tanks and lobbyists is becoming even more incestuous. As investigative journalists .Brooke Williams and Ken Silverstein recently revealed,[50] dozens of think tank scholars working at high-profile American think tanks also manage their own lobbying firms. Although moonlighting as a lobbyist might not be considered illegal, it raises serious ethical and conflict-of-interest issues about the nature and degree of interaction between think tank staffers and policy-makers. Moreover, in a recent exposé, Williams and two of her colleagues documented the formal agreements that several foreign governments have brokered with prominent Washington-based think tanks to lobby on behalf of their interests.[51] Their research will undoubtedly attract the attention of the IRS and will once again call into question the priorities of think tanks. The story has already attracted the attention of several members of Congress, including Representative Jackie Speier (D-CA) who, shortly after the report about foreign government funding of think tanks was released, submitted a proposal that would require all think tank scholars testifying before Congress to disclose their sources of funding. The proposal won immediate bipartisan endorsement and was passed into law on 5 January 2015.[52]

It is not surprising that policy experts who work at think tanks inside the Beltway are attracted to the world of lobbying. In fact, before they take up residence at one of the many think tanks in or around Washington, several of them have spent years on Capitol Hill, in the White House, and/or in the bureaucracy. Along with this experience, policy experts at think tanks usually possess an intimate knowledge of the inner workings of government, and have strong connections to those in positions of power. With this background, becoming a lobbyist makes perfect sense,

and it explains why think tank staffers looking to embark on a new
career path often find gainful employment with lobbying companies, law
firms, and government relations firms that assist clients as they manoeuvre their way through the policy-making process.

Once again, though, it is important to point out that lobbying and
government relations firms do not masquerade as think tanks. For
example, Hillwatch, Global Public Affairs, and Policy Concepts represent a handful of government relations companies in Canada that offer
a wide range of services to clients, including advising them on how various bills in Parliament could affect their financial interests. While these
and similar organizations have expertise in advocacy and communications, they rarely distinguish themselves as leaders in policy research.

In this chapter, we have discovered that determining what a think tank
is and is not is anything but straightforward. To remedy this, I have outlined five defining characteristics to allow us to distinguish think tanks
from the other organizations with which they are often compared. We
can now discuss how think tanks differ from each other.

2

Are All Think Tanks Alike?

In the previous chapter, we devoted considerable attention to explaining the differences between think tanks, interest groups, lobbying, and government relations firms, and other organizations that compete among themselves and each other to influence public policy. Armed with a deeper appreciation for what a think tank is and isn't, the next step is to determine the best way to distinguish one from another. Although think tanks share a common desire to influence public opinion and public policy, and rely on similar tactics to achieve their goals, no two are exactly alike.

Think tanks in Canada, in the United States, and throughout the globe vary enormously in their size, mandate or mission, financial resources, areas of specialization, ideology, and the quality and quantity of the research they generate. They also differ dramatically in the priority they place on policy research and political advocacy, a subject that we will return to below. While these and other traits help scholars to classify think tanks according to specific criteria, it is also important to consider how these institutions are governed, the niche they are attempting to fill, and the extent to which policy experts engaged in research at various think tanks exercise control over the projects they pursue. Moreover, in the process of identifying the types of think tanks that populate the policy research community, it is useful to differentiate those that resemble traditional academic departments from those that have embraced the corporate culture and hierarchical management structure found in many Fortune 500 companies. How think tanks are organized and the way in which they make decisions about policy research and advocacy have a profound impact on how these organizations manage themselves and the stakeholders with whom they interact.[1]

According to the 2008 *Global Go To Think Tanks Index Report*, there were 5,465 think tanks worldwide.[2] Six years later, the authors of the highly publicized study maintained that this number had grown to 6,618.[3] While these figures might be exaggerated,[4] there is little doubt that in virtually every region of the globe, think tanks are on the rise. Not surprisingly, as their numbers grow, they are becoming increasingly diverse. This explains in part why scholars in the field have constructed typologies to identify and document the kinds of think tanks that have taken root in recent decades.[5]

Less than twenty years ago, think tanks tended to fall into one of three categories: policy research institutions that placed a premium on generating rigorous policy research; government contractors or specialists, think tanks that were largely funded by government to undertake research for different government departments and agencies; and advocacy think tanks, known for their ability and preference for combining policy research with aggressive marketing. Think tanks were soon divided into even more categories, and scholars have continued their search for the newest breed of think tank. Among the most notable additions in recent years has been the "think-and-do tank," organizations committed to transforming ideas into action. For instance, some think tanks marketing themselves along these lines have taken credit for helping local communities improve their transportation and energy infrastructure. In a handful of cases, think tanks that embrace a more hands-on approach to problem solving have invested considerable resources working with rival political factions in less developed countries to create a consensus on emerging policy issues.[6]

The purpose of this chapter is not to construct a detailed narrative on the benefits and drawbacks of classifying think tanks, nor is it to chronicle the origin of several hundred think tanks that have been established since the turn of the twentieth century. Rather, my goal is to demonstrate the diversity of think tanks in Canada and in the United States by focusing on four important and distinct periods of their development and evolution: 1900–46, 1947–70, 1971–89, and 1990–2015. The chapter begins by setting out a typology of think tanks that can be employed to describe the different types of policy institutes in the two countries. Although not without its limitations, it is useful in identifying the major types of think tanks that are often associated with the four time periods outlined above: universities without students, government contractors/ specialists, and advocacy think tanks.

CLASSIFYING THINK TANKS IN CANADA AND THE UNITED STATES

Along with designing various typologies to account for the diversity of policy institutes, several scholars have also attempted to identify the key motivations and institutional traits associated with each generation, or wave, of think tanks. For example, in his 1989 article examining the evolution of American think tanks,[7] Kent Weaver, a professor of public policy at Georgetown University and a senior fellow at the Brookings Institution, has identified the three types of think tanks mentioned above as the most significant kinds of research organizations populating the policy-making community. James McGann, however, contends that at least seven categories of think tanks are necessary to account for the entire spectrum in the United States: academic diversified, academic specialized, contract/consulting, advocacy, policy enterprise, literary agent/publishing house, and state-based.[8] While there is some merit in expanding the spectrum of think tanks, as McGann has done, Weaver's typology provides a more manageable and less cluttered framework within which to evaluate the evolution and transformation of think tanks in North America, Europe, and other regions that boast healthy populations of think tanks. It is for this reason that I rely on his typology, albeit with some modifications, to assess the development of think tanks in Canada and the United States. Before chronicling the different kinds of policy institutes associated with the four major waves of think tank growth, I will outline a classification that highlights some of the similarities and differences between the major types of think tanks in the two countries.

Universities without Students

Unfortunately, the think tanks revered by Weaver and other scholars as universities without students are becoming an endangered species. They catapulted onto the American political landscape during the progressive era (1880–1920), and, in many respects, epitomized what a think tank could and, according to some, should be: a sanctuary for experts committed to producing rigorous policy research. These were the kinds of organizations Andrew Carnegie, the Scottish-American steel tycoon, Robert Brookings, the St Louis businessman, and Herbert Hoover, the mining engineer who would become the 31st president of the United States, had in mind when they considered what government required to think its way through a host of domestic and foreign policy challenges.[9] For these and other philanthropists who helped lay the foundation for what would become the golden age of think tanks, the solution was clear, and, with sufficient financial support and sound leadership, entirely feasible: create an environment where academics from various disciplines could apply their scientific expertise to the public policy issues of the day. Recruited from many of the best universities in the United States and abroad, Carnegie and his compatriots believed that a different setting was required for experts to generate the kind of research that would benefit policy-makers – one that fostered and cultivated the intellectual rigour of a university, without the distractions scholars would be subjected to as members of the academy. In this type of think tank, which, in many ways, resembled typical academic departments, dozens of policy experts with advanced degrees (usually PhDs) were hired primarily, though not exclusively, to write books, refereed journal articles, and other scholarly studies that focused on domestic and foreign policy. Decades later, Bill Gates, Steve Jobs, and other entrepreneurs would create similar environments, where programmers, design and software engineers, and other Microsoft and Apple employees had the freedom to explore and test new ideas.

The opportunity to devote most of their waking hours to research without being sidetracked by, or saddled with, teaching and administrative commitments is for many academics a dream come true, and may in part explain the appeal of student-less universities. As is the case when scholars take up appointments at universities, researchers who gravitate to these organizations may pursue projects of their choosing (subject to financial and other considerations). The difference is that in the process of conducting research, they can insulate themselves from the day to day politics of university life. Moreover, unlike universities, the seminars and workshops think tanks offer, and the studies they produce, are usually intended for policy-makers, not students. Supported in large part by funding from the private sector (with varying mixtures of foundation, corporate and individual funding), scholars working at these institutions regard book-length studies as their primary research product.[10] The Brookings Institution and the Hoover Institution, two of the largest private research institutions in the United States, are among the few think tanks that fall into this category, although even these institutes also devote considerable resources to advocacy.[11]

The Brookings Institution, the Hoover Institution, and other research-driven institutes have long been permanent fixtures in the United States, but these types of think tanks are noticeably absent in Canada. Despite recommendations made to the federal government in the late 1960s to create an independent interdisciplinary think tank on the scale of the Brookings Institution, Canada has yet to be home to a university without students. There are several think tanks, including the C.D. Howe Institute, the Mowat Centre, the Institute for Research on Public Policy,[12] CIGI, and the Parkland Institute, that regard academic or policy-relevant research as one of their principal functions, but none that resemble the largest and most distinguished research-oriented think tanks in the United States in size and scope. The Mowat Centre and the Parkland Institute are housed at universities with students, and the scholars who conduct research at CIGI are drawn from various departments at the University of Waterloo and Wilfrid Laurier University. Therefore, in a Canadian context, it might be more appropriate to refer to these types of think tanks simply as policy research institutions instead of as "universities without students." Institutions in this category are staffed by economists, political scientists, and other trained academics, who conduct research on a diverse range of policy issues. Most of their resources are devoted to research, although book-length studies are not regarded as their primary outputs. The Ottawa-based Conference Board of Canada, well-known for its expertise in providing economic forecasting to policy-makers and business leaders, is one think tank that would warrant this classification.

Government Contractors

What distinguishes government contractors from the preceding category is not the type of research they undertake (although much of the research that government contractors generate is confidential), but their principal client and primary source of funding. Think tanks like RAND and the Urban Institute, two of the leading government contractors in the United States, also rely primarily on government departments and agencies to sustain their operations.[13] Similarly, there are several examples of think tanks in Canada whose work is, or was, almost entirely funded by government sources. In fact, during the 1960s, a handful of think tanks or "government councils" were created by the federal government to provide advice in specific policy areas. Many of these institutes, including the Economic Council of Canada and the Science Council of Canada, were disbanded in the early 1990s, victims of budget cuts announced by the Mulroney government in 1992. These cuts claimed several other victims as well, most notably the Canadian Institute for International Peace and Security (CIPS), Canada's premier foreign policy think tank. In the fall of 2014, the North-South Institute (NSI), a fixture in Canada's think tank community for forty years, and a leading voice in the field of international development policy, succumbed to a similar fate when the Harper government decided not to renew federal funding (through the Canadian International Development Agency [CIDA]) to NSI. Unable to secure adequate funds from alternate sources, the NSI had no choice but to close its doors. As Roy Culpepper, former president of the NSI, acknowledged in an interview with the author over a decade ago, when you depend on the government for about half your funding, "it is both a blessing and a curse."[14]

Advocacy Think Tanks

Since the early 1970s, the most common type of think tank to emerge in both Canada and the United States has been what Weaver refers to as the advocacy think tank. Advocacy think tanks, as the name implies, "combine a strong policy, partisan or ideological bent with aggressive salesmanship [in] an effort to influence current policy debates."[15] Recognized for being politically savvy, and having an acute sense of how to market ideas, advocacy think tanks are highly skilled at self-promotion. With a flair for recycling and repackaging ideas, they have played a critical role in transforming the makeup of the policy research community, a subject that will be explored in more detail in chapter 4. Advocacy think tanks place a premium on producing brief reports for policy-makers and their staff, rather than devoting precious institutional resources to preparing book-length studies. The reason for doing this is clear: in addition to the considerable expense incurred in providing staff with the time and resources necessary to research and write books, advocacy think tanks are well aware of the many demands policy-makers must respond to on a daily basis. Knowing that most elected officials do not have the time, inclination, or desire to plough through weighty tomes, think tanks that are more advocacy-oriented prepare short, pithy, and accessible briefs to enlighten politicians about a range of policy issues. It stands to reason why think tanks that are more concerned about recycling ideas than developing new and innovative ones would be intent on distilling complex problems into a handful of pages. Better still, by inserting policy recommendations into their policy briefs, advocacy think tanks soon realized that they had discovered a winning formula: policy-makers, like high school students skimming *Cole's Notes* before an exam, could familiarize themselves with current policy issues in a matter of minutes. They would not find themselves overwhelmed by dense prose and volumes of information and, in a short time, would have the confidence to share their new-found knowledge with colleagues and constituents. Grateful for being educated in the time it takes to drink a cup of coffee and consume a stack of pancakes, policy-makers would then, in all likelihood, develop more of an affinity for similar products distributed by advocacy think tanks. At least, this was the game plan advocacy think tanks had in mind, and, to their delight, it worked. In addition to preparing user-friendly material for policy-makers, advocacy think tanks place a premium on gaining access to the media. In these institutions, staff publish op-ed articles in newspapers with great regularity, write blogs for various publications, and appear on network newscasts and political talk shows to share their insights on a wide range of topical policy issues.

It may also be useful for comparative purposes to add a fourth and possibly fifth and sixth category to Weaver's typology – vanity or legacy-based think tanks, policy clubs, and think-and-do tanks. Legacy-based think tanks are created by aspiring office-holders (or their supporters) and by former leaders who are intent on advancing their political and ideological agendas well after leaving office. Although far more numerous in the United States, there are a few examples of think tanks in Canada that fall into this category. A fifth category – policy clubs – may, according to Evert Lindquist of the University of Victoria, best describe several think tanks in Canada.[16] In his assessment of the impact of Canadian policy institutes, Lindquist suggests that it may be more appropriate to portray think tanks in Canada as policy clubs (where academics, policy analysts, and, occasionally, policy-makers meet to discuss public policy issues) than as policy research institutions capable of providing long-term strategic analysis. Since they are unable to compete with the institutional resources available in several bureaucratic departments and large trade associations, Lindquist contends that the nostalgic vision of think tanks as creators of new and innovative ideas simply does not conform to the experience of most Canadian policy institutes. Although he bases his observations on the work of several policy institutes created in the early 1970s, Lindquist's insights about think tanks as policy clubs can also account for the activities of the handful of small policy shops created in the early twentieth century. A final category is what some

scholars and pundits have described as think-and-do tanks: organizations that make a conscious decision to put ideas into action. There do not appear to be many of these institutes in either Canada or the United States, but they are worth considering as we delve more deeply into the think tank population.

Think Again: The Limits of Think Tank Typologies

Classifying generations of think tanks according to specific institutional criteria may help scholars to distinguish one type of think tank from another, and typologies may be useful in comparing think tanks in different countries; nonetheless, problems can, and often do arise in making such classifications. To begin with, since some organizations possess characteristics common to more than one type of think tank, they often fall into several categories. For instance, while few observers are likely to have trouble distinguishing between the work of the Conference Board of Canada and the Fraser Institute or between the Brookings Institution and the Heritage Foundation, these think tanks engage in similar activities: both undertake research and analysis, and to varying degrees, market their findings. The main difference is in the emphasis they place on pure research and political advocacy, and the resources they assign to each. To argue, then, that the Conference Board of Canada and the Brookings Institution are policy research institutions and the Fraser Institute and Heritage Foundation are advocacy think tanks would be misleading. Both could conceivably be classified as policy research institutions and advocacy think tanks.

This potential shortcoming cannot be overstated. How scholars and journalists classify institutes can have a profound impact on the way different think tanks are perceived in the media, by the public, and by the individuals, corporations, philanthropic foundations, and the governments that may decide to fund them. Referring to the Brookings Institution as a world-renowned policy research institution enhances its credibility and respectability and stock in the policy-making community. It creates the impression, rightly or wrongly, that the institution produces objective, neutral, and balanced research, hence its moniker: quality, independence, impact. Conversely, describing the Heritage Foundation and the Fraser Institute as well-known advocacy think tanks suggests that their views should be taken less seriously or with a grain of salt. At the very least, the term "advocacy" implies that they are more committed to advancing their ideological agenda than to pursuing scholarly research.

The problem of classifying think tanks incorrectly may become more pronounced as these organizations adopt similar strategies to convey their ideas. Like chameleons constantly changing their colours to suit new environments, think tanks frequently alter their behaviour to become more competitive in the marketplace of ideas. For example, to enhance their profile, some early think tanks now rely on strategies employed by newer generations of institutes. And some newly created institutes have looked to older generations of think tanks for ideas on how to manage their operations. In short, despite the diverse nature of think tanks, it is becoming increasingly difficult to isolate their unique institutional traits.

In the process of identifying different types of think tanks, and placing them in a particular category, scholars run the risk of mislabelling them. This problem might be unavoidable, given the methodological problems often encountered in classifiying them; nevertheless, typologies can still be useful in identifying the kinds of think tanks that emerged during particular periods. As the section below illustrates, think tanks associated with each of the four waves of think tank development possessed certain defining characteristics. It is these characteristics that allow a new generation of think tanks to be identified.

Thinking Back: The Evolution of Think Tanks in the United States and Canada

THE FIRST WAVE: 1900–45
The first decades of the twentieth century were a formidable period for think tank development in the United States. Although several prominent universities existed at the time, including Harvard University, Johns Hopkins University, and the University of Chicago, a small group of philanthropists and policy-makers armed with vision and determination believed that what was needed was institutions whose primary focus was not teaching, but research and analysis. Guided by the belief that modern science could be used to solve social, economic, and political problems, a philosophy that was widely embraced during the Progressive era,[17] this group set out to establish privately-funded research institutes ostensibly dedicated to serving the public interest.[18] With generous funding from Robert Brookings, Andrew Carnegie, Herbert Hoover, John D. Rockefeller, Sr, and Margaret Olivia Sage, among others, several of America's most venerable institutions were created. These included the Russell Sage Foundation (1907), the Carnegie Endowment for

Table 2.1 Profiles of selected Canadian think tanks – overview

Institution	Location	Founded	Operating budget	Staff*	Publication type	Area of expertise
Asia Pacific Foundation of Canada	Vancouver, BC	1984	$6 million	30	Journal, policy brief/report, research	Canada-Asia relations
Atlantic Institute for Market Studies	Halifax, NS	1994	$1–$1.5 million	6	Books, papers, research reports	Atlantic Canada social and economic issues
Atlantic Provinces Economic Council	Halifax, NS	1954	$1–$2 million	8	Magazine, research/issue annual reports	Advocate for economic dev't in Atlantic Canada
C.D. Howe Institute	Toronto, ON	1973	$3.5–$4 million	25	Annual, monthly and issue reports, news releases	Fiscal, tax, social, trade policy, innovation and growth
Caledon Institute of Social Policy	Ottawa, ON	1992	$500,000–$1 million	5	Issue/research reports	Poverty and social policy
Canada West Foundation	Calgary, AB	1971	$2.5–$3 million	19	Annual and issue reports	Public policy issues of interest to Western Canada
Canadian Centre for Philanthropy/ Imagine Canada	Toronto, ON	1981	$4–$4.5 million	37	Issue alerts	Not-for-profit sector, charitable organizations
Canadian Centre for Policy Alternatives	Ottawa, ON	1980	$5–$6 million	40	Journal, research/issue reports	Issues of social, economic and environmental justice
Canadian Constitution Foundation	Calgary, AB	2006	$0.5–$1 million	4	Research reports/studies/articles	Individual rights and freedoms, court challenges
Canadian Council on Social Development	Ottawa, ON	1920	$1.5–$2 million	6	Issue/research reports, annual reports	Social policy

Organization	Location	Year	Budget	Number	Publications	Focus
Canadian Defence & Foreign Affairs Institute / Canadian Global Affairs	Calgary, AB / Ottawa, ON	2002	$500,000–$1 million	5	Research/policy papers, monthly publication	Canadian foreign and defence policy, international aid
Canadian Institute for Advanced Research	Toronto, ON	1982	$16 million	36	Journal/magazine, annual and issue reports	Knowledge creation
Canadian International Council	Toronto, ON	1928	$1.5–$2 million	11	Reports	International Affairs
Canadian Tax Foundation	Toronto, ON	1945	$5–$5.5 million	15	Journal, newsletter	Tax research
Canadian Urban Institute	Toronto, ON	1990	$3–$5 million	19	Research/issue reports	Planning and policy for improvement of urban areas
Centre for International Governance Innovation	Waterloo, ON	2001	$26.5–$27 million	80	Policy briefs, research and issue reports	International governance
Centre for the Study of Living Standards	Ottawa, ON	1995	> $.5 million	4	Journal, research/issue reports, newsletter	Productivity, living standards, economic, social well-being
Conference Board of Canada	Ottawa, ON	1954	$38–$40 million	200	Issue reports	Economic trends, public policy, organizational performance
Couchiching Institute on Public Affairs	Toronto, ON	1932	$100,000–$250,000	N/A	Conferences, annual reports	Canadian public affairs
Fraser Institute	Vancouver, BC	1974	$8–$9 million	55	Magazine/journal, issue reports	Effects of economics and public policy on society
Frontier Centre for Public Policy	Winnipeg, MB	1997	$1 million	8	Policy briefs, research and issue reports	Western Canadian issues
George Morris Centre	Guelph, ON	1998	$1–$1.5 million	9	Research/issue reports	Canadian agri-food industry
GPI Atlantic	Glen Haven, NS	1997	>$5 million	7	Research/issue reports	Genuine Progress Index

Table 2.1 Profiles of selected Canadian think tanks – overview (*continued*)

Institution	Location	Founded	Operating budget	Staff*	Publication type	Area of expertise
Institute for Research on Public Policy	Montreal, QC	1972	$2–$2.5 million	15	Journal	Canadian public policy
Institute on Governance	Ottawa, ON	1990	$1.5–$2 million	22	Issue/research reports	(Better) governance
International Institute for Sustainable Development	Winnipeg, MB	1990	$17 million	200	Research reports/policy briefs	Promote sustainable development
Macdonald-Laurier Institute for Public Policy	Ottawa, ON	2010	$1 million	5	Research reports/commentaries/magazine	Issues relating to domestic and foreign policy
Mackenzie Institute	Toronto, ON	1986	$100,000–$250,000	3	Commentaries, newsletters, policy briefs	Issues of public instablility and organized violence
Montreal Economic Institute	Montreal, QC	1999	$2.25 million	13	Research/issue reports	Public policy in Quebec, Canada, wealth-creating reforms
Mowat Centre	Toronto, ON	2009	$2.5 million	18	Research/issue reports	Public Policy in Ontario
Parkland Institute	Edmonton, AB	1996	>$500,000	6	Research/issue reports	Economic, social, political issues of Alberta, Canada
Pembina Institute	Calgary, AB	1985	$4–$5 million	50	Research/issue reports	Environmental, clean energy, recycling & conservation
Public Policy Forum	Ottawa, ON	1987	$3.5–$4 million	22	Research/issue reports	Quality of government, Canada
Vanier Institute of the Family	Nepean, ON	1965	>$1.3 million	8	Research/issue reports	Canadian families
Wellesley Institute	Toronto, ON	2006	$1.5–$2 million	10	Research/issue reports	Population health

Table 2.2 Profiles of selected Canadian think tanks – contact information

Institution	President/director	Mailing address	Email	
Asia Pacific Foundation of Canada	Stewart Beck	220-890 West Pender Street, Vancouver BC, V6C 1J9	info@asiapacific.ca	(604) 684-5986
Atlantic Institute for Market Studies	Marco Navarro-Genie	287 Lacewood Drive, Suite 204, Park West Centre, Halifax, Nova Scotia B3M 3Y7	aims@aims.ca	(902) 429-1143
Atlantic Provinces Economic Council	Elizabeth Beale	5121 Sackville Street, Suite 500, Halifax NS, B3J 1K1	info@apec-econ.ca	(902) 422-6516
C.D. Howe Institute	William B.P. Robson	67 Yonge Street, Suite 300, Toronto ON, M5E 1J8	cdhowe@cdhowe.org	(416) 865-1904
Caledon Institute of Social Policy	Ken Battle	1354 Wellington Street West, 3rd Floor, Ottawa ON K1C 3C3	caledon@caledoninst.org	(613) 729-3340
Canada West Foundation	Dylan Jones	900-105 12th Avenue SE, Calgary AB, T2G 1A1	cwf@cwf.ca	(403) 264-9535
Imagine Canada	Bruce MacDonald	65 St. Clair Avenue East, Toronto ON, M4T 2Y3	info@imaginecanada.ca	(416) 597-2293
Canadian Centre for Policy Alternatives	Bruce Campbell	251 Bank Street, Suite 500, Ottawa ON, K2P 1X3	ccpa@policyalternatives.ca	(613) 563-1341
Canadian Constitution Foundation	Christopher Schafer	1830-52 Street SE Suite 240 Calgary AB, T2B 1N1	info@the ccf.ca	(888) 695-9105
Canadian Council on Social Development	Peggy Taillon	P.O. Box 13713, Kanata ON, K2K 1X6	taillon@ccsd.ca	(613) 236-8977
Canadian Defence & Foreign Affairs Institute/Canadian Global Affairs Institute	Robert Millar	Suite 1600, 530 8th Avenue SW, Calgary AB, T2P 3S8/ 8 York St., 2nd floor, Ottawa, ON, K1N 5S6	contact@cgai.ca	(403) 231-7605/ (613)288-2529

Table 2.2 Profiles of selected Canadian think tanks – contact information (*continued*)

Institution	President/director	Mailing address	Email	
Canadian Institute for Advanced Research	Alan Bernstein	180 Dundas Street West, Suite 1400, Toronto ON, M5G 1Z8	info@cifar.ca	(416) 971-4251
Canadian International Council	Jo-Ann Davis	#210, 42 Wilcocks Street, Toronto ON M5S 1C7	info@opencanada.org	(416)-946-7209
Canadian Tax Foundation	Larry Chapman	595 Bay Street, Suite 1200, Toronto ON, M5G 2N5	lchapman@ctf.ca	(416) 599-0283
Canadian Urban Institute	Peter Halsall	555 Richmond Street West, Suite 402, P.O. Box 612, Toronto ON, M5B 3V1	sclarke@canurb.org	(416) 365-0816
Centre for International Governance Innovation	Rohinton Medhora	57 Erb Street West, Waterloo ON, N2L 6C2	N/A	(519) 885-2444
Centre for the Study of Living Standards	Andrew Sharpe	151 Slater Street, Suite 710, Ottawa ON, K1P 5H3	info@csls.ca	(613) 233-8891
Conference Board of Canada	Daniel Muzyka	255 Smyth Road, Ottawa ON, K1H 8M7	contactcboc.conferenceboard.ca	(866) 711-2262
Couchiching Institute on Public Affairs	Adam Redish	250 Consumers Road, Suite 301, Willowdale ON, M2J 4V6	couch@couchinginstitute.ca	(416) 642-6374
Fraser Institute	Niels Veldhuis	4th Floor, 1770 Burrard Street, Vancouver BC, V6J 3G7	info@fraserinstitute.org	(604) 688-0221
Frontier Centre for Public Policy	Peter Holle	203-2727 Portage Avenue, Winnipeg MB, R3J 0R2	manitoba@fcpp.ca	(403) 400-6862
George Morris Centre	Barb Miller	225-150 Research Lane, Guelph ON, N1G 4T2	info@georgemorris.ca	(519) 827-6239
GPI Atlantic	Ron Colman	535 Indian Point Road, Glen Haven NS, B3Z 2T5.	info@gpiatlantic.ca	(902) 823-1944

Organization	Contact	Address	Email	Phone
Institute for Research on Public Policy	Graham Fox	1470 Peel Street, #200, Montreal QC, H3A 1T1	irpp@irpp.org	(514) 985-2461
Institute on Governance	Maryantonett Flumian	60 George Street, Ottawa ON, K1J 1J4	info@iog.ca	(613) 562-0090
International Institute for Sustainable Development	Scott Vaughan	161 Portage Ave, East, 6th floor, Winnipeg MB R3B 0Y4	info@iisd.org	(204) 958-7700
Mackenzie Institute	Andrew Majoran	P.O. Box 338, Adelaide Station, Toronto ON, M5C 2J4	institute@mackenzieinstitute.com	(416) 686-4063
Montreal Economic Institute	Michel Kelly-Gagnon	910 Peel Street, Suite 600, Montreal QC, H3C 2H8	info@iedm.org	(514) 273-0969
Mowat Centre	Matthew Mendelsohn	720 Spadina Avenue, Suite 218, Toronto ON, M5S 2T9	info@mowatcentre.ca	(416) 978-7858
Parkland Institute	Trevor Harrison	110045 Saskatchewan Drive, Edmonton AB T6G 2E1 (another office in Calgary)	parkland@ualberta.ca	(780) 492-8558
Pembina Institute	Ed Whittingham	219 19th Street NW, Calgary AB, T2N 2H9	lastname@pembina.org	(403) 269-3344
Public Policy Forum	Larry Murray	130 Albert Street, Suite 1405, Ottawa ON, K1P 5G4	mail@ppforum.ca	(613) 238-7160
Vanier Institute of the Family	Nora Spinks	95 Centrepoint Drive, Ottawa ON, K2G 6B1	info@vanierinstitute.ca	(613) 228-8500
Wellesley Institute	Kwame McKenzie	10 Alcorn Avenue, Suite 300, Toronto ON, M4V 3B1	contact@wellesleyinstitute.ca	(416) 972-1010

International Peace (1910), the Conference Board (1916), the Institute for Government Research (1916; became the Brookings Institution in 1927), the Hoover Institution on War, Revolution and Peace (1919), the National Bureau of Economic Research (1920), and the Council on Foreign Relations (1921).[19] Although these and other think tanks created during this time have unique institutional histories, they shared a commitment to debating and investigating a wide range of domestic and foreign policy issues in the hope of improving governmental decision making. With the support of dozens of scholars recruited primarily from the social sciences, the think tanks created during this era claimed to place a premium on producing objective and neutral policy research. However, as previous studies have revealed, their goals, and those of their generous benefactors, were not always entirely altruistic.[20]

While many of the studies produced by these institutes adhered to the highest scholarly standards, the institutes themselves can hardly be regarded as value-neutral research bodies. The Brookings Institution is a case in point. One of America's oldest and most iconic think tanks, Brookings has cultivated a reputation as an independent institute committed to providing objective research and analysis. This commitment was reaffirmed by Brookings president Strobe Talbott following the publication of a 6 September 2014 New York Times article which documented the millions of dollars in funding donated by foreign governments to several high-profile US think tanks. The article, co-written by investigative journalist Brooke Williams, a fellow at Harvard's Edmond J. Safra Center for Ethics, claimed that in return for the sizeable donations, the governments of Qatar and Norway expected the Brookings Institution to lobby on their behalf.[21] In a formal statement issued the morning after the publication of the New York Times article, Talbott wasted little time in addressing these serious allegations. He stated: "Brookings has over 200 scholars and more than 700 funders for hundreds of research projects. Our scholars determine our research and policy recommendations, not our contributors. We accept funding from foreign governments with the understanding that they are supporting our independent research."[22]

Preventing its board of directors from interfering in the research agendas of its scholars is another safeguard Brookings has in place to maintain its intellectual independence. Nonetheless, being independent and producing objective research are two different things. Until recently, few scholars studying think tanks have questioned Brookings's institutional independence, but on several occasions its researchers have made their policy preferences well-known. As early as 1920, a handful of scholars at the Institute for Government Research, one of the institutes from which Brookings evolved, engaged in an aggressive lobbying campaign to convince the federal government to adopt a national budget system. The result was the passage of the Budget and Accounting Act of 1921.[23] Since then, Brookings scholars have been at the forefront of hundreds of major domestic and foreign policy debates, including providing a justification for the Bush administration's war in Iraq.[24] What distinguishes Brookings and other early-twentieth-century policy institutes from more contemporary think tanks is not their reluctance to become involved in the political arena – after all, Brookings has become far more advocacy-oriented in recent years – but the emphasis Brookings continues to place on engaging in medium- and long-term research. In short, unlike the Heritage Foundation and its many disciples who focus on what is commonly known as "quick response policy research" – publications that can be produced quickly for elected officials – many first-generation think tanks focus on issues that policy-makers may want to analyze for years to come. By undertaking more systematic, long-term thinking, think tanks can make an important contribution to improving the quality of public policy by reminding policy-makers of the lessons of history. But to help government situate current policy challenges in their proper historical context, think tanks must avoid becoming bogged down and consumed by the vicissitudes of politics. This is not always easy for organizations intent on marketing themselves as repositories for generating timely and relevant policy ideas.

Despite gaining national prominence in the United States, major research-oriented think tanks were noticeably absent in Canada during the early 1900s.[25] There were a handful of small organizations concerned about Canadian foreign policy. These included the Round Table Movement, the Canadian Association for International Conciliation, the Institute of Pacific Relations – which enjoyed strong Canadian representation[26] – and the Canadian Institute of International Affairs (CIIA). Yet, unlike Chatham House, which is widely considered among the top research think tanks in the world,[27] the CIIA was created more as a "club" of influential Canadians interested in the study of international affairs and Canada's role in the world[28] than as a policy research institution where scholars would dedicate themselves to preparing detailed analyses of world events.[29] After a distinguished history, which spanned close to eighty years, the members of the CIIA voted in November 2007 to change the institute's name to the Canadian International

Council (CIC), which is now housed at the University of Toronto's Munk School of Global Affairs. A year later, in 2008, the Canadian Institute of Strategic Studies (CISS), another Toronto-based think tank, closed its doors and folded its operations into the CIC's Strategic Studies Working Group. Despite these significant changes, the core mission of the CIIA, and now the CIC, has remained relatively intact, although the CIC has made a much stronger commitment to funding and generating policy research. As Jim Balsillie, co-founder of Research in Motion, and the inaugural chair of the CIC, observed in the organization's first annual report, the CIC is "a non-partisan, nationwide foreign policy council established to strengthen Canada's foreign policy. It promotes research and dialogue on international affairs issues through a national network that crosses academic, policy areas, and economic sectors."[30] Balsillie's motivation for helping to create the CIC, CIGI, and the Balsillie School of International Affairs, will be discussed in the relevant think tank profiles.

Some organizations were committed to the study of domestic policy as well. The National Council on Child and Family Welfare, which eventually led to the creation of the Canadian Council on Social Development (CCSD), was formed in 1920.[31] As associations of interested individuals and groups, they may not have looked like "policy" think tanks when compared with those south of the border; nevertheless, they undertook important networking functions, and they did commission some research outside the government. Still, with few exceptions, the think tank landscape in Canada remained nearly barren until the early 1960s.

THE SECOND WAVE: 1946–70
By the end of the Second World War, a new wave of think tanks was emerging in the United States, largely in response to the growing international and domestic pressures confronting American policy-makers. Acknowledging the invaluable contribution that defence scientists had made during the war, the Truman administration considered the enormous benefits that could be derived by continuing to fund private and university-based research and development centres. By tapping into the expertise of engineers, physicists, biologists, statisticians, and social scientists, policy-makers hoped to meet the many new challenges they had inherited as the United States assumed its role as the hegemonic power in the atomic age. It was in this environment that the idea for creating the most prominent government contractor, the RAND Corporation (RAND is an acronym for research and development), was born in 1948.[32]

In addition to making many important contributions to American defence policy, RAND was a prototype for other government contractors, including the Hudson Institute, founded by Herman Kahn, and the domestic-policy-oriented Urban Institute, whose creation was strongly endorsed by President Lyndon Johnson.[33]

In the post–Second World War era, policy-makers in Washington, like the philanthropists of the early twentieth century, recognized the important role think tanks could play in several crucial policy areas. They also recognized the potential benefits of drawing on the expertise of independent research institutes, which had the luxury of engaging in medium- and long-term strategic research instead of relying on government officials drowning in daily paper work. Particularly in this policy area, it was crucial for the government to be able to rely on think tanks that had assembled some of the best minds in the country and who, unlike policy-makers and bureaucrats in Washington, were less likely to be influenced by partisan interests; however, this was not always possible; the political leanings of some of America's leading scientists often influenced their policy recommendations. Much has been written about the political views of J. Robert Oppenheimer, director of the Manhattan Project, who would later assume the directorship of the Institute for Advanced Study at Princeton. Along similar lines, studies have documented the politics of Herman Kahn, and of Edward Teller, father of the hydrogen bomb. Both scientists enjoyed long careers at some of America's leading think tanks.

The United States had entered an era in which its defence and foreign policy would have a profound impact on shaping world affairs. What it required was sound informative policy advice, and, for much of it, it turned to RAND and the Hudson Institute. But just as the federal government relied on these and other think tanks for advice on defence and security issues, President Johnson looked to the Urban Institute to suggest ways to alleviate the many economic, social, and political problems that were contributing to urban unrest throughout the turbulent decade of the 1960s. For Johnson, the war waging inside the United States deserved as much, if not more, attention as the conflicts taking place beyond America's borders. The onset of the Cold War and the War on Poverty placed new demands on the United States government and provided greater opportunities for think tanks to make their presence felt. Like the generation of think tanks before them, government contractors began to fill a void in the policy-research community.

The postwar period in the United States also witnessed the emergence of several other think tanks, including the Center for Strategic and

International Studies (CSIS) and the Institute for Policy Studies (IPS), which were not established as government contractors, but nonetheless quickly became immersed in Washington's policy-making community. Founded in 1962 and home to such luminaries as Zbigniew Brzezinski, national security adviser to President Carter; Admiral William Crowe, former chairman of the Joint Chiefs of Staff; and James Schlesinger, former secretary of defense, CSIS often works closely with incoming administrations to outline foreign and security policy issues. In many respects, CSIS functions both as a research institution and as an advocacy think tank, and is a favourite among foreign governments looking for more leverage and influence on Capitol Hill.[34] Several foreign governments, including Qatar, have made large gifts to CSIS, which undoubtedly helped in the 2014 construction of CSIS's new headquarters on Washington, DC's Rhode Island Avenue. It has established an impressive research program but has also undertaken great efforts to market its ideas. The Institute for Policy Studies (IPS), created in 1963 by Marcus Raskin and Richard Barnett, is another Washington-based think tank known for its interest in American foreign policy; however, unlike the more mainstream CSIS, the IPS has developed a reputation as Washington's think tank of the left for its Marxist/radical approach to US foreign policy. Few would dispute its status as an ideologically driven advocacy think tank.[35]

Several think tanks also emerged in Canada in the postwar period. The Toronto-based Canadian Tax Foundation (CTF) was founded in 1946 by representatives of the national law and accounting societies to conduct and sponsor research on taxation. Eight years later, a branch office of the New York–based Conference Board was established in Montreal to serve its Canadian members. The Conference Board of Canada has since evolved into Canada's largest policy institute, with close to 200 staff and a budget exceeding $25 million.[36] In 1954, the Atlantic Provinces Economic Council (APEC) was formed to promote economic development in the Atlantic region. And in 1958, the Private Planning Association of Canada (PPAC) was founded as a counterpart to the National Planning Association (NPA) in the United States. PPAC was created by "business and labour leaders to undertake research and educational activities on economic policy issues."[37] It was also intended to support the Canadian-American Committee and two other committees of the NPA, to help foster dialogue among representatives from business, labour, and government.[38]

The growth of think tanks in postwar Canada did not end there. The Vanier Institute of the Family was established in 1965 by Governor General Georges Vanier and Madame Pauline Vanier to study "the demographic, economic, social and health influences on contemporary family life."[39] In 1968, the Parliamentary Centre for Foreign Affairs was created to provide research support to parliamentary committees and government departments examining various foreign policy issues.

By the early 1960s, the Canadian government had also begun to demonstrate interest in creating research institutes. The federal government had traditionally relied either on bureaucratic departments or on royal commissions and task forces to advise it on key policy matters. It now began to consider other ways to enhance its policy capacity.[40] But unlike the American government, which relied heavily on private think tanks for research and analysis, the Canadian government decided to establish its own network of policy research institutes. It created several government councils, including the Economic Council of Canada (1963), the Science Council of Canada (1966), the National Council of Welfare (1968), and the Law Reform Commission of Canada (1970), to advise it on a host of policy issues. As Abelson and Lindquist point out:

These organizations received government funding in amounts that most nongovernmental think tanks could only dream about, but operated at an arm's length relationship inside the government (full-time staff were public sector employees). Research activities, including work undertaken on contract by academics and other researchers outside government, were overseen by councils consisting of representatives from the private and nonprofit sectors reflecting different constituencies and elements of society. The councils identified new research initiatives, oversaw a rolling portfolio of projects, and produced consensus reports informed by commissioned research studies. Although the councils were independent, members were appointed for fixed terms by the Prime Minister and governments could request that new research initiatives be undertaken by the councils.[41]

Although they operated at arm's length from their employers, tensions between the councils and various governments eventually began to surface. The system of parliamentary and responsible government was simply not conducive to allowing organs of the state, no matter how

independent, to express views on public policy that were at variance
with government priorities and policies.[42] In its budget of February
1992, the Mulroney government took drastic measures to sever its
institutional ties with the various councils: the government disbanded
close to two dozen policy institutes, including the Economic Council of
Canada, the Science Council of Canada, the Law Reform Commission,
and the Canadian Institute for International Peace and Security. The
Chrétien government took steps to remedy some of that damage, including supporting the Privy Council Office's Policy Research Initiative
(PRI).[43] The PRI was intended to rectify the diminished policy capacity
of government by strengthening the ties between several federal departments and agencies and the external research community. As part of this
initiative, a number of think tanks were called upon to help the government think more strategically about the long-term impact of various
economic and social policies.

THE THIRD WAVE: 1971–89
The second wave of think tank development – the emergence of government contractors and government councils – hit the United States
and Canada at about the same time; yet by the time the third wave was
making its presence felt in the United States, multiple waves were hitting
Canada simultaneously. In the United States in the mid-1970s and
1980s, a new breed of policy institute – the advocacy think tank – was
beginning to get a lot of exposure. What distinguished advocacy think
tanks from the earlier types of think tanks already established in the
United States was not their desire to study public policy issues, but their
determination to market their ideas to various target audiences. Rather
than reflecting on important policy issues from the comfort of their
book-lined offices, advocacy think tanks embraced an entrepreneurial
spirit by immersing themselves in the political arena. Ideas in hand, they
began to think strategically about how to most effectively influence
policy-makers, the public, and the media. Dipping into the American
Enterprise Institute's (1943) playbook, the Heritage Foundation, founded
in 1973, was at the forefront of this new wave, elevating political advocacy to new heights.[44] Specializing in quick-response policy research,
Heritage, before the dawn of the Internet, stressed the importance of
providing members of Congress and the executive with hand-delivered
one-to-two-page briefing notes on key domestic and foreign policy
issues. Encouraged by the critical role Heritage had played during the
Reagan transition of 1980,[45] dozens of think tanks combining elements

of scholarship with aggressive marketing techniques began to take root throughout this period. These included the Rockford Institute (1976), which enjoyed close ties to Reform presidential candidate Pat Buchanan; the libertarian Cato Institute (1977); and the Economic Policy Institute (1986).

As this new wave of think tanks was hitting the United States, three distinct waves of think tank development were emerging in Canada. In the first, the federal government had come to realize by the late 1960s the potential benefits of having a large independent research institute in Canada similar to the ones created in the United States during the early 1900s. In 1968, Prime Minister Trudeau, familiar with the work of the Brookings Institution and painfully aware of the absence of such an institution in Canada, commissioned Ronald Ritchie, an economist, MP, and public servant, to consider the feasibility of creating an independent interdisciplinary policy institute. The resulting report, submitted the following year, led to the creation of the non-profit Institute for Research on Public Policy in 1972, with endowment funding from the federal government and plans to receive additional support from the private sector and provincial governments.[46]

In the second, four established organizations underwent significant transformations into modern think tanks during this period, and several new ones were created: the Canadian Welfare Council (CWC), established in 1920, was transformed into a social policy institute called the Canadian Council on Social Development (CCSD); the small Montreal office of the New York–based Conference Board relocated to Ottawa, allowing it to contribute to its growing expertise in developing economic forecasting models for both the public and private sectors; and the C.D. Howe Research Institute was formed in 1973 (following a merger of the Private Planning Association of Canada [PPAC] and the C.D. Howe Memorial Foundation) to become a centre for short-term economic policy analysis.[47] Finally, the profile of the Canadian Tax Foundation increased significantly during the early 1970s, due to a national debate stimulated by the Royal Commission on Taxation.

Several new think tanks in Canada were created as well. Two new foreign policy think tanks were established in 1976: the Ottawa-based North-South Institute, which, as noted, was forced to close its doors in 2014; and the Canadian Institute of Strategic Studies (CISS), which, as of 2008, became part of the Canadian International Council. The Canadian Centre for Philanthropy (now called Imagine Canada) was formed in 1981 to advance "the role and interests of the charitable sector for the benefit of Canadian communities."[48] The following year witnessed the creation of the Toronto-based Canadian Institute for Advanced Research (CIFAR), which supports global networks of researchers in their quest for answers to some of the world's most pressing scientific, environmental, and social problems. And, with an eye to resolving several other issues that were plaguing the international community, the federal government, following Prime Minister Trudeau's North-South initiative, agreed to establish and fund the Canadian Institute for International Peace and Security (CIIPS) in 1984. CIIPS was neither a government council, nor, as it discovered after being dismantled in 1992, as independent as the Institute for Research on Public Policy. In 1985, the Calgary-based Pembina Institute was established, to study, among other things, clean energy. And in the following year, the Mackenzie Institute began its operations in Toronto. Notwithstanding its modest resources, the Mackenzie Institute has made a name for itself in the field of terrorism and radical ideologies, a research area that has, since the events of 9/11, continued to generate widespread interest. As long as radical extremists wreak havoc in the world, there is no doubt that the institute will have plenty of opportunities to contribute to important policy debates about these and related issues.

In 1987, the Public Policy Forum (PPF) was established to improve public-policy making by providing a forum for representatives from the public, private, and non-profit sectors to consider a wide range of policy initiatives. And in 1990, the Institute on Governance (IOG), currently located in Ottawa's historic ByWard Market, was formed to promote effective governance. Among other things, the IOG advises the Canadian government and the governments of developing nations on how to better manage public services and train executives, and often serves as a broker for Canadian agencies seeking to assist developing governments.

In the third, several institutions devoted to the advocacy of particular points of view, reflecting the latest wave of US think tank growth, were created. The Canada West Foundation (CWF) was established in Calgary in 1971 to inject Western perspectives on national policy debates. The Fraser Institute opened its doors in 1974 to promote the virtues of free-market economics. And finally, the Canadian Institute for Economic Policy (CIEP) was formed in 1979 by Walter Gordon, a former Liberal finance minister, to sponsor a five-year research program on the themes of economic nationalism. In 1980, the Canadian Centre for Policy Alternatives (CCPA) was established by supporters of social democratic principles as a counterweight to the free-market leanings of the Fraser

Institute. The CCPA has worked closely with the leadership of the New Democratic Party and with several public advocacy coalitions, including the Council of Canadians, to convey its concerns on issues ranging from the growing gap between rich and poor to protecting the environment. The trend toward more advocacy-driven think tanks also appealed to the Progressive Conservative party. Following its defeat in 1980, several party members supported the creation of a think tank on economic, social, and international issues, but the initiative floundered when the party chose a new leader. However, conservatives looking for fresh ideas have not been left out in the cold. Since 2005, former Reform leader Preston Manning has welcomed conservatives, both young and old, to participate in activities sponsored by the Manning Centre for Building Democracy (which doesn't appear to satisfy the requirements for being a think tank), and the Manning Foundation (which does). Once a year, the Manning Centre holds a national networking conference in Ottawa, an event that attracts close to 1,000 participants. In the interests of full disclosure, at the 2014 Manning Networking Conference (MNC), I participated in a panel with Niels Veldhuis, president of the Fraser Institute, to discuss the influence of think tanks. As was to be expected, we had very different opinions about how to measure the influence of think tanks. Veldhuis was convinced that his institute has had and continues to have an enormous effect on shaping public opinion and policy. In the absence of any empirical evidence to support his grand claims, I was more skeptical. However, Veldhuis's observations about how and why the Fraser Institute has decided to target the Canadian public instead of policy-makers were very telling and worthy of further consideration. It is a subject that we will return to in chapter 7.

The think tank population in the United States and Canada grew considerably during the 1970s and 1980s as both policy-makers and policy entrepreneurs began not only to identify the need for independent policy advice, but to discover how effective think tanks could be in influencing public opinion and public policy. The growth of conservative advocacy institutions, in particular, was largely driven by generous benefactors who believed that with sufficient funding think tanks could have a significant effect on shaping the political dialogue. Think tanks continued to spring up in both countries in the 1990s and into the 2000s, and, in many cases, are making their presence felt. Although many recent think tanks share much in common with earlier generations of policy institutes, there are, as the most recent wave of think tank development reveals, some notable differences.

THE FOURTH WAVE: 1990–2015

Over the past twenty-five years, different varieties of think tanks have emerged, some resembling a hybrid of previous generations, contributing to an increasingly diverse population. Although they may not constitute a new wave, vanity or legacy-based think tanks, which can be found both in the United States and Canada, deserve some recognition. In the United States, legacy-based think tanks such as the (Jimmy) Carter Center (1982) at Emory University and the (Richard) Nixon Center for Peace and Freedom (1994), renamed the Center for the National Interest in 2011, have developed a wide range of research programs to help advance the legacies of their founders. In contrast, vanity think tanks, usually established by sitting, aspiring, or retiring office-holders, are more concerned with framing ideas and issues that will help lend intellectual credibility to their political platforms, a function no longer performed adequately by mainstream political parties.[49]

Some have claimed that vanity think tanks have also been established to circumvent spending limits imposed on presidential candidates by federal campaign finance laws.[50] Examples include: former Senator Bob Dole's (R-Kansas) short-lived institute, Better America; the Progress and Freedom Foundation (1993), an organization with close links to former Speaker of the House and Republican presidential candidate Newt Gingrich; United We Stand, established by Texas billionaire Ross Perot; and Empower America, founded in 1993 by an impressive band of neo-conservatives, including the late Jeanne Kirkpatrick, William Bennett, and former Republican vice-presidential candidate Jack Kemp. In July 2004, Empower America joined forces with Citizens for a Sound Economy to form FreedomWorks, a Washington, DC, conservative and libertarian lobby group which, to its credit, does see itself primarily as a think tank.

Legacy-based think tanks have also taken root in Canada. In recent years, some notable additions have made a splash, including the Manning Centre for Building Democracy, its research arm, the Manning Foundation, and the Broadbent Institute. Other think tanks that could conceivably fall into this category include the C.D. Howe Institute, named after its founder, a former Liberal cabinet minister and so-called minister of everything during the Second World War, and the Pearson-Shoyama Institute (created in Ottawa in 1993 to examine issues related to citizenship and multiculturalism and named after former prime minister Lester Pearson and former federal deputy finance minister Thomas Shoyama). The closest examples of legacy think tanks were the Canadian Institute for

Economic Policy, formed, as noted, by a former finance minister to further his ideas on economic nationalism, and the Canadian Institute for International Peace and Security, whose creation was, as noted, largely inspired by Prime Minister Trudeau's 1984 North-South initiative.

A more significant trend in Canada at the end of the twentieth century was the privatization of existing government research. In 1992, the Caledon Institute of Social Policy was created in Ottawa, with support from the Maytree Foundation, to enable Ken Battle, a former executive director of the National Council of Welfare, to develop a research agenda without the constraints of serving a government council. In 1994, the Canadian Policy Research Networks, Inc. (CPRN) was created by Judith Maxwell, former head of the Economic Council of Canada, to sponsor longer-term, interdisciplinary policy-research programs on social and economic policy issues and to lever research capabilities from across Canada. CPRN closed its doors in December 2009, unable to remain financially viable. Several other institutes were created in the 1990s: the Atlantic Institute for Market Studies (AIMS, 1994); the Canadian Council for International Peace and Security (CCIPS, 1995), which evolved from the Canadian Centre for Arms Control and Disarmament and the Canadian Centre for Global Security; the Centre for the Study of Living Standards (1995); and the Canadian Centre for Foreign Policy Development (1996), housed until recently in the Department of Foreign Affairs and International Trade (DFAIT), and now called Global Affairs Canada, one of the many federal government department name changes instituted by Prime Minister Justin Trudeau when he took office in the fall of 2015.

The growth of think tanks did not end there. In 1997, the Winnipeg-based Frontier Centre for Public Policy was established, and in the following year in neighbouring Saskatchewan, the Saskatchewan Institute of Public Policy (SIPP) was born. As of 2008, SIPP has operated under the auspices of the Johnson-Shoyama Graduate School of Public Policy at the University of Regina. In 1999, the Montreal Economic Institute (MEI) was founded, offering Quebec an alternative voice to the policy recommendations of Montreal's Institute for Research on Public Policy. Although several of the organizations created in the early 1990s no longer exist, those that followed them have continued to maintain active research programs.

The proliferation of think tanks in the United States and in Canada showed few signs of slowing down as we entered the new millennium. In the United States, a handful of newcomers, including the Center for a

New American Security (2007), a think tank with close ties to the Obama administration,[51] was making an impression. But ironically, it was in Canada where much of the buzz about several new think tanks on the block was being heard, with good reason. In 2001, Jim Balsillie and Mike Lazaridis, then co-CEOs of the Waterloo-based company Research in Motion, creators of BlackBerry, provided a $30 million endowment to launch the Centre for International Governance Innovation (CIGI). In the same year, two other think tanks with considerably fewer resources at their disposal were founded: the Parkland Institute at the University of Alberta in Edmonton, and the Canadian Defence and Foreign Affairs Institute (CDFAI), in Calgary. With a second office in Ottawa, the CDFAI (now named the Canadian Global Affairs Institute) boasts several distinguished scholars and former government officials on its roster of research fellows, including Jack Granatstein, David Bercuson, and Colin Robertson, a former Canadian diplomat with considerable expertise in Canada-US relations. No sooner did these think tanks begin to gain momentum than three other organizations joined the policy research community: the Wellesley Institute (2006), dedicated to addressing "urban health disparities" in southeast Toronto, a think tank that, ironically, owes its existence to the closure of the Wellesley Central Hospital in 1998; the Mowat Centre, housed at the University of Toronto (2009); and the Macdonald-Laurier Institute (2010), led by Brian Lee Crowley, a well-known figure in the think tank community and former director of the Atlantic Institute for Market Studies (AIMS).

The emergence of some of the aforementioned think tanks was influenced by important and telling developments in public-sector think tanks. As noted, the federal government, as part of the first wave of serious budget cutting in 1992, eliminated several think tanks – leaving only the tiny National Council of Welfare untouched. This changed in 2012, when the National Council of Welfare joined the list of other think tanks eliminated by the Harper government.[52] The creation of the Caledon Institute and the now-defunct Canadian Policy Research Networks, Inc., were direct reactions to these eliminations. The irony was that the Mulroney government justified its decision not simply in terms of savings, but also because of the large number of think tanks that had emerged in Canada since the 1960s. Among other things, Prime Minister Mulroney and his colleagues argued that in the 1990s there was sufficient policy capacity located outside government to supplement the research needs of federal departments and agencies. This claim was widely disputed in the media and in some academic circles.[53] Prime

Minister Harper demonstrated even less patience and concern for the welfare of think tanks, particularly those on the left, which required significantly more funding from the federal government to keep them afloat. As some critics of the Harper government have argued, the prime minister was willing to cultivate ties with think tanks that shared his ideology,[54] but was even more willing to undermine those that did not endorse his policy prescriptions.

In reviewing these waves of think tank growth, it is important to keep in mind that each new period of think tanks has not supplanted the institutions that preceded it, but has added new patches to an already complex and colourful quilt. Moreover, older types of think tanks have continued to be created in recent years in both countries. For example, although CIGI is based at a university, it shares many of the guiding principles that helped distinguish the think tanks of the early twentieth century, including a commitment to rigorous research. At the same time, however, a more crowded marketplace of ideas has increased competition for funding and modified the practices of the older institutions, creating a greater awareness of the need to make findings accessible to and easily digested by policy-makers. This lesson has not been lost on several new members of the think tank community in Canada and the United States, including those that want to think about policy solutions and do something about them – such as the "think-and-do tanks," like the Washington-based Center for Global Development. The institutes that comprise the think tank community in both countries may have been created at different times and with different goals, but they all recognize the importance of adopting the most effective strategies to convey their ideas. The question that we must now address is what exactly think tanks do, and how they go about doing it.

3

How Has the Role of
Think Tanks Changed?

In the previous chapter, we chronicled the growth and evolution of think tanks in Canada and in the United States during four distinct waves or periods. This allowed us to acquire a deeper appreciation for the diverse nature of the think tank population and the lengths to which scholars have gone to highlight their similarities and differences. When academics began thinking and writing about think tanks in the late 1960s and early 1970s, many of their observations about how policy institutes interacted with state and non-state actors were deeply rooted in liberal theories of the state: elite theory, pluralism, and statism. Although admittedly dated, these theories continue to find their way into the literature that seeks to evaluate the role, significance, and impact of think tanks in the policy-making community. In the pages that follow, we consider the strengths and limitations of these theories, and what steps can be taken to provide more informed insights about how think tanks attempt to influence public opinion and public policy. In the process, we will offer suggestions as to how these organizations can be examined in a more integrative way. We will come to the realization that it is not simply the terminology that political scientists and sociologists use to describe how think tanks engage different communities that has changed. The continued growth and increased presence of think tanks on the political landscape, and their desire to become more advocacy-oriented, compel us to re-evaluate what they do, how their role has changed, and the extent to which they have become more entrenched in policy-making.

ELITE THEORY

As noted, in several of the earliest studies of think tanks, which focused predominantly on policy institutes in the United States, discussions about how and why these organizations enjoyed privileged status, and were rewarded with preferential access to powerful members of the bureaucracy, Congress, and the White House, were linked to liberal theories of the state. For example, elite theorists posited that many of those who occupied key positions in think tanks, or donated large gifts to sustain their operations, travelled in the same social and financial circles, attended many of the same Ivy League institutions, and belonged to social clubs where the country's leading political figures congregated. Theorists argued that, moreover, by virtue of these strong and overlapping ties, think tanks were provided with the access and opportunities they required to advance both their institutional interests and those of their corporate and philanthropic donors. Several American scholars, including C. Wright Mills, relied heavily on elite theory to analyze the US military–industrial complex in the mid-1950s. Indeed, Mills's seminal 1956 work on the topic, *The Power Elite*,[1] caused quite a stir in both academic and policy-making circles when it first appeared. His growing concerns about how the US Congress, the Pentagon, and defence contractors worked together to fuel the Cold War was not lost on President Dwight Eisenhower: in his farewell address on 17 January 1961, Eisenhower warned the American people about the dangers of the military–industrial complex.[2] Over half a century later, similar concerns are being expressed by journalists and scholars all too familiar with what and who are driving US foreign policy.[3] Studies on elite theory may not generate the scholarly attention they once did, but much of what Mills and his contemporaries revealed still deserves our consideration. Although some of the terms used to describe elites might be outdated, the assumptions underlying this theory have remained largely intact. In fact, elite theory has helped to fuel other theories, some rather fanciful, others not, about how think tanks, in cooperation with other key stakeholders, assist governments in convincing the public to embrace controversial domestic and foreign policies.

Pluralism

As tempting as it is to assume that think tanks are an elite set of actors that enjoy unlimited and unfettered access to the corridors of power, and as much as directors of think tanks would like to be treated like royalty in the White House and on Capitol Hill, some observers are not convinced that they should be perceived differently from other groups competing for attention in the policy-making community.[4] Rather than elevating think tanks to a status usually reserved for a handful of

organizations at the highest levels of government, those embracing the
tenets of pluralism[5] argue that policy institutes, like interest groups, trade
unions, human rights organizations, environmental associations, and a
host of other institutions committed to influencing public policy, face
similar hurdles as they try to navigate their way through the policy-
making process. That some organizations are more effective than others
in capturing the attention of policy-makers does not concern pluralists, as
long as the rules established by government to oversee the participation
of non-governmental organizations in the policy process are followed.

For pluralists, what matters is not that non-governmental organizations have different resources at their disposal, but that they have the
opportunity to compete on a level playing field. As discussed in chapter 1, by imposing restrictions on political and partisan activities, legislative bodies, with the support of government departments and regulatory
agencies, attempt to exercise control over policy inputs (who contributes
to public policy), not policy outcomes (the actual decisions of government). In other words, pluralists contend that policy-makers simply
want to ensure that the guidelines non-governmental organizations must
follow to participate in the policy-making process are fair and transparent. They also claim that policy-makers are less invested in who ultimately succeeds in influencing policy decisions, an assertion disputed
by elite theorists, who recognize that how governments control policy
inputs influences policy outcomes.

Statism

Third, there are a handful of scholars who acknowledge the presence of
think tanks and other non-governmental organizations in the policy-
making community, but who suggest that they play a very modest role in
shaping public policy. Contrary to the assertions of scholars who argue
that public policy is controlled and manipulated by elites and/or by
special interest groups, those embracing the "statist paradigm" maintain
that the state can and does act independently of various societal and
bureaucratic pressures.[6] In short, they argue that the fate of the nation
rests in the hands of presidents, prime ministers, and their cabinets, not
by external groups seeking to impose their agenda on the state.

Institutionalists

And finally, there are scholars who focus less on the elitist, pluralist, or
statist nature of think tanks and the policy environment they inhabit,

and more on the institutional structure and orientation of the organizations themselves. Scholars influenced by the "institutionalist" tradition pay close attention to the mandate and resources of think tanks, and to the many factors that influence the strategic choices they make to become involved at different stages of policy-making.[7] It is to these particular approaches that we now turn.

THINK TANKS AS POLICY ELITES

For some scholars, including Joseph Peschek, Thomas Dye, William Domhoff, John Saloma, and William Minter,[8] think tanks not only regularly interact with policy elites, they also comprise part of the nation's power structure. For example, in the United States, where think tanks frequently serve as talent pools or holding tanks for incoming presidential administrations and as retirement homes for former high-level policy-makers, think tanks are considered elite organizations that are both able and willing to influence public policy. The multimillion-dollar budgets at the disposal of a handful of American think tanks, and the many prominent and distinguished business leaders and former policy-makers who serve on their boards of directors and trustees help reinforce this image. The close ties between think tanks and the corporate and philanthropic donors and foreign governments who fund them[9] suggest to Marxists and elite theorists[10] that think tanks are indeed instruments of the ruling class. These theorists argue that by virtue of the unique space they occupy at the intersection of the academic and policy-making worlds, think tanks are more than capable of advancing the interests of those with economic and political power. The argument advanced by scholars in this field is straightforward: in exchange for large donations, think tanks use their policy expertise and connections with key policy-makers to advance the political agendas of their generous benefactors. On the surface, this seems entirely plausible. After all, it is unlikely that corporations and philanthropic foundations would donate thousands, and sometimes millions, of dollars to think tanks that are acting contrary to their interests. They fund think tanks that share similar ideals and concerns, and those they believe are capable of affecting policy change. As David Roodman, formerly of the Washington, DC–based Center for Global Development, observes, "Every funder has motives. Every funder of a policy-influencing think tank can therefore be described as "buying influence."[11] However, it is important to question the type of return that donors expect on their investment. To quote Enrique Mendizabal, founder of the blog On Think Tanks, "Domestic or foreign, nobody hands over money to think tanks without wanting [something] in return. They may want to influence certain policy decisions or they may just want to see their name outside an office in the think tank's new building. They all want something."[12]

While it makes sense for philanthropic foundations, corporations, and leaders of foreign governments to fund think tanks that can frame issues in ways that will help advance their core interests, it is less important for these and other donors to rely on them to help establish contact with senior-level policy-makers. Through their sizeable donations to congressional and presidential candidates, not to mention their personal friendships and social ties to dozen of politicians, it is unlikely that donors with this kind of cachet would require think tanks to introduce them to government officials. This is not to say that think tanks are unwilling to make introductions – they often do. The point is whether it is necessary for them to do so. Moreover, since corporations and foreign governments can and do hire lobbyists to represent their interests on Capitol Hill and on Parliament Hill, it is unlikely that they would turn to institutions like think tanks, which are prohibited under the Internal Revenue Code and the Income Tax Act, from engaging in overt political lobbying. And since professional lobbyists have an incentive to work tirelessly on behalf of their clients, what can think tanks offer corporate America and Canada that lobbyists cannot? The answer is simple: credibility and respectability, or what Joseph Sandler, an American lawyer with expertise on statutes that govern lobbying, refers to as a "patina of academic neutrality and objectivity."[13]

Corporations and philanthropic foundations turn to "elite" think tanks such as Brookings, the Carnegie Endowment, and the Hoover Institution not so they can take advantage of their political connections (although this could help periodically), but so they can benefit from the relationships these and other think tanks have with the media, universities, and other power centres in Canada and in the United States. But even more important, corporations and philanthropic foundations can take advantage of the reputation that think tanks have cultivated as scientific, neutral, and scholarly organizations to more effectively influence public opinion and public policy. Writing large cheques to political campaigns may provide corporations with access and political capital, but it does not necessarily buy them credibility, which, like valuable information, can prove to be a commodity more precious than money. On the other hand, supporting think tanks that supply the media and policy-makers with a steady stream of information, expertise, and policy recommendations might allow donors to secure both. This could explain in part why corporations and philanthropic foundations also lend a helping hand to other types of research organizations and university departments who can draw on their reputations as scholarly institutions to influence both the policy-making environment and actual policy decisions.

By closely examining the interaction between the largest think tanks in the United States and Canada and key officials in government, scholars may be justified in concluding, as some have, that think tanks play a critical role in influencing public policy. However, since few institutes in Canada or in the United States have resources comparable to the Brookings Institution, the Heritage Foundation, or the RAND Corporation, we must question the utility of employing an approach that assumes that think tanks, by their very nature and purpose, are capable of promoting the interests of the ruling elite. We must also question whether think tanks, as charitable organizations engaged in policy analysis, should be treated as elites.

Think tanks are in the business of shaping public opinion and public policy, but, as noted, have very different ideas of how various domestic and foreign policies should be formulated and implemented. Several think tanks, for example, embrace the views of some elites that free market solutions to economic problems should be pursued. The C.D. Howe Institute, the Fraser Institute, the Montreal Economics Institute, and the American Enterprise Institute in Washington, DC, among others, would certainly favour such an approach. But there are many other think tanks, including the more progressive Canadian Centre for Policy Alternatives (CCPA), the Parkland Institute at the University of Alberta, and the Washington-based Institute for Policy Studies, that have profoundly different views of how governments should resolve economic and social problems. These think tanks go to great lengths to address widespread inequality. Should think tanks that regularly oppose the interests of the ruling elite and work tirelessly on behalf of those who are marginalized in our country, then, be considered part of the elite?

Despite some limitations, which will be explored in more detail below, adopting an elite approach to the study of think tanks has some advantages. As Domhoff and others have discovered,[14] examining the close and interlocking ties between members of think tanks and leaders in business and government can provide interesting and useful insights into why some policy institutes may enjoy far more visibility and notoriety than others. Moreover, by keeping track of who sits on the boards of directors of think tanks, we may be able to explain why some institutes

generate more funding than their competitors. Nonetheless, it is important to keep in mind that while members of think tanks frequently interact with high-level business leaders and policy-makers, their connections
to key figures do not necessarily allow them to exercise influence over
policy. The networks they have established may facilitate access to
important officials on Capitol Hill and Parliament Hill, but their ability
to influence public policy depends on a wide range of factors.

By portraying think tanks as policy elites, scholars can make sweeping
assertions about who controls public policy. But as appealing as this
might be, it is also problematic because it tells us little about the ability or inability of think tanks to exercise influence at different stages of
the policy cycle. It tells us even less about how to assess or evaluate the
impact of think tanks in policy-making. An elite approach assumes, in
short, that with the right connections, think tanks can and will be able
to influence public policy but, unfortunately, it offers little insight into
how this will be achieved.

THE PLURALIST TRADITION: ONE VOICE AMONG MANY

Members of think tanks may occasionally travel in elite policy circles,
but according to some political scientists, including David Newsom,[15]
they represent but one of many types of organizations that populate
the policy-making community. According to this perspective, which is
deeply rooted in the American pluralist tradition,[16] think tanks compete
among themselves and other non-governmental organizations for limited resources. The gains achieved by one group or organization are
frequently offset by costs incurred by others.[17] Since policy-makers, and
the governments they represent, are assumed to behave as moderators or
referees monitoring the competition among groups, pluralists devote
little attention to assessing government priorities. They view public policy not as a reflection of a specific government mandate, but, rather, as
an outcome of the struggle between competing interests.

Studying think tanks within a pluralist framework has its advantages.
For one thing, it compels scholars to acknowledge that, despite the
widely held view that think tanks enjoy preferential access to policy-
makers and other key stakeholders, they constitute only one of many
organizations intent on leaving a mark on public policy. This approach
also serves as a reminder that think tanks, like interest groups and other
non-governmental organizations, rely on similar strategies to shape public policy, a subject that will be explored further in chapter 4.

The pluralist approach, however, has serious weaknesses. To begin with, although disciples of pluralism assume that, in the final analysis, decisions on domestic and foreign policy matters reflect the outcome of an ongoing struggle among groups to advance their respective interests, pluralism sheds little light on why some organizations may be better positioned than others to influence public attitudes and the policy preferences and choices of decision makers. Is it simply a matter of which groups have the largest budgets and staff resources, and most extensive research programs that determines who has influence and who doesn't? Or do other factors such as access to the media, policy-makers, and affluent donors offer better clues as to which group or groups are destined to succeed or fail in the political arena?

The major deficiency of pluralism is not that it assumes that all groups are able to influence public policy equally. On the contrary, pluralists acknowledge that non-governmental organizations vary enormously in terms of size, resources, and expertise, important factors that can account for how successful organizations are in achieving their desired goals. The problem with pluralism is that it exaggerates the virtues of a level playing field while ignoring how groups with vastly superior resources at their disposal can easily outrun or out manoeuvre their opponents. To put it another way, pluralists are so concerned about following the rules of the policy game that they pay little attention to why some organizations always seem to cross the finish line first. For pluralists, process matters far more than outcomes. By the same token, if pluralists treat think tanks as simply one of many voices in the policy-making community without recognizing what makes them unique, they will overlook why, at times, some policy institutes have more opportunities to influence public policy than interest groups and other non-governmental organizations. Think tanks may indeed be part of the chorus, but they possess certain attributes that allow them to stand out. By virtue of their expertise and close ties to policy-makers, think tanks may compete among themselves for prestige and status, but they do not necessarily compete with the hundreds of other participants in the policy-making community. In fact, in some policy areas, think tanks may face little competition at all.

Pluralists also need to acknowledge that, as committed as policy-makers might be to ensuring fairness and transparency in the policy-making process, they often have a vested interest in influencing the outcome of group competition. Instead of behaving as referees, policy-makers representing various government branches and departments can and do rely heavily on select organizations to achieve their goals. Many of these organizations are also closely aligned with large voting blocs in congressional districts and/or parliamentary ridings that elected officials cannot afford to ignore. As we will discuss in chapters 5 and 6, at critical stages of the policy-making process, members of the US Congress and the Executive, and their counterparts in Parliament, regularly turn to specific think tanks for advice on how to tackle thorny policy issues or to help frame the parameters of important policy debates.

Marxists and pluralists disagree about the extent to which think tanks are entrenched in the policy-making process and the willingness of the state to embrace their ideas. However, both acknowledge that think tanks have the ability to play a vital, and, at times, decisive role in public policy, a position that has been questioned by proponents of state theory. While scholars employing the first two approaches focus on various societal and bureaucratic pressures to reveal how public policy is shaped and molded, those advancing the statist paradigm look no further than the state to explain who makes policy decisions.

IN THE NATIONAL INTEREST: A STATIST APPROACH

As multinational corporations, media conglomerates, and powerful special interest groups have established a strong foothold in the Western world, it is not surprising that we have lost sight of who is ultimately entrusted with protecting the national interest, a concern raised most recently by several scholars in the United States.[18] But despite their global reach and visibility, it is not Bill Gates, Warren Buffett, or leaders of other blue chip companies who speak on behalf of the United States and take steps to promote its economic, political, and security interests. It is the president and the people who surround him or her. To remind us of this, a handful of scholars, including Theda Skocpol and Stephen Krasner, have emphasized the relative autonomy of the state in making difficult policy decisions.[19] State theory, according to Aaron Steelman, advances the argument "that while the public can indeed impose some restraint on the actions of the bureaucracy and elected officials, the state retains a degree of autonomy and works according to its own logic."[20]

In his book *Defending the National Interest*, Stephen Krasner elaborates on the theory of statism. He notes: "[Statism] is premised upon an intellectual vision that sees the state autonomously formulating goals that it then attempts to implement against resistance from international and domestic actors. The ability of the state to overcome domestic resistance depends upon the instruments of control that it can exercise over groups within its own society."[21] For Krasner, it is the central state actors in the US – the president and the secretary of state – and the most important institutions – the White House and the State Department – that control foreign policy.

If Krasner, Skocpol, and other proponents of state theory are correct, what impact could think tanks possibly have on influencing state behaviour? Although one might assume that think tanks would be relegated to the sidelines, Steelman suggests that state theory leaves ample room for think tanks to make their presence felt: "State theory can help explain the seeming anomalous cases of former think-tank staffers who enter government pledging to work for a certain set of ideas and then enacting policies that are quite different. In some cases, these individuals have been co-opted by the system; in others, they are generally doing their best to reach their goal, however slowly or circuitously. But either way, the state itself is an important actor."[22]

There are several advantages to incorporating state theory into studies of think tanks. First, it helps to explain how think tank staffers can become directly involved in making key policy decisions. If we accept Krasner's argument that the president and the secretary of state, and the two institutions they represent – the White House and the State Department – are the most important participants in the foreign-policy-making process, it becomes very clear which think tanks have or do not have access to the highest levels of government. Rather than trying to monitor the efforts of think tanks to influence Congress and the media, scholars could simply explore the relationship between the president, the secretary of state, and their closest advisers. If it appears that members from think tanks have served as advisers, or have been recruited to serve in the White House or the State Department, we could assume that they have had direct access to the policy-making process. After all, if the president and secretary of state (along with the secretary of defense, joint chiefs of staff, and national security adviser) are the most influential participants in foreign- and defence-policy-making and often rely on think tank experts for advice, it would be logical to conclude that think tanks are in a position to influence policy decisions. Conversely, if there is little evidence to suggest that think tanks have gained access to the upper echelons of government, scholars could, according to state theory, conclude that they have had little impact in influencing state conduct. In short, state theory, whether it is applied to domestic or foreign policy decision-making in the United

States, Canada, or other democracies, can explain when think tanks have been influential and when they have not.

However, state theory is not without its limitations. It may be useful in explaining why some presidents, such as Richard Nixon, were able to insulate themselves from Congress and the American people.[23] But by the same token, it is less helpful in explaining why many recent presidents have gone to great lengths to consult with the public, members of Congress, foreign governments, international organizations, and a host of non-governmental organizations before making important policy decisions. President George H.W. Bush's efforts in 1990–91 to secure an international coalition to deter Iraqi aggression is a case in point. Before deploying US armed forces to the Persian Gulf, President Bush made sure he had the support of the United Nations and several of its member states, a strategy that his son considered, but later abandoned, before invading Iraq.[24] As the foreign-policy-making process has become more transparent over time and as more governmental and non-governmental organizations have sought to become involved in shaping world affairs, proponents of state theory have had a more difficult time defending the relative autonomy of the state. They have certainly had difficulty explaining why the US Congress appears to have taken a more active interest in foreign policy.[25] In the final analysis, both advocates and critics of state theory acknowledge that the president makes decisions that can profoundly influence America's conduct in the international community. Yet, as we have witnessed in recent years, how presidents make policy decisions ultimately depends on their management style and willingness to listen to their inner circle of advisers. State theory might help to account for how US foreign policy under President George W. Bush was managed, but might do little to shed light on how Presidents Clinton and Obama governed the nation.[26]

Thus far, we have looked at three different theoretical approaches and how they can be employed to study think tanks. Before considering how it might be possible to integrate them more effectively, it is important to consider a fourth approach that has attracted considerable attention: focusing on think tanks as a diverse set of organizations with very different priorities and concerns, rather than as a member of the policy elite, the state, or the broader policy-making community. This approach appears more promising. As we will discover below, a more informed understanding of how think tanks function at various stages of the policy-making process can allow scholars to identify where these institutions have the greatest impact.

DIFFERENT THINK TANKS, DIFFERENT PRIORITIES:
AN INSTITUTIONAL APPROACH

Three distinct institutional approaches to the study of think tanks have surfaced in the literature in recent years. The most common approach focuses either on the history of particular think tanks or on their evolution and transformation in particular countries. Several scholars have written institutional histories of the Brookings Institution, the Council on Foreign Relations, the Heritage Foundation, and RAND.[27] A number of studies have also detailed the rise of think tanks in the United States, Canada, and other advanced as well as developing countries.[28] The obvious advantage of providing detailed histories of think tanks is that they offer a wealth of information on the nature and mandate of organizations, the research projects they have conducted over time, and the various institutional changes they have undergone. The main disadvantage, however, is that many of these studies are simply histories and offer few concrete data to support or deny claims that particular think tanks have played a major role in shaping public policies.

The second and more systematic institutional approach has concentrated on the involvement of think tanks in what students of public policy commonly refer to as epistemic or policy communities.[29] These communities consist of individuals and organizations that, by virtue of their policy expertise, are invited to participate in policy discussions with government decision makers. The formation of policy or epistemic communities is often seen as a critical stage in policy formulation and regime formation. This approach has been undertaken by a handful of political scientists, including Hugh Heclo, Evert Lindquist, and Diane Stone, who regard think tanks as important participants in these communities.[30]

By examining think tanks within a policy or epistemic community framework, scholars can make several important observations. To begin with, by focusing on policy issues, such as the abrogation of the Anti-Ballistic Missile Treaty or the drafting of the controversial Helms-Burton legislation in the United States, scholars can more accurately identify the key organizations and individuals who have been invited to share their thoughts with policy-makers. In addition to determining which groups and individuals participate in the "sub-government" – a term used to describe the various non-governmental and governmental policy experts who coalesce around particular policy issues – this approach offers better insight into the nature of the policy-making process itself. Among other things, a policy or epistemic community framework compels scholars to delve far deeper into the mechanics of policy-making. Rather than treating policy decisions as an outcome of interest group competition or as a reflection of elite interests, this approach requires scholars to think seriously about how policy decisions can be influenced through discussions between non-governmental and governmental policy experts.

There are other advantages to adopting this approach as well. Once the actors participating in the sub-government have been identified, it is possible to compare the recommendations made by participants to the actual policy decisions that were made. Access to minutes of meetings, personal correspondence, testimony before legislative committees, published recommendations, and other information may not enable scholars to come to definitive conclusions about which participants in a policy community were the most influential but these and other materials can offer useful insights into whose views generated the most support.

Given the involvement of policy experts from think tanks in different policy communities, it is not surprising that this framework is being used more often. It is important to keep in mind, however, that while this approach may be better suited to the study of think tanks than either an elite or a pluralist framework, it too has its shortcomings. Examining think tanks within a policy community is useful in identifying which institutes are called upon to offer their expertise at an important stage in policy formulation. Unfortunately, it does not tell us what impact, if any, think tanks inside policy communities or those operating outside the sub-government have in shaping public attitudes and the policy preferences and choices of policy-makers. In short, this approach may tell us who is sitting at the table when key issues are being discussed, but it does not tell us whose voices have struck a responsive chord with those in a position to influence policy decisions. Since we cannot assume that all, or any, important policy decisions are made inside specific policy communities – after all, it is politicians, not policy experts, who cast votes in the legislature – a third group of scholars have begun to consider using a more inclusive approach in studying the involvement of non-governmental organizations in policy-making.

Recognizing that non-governmental organizations vary enormously in terms of their mandate, resources, and priorities, John Kingdon and Denis Stairs, among others, suggest that rather than trying to make general observations about how much or how little impact societal groups have on shaping policy-making and the policy-making environment, scholars should examine how groups committed to influencing public policy focus their efforts at different stages of the policy cycle.[31] Although Kingdon and Stairs do not write specifically about think tanks, their approach to studying how groups seek to place issues on the political agenda and how they try to convey their ideas to policy-makers throughout the policy-making process is well-suited to the study of think tanks.

POLICY CYCLES AND POLICY INFLUENCE: A HOLISTIC APPROACH

For Kingdon and Stairs, trying to determine which domestic and external forces shape public policy constitutes an at times overwhelming undertaking. In fact, as the policy-making community in the United States and in Canada has become increasingly crowded, it has become difficult, if not impossible, to identify those groups that have had a direct impact on policy issues. As a result, instead of making generalizations about which groups influence public policy, Kingdon and Stairs, among others, recognize that not all organizations have the desire or the necessary resources to participate at each stage of the policy cycle: issue articulation, policy formulation, and policy implementation. Some organizations may have an interest in sharing their ideas with the public, so they place issues on the political agenda by expressing their concerns through a number of channels. This is issue articulation. Others may be more inclined to work closely with policy-makers to formulate or implement policy.

By acknowledging that think tanks do have different priorities and mandates, it is possible to construct a conceptual framework that allows scholars to make more concrete observations about the role and impact of think tanks in policy-making. A framework that recognizes the diversity of think tanks and their distinct missions will, at the very least, discourage scholars from making sweeping and often unfounded observations about their impact.

The conceptual framework employed in this book, which will be expanded upon in the chapters to follow, is based on a simple premise: think tanks in Canada, the United States, and much of Europe represent a diverse set of organizations that share a common desire to influence public policy. However, because of their unique characteristics, each think tank must make strategic decisions about how and where to make its presence felt. In other words, since think tanks possess different resources, which, not surprisingly, affect the nature and extent of activities they undertake, they naturally assign different priorities to different stages of the policy cycle. This becomes particularly important in interpreting data such as media citations and testimony before legislative committees, which can be used to evaluate think tank performance.

After considering the four approaches we have employed to study think tanks and how they affect the policy-making process, one central question remains: Which approach or conceptual framework best explains their role and function? Unfortunately, there is no simple answer. As we have discussed, each approach encourages scholars to move in a certain direction and to ask a unique set of questions. Therefore, the question that should be posed is not which theory best explains how the functional role of think tanks has changed, but which framework helps scholars better understand a particular feature or characteristic of their behaviour. For instance, those concerned about the relationship between think tanks and corporations could benefit far more from drawing on the assumptions underlying elite theory than from tapping into pluralist theories of democracy. On the other hand, scholars interested in explaining why some think tanks seem more preoccupied with working on various policy initiatives than with grabbing the headlines would learn a great deal from Kingdon and other students of public policy who have written extensively about how institutions set priorities.

In examining the efforts of think tanks to influence key domestic and foreign policy debates, an integrated approach is required. This approach would draw on the observations showcased by each of the theories outlined in this chapter, but would not adhere exclusively to any particular one. The advantage of relying on multiple theories to explain how the involvement of think tanks affects public policy is that it offers scholars some breathing space to test different hypotheses about when and under what conditions think tanks can have the greatest impact. The alternative is to select a theoretical framework that offers only one perspective on the nature of think tanks and their relationship to policy-makers. For example, Krasner's statist paradigm could be adopted to explain why think tanks and interest groups have had marginal success in constructing and implementing the Obama administration's war on terror. Given the relatively small group of advisers to whom Obama has listened, and the president's decision to continue the war on terror with limited support from the international community, state theory might offer scholars the answers they need. However, the same theory would offer little insight into the debate over national missile defence, which has been kept alive for over three decades by a handful of think tanks, including the Heritage Foundation and the Center for Security Policy. Contrary to the central assumptions underlying state theory, successive US administrations have succumbed to pressure from interest groups, think tanks, and corporate and bureaucratic interests to construct and deploy a missile defence. Rather than looking to Krasner for answers as to why this has occurred, scholars would likely benefit more from reading the work of C. Wright Mills and others who have provided valuable insights about the military–industrial complex.

In the final analysis, scholars must select a theory or theories that will help them to understand the information they have uncovered. They should not rush to find a theory and then hope to gather empirical and statistical evidence to make it more credible. Such an approach may be of little comfort to those looking for a grand theory to explain what think tanks do and how they achieve influence. Still, many experts of American foreign policy and international relations have learned that as tempting as it would be to construct one theory that would reveal the complexity of world affairs, such efforts often amount to little more than an exercise in futility. But before we rush to judgment about which theory or theories best explains how and to what extent think tanks engage in the policy-making process, we need to more fully explore what think tanks do and how they do it. Only then can we determine how the various approaches we discussed in this chapter enhance or obscure our understanding of these unique organizations.

4

What Do Think Tanks Do,
and How Do They Do It?

As the activities and functions of think tanks continue to evolve and expand, it is understandable why so much confusion surrounding what they do and how they go about it persists. Canadians who follow politics at home and abroad undoubtedly have some familiarity with think tanks in Canada, the United States, and beyond. After all, if they watch the news, listen to public radio, browse "political" publications on the Internet, or count themselves among the dwindling population of newspaper readers, it is difficult to avoid the steady stream of information percolating from think tanks. However, even with frequent exposure to these institutions and the opinions of their leading analysts, questions about the priorities, goals, and aspirations of think tanks remain.

Members of the attentive public who may be confused at times as to whether think tanks are similar to interest groups and/or lobbyists, a matter addressed in chapter 1, are hardly alone. Making sense of the various activities that think tanks are expected to undertake is even confusing for policy experts who have toiled at these institutions for years. On any given day, they may be asked to prepare an opinion piece, commentary, or blog for a national or international newspaper and/or online publication, share their insights about a current event on a network newscast or radio program, begin planning a conference, seminar, or workshop that focuses on one of their many research projects, testify before a legislative committee, deliver a lecture, attend a fundraising event, and, when they can take a breath, help coordinate the work of interns and assistants – and all before lunch. If policy experts can manage to take care of these and other responsibilities, they might even manage to steal a few minutes to think about their research. With the growing demands placed on researchers at think tanks, it is not surprising that

Christopher Sands, a respected scholar of Canadian-American Relations at Washington's Hudson Institute, remarked half-jokingly, "I work at a think tank. I don't have time to think."[1]

The opportunity to contribute to timely and relevant research projects may have convinced Sands and his colleagues to seek shelter at think tanks, but over time, they came to the realization that to succeed in what has become an increasingly competitive marketplace of ideas, they had to arm themselves with far more than an advanced degree. Unlike their classmates from graduate school who kept a watchful eye on job postings at various universities, those who sought appointments at think tanks required far more than a master's or PhD to apply. To be employed as a policy expert at a top-tier Canadian or American think tank, it is expected that, at a minimum, applicants possess strong academic credentials and a robust research record, a background deemed critical for enhancing not only their credibility and respectability, but that of the institutions they hope to represent. For think tanks, the ideal applicant is someone who can multi-task. They must possess a comprehensive and diverse skill set that allows them to help their potential employer to educate, disseminate, communicate, prognosticate, advocate, and, yes, indoctrinate. Experience working in government and/or a talent for fundraising is also considered an asset. Ideally, scholars who work at think tanks must present themselves as far more than capable researchers. In a fast-paced and politically charged environment where think tanks are constantly competing for attention and notoriety, those whom they employ must be able to communicate and interact with multiple stakeholders to advance the core mission of their organization. And without the security of tenure, think tank residents have an incentive to become jacks-of-all-trades, and, in a perfect world, masters of them all.

In this chapter, we shift our focus to explaining how think tanks have reinvented themselves as institutions that provide much more than research and analysis. Although developing expertise in one or more policy areas is vital to the success of think tanks, it can no longer be regarded as their sole, or even most important, function. By hiving off resources from research to support other activities, including advocacy, think tanks, argues Tevi Troy, a senior scholar and colleague of Christopher Sands at the Hudson Institute, are devaluing their currency, an observation with which I am in complete agreement.[2] But from the vantage point of many think tanks, it is by diversifying the range of products and services they offer that has *added* value to their currency. As we consider what think tanks do, and how they do it, it is important not to lose sight of these competing perspectives. With this in mind, we may now identify the key functions of think tanks.

MULTIPLE PERSONALITIES IN ORDER:
THE MANY FACES OF THINK TANKS

The ancient Roman god Janus, for whom the month of January is named, is depicted with two faces. With eyes literally on the back of his head, he could simultaneously look to the past and peer into the future. When directors of think tanks look in the mirror each morning, their thoughts may not necessarily turn to Janus, but, consciously or unconsciously, they understand that the future of the institute that they have been entrusted to oversee requires them to both respect past successes and failures, and embrace new opportunities. Whereas the identity of think tanks in the early decades of the twentieth century was often defined by the level and quality of expertise they offered, their contribution is no longer measured solely this way. On the contrary, for think tanks to achieve the kind of influence they truly covet, they must often market themselves as policy shops that provide a range of products and services.

THE FOUR RS — READING, WRITING, ARITHMETIC, AND ...

Andrew Carnegie, Robert Brookings, and Herbert Hoover would have had little difficulty identifying the last word in this phrase, which often appeared in the mission statements of the institutions they helped to endow. Indeed, had they been in a position to draft the guiding principles of the think tanks that bore their name, they likely would have insisted on placing an exclamation mark beside *Research*. The goal of undertaking research that would help to advance the national interest and contribute to a more informed and enlightened public policy was, and remains, the hallmark of think tanks. As discussed in chapter 1, although think tanks vary enormously in terms of the resources they devote to research, generating and producing new and innovative ideas is their raison d'être.

How think tanks conduct research, the areas of specialization in which they concentrate, and the range of publications they produce are all factors they must consider in developing an institutional profile. And, not surprisingly, in Canada, as in the United States, think tanks have embraced different research models. Yet before we discuss the kinds of publications think tanks generate and examples of the research they have undertaken, a few words about how these institutes are managed is in order. As previously noted, in studying how think tanks navigate their way through the policy-making process, it is important to keep in mind whether the organizations themselves resemble traditional academic departments where scholars are free to pursue topics of their choosing, or if stricter controls are placed on the kinds of research topics experts are permitted to undertake, and the form they are expected to take. How think tanks are organized has a profound effect on shaping the institutional culture in which policy experts are expected to conform.[3]

For example, the way in which projects are managed and directed at the Conference Board of Canada or at the Institute for Research on Public Policy[4] is, not surprisingly, very different from how university-based think tanks such as the Centre for Foreign Policy Studies at Dalhousie University and the Centre for Global Studies at the University of Victoria oversee their research. At IRPP, the C.D. Howe Institute, the Canada West Foundation, and most other private or stand-alone think tanks, policy experts usually work in research clusters or designated research programs where they pursue independent and/or collaborative research, and, in consultation with managers and/or directors, investigate topics that have been agreed to, and funded, in advance. How much autonomy and latitude scholars have in selecting their own research projects varies significantly across institutions. According to Jason Clemens, executive vice-president of the Fraser Institute, policy experts at Fraser play an important and active role in deciding which research projects to pursue each year. In what Clemens maintains is a very open and collegial decision-making process, policy experts consult with management, and select seven or eight topics to undertake. Once they have selected from about seventy to eighty potential projects, they turn their attention to locating and securing the funding required to carry out this research.[5] At the Fraser Institute, as in most think tanks that employ a hierarchical, or top-down, decision-making model, careful thought is given to the individuals to whom specific projects are assigned, and the kinds of research outputs they are expected to generate. This model has been adopted by several think tanks in North America, including the Heritage Foundation, which in many ways functions like a medium-sized American corporation.[6]

Inside the boardrooms of Heritage, and other think tanks that resemble corporations, the president leads a senior administrative team that is responsible for, among other things, developing a mission statement, drafting and implementing a strategic plan, and allocating resources in ways they hope will produce optimal results. Moreover, to help achieve their goals, most private think tanks will have the benefit of relying on the advice of an advisory council and board of trustees. Many of the individuals who serve in these capacities may, by virtue of their professional and personal ties to government officials and business leaders, help think tanks elevate their status in the policy research community. In short, from the perspective of those who both fund and operate private think tanks, policy institutes should not be treated any differently than other businesses striving to achieve the highest level of productivity. However, unlike corporations and businesses that measure success by profit margins, the bottom line is far less tangible for charitable organizations such as think tanks. Rather than focusing on a single figure in a ledger column, think tanks evaluate their performance by the extent to which they have influenced public opinion and public policy, a result that does not appear in quarterly reports.

While private think tanks are known to embrace many of the corporate sector's business principles, their counterparts on university campuses are often managed very differently. In addition to being less hierarchical and, of necessity, more collegial, university-based think tanks face a unique set of challenges. This is hardly surprising given that private and university-based think tanks inhabit very different environments which are shaped and influenced by distinct institutional cultures. Although university faculty continue to express concern that their institutions are becoming increasingly corporatized, in reality the academic world remains, in many ways, very different from the private sector.

As salaried employees, policy experts at private think tanks are expected to participate in many of the functions their organizations oversee, functions that, as noted, may require them to wear multiple hats. Opting out is rarely an option, particularly for those who wish to remain on the payroll. In contrast, tenured and tenure-track faculty at universities are paid to teach, conduct independent and/or collaborative research, and contribute some of their time to what is broadly referred to as service. This might entail serving on departmental, faculty, and/or university-wide committees, interacting regularly with the media, and possibly presenting lectures to service and rotary clubs. What they are not expected or required to do is contribute their time and energy to helping think tanks on campus establish an institutional profile. This is something they elect to do. For some faculty, contributing to the research activities of a think tank may allow them to share their work with a larger audience and to network with other colleagues across the university. But if communicating their ideas with the public, with policy-makers, and, potentially, other stakeholders holds little appeal, perhaps an opportunity to receive teaching release time or a modest stipend in exchange for time served with a policy institute might do the trick. To be blunt, the success of university-based think tanks largely depends on the willingness of a select group of faculty and graduate students to buy into the mission of these institutes. Still, even with the support and confidence of key constituencies, university-based think tanks face other challenges.

One of the key challenges of ensuring that university think tanks remain viable and sustainable is to convince faculty that it is in their interest to produce timely and policy-relevant research, conditions that may seem foreign to university researchers but are nonetheless vital to the success of private think tanks. Preparing an article for publication in a refereed scholarly journal or a book chapter in an edited collection, typical outlets for most academics, might take several months and possibly well over a year to produce. Unless scholars are in the habit of submitting commentaries and opinion pieces to magazines and newspapers, something young researchers working toward tenure are discouraged from doing, it might be difficult for them to engage in quick-response policy research, the hallmark of most advocacy-oriented think tanks. For most academics, preparing a 500- to 1,000-word policy brief in a few hours or days, the normal turnaround time for policy experts at private think tanks, would simply be unrealistic.

When it comes to meeting publication deadlines, academics are notorious for submitting their work in a less than timely fashion. Indeed, unlike their colleagues at think tanks, who are required to stay ahead of the curve, academics, because of teaching and administrative responsibilities, often find themselves behind the eight ball. Moreover, scholars in most disciplines are simply not trained or have little interest in writing concise publications for public consumption. They simply do not have the desire or incentive to "dumb down" research they have devoted years to refining. Faculty members would much rather spend their time producing academic publications for academic audiences. This makes perfect sense given that they must produce strong research records to secure tenure and promotion. A handful of single or co-authored studies posted online or distributed in hard copy by think tanks may take up some space on a faculty member's résumé, but they are not the kinds of publications that will, in all likelihood, impress their peers. In the academic world, what matters are university press books, book chapters in edited collections published by prestigious publishing houses, and articles placed in high-profile refereed journals. In short, for most academics trying to make their way through the ranks of the professoriate, spending any significant amount of energy on other kinds of publications (unless they are properly compensated) would not be time well spent.

Naturally, there are exceptions. In some cases, it would make sense for faculty to share their expertise with the broader community. For scholars who have the luxury of tenure, and perhaps have risen to the rank of full professor – the highest rung on the academic ladder – and for those who consider themselves public intellectuals,[7] agreeing to write commentaries, policy briefs, or other kinds of studies for think tanks could pay handsome dividends. Since the role of public intellectuals is, as the term implies, to reach out and educate the wider public, working closely with organizations that are capable of attaching their tentacles to elected officials and to the electorate would be an opportunity they could ill-afford to pass up. Of course, this assumes that think tanks housed at universities are capable of recruiting and retaining a stable of experts who are committed to working on various projects that may take years to complete. Unfortunately, unlike experts employed at private think tanks, scholars affiliated with policy institutes at universities may, for many of the reasons outlined above, remain at these organizations only briefly. This creates formidable challenges for those responsible for organizing and coordinating the research activities of these institutes.

However, even when a small core of faculty agree to participate in the work of university think tanks, considerable challenges remain, not the least of which is securing adequate funding – in all but a handful of cases, they are chronically underfunded. This is certainly not a problem at the Munk School of Global Affairs (MSGA) at the University of Toronto and the Balsillie School of International Affairs (BSIA), a venture supported by CIGI, the University of Waterloo, and Wilfrid Laurier University. Modelled along the lines of the Columbia School of International and Public Affairs and the Harvard School of Government, funds drawn from the MSGA and BSIA multimillion-dollar endowments have been used to support the creation of several institutes, centres (mainly at MSGA), and programs (both at MSGA and BSIA). Although many of these initiatives resemble think tanks in terms of the priority they assign to research and analysis, it is important to keep in mind that the MSGA and the BSIA are, first and foremost, educational institutions that offer a wide range of academic and professional programs. Both institutions support the work of policy institutes, but neither should be regarded as a think tank.

With the exception of one of BSIA's partners, CIGI, whose annual budget is more than $25 million, most university-based think tanks in Canada struggle to keep afloat. The Liu Institute for Global Studies, founded at the University of British Columbia in 1998, has a budget of about $1 million, almost twice the amount available to the Parkland Institute at the University of Alberta. Funding is even more precarious for university-based research institutes with expertise in strategic and security studies. The dozen universities in Canada funded by the Department of National Defence under the Security and Defence Forum Program, established in 1967 "to develop a domestic competence and national interest in defence issues of relevance to Canada's security," must divvy up $2 million, the entire amount set aside for this ongoing initiative.[8] With annual budgets of less than $200,000, participating centres and institutes are expected to organize conferences, seminars, and workshops, provide modest support to graduate students undertaking research on topics related to foreign and defence policy, and generate working papers, edited collections, and other publications that may be of interest to policy-makers and the public. In most cases, a director and administrative assistant (part-time or full-time) are tasked with overseeing the day-to-day operations of these organizations.

Faculty interested in producing policy-relevant research, but concerned about the lack of resources available in most university-based think tanks, may take advantage of other opportunities. For example, several think tanks in Canada, including the C.D. Howe Institute and the Institute for Research on Public Policy, often hire scholars to write studies for various projects they are undertaking. They do this not only because of limited in-house research capacity, but to further enhance their organization's prominence and visibility. Just as corporations and governments reach out to think tanks to bolster their credibility, think tanks are only too willing to forge relationships with distinguished economists, political scientists, historians, and sociologists to give greater weight to their policy recommendations. And why wouldn't they? Securing the participation of well-known scholars increases think tanks' marquee value, and may enhance their cachet with the public and with policy-makers. Assuming the quality and integrity of a think tank's publications are strengthened by the contributions of prominent experts, it may make perfect sense for policy institutes to attach their name to a stable of high-profile scholars. By doing so, they can produce better research, and, quite possibly, influence how the public thinks about particular policy issues. Regardless of think tanks' motivation for courting university faculty – to improve their research capacity or to simply co-opt them as pawns in a carefully planned and executed public relations campaign – it produces a win-win outcome.

Such relationships may also result in favourable outcomes for faculty who are naturally drawn to the kind of research generated by think tanks, and are only too willing to be part of the world they inhabit. They don't regard themselves as dupes, but rather as entrepreneurs in search of opportunities to showcase their ideas to the public.[9] As much as they may enjoy taking part in academic exchanges with students and colleagues, some scholars fear succumbing to what can become a very sheltered, stifling, and claustrophobic life in the academy. To avoid these and other challenges of academic life, scholars often welcome the chance to stretch their legs and breathe in some fresh air. Some, for instance, may decide to spend part or all of their sabbatical as a visiting fellow at a prestigious think tank such as the Woodrow Wilson International Center for Scholars in Washington. This think tank, named for the only US president to hold a PhD, was established in 1968 as part of the Smithsonian Institution. It is also home to the Canada Institute, a research centre directed by Laura Dawson, a specialist on Canada's relationship with the United States. Wilson Center faculty are invited to conduct research, present lectures, and immerse themselves in the policy-making community. In recent years, several Canadian scholars have assumed temporary residency in one of the many institutes funded by the Center.[10]

Thus far, I have highlighted some of the ways in which think tanks in Canada and the United States are governed. As discussed, some prefer a top-down management structure, similar to those found in corporations where individuals occupying senior administrative positions determine how various operations – from research to outreach – are managed. Other think tanks, particularly those found on university campuses, tend to embrace a more collegial and less hierarchical decision-making model. Although there are plenty of examples of both, and many variations in between, it is important to keep in mind that how think tanks are organized influences the culture in which they generate and disseminate research as well as the extent to which they value research.

Before we move on to discuss some of the other key functions think tanks perform, a few words about the kinds of research products think tanks typically generate and the quality of their work is in order. Virtually every think tank website contains an exhaustive list of their various publications that have appeared both in print and/or electronically. Most think tanks also direct visitors to dozens of archived articles and papers.

It does not take long to discover that the vast majority of think tanks publish, in one form or another, policy briefs, position or working papers, newsletters, opinion magazines, and books. Depending on the resources that are earmarked for research, there will be significant variation in the range, diversity, and volume of publications. Not surprisingly, given the high cost of printing and mailing documents, think tanks encourage those interested in their work to download studies from their website. As we will discuss in chapter 7, think tanks closely monitor which publications, and how many of them, are downloaded as one of their performance indicators. Not only does this information provide think tanks with a better sense of which policy issues are generating the most interest and exposure, but it also allows them to construct a profile of those accessing their website. For example, the Center for American Progress (CAP), a Washington-based think tank, has developed highly sophisticated tracking technology to isolate the kinds of policy issues visitors to their website would likely find most interesting and relevant to their work.[11]

Customers who have purchased books or other products from Amazon or Indigo regularly receive recommendations (both solicited and unsolicited) for similar or related items they may wish to consider buying next. The software program employed by these and other companies is intended simply to track the purchase histories of customers and direct them to products they would be most inclined to place in their shopping cart. In a similar fashion, CAP and other think tanks track the publications individuals have downloaded, and notify them through email and social media when similar or related studies become available, one of the many strategies they employ to remain competitive in the marketplace of ideas. Moreover, CAP's tracking technology allows it to gather information about the professional background of individuals accessing their website – academics, journalists, policy-makers, etc. – and to tailor publications according to the demands of specific target audiences. Sending a 200-page study to an elected official who has little time for or interest in sifting through lengthy policy reports will, in all likelihood, result in it being relegated to the trash bin. However, if the same study is directed to academics, non-governmental organizations, journalists, or others working on similar topics, CAP could attract far more exposure, an outcome that, as well as creating a buzz around a particular policy issue, may translate into more funding.

As we will discuss in the following chapters, think tanks have become preoccupied with performance indicators, with good reason. Keeping tabs on how much activity their websites generate may tell directors of think tanks very little about the actual effect their institutions are having on shaping public opinion and public policy.[12] They know it, and those who study think tanks know it. However, in the absence of evidence to support often unsubstantiated assertions that their think tank wields enormous influence, directors are under pressure to provide data to convince donors why they should continue to contribute to, or invest in, their cause. That is why, as we will explore further, monitoring the number of publications downloaded or media citations recorded matter. The more active think tanks are the stronger case they can make for how relevant a role they play in informing and educating the public and policy-makers about particular policy issues. This is a narrative from which think tanks cannot afford to stray.[13]

Without a strong, reputable, and sustainable research program, it is difficult for think tanks to compete in the ideas industry, even if they place a higher premium on political advocacy than policy research. For instance, the Fraser Institute, which by its own admission is far more interested in targeting the public than policy-makers,[14] must continue to engage in various research projects to maintain its status as a credible public policy institute, even though this is a description that has been refuted by many of its critics. It may not be able to compete with the breadth and depth of research being undertaken by several high-profile scholars at CIGI, but its policy prescriptions on a host of economic and social issues, though at times highly controversial and suspect cannot and should not be ignored. The Fraser Institute understands all too well that if the research it produces cannot hold up to scrutiny, its credibility will be compromised. The revered Conference Board of Canada learned this painful lesson in March 2009 when it was found to have plagiarized material from press reports included in a media kit distributed by a US lobbying organization.[15] Although the organization withdrew three of its reports that contained material used without proper attribution, the damage to its reputation had already been done. By committing plagiarism, a serious offence, the Conference Board exposed a fatal weakness in how research is conducted in the vast majority of think tanks, a subject that we will return to shortly.

What was undoubtedly a humiliating episode in the life of this distinguished think tank is nonetheless instructive for those who pass judgment on the quality of a policy institute's research, or where it deserves to be ranked among the world's leading think tanks. In both instances, these opinions are based almost entirely on the reputation of organizations.

While there is no doubt that some think tanks produce higher quality research than others, it is also true that in every organization, some studies will be far more rigorous than others. Although we have come to expect award-winning actors, musicians, novelists, and athletes to produce a body of work that is consistent and praiseworthy, we are often disappointed when our expectations are not satisfied. The same can be said of think tanks that are not necessarily consistent when it comes to producing research of the highest calibre. Of the thousands of reports, working papers, policy briefs, and other materials that emanate from the think tank community each year, there are bound to be plenty of studies that could be more rigorous and intellectually compelling. Unfortunately, each report, regardless of who publishes it, must be judged on its own merits. This is why it is important not to assume that every word and sentence penned by a highly revered think tank should be treated as gospel or that policy recommendations from less prestigious venues should be ignored.

That the Conference Board found itself in hot water when it admitted to plagiarizing material in several of its reports, though disturbing, is not entirely surprising. Unlike academics, whose research in refereed journals and/or university press monographs must undergo a process known as blind peer review, studies published by most think tanks in Canada and the United States are not subjected to rigorous external evaluation. Rather than ensuring that the data they generate, interpret, and evaluate, along with the research methodologies they employ, adhere to the highest scientific standards, think tanks, with few exceptions, do not seek the approval or endorsement of independent experts. Whatever means they rely on to judge the quality and integrity of their work is done internally. Without this added layer of protection that is afforded, though not always guaranteed, by blind peer review, there is a greater likelihood that experts at think tanks will, wittingly or unwittingly, falsify data and manipulate methodologies to support the preferred policy position of their employer and the core interests of their donors. Those who fund think tank research certainly cannot be called upon to verify if studies were prepared properly. In most cases, they do not possess the background or interest to do this. Their primary concern is not the process by which studies were undertaken, but the results. This is not to suggest that think tanks, with the blessing of donors, intentionally or regularly falsify data, although allegations to this effect have been made,[16] but rather that, without a proper system in place to evaluate the quality of their research, they will expose themselves to accusations of impropriety.

Of course, this problem could be rectified, but it is unlikely that organizations intent on producing timely and relevant policy research would subject themselves to the often long and laborious process of peer review. To do so would, in their minds, likely compromise their independence and control over shaping the narrative they have constructed around policy issues, a sacrifice most think tanks would be unwilling to make. As much as think tanks derive credibility from their association with the academic community, unless policy institutes are affiliated with universities, they cannot claim, nor do they want to be restricted by, academic rules and norms.

In Canada, as in the United States and every other country that boasts a healthy and robust population of think tanks, debates about which institutes are the most reputable and produce the highest quality research will undoubtedly continue. But, as part of these discussions, participants also need to remember that carrying out research and analysis on various policy issues is only one of the important functions tackled by think tanks. Without the ability to properly communicate their findings, a skill that is highly valued, think tanks would likely not enjoy the visibility and status on which they have come to depend. It is to a discussion of this vital function that we now turn.

COMMUNICATION, COMMUNICATION, COMMUNICATION

It is often said that when it comes to investing in real estate there are three guiding principles – location, location, location. These principles were closely followed by the Center for Strategic and International Studies (CSIS) when it decided to build its $100 million state-of-the-art headquarters on Washington's Rhode Island Avenue, NW, a stone's throw from Johns Hopkins University's School of Advanced International Studies (SAIS), the Brookings Institution, the Carnegie Endowment for International Peace, the Peterson Institute for International Economics, and a handful of other prominent research institutes.[17] In designing the nine-floor, 12,000-square-metre facility, which boasts 1,000 square metres of Carrara marble, and, dangling above the foyer, arguably the fanciest and most expensive chandelier of any think tank anywhere, Hickok Cole Architects equipped CSIS with everything a policy institute could possibly covet: three floors of conference rooms, a broadcast and recording studio, and an iDeas Lab, "to produce cutting-edge multimedia products."[18]

The decision to build a communications infrastructure that most American and Canadian think tanks could only dream of was not accidental. As CSIS and the other high-powered Washington-based think tanks understand all too well, as important as it is to maintain a rigorous research program and close proximity to policy-makers, ensuring that their scholars can respond to media requests for interviews at a moment's notice and be able to disseminate their findings to journalists and other stakeholders in a timely fashion is critical to their success. This is why several top-tier US think tanks devote millions of dollars each year to communications. In CSIS's case, some of these funds are used to secure access to a satellite that can provide their scholars with detailed information on, among other things, the movement of foreign troops and vessels around the globe.[19] In 2013, the Heritage Foundation, arguably the most high-profile conservative think tank in the world, spent more than $10 million on media and government relations.[20] To put this in perspective, the funds set aside for this one expenditure exceeded the entire budget of the Fraser Institute, Heritage's Canadian ally in the war of ideas. To drive this point home further, Heritage's over $75 million annual budget is greater than the combined resources of the Conference Board of Canada, CIGI, and the Fraser Institute, the three largest think tanks in Canada.

In relaying these figures, it is not my intention to dwell on the huge disparity in resources between the most celebrated think tanks in Canada and the United States. The fact is, when it comes to amassing multimillion-dollar budgets, few Canadian think tanks can compete with Heritage, Brookings, AEI, CSIS, and other research institutes that hover in the upper stratosphere. Yet despite the limited funds available to most Canadian think tanks, they have not lost sight of how important it is to communicate their ideas to different target audiences, and have taken steps over the past several years to pursue a more effective communications strategy. In addition to making their studies available online and live-streaming several of their events, most think tanks are relying more heavily on social media to maintain contact with their followers. Those that can afford to hire one or more communications specialists to prepare newsletters, coordinate the release and distribution of studies, and help organize seminars, conferences, and workshops are only too willing to make this investment. But why go to this trouble and expense? Isn't it enough to simply post studies on a website and allow visitors to browse them at their leisure? Do think tanks really need to hire communications experts to advise them on how to market their ideas? And why cater to high school and university students by informing them about institute activities through Twitter and Facebook? If they are really interested in the work of think tanks, won't they take the initiative to contact individual organizations?

There are many more questions that could prompt think tanks to explain why they have become more media- and technologically savvy, but their answers would likely point to the same conclusion. As an increasing number of organizations compete for the attention of policymakers, the media, and the public, they have no choice but to embrace a more proactive and user-friendly approach to conveying their ideas. As long as constructing, shaping, and massaging the narrative around key policy issues remains a priority for think tanks, and it undoubtedly will, they must adapt to an ever-changing climate that compels them to deliver their message in the most efficient way possible. If this means having to rely more on social media to reach younger generations who are more inclined to access and process information in this manner, so be it. And if it means hiving off resources from research to augment the media relations budget, that may be a trade-off think tanks will have to bear. Think tanks want to influence what and how the public and policy-makers think about health care, education, taxes, threats to global security, and other pressing issues. The challenge for them is to figure out the best way to achieve this while maintaining what Joseph Sandler, whom we referenced in chapter 3, called "a patina of academic neutrality and objectivity."

There is nothing inherently wrong with devoting valuable resources to communications and public relations. However, as some critics of think tanks contend, all things being equal, the more funds set aside for these purposes, the fewer resources there will invariably be for research. Striking a balance between these two critically important functions remains a challenge, but from the perspective of think tanks trying to maintain and enhance their public profile, they have little choice but to invest in communications. For think tanks, it boils down to priorities, which, as noted, vary across institutions. Nonetheless, as Edwin Feulner and the late Paul Weyrich, co-founders of the Heritage Foundation, realized when they secured seed money for their institute in 1973, for think tanks to be recognized and to be heard, they had to aggressively market and promote their ideas.[21] There was no virtue, they believed, in keeping their research a secret, or withholding policy recommendations from policy-makers whom they felt would derive enormous benefit from their wisdom. For Feulner and Weyrich, and the generations of presidents and directors of advocacy think tanks who followed, leaving weighty tomes on book-shelves to gather dust would have all but guaranteed failure.

When the Heritage Foundation opened its doors, it became clear that keeping the media, policy-makers, their staff, and other target audiences up to date about their activities would be a priority. Heritage also made a commitment to ensuring that their experts were always apprised of the many issues being addressed and debated on Capitol Hill. Not only did this help them to produce research that was timely and relevant, but by maintaining close ties to members of the House and the Senate through liaison offices Heritage established, they could tailor publications to the specific needs and demands of elected officials.[22]

To combine policy research effectively with aggressive marketing, the avowed goal of advocacy think tanks, it is essential for researchers and communications specialists to work in concert. After all, as important as it is to generate credible research, for most think tanks, framing their findings in ways that allow them to advance their institutional agenda is even more important. Keeping in mind that think tanks are in the business of shaping public opinion and public policy, how they present themselves and their research to the electorate and to elected officials is critical. Should they fail on both fronts, journalists would waste little time shooting down both the message and the messenger.

It is also necessary to point out that think tanks invest in a communications strategy and personnel for reasons other than presenting themselves in the most favourable light, or determining the most effective ways to frame the parameters around key policy debates. For instance, when think tanks come under fire for making unsubstantiated claims about the causes of an international conflict, or about government waste in the health care sector, or, possibly, for accepting large donations from foreign governments who have every expectation that, in exchange for their generosity, the recipient will lobby on their behalf, it is helpful to have communications and public relations experts on staff to provide damage control. As noted, when investigative reporter Brooke Williams and her colleagues published an exposé in the *New York Times* in the fall of 2014 about foreign governments relying on several high-profile US think tanks for lobbying purposes, it did not take long for Strobe Talbott, president of the Brookings Institution, one of the think tanks profiled in the article, to issue a formal response to the allegations.[23] Rest assured that, not long after the explosive article appeared, the Brookings media team assembled to help advise Talbott on how best to

react. A year later, Talbott was back in the news when he fired Robert
Litan, an economist who had been associated with Brookings for over
forty years, and who, like Talbott, had served in the Clinton administration. Massachusetts Senator Elizabeth Warren insisted that the Brookings's president take action following a barrage of harsh comments she
made in a letter to Talbott in early fall 2015, that Litan had failed to
adequately disclose who had funded a report he had commented on
before Congress. Unaware of a new rule at Brookings that prevented
Litan and other non-resident fellows from acknowledging their Brookings affiliation when testifying before Congress, the economist's ties to
the iconic think tank were terminated.[24] Increasingly sensitive to how
Brookings was perceived in the aftermath of the 2014 *New York Times*
exposé, Talbott appeared to be engaging in damage control once again.

Directors of several Canadian think tanks may not have paid close
attention to the controversy surrounding Talbott and Litan at Brookings,
but policy institutes in Canada that have accepted funds from foreign
corporations and governments, albeit on a much smaller scale, were
watching with bated breath as the story exposing the foreign funding of
US think tanks unfolded. During a fall 2014 episode of TVO's *The
Agenda with Steve Paikin,* three panelists occupying senior positions
with think tanks in Canada were asked about the kind of work their
organizations did internationally, and what, if any, involvement donors
played in decisions regarding the research they were undertaking. One of
the panelists, Jason Clemens, to whom I referred earlier, acknowledged
that 10 per cent of the Fraser Institute's activities had an international
component, and that the institute did indeed accept funds from sources
outside Canada. He said little else.[25] Rohinton Medhora, president of
CIGI, also confirmed that by virtue of his organization's mandate, CIGI
participates in several international initiatives. However, with respect to
funding, whether from domestic or foreign sources, Medhora was
emphatic in stating that donors gave them money "for what we do, not
how we do it."[26] He also made a point of informing viewers that CIGI
received a 5-star rating (the highest possible score) from Transparify, an
organization that rates think tanks according to their willingness to disclose their sources of funding.[27]

In a less explosive and controversial, albeit important, series of newspaper articles, the Canadian Centre for Policy Alternatives was singled
out as one of several charitable organizations being audited by the Canada
Revenue Agency for alleged violations of its registered status under the
Income Tax Act.[28] Speculation that the CRA's audit was initiated in

response to pressure from the Harper government to crack down on the political activities of left-leaning think tanks and other non-governmental organizations, a claim CRA steadfastly denied, most of the press coverage was favourable to the targeted organizations. Moreover, following the announcement of the closure of the North-South Institute in September 2014, a fixture in Canada's think tank community for close to forty years, several journalists expressed dismay over how the federal government could have allowed this to happen.[29] Although staff at the NSI had prepared themselves for this eventuality, and did not want their supporters to engage in a protracted fight with the government, the CCPA was not prepared to remain silent. With the help of several hundred academics who signed a petition opposing the audit, and the assistance of a handful of well-placed journalists, CCPA was able to keep the story about its predicament in the public spotlight. In doing so, the CCPA demonstrated why the relationship between think tanks and the media is vital, and how, with an appropriate communications plan, think tanks can turn even bad publicity into good publicity.

TUNING IN: THINK TANKS AND THEIR NETWORKS

My paternal grandfather Jess, whose formal education ended rather abruptly in grade 8 (a fascinating story that has been told at many family celebrations), often reminded his children and grandchildren what it took to achieve success. With a smirk reminiscent of the one glued to Paul Newman's face in *Butch Cassidy and the Sundance Kid*, an actor whom he both admired and resembled as a young man, he shared his secret: "In life, it's not about who you are. It's who[m] you know."

Although my grandfather spent most of his life in the nation's capital, it is unlikely that he paid much attention to the think tanks that sprouted up in postwar Ottawa. He was a businessman, not a political pundit, but I suspect most think tank directors would agree with his assessment on what it takes to become successful. Think tanks may give the impression that they are lone missionaries travelling across Canada's rugged tundra in search of ideas to promote and individuals to convert. But, despite guarding their independence, which may explain why some think tanks are often reluctant to share information about ongoing research projects with their competitors, they understand what it takes to influence public policy. Significant changes to the country's domestic and foreign policies may occur because of the views of one particular constituency, but this is rare. In most cases, the content and direction of public policy are affected by a vast network of individuals and organizations who readily acknowledge the need for new thinking and are prepared to invest the time, energy, and resources to reach out to the public and to policy-makers. Think tanks often constitute part of these networks, or what are more commonly referred to as civil society and/or social movements.[30]

The Heritage Foundation, which I have made several references to in this and previous chapters, has long been heralded as a leader in the American conservative movement. In cooperation with like-minded think tanks, academics, philanthropic foundations, private donors, religious and educational institutions, interest groups, members of the conservative media, corporations, and a host of non-governmental organizations, it has been able to generate the political and financial support it requires to place and keep several domestic and foreign policy issues on the political agenda. From its ongoing support for free-market solutions to America's economic woes, to its steadfast commitment to fighting terrorism around the globe, Heritage and its many allies are invested in influencing the political climate in Washington. In a similar vein, in Canada, think tanks of all political stripes have made a concerted effort to seek out and work with individuals and organizations who share a similar vision of the principles and values they believe should define our national identity. Although political and ideological divisions exist within these and other networks, movements, and coalitions, think tanks work within these forums to help build a consensus around particular policy issues, a function traditionally performed by political parties. However, unlike parties that have an incentive to mend fences within their ranks before the next election, think tanks need to resist the temptation to focus solely on short-term political and policy victories. For think tanks to establish themselves as key players in the policy-making process, either alone or as part of a much larger constituency of actors, they must make a long-term investment in the ideas they have formulated. Even if think tanks cannot take credit for the ideas they present and repackage for public consumption, they can, at the very least, distinguish themselves as, in the words of historian James A. Smith, "idea brokers."[31]

To effectively broker ideas between different constituent groups, think tanks first have to establish channels through which to share and exchange views on various policy matters. They may do this by simply emailing or posting links of their many publications to journalists, policy-makers, and other interested stakeholders. Given the ease with which documents can be sent electronically, this is a preferred option for many think tanks. Or, depending on their resources, they may elect to organize conferences, workshops, seminars, and roundtable discussions where participants from various organizations are invited to discuss and debate some of the finer details surrounding particular issues. These functions also serve as useful opportunities to expand and strengthen their network of contacts. And if this degree of interaction is not deemed sufficient, think tanks and for-profit educational institutes, such as the Broadbent Institute and the Manning Centre, may decide to organize larger events at which hundreds of policy-makers, academics, journalists, students, donors, and others groups of individuals can interact. This, as noted, is the express purpose of the annual Manning Networking Conference (MNC) held in Ottawa, which Tom Clark of Global TV observed was "like Woodstock for conservative Canadians."[32] The comments of several other journalists highlighting the importance of the MNC appear in the promotional material prepared by the Manning Centre for this gathering.

For think tanks, as with other non-governmental organizations, the importance of creating and expanding networks in which they can share ideas cannot be overstated. Indeed, it is by establishing and nurturing contacts with multiple constituencies that think tanks seek to build momentum or traction around policy issues they hope will strike a responsive chord with the electorate. However, it is important to recognize that creating networks that will expand the shelf-life of key domestic and foreign policy issues is, along with research and communications, simply one tactic employed by think tanks to engage in political advocacy.

THINK TANKS AS POLICY ADVOCATES

When governments make controversial decisions about matters involving armed conflict, or how funds will be allocated for health care, education, social assistance, and crime prevention, discussions invariably turn to who or what was responsible for *influencing* the content and direction of these initiatives, and usually it does not take long for inquiring journalists to round up the usual suspects. After criticizing elected officials for embracing an unpopular approach to addressing one of many domestic and/or foreign policy problems, interest groups, lobbyists, unions, and more recently think tanks find themselves in the crosshairs of political debates. Yet, as organizations that have a vested interest in swaying public opinion and public policy, this is exactly where they should be. Why then does the involvement of think tanks in political advocacy continue to raise suspicion among journalists and ire among scholars? Before I answer this, let me digress.

In his study *Foreign Policy, Inc.*,[33] Lawrence Davidson expresses deep concern for what he believes is the unparalleled and unbridled power and influence of ethnic lobbies over US foreign policy. At a time of growing public apathy and indifference over how the United States manages its foreign relations, Davidson is concerned, among other things, that a handful of well-organized and strongly funded lobbies are able to shape US foreign policy in ways that compromise America's national interest. In what the author refers to as a factocracy, where these and other factions are thought to have a free rein over foreign policy, democracy all but disappears. Although other academics and pundits in the United States and Canada share Davidson's admonitions, much of their animosity and frustration over how domestic and foreign policy is formulated is, unfortunately, misplaced. Rather than directing their anger at nongovernmental organizations that are established for the express purpose of influencing public policy, they should vilify policy-makers and an indifferent public: policy-makers because they, by both omission and commission, have abdicated much of their responsibility for managing the affairs of state; the public because of their lack of interest in the political process.[34]

In the days and weeks following President George W. Bush's decision to invade Iraq, it may have made sense for journalists to write about the Project for the New American Century (PNAC), a small Washington-based think tank with powerful connections to the White House, as a breeding ground for Bush's foreign policy.[35] And in 2006, it might have made sense for journalists to reveal the extent to which the Harper government's economic and social policy agenda resembled many of the policy recommendations of a handful of conservative think tanks in Canada.[36] But, as important as it is to understand the role that think tanks and other non-governmental organizations play in the policy-making process, in the end, it is the policy-makers, and the voters who elect them to office, not policy experts at think tanks, who must claim ownership for formulating and implementing policy decisions.

To further drive this point home, lobbyists should not be blamed for lobbying, interest groups should not be criticized for pressuring elected officials to adopt legislation that would advance the interests of the group or groups they are representing, and think tanks should not be castigated for engaging in political advocacy.[37] After all, how can we berate organizations for doing what they were established to do? As long as they are not violating any laws or participating in what the government considers inappropriate political and partisan activities, why should Davidson and others be concerned? And who decides when these organizations exercise too much influence – scholars, policy-makers, the courts, or the public?

Although this may seem obvious, the reality is that many journalists and scholars, including me, continue to express reservations about the priority that think tanks place on political advocacy. Part of the problem is how we perceive the role of think tanks, and how it has changed over the past few decades. Although the role of lobbyists and interest groups is fairly clear, the role of think tanks remains rather ambiguous. Are think tanks established to produce "applied" policy research or to advocate for what they believe would be better and more informed policy decisions? The short answer is both. It is because think tanks assume the dual role of engaging in both policy research and political advocacy that has caused many observers to question their motivations. It has also tainted how we view political advocacy which, compared with policy research (which can be rigorous or sloppy), tends to be regarded with suspicion. In other words, academics are prepared generally to recognize the valuable contribution the Brookings Institution, the RAND Corporation, the Conference Board of Canada, CIGI, and other research-intensive policy institutes make to public policy, even if the products generated by these organizations tend to be more applied than theoretical. The research produced by think tanks might not often be regarded as ground-breaking or meet the exacting standards of the academy, or even be seen as addressing scientific and legitimate questions, but, for the most part, the pursuit of knowledge is regarded as a virtuous undertaking. In contrast, the pursuit of political advocacy is often seen as far less worthy, self-serving, and sinister. But why is this so?

Just as someone or something can have a positive or negative influence over others, advocating a possible solution to a policy problem may, if adopted by policy-makers, lead to a favourable or less than favourable outcome. However, for reasons not altogether clear, the term advocacy, as it relates to the work of think tanks, often provokes a visceral reaction. This may explain why journalists often describe think tanks they revere as policy research institutions, and those they believe have less than altruistic motives as advocacy organizations. The underlying message is clear: trust the opinions of the former and disregard those of the latter. Doing so, however, would be unwise.

Surely, it is not the willingness of think tanks to engage in advocacy that raises eyebrows among long-time observers of these organizations. To advocate or speak up in support of, or in opposition to, various policy initiatives is the hallmark of a healthy democracy. What value could think tanks possibly have if they were discouraged from sharing their research findings with the public and with policy-makers? No, the concern of those who monitor these institutions is not that think tanks participate in political advocacy. Every organization that seeks to influence public policy, including universities and hospitals, is a policy advocate. Rather, the concern that has been expressed over the extent to which think tanks have become increasingly involved in political advocacy is rooted elsewhere. That several think tanks assign a higher priority to advocacy than to research is undoubtedly a source of irritation to those scholars and pundits who may believe that think tanks have an obligation to produce rigorous policy research. But, even more important, critics are concerned about what think tanks advocate for and against. Those opposed to the Bush administration's war in Iraq did not target PNAC because it was a think tank but because it was a well-known and vocal advocate of removing Saddam Hussein from power. Similarly, critics of the Harper government did not castigate the Fraser Institute and other free-market think tanks for being policy advocates but because they disagreed with their policy recommendations.

As participants in the marketplace of ideas, think tanks understand what it takes to be recognized, and as we have discussed in this chapter, this often means placing a premium on political advocacy. Given the success that several advocacy-oriented think tanks in Canada and in the United States have achieved, it is unlikely that they will stray from the course they have set for themselves. Ideally, a sustainable and challenging research program will provide think tanks with credibility and respectability, but it is the attention they devote to advocacy that may enhance the access they have to the public and to policy-makers. Think tanks perform many important functions, including research, communications, networking, and other activities that fall under the rubric of political advocacy. Ultimately, every institution has to decide for itself the kinds of resources to assign to each of these functions. With this in mind, we will now focus on the key stakeholders, or target audiences, with whom think tanks communicate so they can more effectively convey their ideas. In the process, we will acquire an even greater appreciation for why the creation of networks is so vital to what think tanks do and how they do it.

5

With Whom Do Think Tanks Communicate?

The last chapter devoted considerable attention to explaining several of the key functions performed by think tanks. As institutions ostensibly committed to analyzing the many challenges of implementing a wide range of domestic and foreign policy initiatives, it is not surprising that think tanks spend much of their time, and often the bulk of their resources, on activities, such as conferences and workshops, related to various research programs and projects. Finding solutions to complex policy problems does not occur by accident, and think tanks rarely stumble across quick fixes. The ideas they generate often take years to refine and package in a form that is palatable to policy-makers and to the public. In short, for think tanks to achieve lasting policy influence, they must be prepared to make a long-term investment in both their researchers and the research they undertake. But, as we have also discovered, competing in the marketplace of ideas often requires think tanks to do what is expedient. Recognizing the importance of providing policy-makers and other key stakeholders with information that is timely and relevant, some think tanks are only too willing to compromise the integrity and quality of their research. To make their presence felt, think tanks, interest groups, lobbyists, and other organizations jostle, butt heads, and try desperately to outmanoeuvre each other to leave their mark on public policy. With no less than the future of key domestic and foreign policies at stake, think tanks cannot afford to be complacent when it comes to showcasing their findings. Communicating, marketing, and promoting their work to multiple stakeholders, constituencies, or target audiences is critical, to put it mildly, to their success.

In this chapter, we provide more detailed coverage of the key audiences that think tanks target. We also reveal how the relationships think tanks forge with policy-makers, philanthropic foundations, the media, academics, the N G O community, and other stakeholders can be mutually beneficial. Think tanks may often be responsible for waging a war of ideas, but the groups they hope to engage in battle are hardly innocents. Like the think tanks that go to great lengths to win them over, they have their own political agendas, which can often be advanced by uniting forces with high-profile and well-placed policy institutes.

STAKEOUT: THINK TANKS
AND THEIR STAKEHOLDERS

Policy-Makers

For most think tanks, conveying ideas and policy recommendations to elected officials and career bureaucrats remains a priority. Although the nature of the political system that think tanks inhabit will dictate how and to what extent they reach out to office-holders, a subject we will explore in the next chapter,[1] organizations that study public policy must keep a close watch on what policy-makers are thinking about and the issues they will likely have to consider in the near and foreseeable future. Just as government relations firms monitor how the legislative agenda could affect their clients' interests, think tanks cannot lose sight of the issues that preoccupy those in positions of power. Think tanks with the insight and good fortune to anticipate and project the challenges policy-makers will face in the ensuing months and years will likely enjoy a strategic advantage over their competitors. However, even if think tanks can manage to stay ahead of the curve, they cannot expect to make a splash if the issues they tackle have little bearing on the matters weighing heavily on the minds of policy-makers. To ensure that they are generating timely and relevant research, it only makes sense for think tanks to establish extensive contacts throughout government. Not only does this strengthen the lines of communication, it gives think tanks the confidence of knowing that they are on the same page as policy-makers. Elected officials and their staff, policy advisors in the Prime Minister's Office (P M O) and the Privy Council Office (P C O) or, in the United States, experts in various agencies that make up the Executive Office of the President (E O P), employees in government departments and agencies, those who staff important legislative committees, and directors of party research offices can all, at different times, prove very helpful to think tanks.

For many think tanks, establishing and nurturing contacts throughout government is not an afterthought – it is essential, and can, over time, pay handsome dividends. This explains why several high-profile think tanks in the United States allocate millions of dollars annually to government relations. The success of the Heritage Foundation in extending its tentacles deep inside the corridors and conference rooms on Capitol Hill, the executive branch, and the bureaucracy sent a clear signal to other policy institutes that much could be gained by building an extensive and expanding network throughout government. Heritage accomplishes this through several channels that go well beyond simply providing policy-makers with a full range of their publications: they also rely on liaison offices with both houses of Congress to more closely monitor issues that are on the legislative agenda; maintain a database similar to an online dating site that matches job vacancies in government with suitable young conservatives looking to start their careers in the nation's capital; host seminars and workshops for newly elected members of Congress; invite seasoned politicians to participate in their conferences; and provide accommodation for their staff to serve on presidential campaigns.[2]

Several of the strategies Heritage employs have been adopted by other think tanks in the United States, in Canada, albeit to a lesser extent, and around the globe. Even the Brookings Institution, the iconic think tank that continues to be revered in the academic community, occasionally holds focus groups on Capitol Hill with congressional staffers to find out if the research it produces is well-received. Brookings, like manufacturers of brand-name cereals, has a vested interest in making sure it is satisfying consumer demands.

From the vantage point of think tanks, it would be illogical, not to mention counterproductive, to avoid targeting policy-makers. After all, they are entrusted, with the public's endorsement, with the responsibility to implement public policy. So why wouldn't think tanks devote the time, energy, and resources (assuming they are available) to ensure that their voices are heard? While think tanks clearly see policy-makers through their view-finders, policy-makers, interestingly enough, are looking directly back at them. As elected officials and aspiring office-holders have come to learn, policy experts at think tanks can prove to be enormously helpful on the campaign trail and once they have been elected or re-elected to office.

Yet, to maintain their independence and status as registered charities, it is important for think tanks not to align themselves too closely with political parties. Of course, there are exceptions in Canada[3] and in the United States, and in countries like Germany where some think tanks receive funding from the state to serve the needs of political parties.[4] However, unlike Germany, most think tanks in Canada and the United States do not want to be perceived as mere appendages of political parties. This is not to suggest that policy experts from think tanks avoid interacting with party members. As noted, as part of a broad-based and multi-tiered strategy, think tanks provide elected officials with a steady dose of policy advice. Although this channel provides think tanks with valuable opportunities to strengthen their ties to policy-makers, these interactions are often mutually beneficial. Not only can policy-makers benefit from the expertise that is being offered, but both office-holders and those aspiring to replace them can tap into much larger constituencies and networks that think tanks have developed over time. Among other things, think tanks and the interest groups and other civil society organizations with whom they associate, can help mobilize voters to support, or oppose, particular policy initiatives. Such was the case when the NDP government of Premier Bob Rae enlisted the help of several think tanks, including the Canadian Centre for Policy Alternatives, to galvanize Ontario's opposition to the 1994 North American Free Trade Agreement (NAFTA).[5]

For both incumbents and challengers, there are other advantages to maintaining close ties to think tanks. As we will discuss at greater length in the next chapter, during the last several US presidential elections, dozens of policy experts from some of the country's most prominent think tanks played a critically important role in advising candidates.[6] But even when experts from think tanks have not taken a leave of absence to work on presidential campaigns, candidates from both parties have been able to rely on think tanks to help assess the public's reaction to various policy proposals. It goes without saying that on the campaign trail, presidential and congressional candidates can ill-afford to be linked to highly unpopular programs or initiatives. Therefore, rather than risk jumping into unfamiliar waters with both feet, candidates can sit back and watch think tanks test policy ideas with voters. It doesn't cost their campaign valuable resources and they can make strategic decisions about which issues to embrace and to avoid based on the public's reaction to the ideas marketed by think tanks.

In these and other ways, think tanks can wittingly or by sheer luck be a strategic asset for policy-makers. But, as noted previously, they also provide policy-makers with a currency even more valuable than solicited or unsolicited advice: credibility and respectability. Although the golden age of think tanks during the progressive era, when policy institutes' highest priority was helping government think its way through complex policy problems[7] has long passed, think tanks have still managed to preserve some element of credibility and respectability with the public. Realizing this, policy-makers often turn to them or seek their endorsement to garner more traction and support with the electorate. With a dwindling supply of credibility on which to draw, elected officials often seek out think tanks to help elevate themselves in the public eye. This in part explains why presidential candidates are more than willing to invite prominent experts from think tanks to serve on their campaigns and in their administrations. In short, despite the fact that some think tanks are devoting more and more resources to political advocacy, they are still able to create the impression that they are committed to improving the quality of public policy, an assertion that, when made by policy-makers, tends to fall upon deaf ears. Yet, as important as policy-makers are to think tanks and think tanks to policy-makers, neither could function without the support and confidence of the public, a second key stakeholder to which we now turn.

The Public

In the US mid-term elections on 5 November 2014, a meagre 36.4 per cent of eligible voters cast a ballot for their preferred congressional candidates. Two years before, 57.5 per cent of eligible voters turned out for the US presidential election which returned Barack Obama to a second term in office.[8] In Canada, voter turnout in some recent provincial and federal elections was higher – 52.1 per cent in Ontario in 2014, and 61.4 per cent in the 2011 federal election and 68.4 per cent in October 2015.[9] However, when one-half to one-third of the voting public neglects to exercise their democratic right to vote, how invested is the electorate in issues as important as health care, education, taxation, pensions, and peace and security? And if they are indifferent to the various initiatives policy-makers undertake, why should think tanks concern themselves with what the public cares or doesn't care about? In other words, why should think tanks be more committed to shaping public policy than the individuals who will be affected directly by it? Although millions of Canadians do not vote in elections, far more do, which provides an incentive for think tanks to communicate with them.

While there is no doubt that growing public apathy is a widespread phenomenon,[10] it has not discouraged think tanks from trying to engage the public in a dialogue over a myriad of policy issues. For think tanks, it is not about trying to reach the half or more of the population that pay little to no attention to current affairs. It is about creating a conversation with the millions of people who do. And if think tanks are able to hit a nerve with this attentive public as they probe more deeply into the costs and benefits of embracing health care reform, or the advantages of introducing significant changes to how personal income is taxed, their efforts could be handsomely rewarded. To alter the political climate in ways that will advance both their institutional and ideological interests, as well as those shared by their corporate and philanthropic donors, think tanks need to tap into a wellspring of public support. Once the public is prepared to weigh in, or alternatively, to acquiesce, it is only a matter of time before elected officials act accordingly. Such was the case following the events of 9/11 when the US Congress, at the urging of the Bush administration, voted the controversial Patriot Act into law. Playing on Americans' heightened fears and growing anxiety, policy-makers, with the encouragement and blessing of several conservative think tanks, elected to suspend civil liberties in pursuit of the War on Terror. As intelligence and security services were granted more extensive powers to monitor, wire-tap, and surveil them, Americans sat idly by and watched their freedoms curtailed, a mistake Canadians tried to avoid as the Harper government passed its anti-terrorism legislation, Bill C-51, into law in the summer of 2015.[11]

The decision of the Bush administration to ramp up its fight against terror was seen as a victory by the Project for the New American Century (PNAC), AEI, the Heritage Foundation, and other think tanks inside the Beltway who were calling on policy-makers to send a clear message to America's adversaries.[12] But think tanks were not satisfied winning periodic battles. Their goal was to once again claim victory in the war of ideas, something Heritage and the conservative movement celebrated as America moved further to the right during the Reagan-Bush years.[13]

The importance of making a long-term investment in shoring up public support for their policy initiatives has not been lost on Canadian policy institutes. As noted, both the Broadbent Institute and the Manning Centre (although not technically a think tank) understand all too well how critical it is to train future generations of policy experts and policy entrepreneurs to involve the public in ongoing discussions about the future direction of the country. In doing so, think tanks realize that they cannot just focus on supplying ideas, but must assemble sizeable and vocal constituencies that will lend their voice and support to the proposals they hope to advance. To do this, think tanks must introduce and maintain effective ways of communicating with the public.

As we discussed in the previous chapter, think tanks rely on various channels to communicate ideas to the public and to other target audiences. In addition to maintaining websites that keep readers updated about their research projects and publications, think tanks highlight upcoming conferences and workshops, lectures, and any other new initiatives that may be of interest to those who monitor their activities. Think tanks also rely increasingly on social media to share their insights with select audiences, and, of course, take advantage of the print, broadcast, and electronic media to comment on various domestic and foreign policy issues. In short, think tanks recognize the importance of making their work accessible to the public. They also understand that when it comes to educating, informing, and mobilizing the electorate, it makes little sense to bombard them with reams of information they are unable or unwilling to process. The same can be said of policy-makers who, given increasing demands on their time, simply cannot wade through the mountain of documents on their desks. But, if the purpose of think tanks is to generate and disseminate ideas that will influence public opinion and public policy, how can they ensure that the material they circulate is being read? Although think tanks can never be entirely certain whether their work is having the desired effect on their intended target audiences, they can all but guarantee how to discourage potential stakeholders from considering their findings. Unless think tanks produce materials in a form that is specifically tailored to meet the needs and interests of their audiences, their opportunity to make a positive impression will be severely compromised.

When it comes to communicating with the public, think tanks have to be particularly sensitive: they need to strike an appropriate balance between informing the citizenry without overwhelming them with extraneous information. Achieving this balance is not always easy given the complex nature of many policy issues. Nonetheless, it is essential. Think tanks cannot afford to alienate the public or, for that matter, any of their core constituencies. Determining how best to communicate with people who may know little about think tanks, but who wish to remain informed about current affairs, remains a priority for most policy institutes. However, for think tanks to gain visibility, it is not imperative for the public to remember who they are or what they do. Indeed, a telephone survey asking a cross-section of Canadians to list two or three think tanks in Canada would not likely generate positive results. What is more important for think tanks is to plant ideas in the minds of the electorate that may develop and grow over time. If and when this happens, think tanks will not have to look to the public to acknowledge the contribution they have made to generating discussions about pressing policy issues. On their own and/or with the media's assistance, another key stakeholder with whom they target regularly, think tanks will be more than willing to seek out the adulation and recognition they so dearly covet from policy-makers, journalists, academics, and donors.

The Media

At any given time on any given day, policy experts from think tanks may be called upon to comment on breaking news stories. As journalists scrambled to make sense of why a Malaysian commercial airliner was shot down over the Ukraine, or why a gunman killed an unarmed Canadian soldier guarding Canada's National War Memorial and then went on a shooting rampage in the Parliament Buildings, they knew that help was only a few key strokes away. Within a matter of seconds, journalists could phone, text, and/or email experts at any one of dozens of think tanks in North America or around the world. And more often than not, experts at policy institutes are only too willing to oblige.[14] At some high-profile think tanks in the United States, scholars need only walk down the hall to access their institute's television and radio stations where they can speak to the national and international media.[15] Those that do not have their own communication facilities regularly make their way to network news studios to be interviewed. Although disparagingly referred to as "talking heads," think tank experts perform a useful and, at times, valuable public function by making themselves available to the media. However, what is even more important for the think tanks is that in the process of building a stronger media profile, experts are helping themselves and the institutes they represent increase their stature in the policy-making community.

The creation of CNN and other twenty-four-hour news stations was a windfall for both the media and think tanks. With plenty of air time to fill, the media welcomed policy experts from think tanks of all political persuasions who could summarize and explain why viewers should pay attention to unfolding political events at home and abroad. And with the launching of various political talk shows on Fox News, PBS, BBC, CBC, TVO, and other television networks, the opportunities for think tanks to gain access to broadcast media multiplied exponentially. Think tanks, and the domestic and foreign policy specialists they employ, required little encouragement to strengthen their ties to the media. For years, policy experts have contributed op-ed articles to hundreds of newspapers around the globe, and, more recently, have started blogs on their employers' websites. But to further enhance their exposure, think tank scholars take full advantage of opportunities to appear either as guests on network newscasts, or as participants in conferences and seminars that are broadcast or live-streamed by their institute.[16]

Increasing media exposure is not only vital to think tanks as part of their ongoing efforts to affect policy change; it is critically important for attracting donor funding. To assess their policy impact, think tanks rely on different performance indicators, or metrics, including media hits, testimony by staff before legislative committees, the total number of publications downloaded from their website, citations in academic studies, and government reports. In the absence of a bottom line that highlights losses or gains, think tanks, as not-for-profit organizations, are under heightened pressure by their boards of trustees and directors to evaluate their effectiveness. Put simply, think tanks need to demonstrate how they have made a difference. And since directors of think tanks have an incentive to equate public visibility with policy influence, no indicator seems to preoccupy them more than how much media exposure they generate compared with their competitors.[17]

Chatham House, also known as the Royal Institute of International Affairs, is widely considered the leading think tank in the UK, and, according to some indices, ranks among the world's best.[18] Yet, despite its sterling reputation and hefty coffers, the institute, housed in stately quarters overlooking London's St James's Square, does not take its status or financial future for granted. Over the last several years, Chatham House has enlisted the services of a media consultant to track its exposure in newspapers in more than 190 countries. Several times a week, staff in charge of media relations receive a detailed breakdown of how many times the institute and/or one of its studies/scholars have been cited. These data are carefully maintained and monitored. But, as with other high-profile think tanks around the globe, Chatham House does not collect this information so it can pat itself on the back. On the contrary, the figures contained in what has become a massive database are there to remind both current and potential donors how far, and to what extent, its impact is felt.[19]

Directors of think tanks understand better than most that public visibility, often measured by media exposure, does not accurately reflect how much policy influence their organizations wield. But when funding dollars are on the line, it is not the kind of confession they are inclined to make. Rather than point to the innumerable variables that can influence public opinion and the policy preferences and choices of elected officials, they try to keep the message simple: the more exposure we generate, the more likely it is that the public and policy-makers will listen. The more they heed our advice, the stronger the likelihood that through the studies and commentaries we generate, we will be able to shape the political climate and hence public policy. And then comes the pitch, "If you too are concerned about the direction our country is moving in, you may want to consider making a tax deductible gift to ..."

That think tanks have not fundamentally changed the narrative they have so adeptly constructed around the importance of media exposure suggests that their strategy is paying off. They are simply repeating a story that those who are considering investing in them want to hear. Developing and growing a profile that can enhance an institute's power and influence is something donors understand and appreciate. It makes sense, and, after all, it is how many of them achieved personal and professional success. As we will discuss below, donors are not interested in being lectured about the intricacies of domestic and foreign policy, or how difficult it is to compete in the marketplace of ideas. They just want to know what kinds of products think tanks provide and if they are in a position to increase their market. Providing evidence that the media are interested in what they have to say can and does go a long way in helping think tanks make claims of widespread influence.

The interest think tanks have in augmenting their media profile will only continue to grow, as evidenced by the sizeable investments some well-heeled institutes are making in their communications infrastructures. Indeed, if more newspapers close over the next several years, due to dwindling advertising revenues, it is entirely conceivable that some think tanks will step in to fill the void. Since they are already in the business of providing commentaries on current events, it might not be much of a stretch for think tanks to provide readers with a daily dose of news around the globe. This may entail providing news feeds from other media organizations, offering commentaries on various events from their ideological perspective, or even hosting panel discussions that would help to promote the policy recommendations of their institute. Taking on a more active role as a media outlet is clearly something the Fraser Institute and other think tanks are considering.[20] The relationship that has formed between think tanks and the media has clearly served both of their needs. The media depend on information, analysis of current affairs, and succinct commentaries, and think tanks are well-positioned and equipped to meet their demands.

Donors

The Montreal-based Institute for Research on Public Policy (IRPP), CIGI, the Brookings Institution, the Hoover Institution, and a handful of other well-financed think tanks on both sides of the border have the luxury of drawing on interest generated from an endowment to help defray the costs of running their institutes.[21] Most think tanks do not have that security, so there is no alternative but to compete for donor funding. In the United States, several philanthropic foundations, including the Ford, Rockefeller, and Carnegie Foundations, have donated billions of dollars to support America's leading think tanks. With strong support from the corporate sector and from affluent private donors, top-tier US think tanks enjoy multimillion-dollar budgets. However, the vast majority of think tanks in the United States and Canada, whose annual budgets hover between $1 and $3 million, must scrape together sufficient funds to remain afloat. And to avoid the fate of the North-South Institute, think tanks must develop and maintain a diverse funding base.

Without strong donor support, it is unlikely, indeed improbable, that healthy populations of think tanks would have emerged in the United States and Europe over the past few decades. Think tanks need money, and fortunately they have been able to attract the funding they require to make their presence felt. But why, with so many causes to fund, from medical research to enhancing the quality of inner city schools, have donors invested so much and so often in the work of public policy institutes? One possible explanation is that donors, like the think tanks they fund, are committed to helping policy-makers make more informed decisions about public policy. What better way to do this than to support organizations that are well-equipped and well-positioned to exchange ideas with elected officials in the hope of bringing about domestic and foreign policies bearing their own ideological stamp? On the surface, this makes perfect sense. After all, philanthropy is about helping others, so why not use private funds to serve the public interest? Unfortunately, it is not that simple.

Whether they are providing funds to health care facilities, schools, think tanks, or other not-for-profit organizations, donors are astute investors looking to make solid investments. They may decide to allocate funds for more hospital beds and MRIs or state-of-the-art computers in digital labs. They might also make donations to renovate conference rooms, build libraries, and, possibly, to construct entirely new buildings. Still, when donors make large gifts to think tanks, they are expecting far more in return than a charitable tax receipt and a plaque acknowledging their contribution. They are investing in institutions that straddle the academic and policy-making worlds and with the wherewithal and political connections to shape the political climate for a long period of time. By supporting organizations that can alter the very makeup of the political landscape, as the Heritage Foundation and other conservative think tanks have done, donors can amass a currency far more valuable than money – political influence. As Inderjeet Parmar, an expert on think tanks and philanthropic foundations, has observed, donors are intent on creating and sustaining an extensive network of scholars and organizations that can promote and nurture their vision of the world, a world in which they can continue to reap enormous political and economic rewards.[22] They are certainly not investing in those intent on dismantling the society they have tried to build. If Parmar is correct, and I have every confidence he is, we need to consider what, if any, influence and control donors have over the kinds of research findings think tanks disseminate, the main weapon they employ in the war of ideas.

As mentioned in chapters 1, 2, and 4, following the publication of Brooke Williams's *New York Times* article on foreign government lobbying of US think tanks,[23] Brookings president Strobe Talbott wasted little time clarifying the relationship between donors and scholars at his institution. Not known for mincing words, he stated unequivocally that donors have no say in what research Brookings scholars undertake or how they research. Brookings is, as its president pointed out, an independent think tank that produces independent research.[24] Talbott's forceful denunciation of the *New York Times* exposé was predictable. After all, the Brookings president could hardly remain silent when one of the leading newspapers on the planet had given such extensive coverage to the relationship between think tanks and donors. Perhaps he could have ignored the story if it had been buried in the *National Enquirer,* but this was not the case. And, in all fairness, what else could he have said? That with each cheque donors make payable to Brookings, they should expect the institution to do whatever it can to ensure their policy preferences are well received by policy-makers? From his vantage point, the only recourse was to do and say what he did.

Without being privy to Talbott's innermost thoughts and to the conversations in which he took part with donors and key personnel, we can only speculate on the role donors play in shaping the research agenda of his institute. They may indeed play no role at all, but we can never know for sure. The same can be said of what latitude, if any, donors are granted in providing input on the research projects at other think tanks. Nonetheless, in light of the increased importance think tanks, including Brookings, have assigned to political advocacy, the relationship that policy institutes have forged with donors cannot and should not be overlooked. We may not be able to eavesdrop on what is said between donors, think tank presidents, and their fundraisers behind closed doors, but we do know this: donors are not in the habit of continuing to invest in people and projects that don't pay off. The American Enterprise Institute (AEI) learned this painful lesson in the mid-1970s, when several conservative foundations decided to withdraw their funding, leaving the institute on the verge of bankruptcy.[25] As the competition for funding increases,[26] we also know that think tanks have an incentive to keep donors satisfied. Some think tanks might be able to do this by producing high-quality independent research that is reaching its intended audiences and having a discernible impact on the political climate. This should help keep donors at arm's-length. Others, however, may have to be more accommodating of those who fund them, and, in the process, may be required to compromise their autonomy.

The Academy

Policy experts who conduct research at think tanks are intimately familiar with the academic community. Not only have they received advanced degrees from some of the most prestigious universities in North America and Europe, but many of them have held, or continue to hold joint appointments in the academy. Others, perhaps to keep one foot in the academic world, or simply to pursue their true passion, offer part-time or sessional university-level courses. But the links between think tanks and universities do not end there. In their capacity as coordinators of, and/or participants in, various think tank research projects, policy experts often rely on university faculty to contribute to their studies. As previously mentioned, IRPP and C.D. Howe, among others, contract out much of their research to faculty across the country. Scholars may be asked to provide a chapter for an edited collection or an article for a journal or opinion magazine, participate in a seminar, workshop, or conference or even be invited to become an adjunct or non-resident fellow at a think tank. Furthermore, some faculty may decide to spend part, or all, of their sabbatical at a prestigious policy institute.

Scholars who study think tanks need not peer through a crystal ball to figure out why policy institutes have a vested interest in establishing and strengthening ties to the academic community. Indeed, just as policy-makers turn to think tanks in the hope that some of the credibility that policy institutes enjoy will rub off on them, think tanks look to universities and to many of their more accomplished scholars to help bolster their stature in the policy-making community. In a similar vein, universities, in order to create the impression that the work they undertake is relevant to the public and to policy-makers and therefore deserving of increased (not lower) government funding, have demonstrated a growing interest in think tanks and in the many marketing strategies they employ to enhance their visibility. At times, this has resulted in the creation of well-funded think tanks on university campuses, such as CIGI, an organization made possible through significant private and public funding. Other times, universities have simply provided modest funding to support research centres and institutes that, at least on paper, may go some way to enhance their public profile.

Thus far, we have identified four of the key stakeholders with whom think tanks interact, and if I have given the impression that policy institutes make a concerted effort to reach out to these constituencies in order to advance their core institutional interests, then I have accomplished what I set out to do in this chapter. To become even more entrenched in the policy-making community, think tanks need to build alliances. They have done this, with varying degrees of success, with policy-makers, the public, donors, and the academic community. Yet, in recent years we discovered that think tanks have cast their net even wider by integrating with social movements, policy networks, and other fora that give the policy ideas they are advancing even more momentum and traction.[27]

NGOs, Think Tanks, and Fellow Travellers

Think tanks have a vested interest in protecting their intellectual turf and retaining whatever strategic advantage they enjoy over their competitors. But as we discussed in the previous chapter, think tanks are also

creatures of habit and remain committed to pursuing their goal of influencing both the content and direction of public policy. To this end, they
have established relations with domestic and foreign think tanks, interest groups, religious institutions, and a smattering of other NGOs who
share a commitment to shaping the political discourse around a myriad
of policy issues.

Building and expanding networks that comprise these and other organizations can, as several think tanks in Canada and the United States
have discovered, help create the momentum they need to compel policy-
makers to rethink how they approach pressing domestic and foreign
policy challenges. The cliché that there is strength in numbers is particularly appropriate when it comes to generating support for, or opposition
to, government policies, and rarely do organizations engaged in civil
society or in various social movements miss an opportunity to make
their voices heard.

As part of these and other social and political movements, think tanks
are often regarded as centres of intellectual innovation that can provide
leadership and guidance in helping to frame the parameters of key policy
debates. With the assistance of interest groups and advocacy coalitions,
they can play an important role in informing the public about the costs
and benefits of various issues dominating the country's political agenda.
For think tanks and the many organizations with whom they work, the
advantages of participating in common endeavours far outweigh the
drawbacks. By contributing their insights into how to navigate the policy-making process and build coalitions that will lend strength to their
efforts, think tanks, interest groups, and other NGOs might be able to
achieve together what they could not possibly achieve on their own. In
the end, each of the key participants may take credit for swaying public
opinion and public policy, but that is to be expected. For those engaged
in these networks, what matters even more is attaining measurable
results which they can parlay into additional donor support.

Think tanks have not selected the stakeholders they target by accident.
In their own way, each serves a particular purpose. Policy-makers,
donors, academics, NGOs, the public, and the media represent different
pieces of a puzzle that need to fit together to help think tanks achieve
their desired goals. On the surface, the pattern of cooperation and interaction described in this chapter may suggest that a conspiracy is afoot.
However, it may be more accurate to interpret it as a well-conceived
and multi-layered strategy employed by think tanks to enhance their

visibility and project their influence in the policy-making community. It is also a strategy that, as we will discuss in the following chapter, must be tweaked to accommodate different political environments. Because think tanks in Canada are often compared with their counterparts in the United States, a mecca for some of the world's most prominent institutes, our discussion will focus on the challenges and opportunities these organizations face on both sides of the border.

In What Ways Are Canadian
and American Think Tanks Similar?
How Are They Different?

In the more than two decades I have spent writing and speaking about American think tanks, I am often asked, particularly when addressing Canadian audiences, how think tanks in Canada measure up to those in the United States. It is a reasonable question and one deserving of a candid and thorough response. But before I discuss what makes the think tank experience in each of the two countries unique, let me speak more broadly, albeit briefly, about what has historically been one of Canada's favorite pastimes – comparing ourselves with our continental neighbour.

Comparing Canada with the United States has long been a preoccupation of scholars who are intent on isolating the various factors that condition the national identities of the two countries sharing the world's longest border. This fascination has resulted in a rich body of literature that, among other things, explores the extent to which history, geography, economics, politics, and culture have shaped both their destinies, and helped to guide their special yet complex relationship.[1] But lively exchanges surrounding the similarities and differences between Canada and the United States and between Canadians and Americans are not confined to lecture halls and seminar rooms. In the media, in bars, restaurants, and sports arenas, where amateur and professional teams representing the two countries square off, discussions about the relative virtues and vices of Canada and the United States invariably ensue. On topics ranging from the quality of health care and education to gun control, foreign policy, and hockey supremacy, there is rarely a shortage of opinion as to which country deserves the highest praise. And given the propensity of Canadians and Americans to draw comparisons between their political systems and policy priorities, it is hardly surprising how often questions arise about where power and influence is truly concentrated: inside the hallowed halls of iconic government buildings or in the boardrooms of Fortune 500 companies.

In the dozens of textbooks that provide an overview of Canadian and American politics, the question as to where the lion's share of power resides in each system is usually answered within the first few chapters.[2] Indeed, readers are told that in Canada, the prime minister and his or her cabinet exercise considerable political power that is enhanced by the Prime Minister's Office (PMO), the Privy Council Office (PCO), and the many departments and agencies that comprise the federal bureaucracy.[3] Of course, Parliament and the judiciary perform key functions, but when it comes to directing public policy, power generally rests in the prime minister's hands. By contrast, in the United States, where political power is shared among the three branches (the executive, legislature, and judiciary) of government, the question of who is ostensibly in charge is not always apparent. What makes matters even more complicated is tracking the various individuals and organizations operating outside the formal parameters of government who are in a position to wield policy influence.[4]

The realization that power and influence need not necessarily emanate from the same source has contributed to a greater awareness of the important role played by interest groups, lobbyists, and think tanks in setting policy priorities. For example, in debates and discussions surrounding gun control in the United States, much has been made of the widespread influence of the National Rifle Association (NRA) and the many ancillary organizations with which it is aligned.[5] Similarly, when attention turns to the ongoing turmoil in the Middle East, concerns are often expressed about the extent to which various ethnic lobbies attempt to manage US foreign policy in the region.[6] And in light of recent allegations that several high-profile US think tanks are closely linked to foreign governments intent on enlisting their support to lobby government officials,[7] there is an abundance of conspiracy theories about the relationship between policy institutes, policy-makers, and public policy.[8]

The purpose of this chapter, however, is not to malign think tanks for accepting donations from foreign governments, nor is it to fuel conspiracy theories about where true political and economic power resides. These and other storylines are better left to the imagination of writers on *House of Cards, Homeland, 24, Scandal,* and other television series exposing the dark side of political life. Though perhaps less riveting than watching US federal agent Jack Bauer, played by Canadian actor Kiefer Sutherland, foil a terrorist plot, my intent is, rather, to continue our discussion about the involvement of think tanks in public policy by explaining the various challenges and opportunities they face as they try to navigate their way through the policy-making process. By providing a comparative context in which to study think tanks, it is possible to highlight key features that may help explain why policy institutes in some countries are granted more status and standing in the political arena.

A handful of Canadian journalists and academics have shared their impressions of the growing visibility these institutions enjoy on the American political landscape.[9] These impressions are largely consistent with how think tanks are regarded by those in other countries who pay close attention to the think tank population in the United States. Think tanks in the United States are portrayed as large and well-funded organizations, that, by virtue of their privileged access to high-level policy-makers, can exercise considerable influence over policy-making. In contrast, in Canada, and in other countries where think tanks do not tend to have the same notoriety, their role is often perceived as being less critical to policy development.[10] The prevailing narrative surrounding the relative importance and contributions of American and Canadian think tanks thus suggests that while several US think tanks may have a front row seat to important policy discussions, their Canadian counterparts are often relegated to the sidelines, where they are forced to join the ranks of other NGOs marginalized by the political process. However, as we will discuss in this chapter, while the United States is home to some of the most recognized think tanks in the world, most American policy institutes face challenges similar to their Canadian counterparts. Although several features of the American political system help facilitate their access to policy-makers, think tanks in both countries must overcome a series of obstacles to ensure their voices are heard.

Aware of the complexity of the policy-making process, as well as the demands placed on their limited resources, think tanks must make a number of strategic decisions, not the least of which is where in the policy cycle they will seek to have the greatest impact. As I will discuss below, although think tanks in both countries make similar choices, those in the United States have far more opportunities to become involved in policy-making. But why is this the case? Does the highly fragmented and decentralized nature of the US government, combined with a weak party system, provide think tanks and other nongovernmental organizations with more opportunities to influence policy-making?[11] Conversely, do the principles of strong party unity, cabinet solidarity, and the presence of a permanent civil service entrusted with advising senior officials limit opportunities for think tanks in Canada to participate in policy-making, and hence reduce their effectiveness?

Drawing comparisons between the institutional environments in which think tanks in the two countries function offers some insight into why US policy institutes have established a stronger presence than those in Canada. Several features of the US political system have indeed facilitated the access of think tanks to various stages of the policy-making process. However, differences in political structures cannot account entirely for American think tanks playing a more significant role in policy-making than those in Canada, nor can they explain why some institutes in both countries are more influential than others. In fact, as some heads of Canadian think tanks, including David Zussman, former president of the Public Policy Forum, have argued, the structure of the Canadian government may have very little to do with whether think tanks are effective or ineffective at conveying ideas. The political structure of a country may influence the types of strategies non-governmental organizations use to reach policy-makers, but, according to Zussman, it is the modest resources available to most policy institutes that have limited their impact far more than the political system in which they operate. Gaining access to policy-makers in Canada is not a problem, Zussman claims. The more acute problem is securing adequate funds to engage in long-term research and analysis.[12]

If Zussman is correct, then it is important to draw a distinction, as this chapter does, between opportunities for think tanks to participate in policy-making and the constraints that may undermine their effectiveness. It can thus be demonstrated, as Diane Stone has done in a study comparing think tanks in Great Britain with those in the United States, that the structures of parliamentary democracies may not pose as much of a barrier to think tank access as previously thought.[13]

OPPORTUNITIES FOR THINK TANKS
IN THE UNITED STATES AND CANADA

It is difficult to isolate parts of the policy-making process or a branch or department of the US government where think tanks have not made their presence felt.[14] Think tanks specializing in a wide range of domestic and foreign policy areas have conveyed their ideas to key policy-makers in Congress, the executive, the bureaucracy and, more recently, the judiciary.[15] There are also think tanks at the state level, including the New York–based Manhattan Institute, which has established strong ties to local government leaders, including former New York City mayor Rudy Giuliani.[16] As will be discussed later in this section, dozens of staff from think tanks have become policy-makers themselves.

Among the many factors that have contributed to the proliferation of think tanks in the United States is the structure of the political system, which is characterized by its highly fragmented and decentralized character. As several scholars have observed, few other countries provide an environment more conducive to the development of think tanks.[17] With a government based on separate branches sharing power, a party system in which members of Congress are not bound by party unity, and a growing tendency among presidential candidates to test various ideas on the campaign trail, think tanks have multiple opportunities to shape public opinion and public policy. There are 535 elected officials in Congress alone, not to mention hundreds of staff and committee aides, whom think tanks can approach to consider their policy ideas.[18] Recognizing this, think tanks have, as noted, employed several strategies to attract attention, ranging from testifying before congressional committees and providing concise summaries of key policy issues to members of Congress, to inviting representatives and senators, as well as their staff, to participate in seminars and workshops.

Since members of Congress are not obligated to vote along party lines, they need not be concerned that their association with particular think tanks or their endorsement of some of their policy ideas would undermine party cohesion. Rather than evaluating ideas from think tanks as to whether they are compatible with party interests and policies, they can evaluate them on their own merits. Moreover, as Weaver and others have argued, the weak party system in the United States not only provides opportunities for think tanks to influence policy-making, but has, in some ways, increased the demand for them.[19] In Germany, political parties have created their own think tanks or foundations to conduct research and analysis; political parties in the United States have not.[20] There are a handful of congressional research institutes, public think tanks, including the Congressional Research Service and the Congressional Budget Office, from which members of Congress can request information.[21] However, unlike many independent think tanks, these bodies cannot be expected to provide timely and policy-relevant research.

A number of think tanks, including the Heritage Foundation, assign the highest priority to influencing Congress. Nonetheless, they also recognize the importance of solidifying ties to the bureaucracy, the executive, and the many agencies that advise the president. The Executive

Office of the President (EOP), which comprises several important agencies, including the National Security Council, the Council of Economic Advisers, the Office of the United States Trade Representative, and the Office of Management and Budget, provides think tanks with further opportunities to influence government. During several recent administrations, for instance, presidents have appointed senior staff from think tanks to serve on these and other agencies, and on various advisory boards and executive agencies.[22] Many of these appointees have previously served on policy task forces and on transition teams in presidential elections, a subject that will be discussed in more detail below.[23]

It is not uncommon for presidential candidates to establish task forces during the primaries and general elections to investigate policy concerns. These groups are particularly important for challengers who lack the resources available to an incumbent president or who lack experience in federal politics. For instance, during the presidential campaign of 2000, then-Governor George W. Bush enlisted the support of scholars and policy analysts from a handful of think tanks, including the Hoover Institution and the American Enterprise Institute.[24] In 2008, then-Senator Obama pursued a similar strategy by reaching out to a stable of policy experts with close ties to leading Washington think tanks.[25] And during the 1980 presidential campaign, Martin Anderson and Richard Allen of the Hoover Institution were responsible for organizing close to fifty task forces on domestic and foreign policy to advise then-Governor Reagan on a host of issues.[26]

In Canada, however, it is rare for federal party leaders to organize task forces during election campaigns. Part of the problem is logistical: the election period is far shorter in Canada – it typically lasts thirty-six days, from the time the prime minister advises the governor general of his or her intention to call an election to the day Canadians vote – compared with the lengthy primary season and general election in the United States.[27] Despite the passage of the fixed election law of 2007, some legal scholars, including Errol Mendes of the University of Ottawa, believe that the government can call an election at any time during its mandate, up to a maximum of five years after taking office, a provision enshrined in our Constitution.[28] This element of uncertainty potentially poses, as it has in the past, more problems for think tanks contemplating a more active role during elections. In addition, most Canadian party leaders do not turn to the broader policy community for advice, but rely on their own staff, party research caucus, and party members instead.[29] The prime minister may have even less need of policy task forces during campaigns, because as well as his or her own staff, the prime minister enjoys the support of the Prime Minister's Office (PMO), which serves as a "practical policy think-tank charged with an advisory capacity on the political fortunes of the prime minister and his cabinet."[30] With a staff of over one hundred, including about a dozen researchers, the prime minister has little incentive to seek the advice of think tanks during campaigns. Staff from think tanks are more likely to be called on when the prime minister establishes a royal commission or commission of inquiry to study a particular policy issue, such as free trade or the creation of a security intelligence agency.[31]

While there is little to prevent think tanks in Canada from releasing studies before or during elections or discussing ideas with party members, they do not, for the reasons given above, engage as actively in electoral politics as some of their US counterparts. Yet it is important to point out that while institutional and logistical constraints may limit the involvement of think tanks during elections, so too does the desire of some think tanks, primarily for legal and political reasons, to maintain an arm's-length relationship with political parties.[32] The Vancouver-based Fraser Institute is a case in point. Although the free-market think tank may on occasion try to conceal its conservative leanings,[33] it remained largely supportive of the policies and principles advanced by Harper's Conservatives. Nonetheless, the institute was reluctant, for political and legal reasons, to be seen as a mere appendage of the Conservatives. For similar reasons, it was also careful to avoid becoming too closely aligned with the now-defunct Canadian Alliance. According to Paul Wilson, former director of research for the Canadian Alliance, while there ha[d] been some interaction between members of his party and the Fraser Institute, "Fraser is concerned about being too close to us. They do not want to be seen as a Reform [or an Alliance] mouthpiece. We, on the other hand, are less choosey about the [think tanks] we talk to. Parties are like intellectual prostitutes. We will take good ideas from any source."[34] If Wilson's provocative, tasteless, and sexist comments about the manner in which political parties operate is indeed accurate, think tanks may want to reconsider what kinds of ties they can afford to establish with them. Of course, that depends on how think tanks see themselves. Clearly, some think tanks appear less concerned about their ties to political parties; the Ottawa-based Canadian Centre for Policy Alternatives (CCPA), for instance, maintains very close links to the New Democratic Party (NDP). As Judy Randall, a veteran senior researcher with the NDP Caucus Research Office, who retired in

2004, acknowledged, "Our strongest link to a think tank is the CCPA, although we also use a lot of the work done by the Canadian Council on Social Development, the National Council of Welfare, the National Anti-Poverty Organization and other organizations ... Several of our members have served on [the CCPA's] Board of Directors and their executive director Bruce Campbell worked for us."[35]

There appear to be both external and internal limits to how much direct access think tanks have to party leaders during campaigns. There also appear to be limits to how much impact think tanks have during government transition periods. As previously mentioned, a handful of think tanks, including the Heritage Foundation and CSIS, have played key roles in assisting incoming presidential administrations make the transition to power. Several think tank scholars have also identified topical issues and have advised on placing appropriate people in the hundreds of vacant positions that become available when governments change. These functions provide such think tanks with further opportunities to influence policy.

In contrast, think tanks in Canada rarely offer or are called upon to assist in transition planning, although some, including the Ottawa-based Public Policy Forum (PPF), have undertaken major projects on managing transitions.[36] Again, there are several reasons for this. First, unlike the United States, the transition period before a new government assumes power in Canada does not take three months; it is completed in less than two weeks. This short time frame makes it extremely difficult for think tanks to communicate their ideas to transition leaders. Second, few Canadian think tanks have the resources or expertise to arrange the types of transition planning seminars organized by the Heritage Foundation, the Brookings Institution, and CSIS.[37] Third, and perhaps more important, the federal transition process is overseen and orchestrated by the Privy Council Office (PCO), which is "staffed by career civil servants [and serves as] a major policy-advising agency of the federal government."[38] Furthermore, unlike US think tanks, which take advantage of transition periods to fill vacant positions in the bureaucracy, either with their own staff or with like-minded colleagues, Canadian think tanks have little incentive to closely monitor job vacancies after an election. An incoming US president must identify hundreds of people to assume vacant positions in a new administration, but a Canadian prime minister has the power to fill only a limited number of senior bureaucratic positions after an election, usually at the level of deputy minister. Most individuals who obtain these positions are career civil servants, not think tank staffers.

If think tanks in Canada do not make their presence felt during elections and transitions, where do they have an impact? Canadian think tanks, like many in the United States, do not always select the same target audiences or stages in the policy cycle to become most actively involved. Where and how they exercise policy influence ultimately depends on their mandate and resources, which, as the previous chapter demonstrated, vary enormously.

The priority for some think tanks in Canada, including the IRPP, the Macdonald-Laurier Institute, the CCPA, and the C.D. Howe Institute, is to influence both the policy-making environment and the policy-making process. As a result, these and other institutions welcome opportunities to enhance their visibility by submitting articles to newspapers or by giving interviews on radio and television. Moreover, they acknowledge how critical it is to secure access to the cabinet and senior levels of the bureaucracy, where political power in Canada is concentrated. Although think tanks frequently testify before parliamentary committees and provide party research offices, middle- and senior-level policy analysts in government departments, and members of Parliament with their publications, they devote less attention to influencing the fate of bills being considered by Parliament. They are reluctant to devote resources to shaping debates in the House of Commons, particularly after a bill has passed first reading, largely because of the strong party system. The time to affect the content and direction of a proposed bill is before it reaches the floor of the House. Once the government (assuming it has a majority of seats) has endorsed a bill, there is little that opposition parties can do to prevent its passage.

Publishing op-ed articles in newspapers and other print and online publications and testifying before Parliament might be useful ways of reaching policy-makers, but to have a real impact, think tanks must get further inside the policy-making process. Ken Battle, the long-serving president of the Caledon Institute, realized this shortly after he published an article in the *Globe and Mail* in late 1993 on the ill-fated seniors' benefits. As a result of his article, Battle was approached by several provincial premiers for advice, and, later, by some senior cabinet ministers interested in drawing on his expertise in these and related areas.[39] Battle said, "I recall getting a call at home one afternoon from Paul Martin [the Liberal finance minister], who proceeded to grill me for the better part of an hour on a piece I wrote on the social security review. It was worse than the grilling I took during oral exams at Oxford."[40]

Judith Maxwell, founding president of Canadian Policy Research Networks, Inc., which disbanded in 2009, acknowledges that to have an impact in policy-making, think tanks must rely on diverse and, at times, less visible forms of policy influence. Although Maxwell does not downplay the importance of media exposure, she maintains, as Battle and Zussman do, that think tanks exercise the most influence when they work with key stakeholders behind the scenes, not by discussing policy issues with reporters.[41] Maxwell believes that part of the CPRN's role was to bring together senior bureaucrats, academics, and representatives from the private and non-profit sector in closed door meetings to discuss social and economic policy issues: "We [were] interested in creating new mental maps for policy makers. Our research [and workshops] [were] not intended to simply summarize issues, but to generate new thinking. We want[ed] to help start conversations between people that would have never taken place before."[42]

Canadian think tanks may not have as many channels to shape public policy as those in the United States, but the political structure in Canada does not hinder their access to policy-makers as much as some have suggested. As noted, what may hinder their impact even more than the political environment they inhabit are the limited resources that most Canadian and, indeed, American think tanks have at their disposal, a painful lesson learned by several policy institutes, including CPRN, Inc., the National Council of Welfare, and the North-South Institute.

CONSTRAINING IDEAS: DO CANADIAN AND AMERICAN THINK TANKS FACE SIMILAR CONSTRAINTS?

Different types of political systems impose different types of constraints on non-governmental organizations seeking access to power. Clearly, the political system in the United States is more permeable than the system in Canada and in some other parliamentary systems. Nonetheless, to better understand why US think tanks appear to be more firmly entrenched in the policy-making community than those in Canada, several factors unrelated to the institutional structure of the Canadian and American government must be considered.

In Canada, as in the United States, most think tanks possess modest financial and human resources. The Brookings Institution, with its sizeable endowment, multimillion-dollar operating budget, and over two hundred staff and researchers is sometimes mistakenly regarded as a typical US think tank. However, as noted, Brookings and the handful of other institutes with comparable resources are anything but typical. The typical think tank in Canada and the United States has about a dozen staff and a budget between $1 and $3 million, fewer resources, in fact, than several trade associations, including the Ontario Federation of Labour and the Canadian Manufacturers and Exporters, which boast much larger budgets and staff resources.

The major difference between think tanks in the two countries is that while the United States has such prominent repositories of policy expertise as Brookings, the Center for American Progress, the Hoover Institution, the Heritage Foundation, and RAND, think tanks that generate considerable attention in the media and in some scholarly circles, Canada has few, if any institutes of comparable size and stature. Even its largest institute, the Conference Board of Canada, functions more as a business-oriented planning organization than as a traditional interdisciplinary policy research institute like Brookings.[43]

The absence of a think tank of this scale in Canada cannot be attributed to the lack of qualified individuals to staff it; for decades Canada has had a surplus of postgraduates with PhDs in the social sciences – the degree most policy research institutes in the United States require of applicants. The pool of graduating PhDs in the social sciences in the United States and in Canada has remained relatively constant over the past several years. Although three-quarters of the approximately 4,000 doctorates awarded in Canada in 2004 were in science and engineering, hundreds more students graduated with PhDs in the social sciences and arts and humanities, all of them fields appropriate for undertaking research at public policy institutes.[44]

Finding qualified people to staff think tanks in Canada is not the problem. Indeed, several directors and presidents of Canadian think tanks, including Brian Lee Crowley of the Macdonald-Laurier Institute and Marco Navarro-Génie of the Atlantic Institute for Market Studies (AIMS), hold doctorates; the problem is finding sufficient sources of funding to hire them and their colleagues. CIGI, the Canada West Foundation, the Institute for Research on Public Policy (IRPP), and the Caledon Institute are among the few think tanks in Canada whose core funding is secured through endowments. The current market value of the IRPP's endowment, provided primarily through government funds, is about $40 million. In the 2013–14 fiscal year, the endowment generated the bulk of IRPP's $2.2 million budget.[45] The Caledon Institute's endowment from its co-founder, the Maytree Foundation, pales in comparison: in 2014, it was about $700,000.

Without endowments on which to draw, think tanks in Canada and in the United States must access alternative sources of revenue. For some, including the recently disbanded North-South Institute and the government-funded defence and foreign policy institutes housed at over a dozen Canadian universities, this has meant relying heavily on public funding while trying to supplement their modest budgets with contracts, grants, and donations from private foundations, corporations, and individual donors. But the continued dependence of many think tanks on public funding exposes their vulnerability. Since government agencies and philanthropic foundations often have vested interests in ensuring that their recipients express views consistent with their priorities, think tanks are mindful of the danger of advocating policy recommendations that may alienate them. As several government-funded institutes experienced firsthand following the 1992 Canadian federal budget and in the aftermath of budget cuts implemented by the Harper government, their fate can be determined by the stroke of a pen.

Think tanks that receive little or no government funding may also find themselves in difficult financial straits. These organizations must then turn to the private sector, to individuals, and to foundations for support. In the United States, the Ford, Rockefeller, and Carnegie Foundations, among others, have long supported social science research, much of which has been carried out at think tanks.[46] This generous tradition of philanthropic support in the United States, however, has not taken root to the same extent in Canada, where most think tanks struggle to keep afloat.

Relying too heavily on philanthropic foundations and corporations can also be risky, of course. As with governments that require foreign aid recipients to make certain concessions, philanthropic foundations and large corporate donors must be satisfied that the organizations they deem worthy of funding are acting in a manner consistent with their broader institutional mission and priorities. Failing to appease the political agenda of philanthropic and corporate donors can, as the American Enterprise Institute discovered in the mid-1980s, have serious repercussions. When AEI's president, William Baroody Jr, was unable to convince the Olin Foundation, the Reader's Digest Foundation, and other like-minded donors that his institute was committed to pursuing a truly conservative agenda, they and other like-minded donors withdrew their significant financial support. As a result, AEI, long recognized as a pillar of the conservative think tank community, was brought to the verge of bankruptcy.[47] In recent years, Washington's libertarian Cato Institute has faced its share of political disputes with key supporters as well. Tension between the multibillionaire Koch brothers, who have donated over $30 million to Cato, is hardly a secret in the nation's capital, although a change in leadership at the institute appears to have helped get the relationship back on track.[48]

Succumbing to pressure from donors to embrace principles that are more clearly aligned with their long-term goals will undoubtedly compromise the independence and integrity of think tanks. But it is a price some policy institutes are only too willing to pay in return for a high enough pay-off. The conservative think tank Citizens for a Sound Economy (CSE), which merged with Empower America to create FreedomWorks in 2004 – another think tank generously supported by the Koch brothers – was well aware of this when it began its campaign to derail a multibillion-dollar federal plan to restore the Florida Everglades in 1998. For its efforts, CSE received $700,000 in contributions from Florida's three largest sugar enterprises, "which stand to lose thousands of acres of cane-growing land to reclamation if the Army Corps of Engineers plan goes into effect."[49] Yet even this amount represents only a fraction of the millions of dollars some foreign governments and private individuals, including the Koch brothers and the late Richard Mellon Scaife, one of the Heritage Foundation's principal donors, have invested in top-tier US think tanks.

While the gap between the wealthiest think tanks in the US and most policy institutes continues to widen, achieving financial independence remains the most significant obstacle think tanks in both countries must overcome to ensure a strong presence in the policy-making community. Without a sizeable budget, think tanks are simply unable to mount the extensive research and media relations programs necessary to attract the attention of policy-makers and other key stakeholders. More important, without ample resources to draw on, think tanks will not be able to recruit the types of people most qualified to produce policy-relevant research, as will be discussed in more detail shortly.

Some consideration should also be given to important cultural differences between Canada and the United States, which could also affect the prominence of think tanks in the policy-making process. One significant cultural factor that may account for their playing a less visible role in Canada is the relative absence of a strong, vocal entrepreneurial class in the private sector. As Abelson and Carberry point out,

In the US, independent policy entrepreneurs have provided important leadership in the formation of think tanks dedicated to providing information and advice to government. In Canada, on the
other hand, such leadership is likely to come from the government
itself or from senior public servants. This difference reflects both
the incentives created by the institutional structure of each form of
government as well as cultural understandings of the appropriate
repositories of policy expertise.[50]

John Kingdon's work on policy entrepreneurs, defined as "advocates
for proposals or for the prominence of an idea," demonstrates how these
individuals can have an important impact on policy issues: "Their defining characteristic, much as in the case of a business entrepreneur, is their
willingness to invest their resources – time, energy, reputation, and sometimes money – in the hope of a future return."[51] Why do policy entrepreneurs undertake these investments? They do so, according to Kingdon,
"to promote their values, or affect the shape of public policy."[52]

Without effective and meaningful government initiatives to establish
policy institutes like IRPP, leadership must come from one or more policy
entrepreneurs. According to the limited research conducted in this area,[53]
there is some evidence to suggest that, at least with respect to the private
sector, these entrepreneurs are likely to be more prominent in the United
States than in Canada. In their study of the environmental agenda in
the two countries, Harrison and Hoberg observed a difference in policy
entrepreneurship.[54] Among other things, they discovered that policy
entrepreneurs in the United States played an important role in the promotion of certain environmental issues, particularly the effects of radon, and
were able to put their discussion on the political agenda. They also noticed
an absence of similar activity in Canada. Harrison and Hoberg note how
the presence of policy entrepreneurship is, in a certain sense, tied to the
institutional arrangements of each political system.[55] The highly fragmented American political system, combined with an absence of strong
party unity, provides private policy entrepreneurs with incentives to shape
the political agenda. The relatively closed and party-driven system in
Canada, by contrast, offers few allurements to such entrepreneurs.

As noted at the beginning of this study, several think tanks in the
United States owe their existence and, indeed, their success, to the efforts
of policy entrepreneurs committed to injecting their political and ideological views into the policy-making process. Robert Brookings, Andrew
Carnegie, and the Heritage Foundation's Edwin Feulner represent but a

handful of such entrepreneurs who have created think tanks as institutional vehicles to promote their beliefs. This entrepreneurial spirit is also evident in the vanity and legacy-based think tanks in the United States.

By way of comparison, few think tanks in Canada are the direct creation of *private* sector policy entrepreneurship.[56] The Fraser Institute, under the initial guidance of Sir Antony Fisher, Patrick Boyle, and economists Sally Pipes and Michael Walker, and the defunct Canadian Institute for International Peace and Security (CIIPS), which was inspired by Prime Minister Pierre Trudeau's global peace initiative, are notable exceptions.[57] On the other hand, the *public* sector has been a viable source of leadership. Senior public servants, including Michael Pitfield and Michael Kirby,[58] played important roles in creating the IRPP, the Economic Council of Canada, the Science Council of Canada, and other governmental advisory bodies.[59]

The fact that major initiatives for creating Canadian centres of policy expertise come from inside the government and not from the private sector, as in the United States, is not surprising given the importance granted to bureaucratic and party policy advice in the parliamentary process. In part, it reflects the differences in culture in both countries in how policy expertise is provided to the government. Colin Gray, former chairman of the Virginia-based National Institute for Public Policy, has suggested that the culture of "officialdom" in the Canadian and British bureaucracies discriminates against groups seeking to provide external advice to government. This ethos of officialdom contrasts with the relatively open access of the US system, in which the role of the bureaucracy in providing policy advice is often overshadowed by the presence of "independent" advisors operating in the private sector.[60]

The difference in think tank development in the two countries, particularly in the source of their creation and growth, may reflect broader societal trends: sociological analyses of Canadian and American societies provide an interesting comparison. Canada has long been viewed as more "conservative, traditional ... statist, and elitist" than the United States.[61] In contrast, American attitudes about individualism and the limited role of the state have supported a culture encouraging private entrepreneurship. As Lipset argues, "If one society leans toward communitarianism – the public mobilization of resources to fulfill group objectives – the other sees individualism – private endeavor – as the way an 'unseen hand' produces optimum, socially beneficial results."[62]

In sum, think tank development in the United States is supported by cultural influences: a value system that stresses individual effort, a tradition of philanthropy, and independent advisors operating alongside the bureaucracy. This has encouraged policy entrepreneurship from the private sector, with think tanks originating from society. The Canadian cultural context provides a different environment for think tanks, particularly its bureaucratic ethos, which, at times, discourages external advice. Governments in Canada have taken, and continue to take, an active role in their formation and maintenance, as evidenced by the federal government's support for CIGI and other policy institutes. This does not mean that private entrepreneurship is unwelcome, but that it may face substantial challenges to overcome both the cultural climate and institutional arrangements in order to secure a meaningful role in policy debates.

The opportunities for think tanks to convey their ideas to policy-makers and the constraints that may undermine their efforts help to shed light on some of the differences between them in Canada and the United States. It is also important to consider another issue – the incentives for government officials to turn to think tanks for advice. A closer look at this factor may help to better explain why think tanks in the United States appear to be more relevant in policy-making than those in Canada.

EXPLORING INCENTIVES:
WHY POLICY-MAKERS TURN TO THINK TANKS

There are several reasons why policy-makers in the United States would turn to think tanks for information and advice. To begin with, a number of US think tanks have established impressive research programs in domestic and foreign policy by recruiting not only first-rate academics, but many former high-level policy-makers to their institutions. The presence of former cabinet secretaries and other seasoned policy-makers also provides an incentive for members of Congress, the executive, and presidential candidates to solicit their advice. Access to present and former think tank luminaries, including Robert Kagan, Strobe Talbott, Michelle Flournoy, Francis Fukuyama, Zbigniew Brzezinski, and Condoleeza Rice, may help to open other doors for office-holders or for those aspiring to become policy-makers. In short, members of Congress, the executive, and the bureaucracy can benefit from the wealth of expertise and the extensive network of contacts available at several US think tanks. Moreover, unlike most university professors, who have little incentive to produce timely and policy-relevant research, scholars at think tanks are more sensitive to the policy needs of elected officials. They can provide decision-makers with what they need – clear and concise summaries of the costs and benefits associated with particular policy proposals, not to mention the credibility and respectability that policy-makers can derive through their association with prominent policy institutes.

There are other incentives as well. As previously mentioned, several think tanks have been able to assemble talent pools of scholars for incoming administrations to draw on to fill important positions in government. For instance, during the Carter, Reagan, Clinton, Bush, and Obama administrations, many think tanks, including the Brookings Institution, the Hoover Institution, the Center for American Progress, the Center for a New American Security, and the American Enterprise Institute, contributed key people.[63] Politicians and aspiring office-holders can also turn to think tanks for ideological support: advocacy-oriented think tanks like the Heritage Foundation often help to validate or reinforce the ideological views of incumbents and challengers.

It is less clear why policy-makers in Canada would turn to think tanks for advice. To begin with, some preliminary data reveal that most of those conducting research at private think tanks in Canada, unlike their colleagues at equivalent institutions in the United States, do not possess doctorates, despite the availability of individuals with PhDs in Canada. Most researchers have an undergraduate or master's degree in the social sciences.[64] Furthermore, unlike most policy experts at top US think tanks, who have held several important government positions, most think tank analysts at Canadian think tanks, with few exceptions, have limited experience at the municipal, provincial, or federal level. This does not mean that analysts need prior government experience to provide informed observations about government or the issues confronting elected officials, but it does suggest that policy-makers may be more inclined to rely on think tank personnel who have worked in government in some capacity and who have some direct experience working with stakeholders. His extensive government experience may in fact explain why Ken Battle is often approached by cabinet ministers and senior officials for advice. It may also explain why, compared with several other think tanks, the Caledon Institute has become so firmly entrenched in the policy-making process. Second, unlike the United States, where there appears to be a revolving door between think tanks and government, it is rare for think tank scholars in Canada to be recruited into senior positions in the bureaucracy or for former cabinet ministers, bureaucrats, and experienced parliamentarians to go to think tanks after leaving public office.[65]

Some directors of Canadian think tanks have, as noted, held important government positions. However, few think tanks have been able to hire leading policy experts, in large part because of limited financial resources. Others, like the Public Policy Forum, elect not to actively recruit high-profile policy analysts, preferring instead to hire individuals with an array of talents, that include effective networking, fundraising, and well-honed communication skills. Regardless of the importance directors of think tanks place on hiring prominent academics or policy-makers, the absence of well-known experts may discourage some government officials from using think tanks – but so, too, will the uneven quality of research being produced at some institutes. As Lindquist has noted, to be relevant, think tanks must produce work that contributes to a better understanding of the intricacies of important policy issues. But as he discovered in his detailed examination of Canadian policy institutes, it is questionable how much some think tanks have added to major policy debates.[66] Finally, although many think tanks in the United States may lend intellectual credibility to the ideological agenda of policy-makers or aspiring office-holders, this function is less critical for policy-makers in Canada. Members of Parliament may benefit from and, indeed, welcome ideological support from think tanks, but it is the party caucus, not independent think tanks, that determines the party line.

Comparing think tanks across nations and understanding how political structures can promote or impede their access to policy-makers is invaluable in explaining why, for instance, think tanks in the United States and in other democracies enjoy more opportunity to shape public opinion and public policy than independent institutes operating in countries with totalitarian and authoritarian regimes. Yet, as this chapter has illustrated by comparing the US and Canada, it is important not to exaggerate the extent to which institutional differences are responsible for elevating or diminishing the profile of think tanks. In other words, the significant differences in the governmental systems of the United States and, say, Japan, helps explain why, compared with US think tanks, those in Japan enjoy only modest visibility. On the other hand, the differences in the political systems of the United States and Canada cannot account entirely for Canadian think tanks' lesser prominence. Several features of Canada's parliamentary system have indeed limited their opportunities to influence policy-making, but far more decisive factors in determining their success or failure are their effective use of often modest resources to advance their goals, and the willingness of policy entrepreneurs and philanthropists to support their mandate.

Gray has noted that "American-style think-tanks could not function in Canada or Great Britain ... because of the differences in political culture and government structure."[67] But, as this chapter has demonstrated, the same types of think tanks that exist in the United States have not only emerged in Canada, but have contributed in some instances both to policy-making and to shaping the policy-making environment. They have accomplished this in many ways: by advising cabinet ministers, as Ken Battle and others have done; and by helping to increase public awareness about the costs and benefits of introducing different pieces of legislation by sharing their ideas with the media, as the Fraser Institute, the C.D. Howe Institute, and others frequently do. But how much influence do think tanks in Canada wield, and should we believe what directors of policy institutes tell us about the impact their organizations have on shaping public opinion and public policy?

How Do Think Tanks Evaluate Their Impact, and Why Should We Be Skeptical?

Over the last two decades, as an increasing number of scholars from various academic disciplines have immersed themselves in the study of think tanks, considerable progress has been made in furthering our understanding of the role these organizations play in policy development. However, despite scholars providing a more detailed and comprehensive explanation as to why think tanks have emerged in significant numbers, and why some regions are particularly well-suited for their development, questions surrounding how much or how little influence they have in affecting policy change persists. But, interestingly enough, determining how to assess or evaluate the impact think tanks have in shaping public opinion and public policy has not only become a preoccupation of scholars; it has also become a pressing concern for directors and presidents of think tanks, who must keep their boards of directors and trustees apprised of how their organization has fared compared with their competitors. In addition to satisfying their boards and directors, presidents of think tanks have the added pressure of convincing donors and other key stakeholders to support the work of their institute. To do this, they rely on what are commonly referred to as performance indicators, or metrics, such as media citations, the frequency with which their staff testify before legislative committees, and the number of publications downloaded from their website. What they are trying to measure, albeit indirectly, is their organization's influence on public opinion and public policy.

Some think tank leaders, such as Brian Lee Crowley, managing director of the Macdonald-Laurier Institute, acknowledge how difficult it is to measure influence. Crowley readily admits, "It is far from a perfect science."[1] But Crowley, a recognized veteran in the think tank world who served as founding president of the Atlantic Institute for Market Studies (AIMS), also appreciates why it is critical for policy institutes to promote themselves and the products they generate. And if this means taking credit (whether deserved or not) for successful policy initiatives or celebrating a high ranking in a think tank survey, so be it. In the final analysis, as discussed in previous chapters, trying to convince policy-makers, the public, and other stakeholders that your institute has been able to shape the discourse about key policy issues is half the battle. For think tanks, it is about creating the illusion of policy influence.

In some respects, think tanks are no different from the corporations and private businesses that fund them. They have a product to sell and an image to project in a marketplace that rarely rewards complacency. As a result, we should be not surprised when think tank directors embellish their institutes' achievements. After all, their reputation and success ultimately depend on how their institute performs. It is thus important for those who study think tanks and read their news releases and publications to understand what motivates them. To this end, I begin by providing examples of how some directors and presidents of think tanks have tried to portray their institute in the most favourable light. I do this not to castigate or ridicule them (although I would be lying if I didn't acknowledge how much I enjoy doing this), but to remind readers how important it is to read between the lines. Not surprisingly, the examples I have selected are based on the reactions of two think tanks to the favourable rankings they received in the *Global Go To Think Tanks Index Report*. This annual survey has become think tanks' equivalent of the Oscars, Emmys, Tonys, Grammys, Junos, and Golden Globe Awards all wrapped up into one. The public release of the global rankings may not give think tank directors an opportunity to schmooze on the red carpet, but for many of them, being recognized as one of the world's leading think tanks is worth its weight in gold (or gold plate, as is often the case).

AND THE WINNER IS?

It did not take long for David Bercuson, one of Canada's most renowned military historians and the former director of programs at the Calgary-based Canadian Defence and Foreign Affairs Institute (CDFAI)[2] (recently renamed the Canadian Global Affairs Institute [CGAI]) to share the good news he received from the 2012 *Global Go To Think Tanks Index Report*.[3] Indeed, shortly after the preliminary findings of the annual

index and rankings of over 6,000 think tanks had been circulated, the
CDFAI issued a press release proclaiming, "CDFAI ranked one of the
top think tanks in the nation."[4] On the surface, Bercuson had cause for
celebration. His institute, which had been founded in 2001 "to be a catalyst for innovative Canadian global engagement,"[5] had ranked 7th on
the list of the top thirty think tanks in Canada and Mexico,[6] a considerable improvement over the 30th place ranking CDFAI had received a
year before.[7] Fourth overall among Canadian think tanks – after the
Fraser Institute, the Centre for International Governance Innovation
(CIGI), and the North-South Institute (NSI)[8] – CDFAI had clearly made
an impression on the more than 1,500 experts called upon to rank the
world's top think tanks.[9] What must have been even more gratifying to
Bercuson was the fact that CDFAI placed higher than several larger and
more established think tanks, including the C.D. Howe Institute, the
Canadian International Council (formerly the Canadian Institute of
International Affairs [CIIA]), and the Institute for Research on Public
Policy (IRPP).[10]

Bercuson attributed the organization's success to "the many people –
Fellows, Advisory Council, Board members and staff – who have worked
tirelessly to achieve maximum results with minimal resources." However,
he made no mention of how CDFAI had fared in several other categories
included in the report. For example, among the "Top 70 Security and
International Affairs Think Tanks" in the world, a grouping where one
would expect to find CDFAI given its defined areas of expertise, the
institute was noticeably absent.[11] Although several American and
European think tanks, including the RAND Corporation, the Center for
Strategic and International Studies (CSIS), the Brookings Institution,
and Chatham House, found themselves atop this star-studded list, no
Canadian think tank appeared on the roster. Ironically, it was a Russian
think tank that provided the only reference to Canada. The Moscow-
based Institute for US and Canadian Studies ranked 62nd.[12]

The CDFAI was also overlooked in several other categories highlighted in the report. In what the authors of the publication referred to
as "Special Achievements," where think tanks were recognized for,
among other things, the best use of the media (print and broadcast), best
external relations/public engagement, most innovative policy ideas and
proposals, outstanding policy-oriented research programs, best use of
the Internet or social media, and most significant impact on public policy,
CDFAI did not receive a single mention.[13] However, there was some
consolation for the Canadian think tank community as the Fraser

Institute, the North-South Institute, and IRPP managed to garner some attention. To be fair, ranking 7th among the top thirty think tanks in Canada and Mexico may have been newsworthy, but Bercuson's comments provided only a glimpse of where CDFAI stood relative to its competitors. As is typical for think tanks when they showcase their accomplishments, it is usually what is not said that deserves closer consideration. Interestingly, after CDFAI saw its ranking slip to 8th place among the top think tanks in Canada and Mexico in the 2013 and 2014 editions of the *Global Go To Think Tanks Index Report*,[14] it issued a more restrained and somewhat misleading press statement when the report's 2014 findings were released. Rather than acknowledging that CDFAI had placed 8th out of the top thirty think tanks in Canada and Mexico (there is no separate table for think tanks in Canada), CDFAI announced that it "ranked among the top five think tanks in Canada."[15]

It is true that CDFAI placed among the top five Canadian think tanks listed in this combined category. Still, it is questionable, given the ad hoc, arbitrary, and impressionistic nature of the rankings and the less than rigorous process that generates them, whether CDFAI would have secured a similar position in a category devoted exclusively to Canadian think tanks. Since many of the experts called upon to rank think tanks in this global survey possess little knowledge of think tanks in Canada, it is uncertain where CDFAI would find itself among its competitors. This problem has become particularly acute in surveys of this kind where experts are not required to undertake a detailed assessment of hundreds of institutes, but simply to provide their impressions of think tanks. With little detailed knowledge of what particular think tanks do, or the quality of work they produce, experts often base their decisions on their reputation. This may explain why the Brookings Institution and Chatham House consistently receive the highest rankings in this survey. It would also explain why the Fraser Institute, admittedly Canada's best-known think tank, is also consistently rewarded with a favourable ranking.

As noted, think tanks understand the shortcomings of the global think tank survey, and recognize that its findings are not the result of rigorous science, but random selection. However, this has not discouraged CDFAI and others that have received favourable rankings from showcasing their good fortune. As with most think tanks intent on elevating their status in the eyes of key stakeholders, putting a positive spin on the much touted global think tank rankings was a play CDFAI was only too willing to make. In concluding its brief statement following the release of the 2014 report, CDFAI added, "With your help, we look forward to making 2015 an even better year."[16] But better for whom? For the federal government as it continues its efforts to protect Canada's defence and foreign policy interests, or for CDFAI as it looks to improve its standing in these and other rankings? Perhaps both. As Bercuson observed in the fall of 2014, "I think we've [CDFAI] had some impact on the way defense and security policy has evolved in Canada over the last 10 years or so."[17] Not surprisingly, Bercuson did not elaborate on what kind of impact his institute has had.

The Fraser Institute was far less modest in publicizing the results of the 2014 survey. In a press release issued on 22 January 2015, a day before the *Global Go To Think Tanks Index Report* was unveiled in more than sixty cities, Fraser Institute president Niels Veldhuis proudly proclaimed that Fraser was "first among the nearly 100 think tanks in Canada for the seventh consecutive year and 19th out of 6,618 think tanks from 182 countries worldwide."[18] He added, "Being recognized as one of the top 20 think tanks in the world and the only Canadian think tank in the global top 40 speaks volumes about the quality of research and programs produced by our diverse staff and senior fellows across Canada and the United States."[19] And if this wasn't enough praise to heap on his institute, Veldhuis offered the following: "The University of Pennsylvania ranking is validation that the Fraser Institute continues to successfully study, measure and broadly communicate the effects of government policies and entrepreneurship on the well-being of Canadians."[20]

It would be tempting, and, frankly, justifiable (for some jaded political scientists), to indict Bercuson, Veldhuis, and other think tank directors and presidents for exaggerating their institutes' achievements in the press and on their websites. But, as we will discover in the pages that follow, this is exactly what leaders of think tanks are expected to do. In what has become an increasingly competitive marketplace of ideas where think tanks must secure funds to keep afloat, directors have an obligation, and, to be blunt, an incentive to cast their organizations in the most flattering light. To dismiss or downplay the kind of public recognition that comes from widely-known publications such as the annual *Global Go To Think Tanks Index Report* would likely not sit well with the boards of directors and funders who support the work of these institutes. In fact, to do otherwise would be foolhardy.

By pointing out how cavalier directors of think tanks can be when it comes to highlighting or ignoring data that suit their organizations' interests, it is not my intention to cast aspersions on, or to in any way discredit, those entrusted with overseeing the nation's think tanks. There are plenty of political pundits who are willing to take up this cause. Rather, by demonstrating how easily rankings and other measurements of think tank influence can be manipulated, I would like to focus attention on one of the fundamental problems encountered by scholars and journalists in evaluating the contributions of think tanks to public policy. As we will discuss in this chapter, influence is, by its very nature, subjective. However, this has not discouraged think tanks, or the various organizations that monitor them, from making unfounded assertions about their efforts to shape specific policy issues and the political environment in which they inhabit. We have good reason to be skeptical.

WHY IS IT SO IMPORTANT TO THINK TANKS
TO MEASURE THEIR INFLUENCE?

As a die-hard hockey fan, I regularly browse the NHL.com website to check on how my favourite players are doing. It's not because I take part in any hockey pools – my son has a far better handle on how they work than I do. I just want to know how many goals and assists Sidney Crosby, Jordan Eberle, and Nazem Kadri have tallied. But since hockey is a team sport, why should individual statistics really matter? Why should I not simply focus on the standings? In a similar vein, why have think tanks, as non-profit organizations, become so consumed with measuring their performance when they are, ostensibly, committed, as countless other organizations are, to improving public policy? After all, unlike professional hockey players, who have incentive clauses built into their contracts that, if met, could pay handsome dividends, resident scholars at think tanks do not generally receive bonuses for having their publications cited in the press or in academic indices. So why should it matter if some think tanks generate more media citations than their competitors or have staff who testify regularly before legislative committees? As long as policy-makers enact legislation that will serve the public interest, isn't that enough?

The reality is that as much as players are committed to helping their team win and as much as think tanks celebrate positive policy change, they are motivated by competing and often conflicting objectives. For players, it is about posting numbers that will translate into more lucrative contracts. Similarly, for think tanks, it is about compiling and massaging performance indicators that will impress current and potential donors. But unlike player statistics that can be verified, claims about how much influence think tanks wield cannot. Still, this has not discouraged think tanks from highlighting their accomplishments. They understand all too well that the more exposure and attention they generate, the easier it is for them to attract funding. And with more financial resources at their disposal, think tanks can establish a more visible presence in the political arena. This, in turn, may allow them to establish a stronger platform from which to shape the political climate. But does greater visibility, exposure, and favourable rankings in various think tank indices necessarily translate into policy influence?

Presidents and directors of think tanks would like us to believe that performance indicators such as the ones I have referred to are evidence of the policy impact they enjoy, a topic that we will return to shortly. They regularly make such claims in annual reports and rarely hesitate to boast about their institute's achievements in public gatherings. For instance, at the annual Manning Networking Conference held in Ottawa in March 2014, Veldhuis went to great lengths to extol the virtues of his organization.[21] During his thirty-minute presentation, he claimed, among other things, that while Fraser pays far less attention to influencing policy-makers than it once did, it continues to set its sights on shaping public opinion, something, he argued, that his organization has had considerable success doing.[22] However, despite his grand assertions, Veldhuis did not provide a shred of empirical evidence to support his conclusions (since he didn't have any), something I, as a co-panellist asked to speak about the role and influence of think tanks in Canada and the United States,[23] found rather telling. But to be fair, Veldhuis's motivation in constructing a narrative that celebrated, and, to be clear, embellished the Fraser Institute's success, was not meant to be subjected to close scholarly scrutiny. Rather, his comments were intended to impress the largely conservative faithful in attendance to invest both ideologically, and possibly financially, in the efforts of the free-market institute.

Veldhuis's analysis of how the Fraser Institute has become a pillar of the conservative movement in Canada is instructive in as far as it emphasizes the importance of developing a comprehensive and well-coordinated approach to engaging in political advocacy. However, it is questionable whether his statements about the influence of his institute would fool even the most basic polygraph. This begs us to ask whether he sincerely believes that Fraser has widespread influence, despite the absence of empirical data to support such claims, or if he has simply adopted a posture that presidents of any corporation, or government agency for that matter, would be expected to embrace.

WHAT RANKINGS AND OTHER PERFORMANCE INDICATORS
DO AND DO NOT TELL US

When based on concrete data, rankings can prove to be enormously helpful to both public and private institutions. Each year, for example, popular magazines and newspapers such as *US News & World Report*, *Maclean's*, and *The Globe and Mail* conduct surveys of the best universities in the United States and Canada. Although several university presidents have publicly criticized some of the criteria used to establish rankings, they have also come to rely increasingly on various metrics to assess how their institutions are performing relative to their competitors. For instance, in their strategic planning documents, university administrators pay close attention to how many international students are pursuing advanced degrees on their campus and the amount of tri-council support their faculty receive. They also track completion rates for PhD students and enrollment trends among undergraduates. Although these and other data can be interpreted in different ways, at least the actual numbers can be verified. However, as I have pointed out, the same cannot be said for think tank rankings that have been compiled by the University of Pennsylvania, the Center for Global Development,[24] the UK-based *Prospect Magazine*,[25] and other media outlets.

It should not come as a shock to anyone by now that I am not a fan of think tank rankings. My concern, as noted, is not that efforts are being made to track the growth of think tanks worldwide. This is a worthy endeavour, assuming of course that a consensus is reached on what organizations constitute think tanks. As noted, the problem I have is with the arbitrary and ad hoc manner in which think tank rankings tend to be generated. To put this in perspective, to undertake a thorough and systematic assessment of the work produced by hundreds of think tanks in any given year would take teams of researchers several years to complete. A thorough evaluation of even one small to mid-sized think tank would consume hundreds of hours. So how is it that the 1,500 or more so-called experts assembled by the University of Pennsylvania to rank what they consider to be the world's most recognized think tanks (which is problematic for other reasons) can complete their work in a matter of hours or days? Since those willing to participate in the rankings are not being compensated, it is difficult to imagine that they would be willing to invest a significant block of time to complete this task. As a result, one must question how seriously they take their responsibility. The problem is that there is no process in place to monitor how experts arrive at their rankings, that is, no quality control. Individuals who, ostensibly, have some understanding of think tanks (some do but many likely don't) are simply asked to rank policy institutes that appear in different categories. For experts possessing little knowledge of think tanks in particular regions, providing a ranking would be akin to throwing darts at a board. Yet, despite these and other limitations, for the past seven years, as the New Year is ushered in, think tanks have anxiously awaited the results of the global think tank rankings.

For think tanks that consistently receive high rankings, the release of the report is cause for celebration. However, for those of us who have studied these organizations for years, it is cause for dismay. Unless and until a more rigorous process is implemented to properly evaluate the contribution of think tanks to public policy, these and similar rankings should be taken with more than a grain of salt. The authors of the *Global Go To Think Tanks Index Report* would benefit from looking at how the founders of Transparify[26] conduct their survey of think tank transparency. Concerned that many think tank websites do not reveal financial information about their domestic and foreign sources of funding, Transparify established a rating system (similar to a report card) that uses a five-point scale (5 being the highest) to assess the extent to which think tanks are transparent. For example, in 2014, the first year in which this rating system was used, CIGI received a 5-star rating, which it proudly revealed in a news release.[27] Several other think tanks, however, did not fare as well. Similarly, the authors of the think tank report at the University of Pennsylvania could move from a ranking system to a point scale that evaluates think tanks according to an agreed-upon set of criteria. This system may not be as sexy as the model they now have in place, but the results could prove to be far more accurate. The manner in which think tank surveys and rankings are conducted will undoubtedly generate further discussion as policy institutes continue to compete for recognition and prestige in the policy-making community, but so too will the performance indicators upon which they rely to measure their influence. Should we be skeptical of these as well?

During his appearance on *The Agenda with Steve Paikin* during the fall of 2014, Jason Clemens, executive vice-president of the Fraser Institute, commented that the motto of his organization, of which, by his own admission, he regularly reminds his researchers, is that "if it matters, measure it."[28] Although Clemens was referring to a range of social and economic factors that economists often take into account, such as unemployment rates, taxes, and social welfare assistance, his advice about measuring what matters has spilled over into performance indicators commonly used by think tanks. In this regard, the motto for many think tanks, including Fraser, appears to be that if what we do looks impressive and can be measured, measure it. In other words, what matters most to think tanks is whether the target audiences they are trying to reach and win over believe their assertions about the influence they wield. But on what basis do think tanks make such claims? And how do they assess their impact?

ARE THINK TANKS AS INFLUENTIAL AS THEY CLAIM TO BE?

To take stock of what think tanks do and how they can leverage their influence, CIGI sponsored a conference on 20 September 2011 entitled, *Can Think Tanks Make a Difference?*[29] (I gather the title *Do Think Tanks Matter?* was already taken.) In the report that was circulated following the day-long event at its Waterloo headquarters, CIGI made several key points about how think tanks can be effective and what they need to do to maximize their influence. Some of these observations are summarized below:

· To maximize their influence, think tanks need to excel at communicating in plain language to engage both policy influencers [apparently a new word appropriated from the George W. Bush administration] and citizens at large.
· The role of think tanks should be to influence public opinion. If they can do that, governments will act.
· Think tanks have the most influence on public policy when they establish credibility via high-quality timely research and understand the political process.
· Effective think tanks need to leverage social media to engage and involve citizens in dialogue.[30]

The participants in the CIGI conference concluded in a nutshell what scholars who have studied think tanks for years have long observed. In an effort to shape public opinion and public policy, think tanks must engage multiple stakeholders, produce timely and relevant research, and communicate their ideas clearly, accessibly, and cogently. Just think how much money the conference organizers could have saved by issuing this one statement. In any event, CIGI should be credited for being so candid about its intentions – to influence the policy preferences and choices of policy-makers. But what is missing from this document is whether or not CIGI researchers believe they have succeeded in doing so. In response to the title of the conference, the answer is yes – think tanks can make a difference. The more difficult question is: how and to what extent do they measure this?

When it comes to measuring their impact on public opinion and public policy, CIGI finds itself in the same predicament as its competitors. It understands that various performance indicators do not necessarily provide an accurate assessment of its contribution to key policy debates, but in the absence of a better alternative, CIGI, like most think tanks in Canada, the United States, and Europe, feels compelled to draw on data that reflect how active it is around certain policy issues. Yet, as we will discuss below, engagement and visibility should not be confused with policy influence. Although presidents and directors of think tanks have a propensity to equate public exposure with policy influence, establishing a causal relationship between the two is inherently problematic.

Among the most common performance indicators think tanks rely on to impress donors and other key stakeholders is media exposure. Their reason for doing this is simple. It is the easiest way for think tanks to convince their target audiences that what they say and do is relevant and important. And what better way to demonstrate this than to maintain records of how often they are referred to in newspapers, on television, and on radio (see Appendix 1). As noted, think tanks regularly monitor the number of times their institute, staff, and studies are cited in domestic and foreign newspapers so they can compare their exposure to a select group of competitors. Some, including London's Chatham House, engage the services of a media relations company to perform this function, with the results often making their way into its annual reports and promotional materials.[31] But monitoring media exposure is more often conducted in-house. Think tanks can take advantage of online databases such as the Vanderbilt Television and News Archive[32] to track how often their staff appear on American network newscasts. They can also keep a close watch on how many followers they have on Twitter and Facebook, the number of times their organization has been cited in government publications such as *Hansard* and the *Congressional Record*, and the frequency with which their studies are cited in various academic indices.[33] Google Scholar and other search engines are useful in this regard. To provide them with a better sense of how extensive their reach is, think tanks can also record how many visitors access their website, keep a running tally of how many of their studies are downloaded, and track the number of people who subscribe to their online publications. However, while these and other data are readily accessible and can be used by think tanks to elevate their stature in the eyes of stakeholders, it is important to remind ourselves what the public exposure and visibility of think tanks means.

We know why think tanks covet media exposure, but why have the media become increasingly interested in think tanks? What is it about public policy institutes that journalists find newsworthy? As think tanks have become more visible in the political landscape (largely because of their growing numbers and strong ties to policy-makers), it is not surprising that they have commanded more media attention. At times, think tanks generate exposure because they have released a report (the more controversial, the more exposure) that focuses on an issue of concern to policy-makers and the public, such as reforms to health care or post-secondary education. At other times, think tanks may find themselves in the news because they have received a high ranking in a think tank survey or because they are being audited by the Canada Revenue Agency. But more often than not, when think tanks are cited in the popular press, it is simply because one of their policy experts has provided his or her take on a given political development. Yet, regardless of the context in which particular think tanks are referenced, what matters to these institutions is not necessarily why they made their way into a news report or newspaper article, but how often they are mentioned. Receiving a high ranking in a global think tank survey is important to think tanks, but so too is being recognized as one of the most talked about and written about policy institutes. This kind of recognition has its own cachet. With heightened media exposure, think tanks hope to enhance their credibility in the eyes of the public, policy-makers, and other constituencies. With greater credibility, they might be granted more access to policy makers, leverage they can then use to attract additional funding.

The amount of media exposure think tanks generate on a specific policy issue may help scholars identify the organizations most invested and engaged in particular policy debates, but it still does not answer the question as to whether their input mattered. Being quoted in the press or relying on an op-ed to propose recommendations for changing the substance and direction of various policy initiatives is a far cry from being able to influence what the public and policy-makers think about important policy issues. In fact, just because a think tank makes its views known in the press does not mean that large segments of the public or a small group of policy-makers are even aware of them. And even if they were, it does not mean that think tanks are in a position to affect policy change. As students of public policy understand all too well, several factors, at both a micro and macro level, can influence policy decisions. But think tanks know this – they understand the intricacies of the policy-making process, and they are painfully aware that it takes far more than media exposure to leave an indelible mark on public policy. Nonetheless, while they may or may not believe their own hype or the spin they put on their public profile, think tanks recognize how critical it is to convince others that they are well-positioned to exercise influence. For think tanks and other organizations that compete for the attention of the public and policy-makers, media exposure is a valuable tool they can use to elevate themselves in the political arena. As previously discussed, this may explain why some well-heeled think tanks in the United States have invested millions of dollars in developing and expanding their media relations infrastructure. Although few think tanks in Canada are capable of making this kind of investment, they recognize the importance of strengthening their ties to the media.

As important as it is for think tanks to be in the media spotlight, there are other ways for policy institutes and the scholars who participate in their research programs to attract attention, including testifying before legislative committees (see Appendices 2 and 3). Once again, however, it is important to question how this activity may or may not be useful in helping think tanks and the scholars who study them measure their reach and policy impact. In chapter 1, we went to great lengths to differentiate between think tanks, interest groups, lobbyists, and government relations firms, and although we identified many similarities, there were some notable differences, not the least of which was the commitment think tanks ostensibly make to policy research. Why is this important and why is it relevant to our current discussion? The reason I bring this up is to emphasize an earlier point. By marketing themselves as institutions comprising experts engaged in policy analysis, think tanks enjoy a certain status – one that is derived from a widespread belief, nurtured and reinforced by their carefully constructed public relations campaigns, that what they do and how they do it somehow makes them more virtuous. Claiming that they are committed to contributing to better and more enlightened public policies, think tanks wittingly, and at times unwittingly, try to take the high moral ground. Unlike advocacy groups and lobbyists who pursue narrow self-interest, think tanks see themselves as guardians of the public interest. Seen in this light, think tanks take advantage of what many of their competitors appear to lack, respectability and credibility, virtues they can exploit to gain access to various stages of the policy cycle. One of these stages of the policy cycle focuses on policy formation where, in an attempt to engage multiple stakeholders, policy-makers often turn to various organizations with expertise in particular policy areas.[34] Not surprisingly, policy experts at think tanks who possess an intimate knowledge of the domestic and foreign policy issues that have made their way onto the government's agenda are often invited to share their insights with the appropriate legislative committees.

Testifying before high-profile parliamentary or congressional committees provides think tanks with yet another opportunity to showcase their ideas and enhance their visibility. Still, how much of an impact a single appearance before a committee will have on its members or, ultimately, on legislation is difficult to measure. However, while the various factors that might have influenced government policy may preoccupy historians and political scientists for years, the answer is of little concern to think tanks that are more interested in gathering data they can use to impress potential supporters and parlaying those data into greater financial support.

The purpose of this brief discussion is not to leave readers with the impression that think tanks are being entirely disingenuous when they boast about their accomplishments in the political arena. There are many examples of think tanks that have made valuable contributions to important policy initiatives. I simply want to point out that the narrative think tanks construct about the policy influence they wield must be subjected to closer scrutiny. Performance indicators such as the ones outlined above may allow think tanks to acquire a better sense of how they are doing compared with their competitors and may reflect their level of engagement with particular policy issues, but these and similar data do not provide a clear picture of how much or how little policy influence think tanks exercise. Information about the media exposure think tanks generate and the frequency with which their staff testify before legislative committees should, along with the kinds of publications they produce, and the number of followers they have on Twitter and Facebook, be used as a point of departure, not a landing, for a much broader discussion about how public policy is determined.

It is understandable why pundits, journalists, and scholars are among those who believe that think tanks like the Heritage Foundation, the Brookings Institution, the Fraser Institute, and other policy institutes have played a critically important role in shaping public opinion and public policy in the United States and Canada. These think tanks have sizeable budgets, enjoy close ties to policy-makers, have become experts in marketing ideas and themselves, and have become permanent fixtures on the political landscape. And although there is little doubt that in some policy circles they have made their presence felt, they represent but one set of actors competing for policy influence. Scholars who study think tanks are under no obligation, and, in fact, would be foolhardy, to take the claims think tanks make about their impact at face value. When it comes to questioning where true political power resides, scholars' responsibility is to question, to probe, and to analyze. Unfortunately, in the study of think tanks, journalists and scholars have been far too complacent. For instance, when Edwin Feulner, the long-time president of the Heritage Foundation, told a reporter in the early 1980s that an estimated 60 per cent or more of the hundreds of policy recommendations contained in Heritage's mammoth study, *Mandate for Leadership*, had been implemented by the Reagan administration, not a single follow-up question was asked. Rather than challenging this claim, the reporter took Feulner's word as gospel.[35] All the reporter had to do to was ask the interviewee two simple questions: how did he arrive at the conclusion that hundreds of Heritage's recommendations had been adopted by President Reagan and his administration, and what empirical evidence did he have to document the extent of his organization's influence? Perhaps it was in the same file containing the material drawn on by Niels Veldhuis when he enumerated the Fraser Institute's successes.

Those entrusted with managing think tanks[36] have an incentive to portray their institutions in the most favourable light even if this means embellishing their achievements. However, scholars who closely follow their activities have no such incentive. Our responsibility is not to be publicists or spin doctors, but to expose the multiple layers of the policy-making process so that we can reveal the role think tanks play and the contribution they make to public policy. To do this, however, it is necessary to study think tanks from both a quantitative and qualitative perspective.

A TWO-PRONGED APPROACH

Compiling large data sets on the visibility of think tanks, though laborious, is not a difficult undertaking. Several search engines allow users to track the media exposure of think tanks in hundreds of domestic and foreign newspapers. Scholars can, for instance, monitor think tank citations by region, topic, and date, and, depending on the time horizon they select (usually five or ten years), produce a ranking of the most widely cited think tanks. A similar approach can be employed to rank think tanks that are referenced in broadcast media and on countless websites.[37] Moreover, through websites managed by the US Congress and the Canadian Parliament, a list of testimonies provided by policy experts at think tanks can also be easily obtained.[38] With this information in hand, scholars can begin to hypothesize why some think tanks attract more media exposure than others, and why staff from some policy institutes appear with far greater regularity before legislative committees. Still, although these and related data may help inform discussions about think tank visibility and may reflect the extent to which these institutions are engaged in particular policy debates, they are less useful in assessing policy influence. For example, while there appears to be a direct correlation between the number of times think tanks are quoted in the press and the size of their budget,[39] scholars have been unable to detect a causal relationship between public visibility and policy relevance: that is, the most talked about and written about think tanks are not necessarily those that exercise the most policy influence. Indeed, as noted, some think tanks, such as the Caledon Institute, maintain a modest media profile while enjoying considerable access to the high-level policy-makers.[40] Other think tanks also prefer to operate with little fanfare so do not assign a high priority to building a public profile, another reason for questioning the utility or futility of media rankings. Numbers that reveal how much exposure think tanks attract thus do not provide the context scholars require to ascertain how and where in the policy-making process think tanks have the greatest impact. On the other hand, qualitative assessments based on surveys, interviews, and case studies can prove to be enormously helpful in delving more deeply into the extent and nature of think tank influence.

One of the many challenges scholars of think tanks face is resisting the temptation to make general observations about the organizations they study and the kind of influence they exercise. We have already pointed out that no two think tanks are exactly alike. By the same token, the circumstances under which policy institutes are able to contribute to the policy discourse on domestic and foreign policy debates differ dramatically. This explains why Leslie Gelb, former president of the New York–based Council on Foreign Relations, concluded that assessing the policy influence of think tanks is notoriously difficult – it is "highly episodic, arbitrary, and difficult to predict."[41] To achieve policy influence, think tanks need to present the right ideas to the right people at the right time. But even then, their best laid plans may fall upon deaf ears. If there were a five-step program to guarantee that think tanks could leave their stamp on government policies and initiatives, they would trip over each other to sign up. In reality, there is no guaranteed formula for success. Sometimes, think tanks are able to engage policy-makers and the public in ways that provide them opportunities to share their insights about policy issues. At other times, their voices are barely heard. As with other non-governmental organizations that remain vulnerable to changing political conditions, much of what happens in the environment think tanks inhabit is beyond their control. Furthermore, relatively autonomous institutions establish and implement their research programs, and determine how and in what form to release their policy recommendations, but how well their ideas will be received and whether they will be acted upon is hard to predict. Recognizing this, scholars have published an increasing number of case studies on the involvement of think tanks in various policy debates.[42]

Case studies of think tanks and their efforts to involve themselves in key policy discussions can help shed light on the many factors that may facilitate or frustrate their ability to achieve their desired outcomes. Although these avenues of inquiry may provide only a snapshot in time, the picture they reveal at a given moment can go a long way in providing a more systematic examination of public policy institutes. At the very least, a more detailed investigation of particular think tanks and their interaction with key stakeholders may compel scholars to rethink some of their earlier observations about the inner workings of these institutions.

We have clearly made some headway in responding to the questions posed at the beginning of the chapter. By now, readers should have a better understanding of how think tanks attempt to assess their impact, and why, in response to think tank claims about the amount of influence they wield, a healthy dose of skepticism is in order. This is not to suggest that the contribution think tanks make at various stages of the policy cycle should be ignored, or that there is little evidence to suggest that think tanks have left a mark on public policy. On the contrary, think tanks have had a discernible impact on plenty of domestic and foreign policy debates. I am simply suggesting that to assess more accurately how much influence think tanks wield, it is necessary to pay closer attention to their efforts to educate and inform specific target audiences, and to keep in mind that influence is exercised in different ways and takes on different forms. Think tanks may not always be in a position to alter specific policy decisions, but this does not mean that their presence has not been felt. In a similar vein, producing a steady stream of publications, occupying the media spotlight, and hosting policy-makers at high-profile functions, does not mean think tanks are necessarily able to dictate policy outcomes. When it comes to studying think tanks, we should be careful to neither exaggerate their influence nor downplay their significance.

8

Conclusion:
Looking Back and Thinking Ahead:
The Future of Canadian Think Tanks

The first seven chapters of this book have been devoted to answering the most common questions I have been asked about think tanks, beginning with what a think tank is and what it is not. Several chapters later, we concluded our inquiry with a discussion as to why it is notoriously difficult to assess their influence. Along the way, we discovered that no two think tanks are exactly alike and comparing some of the differences and similarities between Canadian and American public policy institutes may be useful in explaining why the behaviour of these institutions has been shaped by far more than the political environments they inhabit.

As we reflect on the ground covered so far, it is important to take stock of what we have learned about think tanks, and how their experience as players in the war of ideas may influence the ways in which they continue to navigate the policy-making process. While those who engage in this field of inquiry continue to devote considerable attention to the rise and influence of American think tanks, they could benefit by taking a closer look at how policy institutes in Canada, and in other countries with healthy think tank populations, have distinguished themselves as vocal and active participants in the policy-making community. Think tanks in Canada may not yet have achieved the visibility and stature of their American counterparts, but, in all fairness, few other countries have a think tank community that can rival, in sheer number and in financial and staff resources, the most prominent policy institutes in the United States. However, though most think tanks in Canada can only dream of achieving the status and perceived influence of the Brookings Institution, the Heritage Foundation, the RAND Corporation, and other top-tier US policy institutes, it would be misleading, and, frankly, inaccurate, to conclude that Canadian think tanks languish in obscurity. As this study has demonstrated, rather than being relegated to the sidelines, several Canadian think tanks have immersed themselves in key policy debates, and in the process have emerged as distinguished players in the political arena. Indeed, on issues ranging from health care and educational reform to enhancing Canada's global competitiveness and restructuring the Canadian military, Canada's think tanks have made their views known and their presence felt.

It is clear that several Canadian policy institutes have developed a unique identity and, in the process, have carved out a niche. It is also clear that every think tank in the country possesses a distinct vision, informed by its institutional history, and a defined set of priorities. Think tanks may share a common desire to influence public opinion and public policy, but when it comes to shaping the political climate, they are not alone. Competing for the attention of policy-makers and other stakeholders are thousands of interest groups, unions, advocacy coalitions, and lobbyists, not to mention a multitude of other non-profit organizations. Yet, as discussed in chapter 1, while think tanks are often mentioned in the same sentence as interest groups and lobbyists, their commitment to providing timely and policy relevant research sets them apart. Thus, in what has become an increasingly congested marketplace of ideas, think tanks have come to occupy an important space that bridges the academic and policy-making worlds. And in this complex environment, they have developed key strategies to engage various stakeholders.

The desire of think tanks to engage stakeholders, and to design effective strategies to affect policy change may, at least on the surface, seem odd to those who perceive think tanks as neutral scientific organizations committed to helping government think its way through complex policy issues. After all, the desire to breathe life into organizations that could dedicate themselves to finding concrete solutions to the nation's ills is what, in part, motivated philanthropists during the progressive era to establish think tanks in the first place. Indeed, if this is what think tanks are supposed to do, then why are scholars who study them employing terminology often found in business textbooks to describe their activities? The short answer is that think tanks have evolved from organizations committed to policy research to those increasingly preoccupied with political advocacy. It is because think tanks have come to place a much higher premium on promoting and marketing their ideas that this book has addressed the seven questions, related to the efforts of think tanks to become more entrenched in the policy-making process.

After isolating the defining characteristics of think tanks, we are better able to discern why, among other things, most think tanks in Canada register as charitable organizations. When we interpreted the language of the Income Tax Act, where it pertains to non-profit organizations, we soon discovered that once a think tank was designated as a registered charity it was given tax-exempt status and the ability to issue tax receipts for charitable donations. But we also learned that in exchange for accepting this status, think tanks then had a legal obligation to remain non-partisan. Although charitable status did not compel policy institutes to renounce their ideology, they cannot openly support or oppose candidates running for public office, nor can they provide funds to political parties. This discussion, along with our evaluation of the differences and similarities between think tanks, interest groups, and lobbyists, helped lay a foundation for our deeper inquiry into the activities of policy institutes.

Following this initial foray into the study of think tanks, we turned our attention to asking whether all such organizations are alike. This compelled us to become familiar with various typologies that have been constructed to describe the different types of think tanks populating the policy research community, and the various benefits and drawbacks of incorporating them in their analyses. With this material in hand, we were able to probe further into the study of think tanks by evaluating the most useful theoretical approaches to observe the role and function of these organizations, a challenging, though not insurmountable, barrier to unlocking the mysterious world they occupy. Having traversed this daunting terrain, we shifted focus from abstract discussions about pluralism and elite theory to the practical realities of think tanks. What do these institutions do, how do they do it, and with whom do they communicate? These and related questions further helped to frame the parameters of our discussion.

Our attention then turned to the differences and similarities between Canadian and American think tanks. It did not take long to discern that most think tanks in Canada do not enjoy the stature or financial resources of the Heritage Foundation, the Brookings Institution, the RAND Corporation, or the other celebrated think tanks inside the Beltway. But it also didn't take a crystal ball to reach the conclusion that, like their US counterparts, Canadian think tanks draw on a range of strategies to ensure that their voices are heard. Having more modest resources does not mean that think tanks have to be modest in their goals and objectives. And finally, we addressed a question that frequently arises with think tanks: How much influence do these organizations wield, and should we be skeptical about how they assess their policy impact? Answering this required a careful and nuanced understanding of how to evaluate the many performance indicators on which think tanks draw to determine the extent to which they shape both the policy-making environment and the policy preferences and choices of policy-makers.

After reading this volume and reflecting on the answers to these questions, I am confident that readers will, at the very least, reconsider how they think about these institutions. If this happens, I will have accomplished my goal. In writing this book, my purpose, as stated, was to provide greater insight into organizations that readers have some familiarity with and, hopefully, a budding interest in. By responding to the most common questions I have been asked about think tanks, it is my sincere hope that this discussion will generate even more reflection.

The evolution and transformation of think tanks in Canada, the United States, and throughout the international community – from institutes engaged in policy research to those that place a higher premium on political advocacy – should remind us of the importance of paying attention to organizations that define themselves by the ideas they generate, and the impact they have on changing the political climate. Ideas do matter, as do the institutes that bring to them to life. Although I still find solace in the glory days of think tanks during the progressive era, I understand all too well that the kinds of think tanks I admired have, with few exceptions, become a distant memory. As think tanks look to the future, it is unlikely that they will spend much time reminiscing about "the good old days" when they considered themselves fortunate if a journalist, scholar, or policy-maker paid attention to one of their studies. Directors of think tanks, like CEOs of major corporations, have little incentive in waiting for their phone to ring: they are policy entrepreneurs who understand how important it is to enhance the visibility of the organizations they are entrusted with.

As we peer into the future, what can we expect from think tanks? At the very least, we can expect them to become even more aggressive in showcasing their ideas. Recognizing the increasingly competitive nature of the policy research community, think tanks will undoubtedly invest more time and energy in courting key stakeholders, including the media, policy-makers, donors, academics, and the public. Securing donor support, expanding their policy networks, and increasing their access throughout government will be critical for think tanks to succeed. But their success will also depend on the willingness of policy-makers and other decision makers to engage in discussions with them about key policy issues. Although there is little doubt that think tanks will continue to construct and advance a narrative about how influential they are, to have a discernible impact they will have to share their insights with the public and with policy-makers in ways that are accessible and meaning-ful, such as speaking to people candidly, explaining the costs and benefits of pursuing different policy options.

The future of think tanks in Canada may seem dire, particularly to supporters of institutes forced to close their doors because of financial hardship. Yet there is reason for optimism with the emergence of several new policy institutes in recent years. As the next section of the book demonstrates, think tanks with expertise in various fields of domestic and foreign policy have made their presence felt on the Canadian politi-cal landscape. They differ dramatically in terms of size, financial resources, and research programs, but all have a common desire to share their insights and expertise with various target audiences.

As Canadians, we are known for being modest and understated. During a class I presided over as a visiting professor at the Université Aix-Marseille in the picturesque city of Aix-en-Provence, France, I recall telling students that if they wanted to get a glimpse of the Canadian character they should watch an animated commercial that Tim Hortons aired in 2013, showcasing things that are uniquely Canadian: the com-mercial showed a flock of Canada geese in flight, and when one goose bumped into another, it simply said "sorry." How typically Canadian.

When it comes to think tanks, however, Canadians have nothing to be sorry for. We may be disappointed in and justifiably frustrated with the steps the Harper government took to cut back on funding to several of our policy institutes. In recent years, too many think tanks in Canada with long and distinguished histories have been forced to close their doors. However, while our population of think tanks, like our popula-tion in general, pales in comparison with the US, it does not mean that our policy institutes are inferior or should be ignored. On the contrary, by looking at the brief profiles of two dozen think tanks in the pages that follow, we should acquire a deeper appreciation of the expertise, rich-ness, and diversity of these institutes. But before we turn to these organi-zations, we need to discuss what steps can be taken to ensure the sustainability and viability of think tanks in Canada.

In the fall of 2015, Justin Trudeau, the eldest son of Pierre Elliott Trudeau, was sworn in as Canada's 23rd prime minister. Although he paid tribute in his victory speech to the thousands of Canadians who helped contribute to an impressive Liberal majority, Trudeau made no mention of his father, or what his father's legacy meant to him or to the country. In all fairness, perhaps it was simply not the right occasion to recognize how Pierre Trudeau's vision and values had rubbed off on him.

After all, Justin Trudeau is not his father, and has his own ideas of what needs to be done to move Canada forward. However, if he is concerned about climate change, the plight of Syrian refugees, and Canada's efforts to combat terrorism, he may want to think seriously about the contribution that Canadian think tanks can and have made to policy development. In this regard, he would certainly benefit from considering what his father did to enhance the role of think tanks in Canada.

Although many Canadians criticized Pierre Elliott Trudeau's efforts to bring about the repatriation of the Constitution and his handling of the 1970 October Crisis, few questioned his intellect and desire to encourage more informed and educated discussions about public policy. A gifted scholar, Trudeau was well aware of the reputation enjoyed by the Brookings Institution and Chatham House, among other top think tanks, on the world stage. Not surprisingly, shortly after he assumed office in 1968, he instructed Ronald Ritchie to lead a commission to explore the possibility of creating a Brookings-like think tank in Canada. The result, as discussed in chapter 2, was the Institute for Research on Public Policy. With a secure endowment, IRPP has undertaken hundreds of studies on key domestic and international issues. But Trudeau's interest in think tanks did not stop there. He was also largely responsible for the creation of the Canadian Institute for International Peace and Security (CIIPS) in 1984, an emerging player in the global think tank community. The CIIPS, along with the Science Council of Canada, the Economic Council of Canada, and several other policy institutes, was closed by the Mulroney government in 1993.

There is no doubt that the fallout from the 1992 federal budget continues to cast a dark shadow over the Canadian think tank community. Although it should have served as a reminder of how eliminating key research institutions can have disastrous consequences for the production and dissemination of public policy research, it did not discourage the Harper Conservatives from targeting even more think tanks over the past few years. If the health of a democracy is measured in part by the number of organizations that contribute to public policy, Canadians need to carefully consider how our think tanks are faring. If we ignore the challenges they face, and the strategic decisions they feel obliged to make to remain relevant, we do so at our peril.

In this study, I have discussed how and why think tanks in the United States and beyond have, in recent years, placed a higher premium on political advocacy than policy research. Think tanks in Canada have not been immune to this reorientation, and indeed in many ways have embraced it. The increased competition in the marketplace of ideas may account for why think tanks have become more advocacy-oriented, but we cannot lose sight of the financial motivation for adopting this posture. Think tanks, like other non-profit organizations, often struggle to keep afloat, and without adequate funding they all but guarantee that their voices will be silenced. In the absence of a sizeable endowment, which few think tanks possess, their existence remains precarious. However, this can change.

Created by an Act of Parliament, CIIPS, unlike IRPP, did not have the luxury of a multimillion-dollar endowment. As a result, from the time it was conceived, its existence remained precarious. If the Canadian government is truly committed to creating world-class think tanks that can attract some of the best and brightest economists, political scientists, sociologists, statisticians, and other scholars, who are capable of producing rigorous public policy research, Canada could become home to one or more think tanks resembling the Brookings Institution. Indeed, it could accommodate several think tanks that have expertise in domestic and foreign policy. We have the Conference Board of Canada – why stop there?

The challenge in creating large and well-funded think tanks will not be identifying talented experts to recruit. There is a surplus of scholars in Canada, the United States, and in many other parts of the world, thanks in part to fewer employment opportunities at universities, who would gravitate to institutions committed to rigorous policy research. Put simply, if we build think tanks with secure long-term funding, they will come. The added benefit of ensuring that long-term funding is in place is that think tanks will not likely feel as tempted or obliged to accommodate the wishes of private donors, or the policy preferences of government officials. For think tanks to fulfill the role for which they were originally established, two things must happen: their funding cannot be threatened, and they must be able to operate at arm's-length to government. This is not to suggest that they would not be accountable – they would certainly be required to report on their activities to an oversight board. But the direction and content of their research could not be compromised by outside forces.

The question that remains is whether the federal government places a sufficiently high value on the kind of work think tanks produce, and the nature of the contribution they make to public policy. If it doesn't, this discussion will fall on deaf ears. But the government needs to know that in the absence of a sustained commitment to the public funding of several think tanks, we will continue to witness what has transpired in recent years. Think tanks financed by private sector interests will continue to become more advocacy-oriented, and the shifting of resources from policy research to advocacy will, in all likelihood, continue to compromise the quality and rigour of studies produced by some institutes. While the increased profile of think tanks may help their bottom line, it is unclear how their visibility will serve the public interest. Of course, for think tanks committed to maintaining a balance between advocacy and research, it is to be hoped that their contribution to public policy will be more pronounced.

It is also important to recognize that secure funding for think tanks may allow these institutions to focus on what is truly important – generating viable solutions for a wide range of policy problems, not convincing themselves and others of how much influence they wield. As noted, in order to generate more funding, think tanks monitor a range of performance indicators from media exposure to the frequency with which publications are downloaded from their websites. Measuring these and other outputs has become as much of an obsession as people tracking how many steps they take during the course of a day. But Fitbits don't work for think tanks, nor does focusing on the exposure they've generated. Before directors of think tanks issue directives to staff to maintain detailed logs on how many journalists and policy-makers they have spoken with in a given month, they may want to remind themselves of an observation often attributed to Albert Einstein: "Not everything that counts can be counted, and not everything that can be counted counts."

Think tanks such as the Fraser Institute, the Atlantic Institute for Market Studies, and many other think tanks in the country may admire, and, indeed, try to emulate what top-tier advocacy think tanks in the US think tanks have achieved, but they may also want to engage in serious and honest discussions about the value they add to contemporary policy debates. Although it is entirely understandable why think tanks compete for attention and prestige, the important position they occupy demands that they think more critically about how they can remedy some of the ills confronting the nation. This kind of thoughtful reflection, along with a commitment from the federal government to provide long-term public funding of institutions whose top priority is to serve the needs of the country, would go a long way to reminding Canadians of the important role that think tanks have to play.

9

Profiles of Canadian Think Tanks

A NOTE ON THINK TANK PROFILES

As noted, one of my goals in writing this book is to introduce readers to the rich and diverse population of Canadian public policy institutes. In this section, I present brief profiles of twenty-four think tanks (which speaks to my obsession with the television show of the same name) that have distinguished themselves as organizations with a sustained interest in shaping public opinion and public policy around important domestic and foreign policy issues. With few exceptions – the Mowat Centre (the University of Toronto), the Parkland Institute (the University of Alberta), and CIGI (which, along with the University of Waterloo and Wilfrid Laurier University, maintains the Balsillie School of International Affairs) – most of the institutes profiled are what I refer to as free-standing, independent think tanks.

In the 2014 *Global Go To Think Tanks Index Report*, the authors concluded that Canada was home to ninety-nine think tanks (how appropriate, given the country's obsession with Wayne Gretzky's iconic number and our beloved game of hockey), making it the tenth-largest think tank population in the world, slightly ahead of Italy (92) and South Africa (87), and behind Japan (108), France (177), the United Kingdom (287), China (429), and the United States (1,830). Unfortunately, as much as I would like to associate Wayne Gretzky with think tanks in Canada, the reality is that several of the organizations listed in the *Index* either are not think tanks or barely have a presence. Indeed, some may exist only in a filing cabinet. Academic bodies such as the Canadian Economics Association which, to my knowledge, has never regarded itself as a think tank, and university-based research centres, including the Centre for International and Defence Policy at Queen's University and the Centre for Global Studies at the University of Victoria, which operate on shoestring budgets, simply should not be included in this list. It is difficult to determine exactly how many think tanks exist in Canada, but it is likely that the figure of ninety-nine has been significantly inflated.

Deciding on twenty-four think tanks to profile invariably meant that some institutes would be left out. For instance, the Broadbent Institute and the Manning Centre for Building Democracy, two institutions that appear frequently on lists of Canadian think tanks, have not been included, in large part because they more closely resemble advocacy organizations. Nonetheless, I have tried to offer a representative sample (based on region, size, and areas of specialization) that would help inform our discussion of think tanks in Canada. In the pages that follow, key facts about their history, mandate, and research programs will be provided. Much of this information has been obtained through think tank websites, personal correspondence, and print and online databases. Because organizations undergo constant change, it is entirely possible that by the time this book appears in print, information on budget, staff size, and other resources will have to be updated. I would thus encourage readers to contact individual think tanks directly. The following think tanks, in alphabetical order, will be profiled:

- Asia Pacific Foundation of Canada
- Atlantic Institute for Market Studies (AIMS)
- C.D. Howe Institute
- Caledon Institute of Social Policy
- Canada West Foundation
- Canadian Centre for Policy Alternatives (CCPA)
- Canadian Council on Social Development (CCSD)
- Canadian Defence and Foreign Affairs Institute/Canadian Global Affairs Institute (CDFAI-CGAI)
- Canadian International Council (CIC)
- Centre for International Governance Innovation (CIGI)
- Conference Board of Canada
- Fraser Institute
- Frontier Centre for Public Policy
- Institute for Research on Public Policy (IRPP)
- Institute on Governance

- International Institute for Sustainable Development
- Macdonald-Laurier Institute for Public Policy
- Montreal Economic Institute (MEI)
- Mowat Centre
- Parkland Institute
- Pembina Institute
- Public Policy Forum
- Vanier Institute of the Family
- Wellesley Institute

ASIA PACIFIC FOUNDATION OF CANADA

Tank Facts

Established: 1984
Location: Vancouver, BC
Budget: > $6 million
Staff: ~ 24; >20 fellows
President/Director: Stewart Beck
Website: www.asiapacific.ca

Established by an Act of Parliament, the Asia Pacific Foundation of Canada Act, the Vancouver-based not-for profit institute, is the country's premier think tank on Canada-Asia relations. With a mandate to "raise awareness and foster informed decision-making" about Canada's ties to this critically important region, the foundation works closely with public and private sector institutions on a wide range of policy issues. Drawing on the expertise of approximately thirty staff and a budget hovering around $6 million, the Asia Pacific Foundation seeks to develop and nurture networks among individuals and organizations committed to establishing a stronger Canadian presence in Asia.

According to the Act, which gave birth to the organization and defined its mission, the Asia Pacific Foundation is responsible for:

(a)   promoting mutual awareness and understanding of the cultures, histories, religions, philosophies, languages, life styles, and aspirations in the Asia-Pacific region and Canada and their effects on each other's societies;

(a.1)   promoting dialogue on, and understanding of, foreign policy issues as they relate to Canada and the Asia-Pacific region, an additional goal articulated in 2005;

(b)   supporting development cooperation between organiza-
        tions, institutions and associations in Canada and in the
        Asia-Pacific region;
(c)   promoting collaboration among organizations, institutions
        and associations in private and public sectors in Canada
        and in the Asia-Pacific region;
(d)   promoting closer economic and commercial ties between
        Canada and the Asia-Pacific region;
(e)   promoting, in Canada, scholarship in and expertise on eco-
        nomic, cultural, social and other subjects relating to the
        Asia-Pacific region, and in the Asia-Pacific region, scholar-
        ship in and expertise on economic, cultural, social and other
        subjects relating to Canada; and
(f)   collecting information and ideas relating to Canada and the
        Asia-Pacific region and disseminating such information and
        ideas within Canada and the Asia-Pacific region.[1]

In August 2014, Stewart Beck, Canada's former High Commissioner
to India and ambassador to Nepal and Bhutan, succeeded Yuen Pau
Woo, an authority on China who served as the Foundation's president
and CEO for nine years and holds the title of Distinguished East Asia
Fellow. The Foundation is governed by a board of directors, which
includes the president and CEO, four other directors appointed by the
governor-in-council, and up to eighteen additional directors. The board
is chaired by John H. McArthur, dean emeritus, Harvard Business School.
Among its directors are: Colin Dodds, president, Saint Mary's University;
Kevin Lynch, vice-chairman, BMO Financial Group; and Indira
Samarasekera, president and vice-chancellor, University of Alberta.
    The Asia Pacific Foundation's funding is drawn primarily from an
endowment provided by the Government of Canada and by corporate
and individual donors. In recent years, donors who have provided
$100,000 or more included: BMO Financial Group, Shell Canada,
Manulife Financial, and Teck Resources Limited. Sizeable donations in
amounts up to $99,999 were also made by HSBC Canada, Port Metro
Vancouver, Air China, Blake, Cassels & Graydon LLP, Canadian Association of Petroleum Producers, Canadian Pacific, Cathay Pacific Air-
ways, Deloitte, Fiera Capital, Husky Energy, Port of Halifax, TELUS,
Vancouver Airport Authority, Westport Innovations Inc., Encana Corporation, Five Stars Travel Limited, Harvest Operations Corporation, The
Japan Foundation, New Routes to the Future Ecological Foundation,

POSCO Canada, Province of Alberta, Salley Bowes Harwardt LC, United Way of Canada, and the University of British Columbia.

The foundation's current research focuses on four themes: promoting trade, investment, and innovation; building skills and competencies; mobilizing energy assets; and understanding Asia. It maintains an active publications program overseen by an editorial team. Experts, both at the foundation and those contracted to undertake research on its behalf, publish a steady stream of research papers, blogs, surveys, and analyses for various audiences on a wide range of social, economic, and political issues affecting Canada's relations in Asia. With extensive expertise on the countries of Asia and Canada's ties to them, experts from the Asia Pacific Foundation are called upon regularly to share their insights with the media. In addition, the Foundation offers post-graduate and research fellowships to academics to produce policy papers. Moreover, to further generate and disseminate its findings, the Foundation engages in the following activities:

- Forum of Discussion – "Disseminating knowledge and raising public awareness through roundtables, panel discussions and speaking engagements."
- Research and Analysis – "Promoting informed discussion on Canada-Asia relations through research reports, publications and opinion editorials."
- Special Research Projects – "Identifying and filling knowledge gaps on issues affecting Canada-Asia Relations"
- Track Two Diplomacy – "Supporting government-to-government processes to encourage and pave the way for new strategic developments."
- Grants and Fellowship Programs – "Providing new-generation researchers and journalists with the opportunity to engage in policy research and media coverage of Asia."[2]

References to the Asia Pacific Foundation of Canada in Selected Canadian Newspapers

CALGARY HERALD

Berthiaume, Lee. "Chinese Leadership Remains a Wild Card; Human-Rights Remain Barrier to Business." 13 November 2012, A4.

Cryderman, Kelly. "Canada's Future Linked to Foreign Investment." 5 January 2013, A4.

Lynch, Kevin, and Pau Woo Yen. "Canada Must Act Before Asia Finds Energy Supply." 20 March 2013, A11.

Yedlin, Deborah. "Access to Asia Requires National Strategy." 9 June 2012, D1.

GLOBE AND MAIL

Berkow, Jameson. "Who's Afraid of China?; Industry Mum as Citizens Worry about Giant's Rising Influence in Oil Sands." 11 May 2012, E6.

Cohen, Andrew. "Emissary Had Brilliant Government Career." 15 November 2012, S8.

Cousineau, Sophie. "Nexen Approval Fails to Provide a Gateway to China." 12 December 2012, B2.

Curry, Bill. "For Flaherty, Promoting Budget in Asia Is Business as Usual." 28 March 2013, A4.

– "Ottawa Must Pursue More Than Just Economic Links with Asia, Study Urges." 6 September 2012, A4.

Curry, Bill, and Sean Silcoff. "Former Finance Minister Urges Debate on New Language Skills." 17 October 2012, A8.

Hoffman, Andy. "Clarity Urged for Foreign Takeovers." 16 August 2012, B4.

Jang, Brent. "The High-Risk, High-Stakes Plan to Export LNG to Asia." 3 April 2013, B4.

Jiang, Wenran. "Beijing and Tokyo Must Back Off." 19 September 2012, A21.

Job, Brian. "Does Ottawa Have Staying Power in Southeast Asia?" 8 August 2012, A15.

McCarthy, Shawn, and Andy Hoffman. "Harper Promises Playbook for Takeovers." 7 September 2012, B1.

McKenna, Barrie, and Greg Keenan. "South Korea Free-Trade Deal 'Very Close.'" 26 March 2013, B1.

Simpson, Jeffrey. "Oil-Patch Ironies Aside, Many Questions for Harper." 28 July 2012, F9.

Vanderklippe, Nathan, Shawn McCarthy, and Jacquie McNish. "Petronas to Sweeten the Payoff if Ottawa Says Yes." 5 December 2012, B1.

Wheeler, Carolynne, Andy Hoffman, and Brent Jang. "What It Means for the Canadian Economy." 16 November 2012, A11.

Yuen, Pau Woo. "A Ring Fence Won't Build National Champions." 19 October 2012, A17.

– "Why Stop There?" 28 September 2012, A20.

NATIONAL POST

Berkow, Jameson. "Benefit Rule Tests China's Patience; Conference Report." 6 July 2012, FP1.

– "Chinese Partnerships 'Have Not Disappointed'; With Huge Cash Reserves, More Sensitivity to IP and Enviable Expertise, Fostering Economic Relationships with China Can Help Increase Canada's Productivity in the Oil Patch." 25 September 2012, FP4.

– "India Finally Bids for Canadian Energy Assets; Following China; 'They Don't Have as Deep Pockets as the Chinese.'" 25 September 2012, FP5.

– "Links with China Bring 'Long-Term Pain': Study; Caution to Ottawa." 7 September 2012, FP1.

– "National Interest Comes First, Report Says Selling Resources." 6 June 2012, FP2.

Berthiaume, Lee. "Canada Joins Pacific Exercise; 1,400 Troops." 17 July 2012, A4.

Cattaneo, Claudia. "Asia Seeking a New Energy Bargain; It Wants to Set Its Own Terms in a Buyer's Market." 6 April 2013, FP5.

Hussain, Yadullah. "What's Next?; Chinese-Canadian Energy Relations Are in the Early Stages of Exploration After Ottawa's Ruling to Allow Majority State-Owned Enterprise Investment in Oil Sands." 8 March 2013, FP7.

Lewis, Jeff. "The Latest M&A Supercycle; Asian National Oil Companies Will Likely Be on the Hunt in 2013." 18 January 2013, FP6.

McMillan, Charles, and George Stalk Jr. "Seize the Continent." 6 March 2013, FP11.

Yuen, Pau Woo. "Muddled Thinking on SOEs; A Few State Takeovers like Nexen Deal Won't Destroy Market." 14 September 2012, FP11.

TORONTO STAR

Dembicki, Geoff. "Riding China's Bumpy Green Wave: Western Firms Find Profit and Peril in Country's New-Found Move." 24 November 2012, S15.

Keung, Nicholas. "Overseas Parents Fret over Students: Canada's Peaceful Name Tarnished by Attacks." 23 July 2012, GT1.

Lewis, Michael, and Vanessa Lu. "Move Signals New Openness: CNOOC and Petronas Approvals Seen as a Shift from 2010's Rejection of Potash Corp. Takeover." 8 December 2012, A6.

Lu, Vanessa. "China Buying into Canada in a Big Way: Last Five Years Have Seen Billions Flow Across the Pacific." 20 July 2012, B1.

McDiarmid, Jessica. "Panda Loan Won't Solve Canada-China Relations: Bringing Bears Here Nice Gesture but Experts Say Work to Be Done." 27 March 2013, GT3.

VANCOUVER SUN
Austin, Jack. "Harper Doctrine a Diving Catch for Canada's Future." 3 January 2013, A15.
Berthiaume, Lee. "Canada Joins Military 'Full-Court Press' in Asia; Growth of Region's Economic and Military Importance Creates Both Opportunities and Concerns." 17 July 2012, B3.
– "China's New Leadership Will Affect Canada; World Would Benefit from Political Reforms That Lead to More Freedom, Respect for Human Rights." 13 November 2012, B1.
– "Harper May Go Political for China Envoy; If the Next Ambassador Is a Senior Tory, It Will Send a Signal of Beijing's Growing Importance." 2 June 2012, B4.
Blair, Dennis, and Kevin Lynch. "Self-Sufficiency Will Open Doors; New Energy Relationship with Asia-Pacific Region Offers Opportunities for Co-operation on Common Objectives." 2 April 2013, A11.
Cayo, Don. "Canada Needs More Asian Engagement." 7 September 2012, F3.
Hamilton, Gordon. "Japan Guarantees $10 Billion to Boost BC Gas Development; Loans Backed to Companies in Effort to Encourage Infrastructure Investments." 6 April 2013, D1.
Hansen, Darah. "Group Formed to Help City Connect with Public; Task Force Represents a Mix of Talent, Age, Diversity and Home Neighbourhoods." 6 December 2012, A2.
O'Neil, Peter. "Deal with China Triggers Public Concern, Lawyer's Warning; Treaty Could Cost Canada Billions if BC Blocks Northern Gateway Project." 26 October 2012, E1.
Yedlin, Deborah. "Canada Must 'Think Big' on Energy Strategy to Tap Asian Markets." 16 June 2012, C4.
Yuen, Pau Woo. "Canada Playing Catch-up in Asia; This Country Needs a Leapfrog Policy to Transform Itself into the Most Asia-Engaged Nation in the Western World." 16 April 2012, A11.

Selected Publications of the Asia Pacific Foundation of Canada

Busza, Eva, Nathan Allen, Matthew Neckelmann, Tiffany Chua, and Kenny Zhang. "Intellectual Property Rights Challenges Facing

Foreign and Canadian Companies in China: Survey Results and Analysis." *Research Reports.* 12 February 2015.

Busza, Eva, Tiffany Chua, and Matthew Neckelmann. "Intellectual Property Rights Challenges Facing Foreign and Canadian Businesses in China: A Survey of Literature." *Research Reports.* 7 October 2014.

Chau, Tiffany. "Conference Report: International Seminar on Innovation, Entrepreneurship, and Open Talent Policy." *Research Reports.* 4 March 2015.

Gould, Douglas. "Canadian Companies That Do Business in India: New Landscapes, New Players and the Outlook for Canada." *Research Reports.* 13 April 2015.

Grafton, R. Quentin and N. Ross Lambie. "Australia's Experience in Developing an LNG Export Industry." *Research Reports.* 17 September 2014.

Kincaide, Heather, Clare Richardson-Barlow, Laura Schwartz, and Vineeth Atreyesh Vasudeva Murthy. "Pacific Energy Forum: New Frontiers in Trans-Pacific Energy Trade." *Research Reports.* 12 November 2014.

Koyama, Ken. "Japan: A High-Value Market for Canadian LNG." *Research Reports.* 30 October 2014.

Singhal, Rajrishi. "India: An Overlooked Opportunity for Canadian LNG." *Research Reports.* 30 October 2014.

Tao, Wang. "Supplying LNG to China: Does Canada Have What It Takes?" *Research Reports.* 30 October 2014.

Williams. Erin. "'Canada's Asia Challenge: Building Skills and Knowledge for the Next Generation' Conference Summary Report." *Research Reports.* 25 February 2015.

ATLANTIC INSTITUTE FOR MARKET STUDIES (AIMS)

Tank Facts

Established:	1994
Location:	Halifax
Budget:	$1.5–$2 million
Staff:	5 staff; 14 research fellows
President/Director:	Marco Navarro-Génie
Website:	www.aims.ca

With a generous start-up grant from the Donner Foundation, a group of Atlantic Canadians set out to create an organization that would encourage policy analysts to address the unique challenges and opportunities facing the region. The result was the Atlantic Institute for Market Studies (AIMS), a think tank committed to broadening "the debate about realistic options available to build [the Atlantic]."[3] To fulfill its mandate, AIMS pursues four main objectives: initiating and conducting research that identifies current and emerging economic and social issues confronting Atlantic Canada; investigating a full range of options for public and private responses to these issues; communicating its research to regional and national audiences in a non-partisan manner; and sponsoring seminars, lectures, and training programs.

Reflecting on the need to create a think tank in Atlantic Canada that examines current and emerging policy issues in the region, Brian Lee Crowley, the founding president of AIMS, who, since 2010, has been managing director of the Ottawa-based Macdonald-Laurier Institute, remarked:

> There are other national think-tanks that aim to stimulate people to think in new and better ways about economic and social policy, to take the long strategic view, to speak out on controversial issues ... The C.D. Howe Institute, the Fraser Institute, the Institute for Research on Public Policy and the [Canadian] Centre for Policy Alternatives spring to mind. But these national organisations can devote little of their time and effort to the particular challenges and circumstances of Atlantic Canada ... regionally, there are other groups, like the Atlantic Provinces Economic Council, that gather and publish the most complete and up-to-date economic data on Regional Development, public academic treatises ... AIMS seeks to do more than provide useful factual information on what's going on in the economy today ... rather, AIMS exists to offer a platform for the best and brightest to put forward their own thoughts and analysis about what to do about our challenges and opportunities, about how we can think and act strategically, and for the long term, to build a more prosperous future for the region.[4]

AIMS relies on several channels to convey its ideas on how best to confront the many challenges in Atlantic Canada. In addition to producing a quarterly newsletter, the *Beacon*, and several other publications, including blogs that are targeted to university students, AIMS regularly holds conferences and seminars to promote exchanges between policy-makers, academics, and leaders from the private and non-profit sectors. AIMS also actively engages the media and encourages its scholars to share their insights with journalists. Funded by foundations, corporations, and individual donors, AIMS maintains an extensive research program that covers a wide range of topics: education, energy, healthcare, security and defence, regional development, and urban affairs. The president of AIMS, Marco Navarro-Génie, a scholar of Latin American politics, society, and culture, is supported by a large board of directors representing several large companies in Canada.

References to the Atlantic Institute for Market Studies
in Selected Canadian Newspapers

GLOBE AND MAIL
Curry, Bill. "Conservatives Set to Give 'Fair Bit of Details' on EI Rules." 24 May 2012, A7.
Ibbitson, John. "Scott Brison Has an Economic Plan to Save the Maritimes from a Greek Tragedy." 19 February 2013, A4.
McKenna, Barrie. "For Government Subsidies, What Price Is Too High to Save a Job?" 1 October 2012, B1.

NATIONAL POST
Holle, Peter. "Artificially Cheap Hydro Power: Your Equalization Dollars at Work." 29 May 2012, A14.
Kheiriddin, Tasha. "How Equalization Hurts Everybody." 12 October 2012, A10.
Kline, Jesse. "Maritimes Need to Help Private Sector Grow; Too Many People in Rural Communities, Researcher Says." 8 February 2013, A7.
Spencer, Juanita. "Pay People, Not Provinces." 30 May 2012, A15.

NEWSPAPERS IN NEW BRUNSWICK
Bennett, Paul W. "In Practice, Theory Never Works." *Telegraph-Journal* (Saint John). 14 June 2012, A11.
"Business Leaders to Discuss Challenges." *The Times & Transcript* (Moncton). 27 April 2013, D2.
Chilibeck, John. "Energy Savings through Sharing Touted." *Telegraph-Journal* (Saint John). 24 October 2012, B1.
– "Save Energy by Sharing, Report Urges; ? AIMS Study Says Atlantic Provinces Should Pool Power Resources." *The Times & Transcript* (Moncton). 24 October 2012, C2.
Cirtwell, Charles. "Economic Zombies Keep Rising from Dead." *Telegraph-Journal* (Saint John). 19 February 2013, B1.

- "Employment Insurance: What's Left to Do?" *Telegraph-Journal* (Saint John). 5 July 2012, A9.
- "Find Revenue from Budget Cuts, Not Taxes." *Kings County Record* (Sussex). 19 February 2013, A9.
- "Find Revenue in Cuts, Not Taxes." *Telegraph-Journal* (Saint John). 15 February 2013, A9.
- "It's Time to Make the Tough Calls." *Telegraph-Journal* (Saint John). 4 February 2013, A7.
- "OK, Taxes Are Up – Now What?" *Telegraph-Journal* (Saint John). 5 April 2013, A9.
- "Why a Hybrid Health-Care System Would Work." *Telegraph-Journal* (Saint John). 6 December 2012, A15.

"Debate Strategy, Not Just Taxes." *Telegraph-Journal* (Saint John). 30 January 2013, A8.

"Easy Way Out?; We Say: Misguided Call for HST Hike Bad for Metro, Bad for N.B." *The Times & Transcript* (Moncton). 15 May 2013, D6.

Enman, Charles. "Observers Endorsing Economic Union; ? Region Will Benefit from Enhanced Economic Co-Operation: CEO." *The Times & Transcript* (Moncton). 19 December 2012, C4.

Gessell, Paul. "A Question of Fairness." *Telegraph-Journal* (Saint John). 7 May 2012, A1.

Hobson, Cole. "HST Hike Touted by AIMS CEO as Revenue Generator." *Telegraph-Journal* (Saint John, NB). 14 May 2013, A4.

Huras, Adam. "HST Referendum Possible." *The Bugle-Observer* (Woodstock). 1 February 2013, A3.
- "Investment Begins with People." *Daily Gleaner* (Fredericton). 17 May 2013, D5.
- "Province Urged to Move on HST; Finance 'Hold a Referendum Now' on Harmonized Sales Tax, Head of Atlantic Canada Think-Tank Says." *Telegraph-Journal* (Saint John). 29 January 2013, A1.
- "Referendum to Hike HST Possible before Election." *Telegraph-Journal* (Saint John). 31 January 2013, A1.

Luciani, Patrick. "Taxes Won't Fix Obesity." *Telegraph-Journal* (Saint John). 20 February 2013, A7.

MacKinnon, David. "Equalization Has Failed Us." *Telegraph-Journal* (Saint John). 3 November 2012, A15.
- "Stop NB's Fiscal Insanity." *Telegraph-Journal* (Saint John). 12 May 2012, A11.

McIver, Don. "Amalgamation: One Size Fits None." *Telegraph-Journal* (Saint John). 30 May 2012, A7.

– "Importing Health Care by Exporting Patients." *Telegraph-Journal*
 (Saint John). 6 July 2012, A7.
– "Try Less Government, Not Less Local Governments." *Telegraph-
 Journal* (Saint John). 27 April 2012, A9.
– "Wanted: A Fundamental Rethinking of Priorities." *Daily Gleaner*
 (Fredericton). 12 April 2012, C7.
– "We Need a Miracle." *Telegraph-Journal* (Saint John). 18 June 2012,
 A5.
"Make Tax Issues a Business Case; We Say: Minister Higgs Should Stay
 the Course; No Tax Hikes." *The Times & Transcript* (Moncton).
 30 January 2013, D6.
"More Taxes Won't Help Us; Petro-Resources Can." *The Times &
 Transcript* (Moncton). 23 February 2013, D6.
Morris, Chris. "Credit Hit Seen as Wake-Up Call; Finance Rating
 Downgrade Should Trigger Revisiting of Government's Expenditure,
 Revenue Budgets: Savoie." *Telegraph-Journal* (Saint John). 11 June
 2012, A1.
– "Mount A's First Aviation Students Ready to Graduate." *The Times
 & Transcript* (Moncton). 4 May 2013, D2.
– "New Kent Distribution Centre in Works." *The Times & Transcript*
 (Moncton). 8 May 2013, C2.
– "Open Transfer Talks: Expert; Funding Knee-Jerk Reaction to
 Maintaining Equalization Status Quo Is Doing Province a Disservice:
 Savoie." *Telegraph-Journal* (Saint John). 11 May 2012, A1.
– "Public Education a Little Too Close to the Private Sector?" *The
 Times & Transcript* (Moncton). 8 March 2013, D7.
– "Rethink Think-Tank Reports." *Telegraph-Journal* (Saint John, NB).
 16 May 2012, B1.
– "Transfer Payment Pressure; Study Newly Formed Coalition Says
 Equalization System Has Hurt Have-Not Provinces More Than It
 Helps." *Telegraph-Journal* (Saint John). 10 May 2012, A1.
Weil, Gordon. "New Energy Act Is Step into the Past Benghazi Attack:
 The Story No One Prefers to Tell." *Telegraph-Journal* (Saint John).
 14 May 2013, A7.
Weil, Gordon L., and Charles Cirtwell. "Pool Power to Meet Region's
 Needs." *Telegraph-Journal* (Saint John). 3 August 2012, A9.

REGINA LEADER POST
Couture, Joe. "Saskatchewan High Schools Ranked." 5 July 2012, A1.

WINNIPEG FREE PRESS
Wilson, James. "Gas Stop on the Road to Economic Prosperity."
30 August 2012, A11.

THE CHRONICLE HERALD (HALIFAX)
"AIMS Floats Municipal Income Tax." 29 November 2012.
Alberstat, Joann. "Impact of Link on Rates Revealed Today; Premier
Says Hikes Will Be Modest, Short Term." 25 January 2013.
– "Report Urges Power Pooling; 'Utilities Lose Nothing ... Customers
Pay Less.'" 24 October 2012.
Bailey, Sue. "Review of Muskrat Falls Reports Urged; Independent
Regulator Should 'Scrutinize' NL Documents, Critics Argue."
2 November 2012.
Bennett, Paul. "SchoolsPlus Has Lost Its Way but It's Expanding
Anyway." 22 June 2013.
Beswick, Aaron. "NSBI Does Well in Report It Ordered." 24 April 2013.
Black, Bill. "Part of Taxes Could Be Based on Road Frontage."
23 March 2013.
Borden, Sherri. "Happy to Be in Scandal-Free Halifax; Flaherty Visits
for Fireside Chat, Says Europe Is His Biggest Worry." 7 June 2013.
"Brison Touts Free Trade for Maritimes; Kings-Hants MP: Region
Should Follow Example of Western Provinces in Setting Up Binding
Deal." 16 February 2013.
Bundale, Brett. "High Hopes for Economy; Shipbuilding Deal; $2b Off-
shore Plan; Subsea Cable: Promises or Prosperity?" 17 November 2012.
– "Municipal Income Tax Already Works in Many Places." 12 December
2012.
Cirtwill, Charles. "Economic Action Plan? Just Watch Him."
24 November 2012.
– "N.S. Resources, Defence Seen as Economic Spurs." 28 July 2012.
– "Think Local Control over Private Means to Public Ends."
25 October 2012.
Fraser, Laura. "Economy, Transit Key Areas of Focus for Halifax's
Savage; Newly Elected Mayor Has High Hopes for City."
29 December 2012.
– "Ideas Abound about Commercial Taxes; Halifax Mulls Linking
Rate to GDP; Businesses Eye Hybrid System." 20 December 2012.
– "Italian Economist Makes Case for Decentralization; Gains Cited for
Education, Healthcare." 30 October 2012.

– "N.S. Urged to Utilize Joint Purchasing; Only Three Made Since Provinces Agreed to Buy in Bulk." 8 December 2012.

Frost, Grant. "AIMS Misses the Mark on Education." 13 February 2013.

"Income-Based Tax Best Model." 2 March 2013.

Jackson, David. "Halifax Think-Tank Head to Join Ontario institute." July 4, 2013.

– "Muskrat Falls Called Lower Risk for NS" 10 October 2012.

Jeffrey, Davene. "Baillie: Hold the Line on Power Rates; Tories Say Freeze Possible Even with More Renewables." 19 November 2012.

Leger, Dan. "Raising Alarms on Equalization, Fairness and Dependence." 7 January 2013.

Mallett, Ted. "Municipal Income Tax System Would Be Unworkable." 4 December 2012.

– "Municipal Taxes; Stop Guessing." 5 December 2012.

– "Property Assessments; Past Time to Reassess System." 17 January 2013.

Stephenson, Marilla. "An Income Tax Won't Cure HRM Woes." 27 February 2013.

Surette, Ralph. "The Maritime Future and a Hostile Ottawa." 23 February 2013.

Willick, Frances. "Passport to the Operating Table; Halifax Well-Positioned to Profit from Medical Tourism, Alberta Doctor Says." 16 November 2012.

– "School Size Debate Tackles Primary Views; Conventional Notions Challenged." 15 September 2012.

Zaccagna, Remo. "NS Bill for Power Project Fluid; Emera Numbers May Affect Cost." 31 October 2012.

Zitner, David. "Health Care for Nova Scotia: It's about Government, Not Patients." 28 July 2012.

– "Lack of Choice, Competition and Confidence in Patients a Prescription for Dysfunction." 13 April 2013.

Selected Publications of the Atlantic Institute for Market Studies

Bennett, Paul W., and Derek M. Gillis. "Education on Wheels: Seizing Cost and Energy Efficiency." *Atlantic Institute for Market Studies Policy Paper*. January 2015.

Eisen, Ben, David Murrell, Shaun Fantauzzo. "Declining Equalization Payments and Fiscal Challenges in the Small 'Have-Not' Provinces."

Atlantic Institute for Market Studies/Frontier Centre for Public Policy Policy Paper. November 2014.

Eisen, Ben, and Mark Milke. "Nova Scotia, New Brunswick, and the Equalization Policy Crutch." *Fraser/AIMS Research Bulletin.* December 2014.

Eisen, Ben, and Shaun Fantauzzo. "The Size and Cost of Atlantic Canada's Public Sector." *Atlantic Institute for Market Studies Policy Paper.* September 2014.

Feehan, James. "Electricity Market Integration Newfoundland Chooses Monopoly and Protectionism." *Atlantic Institute for Market Studies Commentary.* November 2013.

Gross, Michael. "Governance in Health Care." *Atlantic Institute for Market Studies Commentary.* April 2013.

Luciani, Patrick. "Is the Obesity-Industry-Complex Making Us Fat?" *Atlantic Institute for Market Studies Commentary.* June 2013.

Munro, Ian. "Short of the Green. Golf as an Economic Development Tool on Prince Edward Island." *Atlantic Institute for Market Studies Policy Paper.* February 2015.

Murrell, David and Shaun Fantauzzo. "New Brunswick's Debt and Deficit: A Historical Look." *Atlantic Institute for Market Studies Policy Pape.* May 2014.

Weil, Gordon. "Taking Stock of Atlantic Canada's Electricity Sector." *Atlantic Institute for Market Studies Policy Paper.* October 2014.

C.D. HOWE INSTITUTE

Tank Facts

Established:	1973
Location:	Toronto
Budget:	$3.5–$4 million
Staff:	~25
President/Director:	William B.P. Robson
Website:	www.cdhowe.org

Few think tanks in Canada have attracted more attention in the media and in policy-making circles than the Toronto-based C.D. Howe Institute, an organization whose mandate is to help improve living standards in Canada through sound economic and social policy.[5] Named after Clarence Decatur Howe (1886–1960), the Liberal cabinet minister who served continuously in the governments of Prime Ministers William Lyon Mackenzie King and Louis St Laurent from 1935–1957, the institute's origins can be traced to the Private Planning Association of Canada (PPAC), established in 1958 "by business and labor leaders to undertake research and educational activities on economic policy issues."[6] In 1973 the PPAC merged with the C.D. Howe Memorial Foundation (1961) to become the C.D. Howe Research Institute (HRI). Eight years later, when the HRI dissolved, the "Foundation again became a separate entity and the reconstituted PPAC was renamed the C.D. Howe Institute."[7]

Known for its expertise on Canadian economic, social, and trade policy, C.D. Howe has published hundreds of studies and sponsored countless conferences and workshops on virtually every major policy initiative upon which the federal and provincial governments have embarked. In 2013, the institute held "a record 60 policy events and publish[ed] a record of 55 research studies."[8] Many of these studies have been written by its small staff of in-house experts, including C.D. Howe's president William Robson and Wendy Dobson, professor at the Rotman School of Management, University of Toronto, and cover topics ranging from energy and transportation policy and healthcare to payment technology and governance and tax rates and credits.[9] Countless other studies have been contracted out to some of the country's leading economists and political scientists, including David Laidler, Judith Maxwell, Thomas Courchene, Robert Young, Michael Hart, Sylvia Ostry, and Michael Trebilcock.[10] The institute, which devotes approximately 90 per cent of its budget to research and related expenses, and prides itself on publishing high-quality, peer-reviewed studies, does not try to overwhelm readers with monographs of several hundred pages, but relies on brief studies or commentaries to highlight the implications of particular government policies.

The C.D. Howe Institute, unlike many other think tanks, does not assess its influence solely by the number of publications it produces or by the many prominent business leaders who serve on its board of directors. Rather, it evaluates its impact by the contribution it makes to stimulating informed public debate. According to one of its annual reports, "The Institute monitors whether its output measures up to the high standards of its members, the media, policy-makers, and the public. Key indicators of success are strong attendance at Institute meetings, wide news coverage of Institute publications, an improved quality of public debate, and, ultimately, the willingness of policy-makers to listen."[11]

The C.D. Howe Institute follows a simple formula to ensure that policy-makers listen: it outfits "influential decision-makers with concrete research, [and] provide[s] a forum in which they can interact, and mix vigorously."[12] This formula seems to have paid off. Over the years, C.D. Howe has received dozens of endorsements from policy-makers, journalists, and business leaders who have acknowledged the valuable work of the institute. It also continues to enjoy the support of several major donors, including the Donner Foundation, Aurea Foundation, Max Bell Foundation, Lotte & John Hecht Memorial Foundation, and Pfizer Canada Inc. The Institute also receives funding from several corporations and private donors.

Although the institute takes great pride in the research it generates, it pays close attention to how often its studies and conferences are quoted in the press, and how much traffic is generated on its website. According to its *2013 Annual Report*, "C.D. Howe received a total of 1,466 citations across Canadian and international media in 2013 – a 46 percent increase since 2010 ... Online, cdhowe.org surpassed 15,000 monthly visits for the first time."[13]

References to the C.D. Howe Institute
in Selected Canadian Newspapers

CALGARY HERALD

Berthiaume, Lee. "Merkel Courts Canadian Cash." 14 August 2012, A6.

Coyne, Andrew. "Flaherty Needs to Address Long-Term Challenges." 19 March 2013, A10.

Crowley, Brian Lee. "Why We Should Worry about Inflation." 18 September 2012, A10.

Golombek, Jamie. "Taxing Issues in Québec." 6 October 2012, C14.

Henton, Darcy. "Read My Lips – Again – on Sales Tax, Redford Says." 22 February 2013, A1.

Isfeld, Gordon. "Carney Leaving Central Bank Post; Moving to Bank of England." 27 November 2012, C1.

Kennedy, Mark. "Harper, Flaherty Blast 'Partisan' Critics." 6 March 2013, A7.

Morgan, Steve. "MPs Off to a Good Start; Pension Reform Must Extend to Public Workers." 23 October 2012, A14.

– "Ralph's Legacy; Former Premier Made a Sales Tax All but an Impossibility." 25 February 2013, A10.

– "The Wrong Prescription for Our Drug Costs." 5 April 2013, A21.
Shecter, Barbara. "Pooled Pensions 'Tax on Poor': Report." 24 August
 2012, D3.
– "Stay Course Says Ex-Bank Head." 14 December 2012, C2.
Stephenson, Amanda. "EU Says Beef Deal Hinges on Dairy; Ambassador
 Demands More 'Give and Take.'" 29 May 2013, F1.

GAZETTE
Berthiaume, Lee. "Harper and Merkel to Talk Trade and EU Crisis;
 Prime Minister Not Expected to Back Down from Refusal to Provide
 Aid to Europe." 14 August 2012, C10.
Bryan, Jay. "Foreign 'Investment' Isn't Terrible." 2 August 2012, B10.
Busby, Colin, and William B.P. Robson. "How Quebec Can Address
 Rising Health-Care Costs." 15 February 2013, A17.
Coyne, Andrew. "When It Comes to Government Spending, One Plus
 One Equals Three." 23 February 2013, B5.
French, Cameron. "Housing Appraisal Database May Be Faulty,
 Experts Say; Quick Appraisals Often Overvalue Home, Raising Risk
 of US-Style Housing Crash." 24 October 2012, C22.
Hadekel, Peter. "The Federal Government Must Show Leadership in
 Issue of Joblessness." 20 March 2013, A18.
– "PQ Tax-Hike Plan Could End Up Creating a Shortfall, Expert Says."
 10 October 2012, A20.
– "Preview Canadian Universities Can Do Better; Technology Transfer
 to Private Sector Must Improve." 7 June 2013, A16.
Johnson, William. "PQ's Tax Flop Shows Folly of Its Electoral
 Promises." 12 October 2012, A16.
– "There's No Unilateral Right to Quebec Self-Determination."
 8 February 2013, A17.
Shecter, Barbara. "Pooled Pensions Are 'A New Tax on the Poor'; Rules
 Prevent Private-Sector Workers from Saving Enough to Retire."
 24 August 2012, A19.

GLOBE AND MAIL
"Adjusting to a Value-Chain World." 13 August 2012, A10.
Aston, David. "Retirement Is Cheaper Than You Think." 16 March
 2013, B10.
Blackwell, Richard. "The Contenders." 27 November 2012, B4.
Blackwell, Richard, and Tavia Grant. "Preview Obama's Labour Pains:
 Minimum Wage Debate Flares Up." 14 February 2013, B9.

Carmichael, Kevin. "A Call to Action on Fed's Asset-Buying Strategy."
    28 November 2012, B 10.
- "The Case for a Rate Hike from the Bank of Canada." 16 May 2013,
    B 2.
- "Economy's Foggy Future Poses Challenge for Carney." 3 September
    2012, B 1.
- "For Bank of Canada, It's All a Matter of Time." 21 January 2013,
    B 2.
- "How the 'Coyne Affair' Paved the Way for Carney." 15 October
    2012, B 3.
- "Macklem's Bank Shot." 30 March 2013, B 6.
- "Why the Economy Is Stuck in Low Gear." 8 September 2012, B 1.
Chase, Steven. "MPs Face Longer Wait for Pension." 19 September
    2012, A 1.
Chase, Steven, and Daniel Leblanc. "Carney Speaks on Liberal Ties."
    24 January 2013, A 6.
- "Carney's Liberal Ties Irk Tories: Sources." 22 December 2012, A 9.
Curry, Bill, Grant Robertson, and Tara Perkins. "Flaherty Thanks Banks
    For Refusing to Cut Mortgage Rates." 9 March 2013, B 1.
Erman, Boyd. "Don't Hold Your Breath for a Privatized CMHC."
    8 January 2013, B 2.
Grant, Tavia. "Inflation Rates Spark Frequent Debates on Accuracy."
    17 September 2012, B 2.
Heinzl, John. "Can I Take More Risk If I Have a Pension?" 16 February
    2013, B 13.
Herman, Lawrence. "While Governments Dither, Industry Itself Sets
    Standards." 30 August 2012, A 15.
- "How Harper and Obama Are Alike." 8 June 2013, F 9.
- "Howe Institute Dismisses PRPPS." 24 August 2012, B 5.
Howitt, Peter. "Let Curiosity Drive Commerce." 6 June 2013, A 17.
Hunter, Justine. "Where's the Faith?" 18 February 2013, S 2.
Jang, Brent. "Quebec, Alberta Win Dubious Honour." 22 February
    2013; B 7.
Johnson, David. "Middle Schools Should Be the First to Close."
    14 November 2012, A 21.
Laurin, Alexandre. "Flaherty Constrained by Old Goodies, New
    Realities." 22 March 2013, A 19.
Magowan, Paul. "Scary Thought." 28 November 2012, A 18.
Mason, Gary. "One Good Report Won't Restore Voters' Trust."
    19 February 2013, A 6.

Mckenna, Barrie. "Aitken's 'National Champions' Stand Sparks Retort from Manley." 22 September 2012, B3.
– "Apprentice Rules Unhelpful: Report." 2 May 2013, B8.
– "Canada Eager for US to Avoid Fiscal Cliff." 7 November 2012, A5.
– "Higher Prices, Less Choice: Let's Reject Cartels." 26 November 2012, B1.
Milner, Brian. "Dallas Fed President Condemns Washington for Slow Recovery." 5 June 2013, B7.
O'Kane, Josh. "Invest Early, but Not Before Clearing Debt." 11 February 2013, B8.
Parkinson, David. "Canada's Cash Hoard Not the Work of Misers." 17 January 2013, B2.
– "Increased Drug Coverage Makes Economic Sense." 14 June 2013, B2.
– "Made in Canada: Carney Aims to Bring Rate-Pledge Magic to UK." 8 February 2013, B1.
– "Ottawa's Deficit Numbers May Be Underplaying Pension Reality." 29 March 2013, B2.
"Pension Silver Lining in the Omnibus." 22 September 2012, F8.
Perkins, Tara. "Land-Transfer Tax Affects Cheaper Homes Most." 11 October 2012, A17
– "Mortgages Back Under Spotlight." 14 May 2013, B4.
Perkins, Tara, and Grant Robertson. "Canada's $800,000,000,000 Housing Problem." 27 December 2012, B1.
Pitts, Gordon. "He Made Saskatchewan Steel Company into an International Powerhouse." 22 February 2013, S8.
Poschmann, Finn. "Carney, Horseshoes and Canada's Stellar Performance." 13 February 2013, B2.
– "Flaherty Has a Chance to Complete Ottawa's Savings Revolution." 21 March 2013, B2.
– "Indalex Ruling Captures Balancing Act of Bankruptcy Law." 4 February 2013, B4.
– "PPP Canada." 19 March 2013, B5.
– "Preview Up from One-Sided Free Trade." 30 April 2013, A14.
– "Private Sector Should Take Over from CMHC." 4 January 2013, B2.
Ragan, Christopher. "Bank of Canada's Growth View Is Clouded in Hazy Thinking." 28 May 2013, B2
– "Carney's Bold Entrance, Poloz's Measured Exit." 5 June 2013, B2.
Robson, William B.P. "Business Investment: We've Raised Our Game." 4 September 2012, A17.

Silcoff, Sean, and Steve Ladurantaye. "A Consumer Agenda That's Not Quite Complete." 8 June 2013, B9.
– "Time for a More Ambitious Board." 16 March 2013, F9.
Waldie, Paul, and Janet McFarland. "The Taxman Cometh." 5 January 2013, F1.
Yakabuski, Konrad. "Clusters, Right to Work and the 'Prosperity Gap.'" 2 May 2013, A17.

NATIONAL POST
Beaudry, Paul, and Phillipe Bergevin. "The New Rate Normal; The Next Decade Will See Atypically Low Interest Rates." 30 May 2013, FP13.
Bergevin, Philippe, and Benjamin Dachis. "Provinces Must Join Training Effort." 22 March 2013, FP11.
Bergevin, Philippe, and Finn Poschmann. "Reining in BDC; Ottawa Should Wind Back Its Capital Lending Limit." 12 February 2013, FP11.
– "Roll Back Margin Creeps; Crowns' Expanding Mandates Should Be Cut Back to Size." 7 February 2013, FP11.
Bergevin, Philippe, and William B.P. Robson. "The Real Advantages of Real Return Bonds." 2 October 2012, FP13.
Bitti, Mary Teresa. "Commercialization Conundrum; Canada Must Turn Ideas into Social and Economic Value." 3 April 2013, SR1.
Busby, Colin, and Alexandre Laurin. "An HST for Alberta." 6 March 2013, A12.
Corcoran, Terence. "Debt, a Low Rate Mess." 16 May 2013, FP1.
– "Stimulus till the Cows Come Home." 13 December 2012, A1.
Coyne, Andrew. "Back to Work; Productivity Only Fix for Economic Double Whammy." 4 September 2012, A1.
– "Last Chance to Get It Right; Flaherty Should Think Long-Term for Budget Legacy." 19 March 2013, A1.
– "More Phony Forecasts to Sap Public Purse." 23 February 2013, A4.
– "Parliament a Growing Charade; McGuinty, Harper Pushing Us to the Point of No Return." 20 October 2012, A22.
Crow, John. "No Virtue in Expanding BoC's Role." 14 December 2012, FP11.
Deveau, Denise. "Does the Net Benefit Test Make the Grade?; Transparency Issue; A Better Test May Be to Focus on National Interest." 10 April 2013, SR1.

– "NAFTA Paves Positive Path for EU Deal; Patience Needed."
27 March 2013, SR2.

Evans, Charles L. "Easy Money under 'Modern Macro' Theory."
28 November 2012, FP13.

Found, Adam, and Peter Tomlinson. "Ontario School Tax a Burden to
Business." 7 December 2012, FP11.

Frum, David. "Investing in Our Future (Or Not)." 11 August 2012, A23.

Golombek, Jamie. "Taxing Issues in Quebec." 6 October 2012, FP12.

Greenwood, John. "Big Bank in Waiting; The EDC Has Expanded into
an Emerging Global Banking Power. But Should a Crown
Corporation Be in the Lending Business?" 23 February 2013, FP6.

– "It's a Bit of a Problem; For Businesses Built around the Virtual
Currency Bit Coin, Dealing with Real-World Banks Is Proving to Be
Increasingly Difficult." 27 April 2013, FP1.

– "NDP's Mulcair Takes Aim at RBC" 9 April 2013, FP3.

– "Porter 'Obvious Choice' for BMO Chief Economist; Succeeds
Cooper." 15 December 2012, FP2.

Halde, Jean-Ren. "BDC Occupies Unfilled Market Niche." 20 February
2013, FP11.

Heath, Jason. "Annuities." 5 September 2012, FP8.

– "Making Your Home a Target; Report Critical of CPI Methodology."
13 September 2012, FP1.

Herman, Lawrence, and Daniel Schwanen. "Deal a Big Step Forward."
27 October 2012, FP19.

Hopper, Tristin. "Land Transfer Tax Hits Real Estate Sales." 11 October
2012, A8.

Isfeld, Gordon. "Carney Faces 'Enormous Challenges' in UK"
10 January 2013, FP1.

– "Persevere; Crow Sums Up BoC's Monetary Policy." 14 December
2012, FP3.

– "Poloz Sticks to Carney's Script; Long on Assurances, Short on
Detail." 7 June 2013, FP1.

– "Short Timeline Favours Macklem; BoC Governor." 4 January 2013,
FP1.

– "Top Job at BoC Will Be Toss-Up." 27 November 2012, FP1.

– "Uncertain World Faces New Governor; But Unlikely Poloz Will Cut
Rates: Economists." 3 May 2013, FP3.

Ivison, John. "Banker Fits the Political Bill; Surprise Pick for Governor
on Same Page as Tories." 3 May 2013, A1.

– "Liberal Passes Tories on Right; Garneau to Unveil Pro-Investment
Economic Plan." 12 December 2012, A1.

Kheiriddin, Tasha. "Everywhere You Look: A Case for Smaller Government." 2 May 2013, A12.

Lafleur, Steve. "Don't Trash Outsourcing of Garbage Pickup." 4 September 2012, A12.

Laurin, Alexandre, and James Pierlot. "Pooled Pensions Need Tweaking." 27 September 2012, FP11.

Leong, Melissa. "Top Earnerstake Hit." 29 January 2013, FP1.

Marr, Garry. "Looking for Loopholes; Governments Can Search for New Ways to Tax the Rich, but It Doesn't Mean They'll Pay." 21 May 2013, FP3.

– "The Personable Economist; Questions & Answers." 1 February 2013, FP3.

Poschmann, Finn. "Does Debt Slow Growth?; Good Arguments on Both Sides in This Debate." 30 April 2013, FP11.

– "Monetary Apocalypse; Its Horsemen Gather in Moscow on Brink of Currency War." 15 February 2013, FP11.

– "Off Target on Inflation; New Fed Strategy Recalls the Same Low-For-Long Advice to Greenspan That Triggered US Housing Bubble." 14 December 2012, FP11.

– "Ottawa's War on Tax 'Avoision' Is Worrisome." 14 May 2013, FP11.

– "Poloz: A Subtle Shift in Policy?" 3 May 2013, FP11.

– "What If There Were No 1%-ers?; Income Distribution of 99% Remarkably Stable." 30 January 2013, FP11.

Poschmann, Finn, and Daniel Schwanen. "Canada Reaps Ontario's Whirlwind." 1 February 2013, FP11.

Poschmann, Finn, and Phillipe Bergevin. "A Bitcoin Primer; Digital Currency Holds Potential for Good and Bad." 10 May 2013, FP11.

– "The Real Risky Lender; Flaherty Doesn't Have to Look Far for Risky Home Lending." 21 March 2013, FP11.

– "Taxpayer-Lite Housing Finance." 7 June 2013, FP11.

Schwanen, Daniel. "Drop Dogmatism on Chinese Investments." 27 November 2012, FP11.

Shecter, Barbara. "Drastic Spending Cuts May Be Needed; Time to Tighten Our Belts." 30 January 2013, SR.1.

– "Pooled Pensions Remain a Dream." 19 November 2012, FP1.

Shecter, Barbara, and Gordon Isfeld. "PRPPs May Tax Canada's Poor; C.D. Howe Report." 24 August 2012, FP1.

Tedesco, Theresa. "Dickson Steers a Hard-Line Course." 23 May 2013, FP2.

Tedesco, Theresa, and Gary Marr. "Changes atop Shrinking CMHC." 7 May 2013, FP1.

- "US Economy Needs Clear Road Map." 5 June 2013, FP15.
Watson, William. "Quebec's Besieged 'Rich.'" 19 October 2012, FP11.

OTTAWA CITIZEN
Argitis, Theophilos, and Andrew Mayeda. "Lobbyist Mines the Politics
   of Takeovers; Look at How Hill & Knowlton's Wide Range Helps It
   Land Work on Foreign Takeover Bids." 22 August 2012, D1.
Coyne, Andrew. "Aging Population Could Be Flaherty's Final
   Challenge; Tackling Long-Term Issues Best Way to Ensure His Place
   in History." 19 March 2013, A3.
- "Government Candour on Budgets Notoriously Haphazard."
   23 February 2013, B7.
Crowley, Brian Lee. "Why We Should Worry about Inflation."
   15 September 2012, B6.
Heartfield, Kate. "McGuinty Was Long on Ideas, Short on Execution."
   15 June 2013, B1.
Isfeld, Gordon. "'I Think It Was the Right Decision'; Carney Named
   Bank of England Chief." 27 November 2012, D1.
Kennedy, Mark. "Budget Secrecy Emotions Out in the Open; PM,
   · Flaherty under Fire after Calling Two Critics 'Partisan' Liberals."
   6 March 2013, A1.
May, Kathryn. "PS Forced to Scrimp for Retirement." 7 December
   2012, A2.
- "PS Unions Fear Pension Reforms Will Lead to 'Two-Tier'
   Workforce; 'This Takes Us Back to When Women Were Paid Less
   Than Men.'" 26 September 2012, A1.
- "PS Workers to Pay More for Pensions; Conservative Reforms Will
   Also Create Two-Tiered Retirement System." 19 October 2012, A1.
"Reality for MPs." 20 September 2012, A10.
Shecter, Barbara. "Pooled Pensions 'A New Tax on the Poor'; Current
   Plans Resemble RRSPs With a New Coat of Paint." 24 August 2012,
   F1.
- "Warm to the Caribbean." 16 January 2013, A12.

PROVINCE
Brown, Robert. "Canada's Health System Isn't a Ponzi Scheme."
   13 December 2012, A20.
Morgan, Steve. "BC Pharmacare Plan Is Tough Pill to Swallow." 19 June
   2013, A16.
Sutherland, Jason, and Nadya Repin. "Hospital Funding Should Come
   With Strings." 1 May 2013, A16.

TORONTO STAR

Alamenciak, Tim. "How to Pay for the Repairs." 13 December 2012, GT.2.
– "Per-Kilometre Driving Levy Will Face Hard Road Ahead." 4 April 2013, GT.1.
Dachis, Benjamin. "HOT Idea to Ease Traffic Congestion." 15 May 2013, A19.
Flavelle, Dana. "Help Wanted: The Bank of Canada Is Looking for a New Governor. Candidates Must Be Exceptionally Well Qualified, Be an Exceptional Communicator in Both Official Languages, Have the Courage to Take a Stand to Support Principles and Policies, Be a Canadian Citizen." 8 January 2013, B1.
Ferguson, Rob. "Province Urged to Pool Pensions: Annual Savings of $100M Could Be Achieved, Report Says." 17 November 2012, S18.
Flavelle, Dana. "CPP Could Fix Pension Crisis, Says Dodge: Former Bank Governor Disagrees with Ottawa on Merits of 'Pooled' Plans." 28 November 2012, B1.
Goar, Carol. "How to Modernize Canada's Science Policy: Report Sees National Research Council as a Bridge between Science and Industry." 17 June 2013, A15.
– "Serious Think-Tank Invents Fanciful Index." 25 February 2013, A15.
– "Uneasy Truce on Corporate Hoarding." 23 January 2013, A15.
Johnson, David. "Labour Disputes Impair Learning: Research Reveals Negative Impact of School Strikes and Work-to-Rule Campaigns on Students' Performance." 10 December 2012, A19.
Lu, Vanessa, Michael Lewis, and John Spears. "Surprise 'Outsider' Praised: Economists Welcome New Governor's Skills in Trade and Communication." 3 May 2013, B1.

VANCOUVER SUN

Brown, Robert L. "Canadian Health Care System Isn't a Ponzi Scheme." 19 December 2012, A13.
Bryan, Jay. "Don't Be Scared of Foreign Investment." 11 August 2012, D4.
Cayo, Don. "BC May Cope with Aging Better Than Most." 26 January 2013, C4.
– "Competition Law Favours Cartels over Consumers; Price Regulation May Be Justified in Some Natural Monopolies, but When Market Failures Occur, the Rules Often Go Too Far." 28 May 2013, C2.
– "Pension Shortfall Worse Than Ottawa Admits; Collapse of Investment Returns That Set Back Retirement Dreams of Countless Canadians in the Private Sector Has Also Hit Government Plans." 27 December 2012, D7.

– "Perversity of Property Transfer Tax Is Confirmed in Toronto; Report
  Indicates the Fee Has Had a Negative Effect on Home Sales, Which
  May Also Be the Case for British Columbia's Province-Wide Levy."
  13 October 2012, H4.
– "Pooled Pensions May Not Help Low, Middle-Income Workers;
  Much-Touted New Federal Plan Offers Little and Could Be Costly."
  24 August 2012, D6.
– "Property Taxes Combine to Slow Business Development; Provincial
  Levy Once Funded Schools, but Now Goes to General Revenue."
  11 December 2012, C3.
– "Time to Boost Our Flagging International Performance; Canada
  Must Preserve Its Profitable Relationship with the US While
  Developing Stronger Ties with the EU, Asia." 7 August 2012, B9.
– "A Worker Shortage Looms, Yet Young People Can't Find Jobs;
  Commitment to a Long-Term Policy Is Needed to Give Youth a
  Strong Start." 9 April 2013, D1.
Coyne, Andrew. "Government Candour on Budgets Is Haphazard;
  Ottawa, the Provinces Routinely Overspend." 23 February 2013, B3.
Crowley, Brian Lee. "Even Two Per Cent Inflation Will Diminish a
  Pension." 20 September 2012, A13.
Finlayson, Jock. "The Centre of Economic Gravity Is Tilting."
  4 December 2012, A15.
Fontaine, Daniel. "The 'Silver Tsunami' Is Already Here; Community
  Service Providers Help BC's Government Keep Senior Care Costs
  Down, While Maintaining Quality." 15 April 2013, A11.
Gardner, Dan. "Canada's Economic Prudence Is Risky; Caution Has a
  Price." 1 September 2012, D4.
Georgetti, Ken. "Companies Should Return Money to Government to
  Invest." 21 January 2013, A8.
Isfeld, Gordon. "Carney Announces Departure from Bank of Canada;
  Governor Will Step Down June 1 to Take Reins of United Kingdom's
  Central Bank." 27 November 2012, C1.
Lalonde, Marc. "Child Care a Surefire Investment for Government."
  24 October 2012, A11
Martin, Paul. "Pensions: There's More Than One Way to Count Your
  Chickens." 8 November 2012, A16.
McKenna, Barrie. "Apprentice Rules Unhelpful: Report." 2 May 2013,
  B8.
Morgan, Steve. "BC's Fair PharmaCare Fares Poorly Compared with
  Other Systems." 12 June 2013, A14.

- "Pension Reform Must Extend to Public Workers." 25 October 2012, A14.
- "Poloz Urged to Hike Interest Rates." 16 May 2013, C1.

Rainer, Hans. "Canada's Fossil Fuel Policy Myopic and Reckless." 1 December 2012, C7.

Richards, John. "CIDA – Still Avoiding the Dilemmas of 'Effective Aid.'" 15 April 2013, A11.

- "Native Education Faces Obstacles; Generating Better School Outcomes for Aboriginals Will Take a Generation of Hard Work by All Stakeholders." 20 March 2013, A13.

Selected Publications of the C.D. Howe Institute

Blomqvist, Åke, and Colin Busby. "Rethinking Canada's Unbalanced Mix of Public and Private Healthcare: Insights from Abroad." *C.D. Howe Institute Commentary*. 25 February 2015.

Boyer, Marcel. "The Value of Copyrights in Recorded Music: Terrestrial Radio and Beyond." *C.D. Howe Institute Commentary*. 18 February 2015.

Busby, Colin, and Nicholas Chesterley. "A Shot in the Arm: How to Improve Vaccination Policy in Canada." *C.D. Howe Institute Commentary*. 12 March 2015.

Dachis, Benjamin. "Railroad Blues: How to Get Canada's Rail Policy Back on Track. " 2 April 2015.

- "Tackling Traffic: The Economic Cost of Congestion in Metro Vancouver." *C.D. Howe Institute Commentary*. 9 March 2015.

Friesen, Jane, Benjamin Cerf Harris, and Simon Woodcock. "Expanding School Choice through Open Enrolment: Lessons from British Columbia." *C.D. Howe Institute Commentary*. 12 February 2015.

Gros, Barry, Karen Hall, Ian McSweeney, and Jana Steele. "The Taxation of Single-Employer Target Benefit Plans – Where We Are and Where We Ought to Be." *C.D. Howe Institute Commentary*. 4 March 2015.

Protti, Denis. "Missed Connections: The Adoption of Information Technology in Canadian Healthcare." *C.D. Howe Institute Commentary*. 26 March 2015.

Robson, William B.P., and Alexandre Laurin. "Challenges, Growth and Opportunity: A Shadow Federal Budget for 2015." *C.D. Howe Institute Commentary*. 14 April 2015.

Robson, William B.P., and Colin Busby. "By the Numbers: The Fiscal Accountability of Canada's Senior Governments." *C.D. Howe Institute Commentary*. 16 April 2015.

CALEDON INSTITUTE OF SOCIAL POLICY

Tank Facts

Established: 1992
Location: Ottawa
Budget: ~$1 million
Staff: 8
Director/President: Ken Battle
Website: www.caledoninst.org

It is difficult to discuss the Caledon Institute without invoking the name of its director and founder, Ken Battle. In fact, few other think tank directors in Canada have become so closely identified with a public policy institute. Battle's reputation as one of the country's most astute thinkers on social policy is well-known within the nation's capital. He is often invited to advise senior policy-makers on a range of social and tax policies, including old age security and child welfare benefits, and served as director of the now-defunct National Council of Welfare, a citizen's advisory body to the minister of national health and welfare which, due to budget cuts, was forced to close its doors in 2012.[14]

After spending close to fifteen years at the National Council of Welfare, Battle became increasingly sensitive to how critical a publicly funded policy institute could be of government policies. As one of the Mulroney government's most vociferous critics, Battle was convinced that both his position and the future of the National Council of Welfare could be in jeopardy as long as he remained in charge. "At the time, I began looking around for other positions," Battle stated. "I thought for a while that I would try to become director of the Canadian Council on Social Development [CCSD], but then something else came up."[15]

What came up was a meeting with Toronto businessman and philanthropist Alan Broadbent, who wanted to fund a public policy organization that would have an impact. Although Battle initially approached Broadbent for funds to help rebuild the CCSD, Broadbent was more interested in creating a new organization that would study social and welfare policies than in revitalizing an existing institution: "Alan is one of those capitalists with a social conscience who clearly wanted to fund an organization that would make a difference ... When he made me an offer to head up a new institute, I accepted."[16]

Following a handful of meetings with Broadbent, Battle developed the Caledon Institute's mission statement, which reads: "The Caledon Institute of Social Policy is a leading private, non profit social policy think tank that conducts social policy research and analysis. As an independent and critical voice that does not depend on government funding, Caledon seeks to inform and influence public and expert opinion and to foster public discussion on poverty and social policy. As a social policy think tank, Caledon develops and promotes concrete, practicable proposals for the reform of social programs at all levels of government and of social benefits provided by employers and the voluntary sector."[17] Although Caledon may not depend on government funding and "is not affiliated with any political party," it does "welcome charitable donations from individuals and organizations and occasionally undertakes contract projects for governments and nongovernmental organizations on the basis that such work advances Caledon's research agenda, but does not define it."[18]

With roughly $300,000 from Broadbent's Maytree Foundation, Caledon opened its doors in February 1992. It currently has a budget of approximately $1 million that is generated from the Maytree Foundation and from other sources for project-specific funding. From its inception, Caledon has purposely maintained a small and nimble policy shop; its board of directors, which meets once a year, barely satisfies the minimum legal requirement of three people. In addition to Battle, the board consists of Broadbent, a lawyer, and a financial analyst. "The advantage of having a lean operation is that we can change direction fast if we have to," Battle notes. "This allows us to move ahead of the government and influence substantive policies and the political agenda."[19] Caledon maintains a small research staff. Assisting Battle are Sherri Torjman, vice-president of Caledon, who has written extensively on several issues, including social spending, health care, and fiscal arrangements; senior scholar Michael Mendelson, a former deputy secretary of Cabinet Office in Ontario, who has several publications on social and fiscal policy to his credit; two policy associates; and an associate fellow. With modest resources, Caledon has managed to establish an impressive publication program. Its commentaries on various social policy issues, "Caledon's most useful product," according to Battle, are widely circulated to policy-makers, social advocacy organizations, and the media. Caledon's media profile is modest compared with several other think tanks, such as the Fraser Institute and the C.D. Howe Institute, but its contribution to policy formulation is well-recognized by directors of party research offices and senior policy-makers.[20]

References to the Caledon Institute of Social Policy
in Selected Canadian Newspapers

CALGARY HERALD

Farkas, Joan. "Here to Stay." 27 November 2012, A15.

Kennedy, Mark. "Harper Poised to Announce Pension Cutbacks; Budget Set for Thursday Release." 25 March 2012, F1.

GAZETTE

Mendelson, Michael. "Risk Too High for Quebec to Run Its Own Employment Insurance." 17 September 2012, 19.

GLOBE AND MAIL

Galloway, Gloria. "Need for Upgrades on Reserves Can't Wait, Former PM Says." 23 November 2011, A4.

Ibbitson, John. "Premiers to Face Off against Ottawa over Job Program." 22 July 2013, A3.

McKenna, Barrie. "Canada Job Grant Program Is 'Deeply Flawed,' Report Says." 17 June 2013, B5.

Morrow, Adrian, and Bill Curry. "Premiers Seek Opt-Out Clause on Training." 26 July 2013, A3.

Ryell, Nora. "She 'Believed in the Power of Community.'" 22 July 2013, S10.

Torjman, Sherri. "Private Money, Public Programs? There Will Always Be Strings." 8 May 2013, A15.

NATIONAL POST

Coyne, Andrew. "Jobs Grant Plan Needs Adjustment; If Provinces Want Citizens to Benefit, They Can Pony Up." 18 June 2013, A4.

TORONTO STAR

Goar, Carol. "Job Training Plan Needs an Overhaul." 21 June 2013, A23.

– "Defunct National Welfare Council Finds a Saviour." 29 May 2013, A19.

– "Harper Makes Unexpected Breakthrough." 16 December 2011, A23.

Monsebraaten, Laurie. "Institute Takes on Some Work From Welfare Council." 30 June 2012, A11.

Torjman, Sherri. "Home-Care Crunch Coming: Elderly Woman's Case Highlights Need to Put Supports in Place." 6 October 2012, IN6.

Whittington, Les. "Governments Eye Social Financing: May Take Years to See if This Experiment, Which Began in UK, Will Work." 10 November 2012, A10.

– "Qualifying for Benefits Gets Tougher: Budget Pushes Jobless to Prove They're Not Passing Up Work." 13 April 2012, A6.

VANCOUVER SUN

Fekete, Jason. "What Will OAS Deferral Mean?; Action Announced in the Budget Will Affect Canadians Now under Age 54." 31 March 2012, B2.

Jarvis, Lee. "Why a Genetically Modified Pig Is a Waste of Money." 14 April 2012, D3.

Selected Publications of the Caledon Institute of Social Policy

Battle, Ken. "Child Benefits and the 2015 Federal Budget." *Caledon Institute of Social Policy*. April 2015.

Battle, Ken, and Sherri Torjman. "If You Don't Pay, You Can't Play: The Children's Fitness Tax Credit." *Caledon Institute of Social Policy*. October 2014.

Battle, Ken, Sherri Torjman, and Michael Mendelson. "The 2015 Deficit-of-Ideas Budget." *Caledon Institute of Social Policy*. April 2015.

Hayes, Brigid. "What You Need to Know about the Canada Job Fund." *Caledon Institute of Social Policy*. December 2014.

Kesselman, Jonathan Rhys. "Family Tax Cuts: How Inclusive a Family?" *Caledon Institute of Social Policy*. November 2014.

Makhoul, Anne. "Social Assistance Summaries." *Caledon Institute of Social Policy*. March 2015.

Torjman, Sherri. "Cut the Tax Cut." Caledon Institute of Social Policy. January 2015.

– "Liveability – For Whom?" *Caledon Institute of Social Policy*. February 2015.

– "Symposium on Children of the Recession." *Caledon Institute of Social Policy*. January 2015.

Tweddle Anne, Ken Battle, and Sherri Torjman. "Welfare in Canada 2013." *Caledon Institute of Social Policy*. November 2014.

CANADA WEST FOUNDATION

Tank Facts

Established: 1971
Location: Calgary
Budget: $1.5–$2 million
Staff: 19 .
Director/President: Dylan Jones
Website: www.cwf.ca

The Canada West Foundation traces its origins to the One Prairie Conference held in Lethbridge in 1970. A consensus developed at the conference that research on Western Canadian concerns should not only continue, but be expanded. This decision led to the formation of the Canada West Council, which in turn developed the mandate for the Canada West Foundation. The Canada West Foundation is governed by the Canada West Council, "which provides direction on the current and future education and research activities of the Foundation."[21] The Foundation's budget of approximately $2 million is drawn from several sources, including the interest generated from an endowment created in 1996 which, in 2013, was valued in excess of $8.5 million.[22]

The Foundation pursues three main objectives: "to initiate and conduct research into the economic and social characteristics and potentials of the West and North within a national and international context; to educate individuals regarding the West's regional economic and social contributions to the Canadian federation; and to act as a catalyst for informed debate."[23]

Its mandate is "to explore public policy issues of particular interest to western Canadians, to test national policies against regional aspirations and to ensure an effective regional voice in national policy discussions and the national political process."[24]

Canada West maintains an active research program, and in 2013, added three new policy research centres focusing on trade and investment; natural resources; and human capital.[25] Since its inception, the organization has published hundreds of studies on issues ranging from the effects of free trade on the western economy to the regulation of charities in Alberta to investment opportunities for the western provinces in Mexico. It also publishes a quarterly magazine, *Window on the West*, which explores a wide range of social, economic, environment, and political issues of interest to Western Canada. A passionate advocate for greater western representation in Parliament, the Foundation has sponsored publications and conferences that have focused on the prospects for constitutional reform in Canada. However, in recent years, Canada West has diversified its research program by moving beyond the West's role in the Canadian federation. Supported by a large board of directors with representatives from Alberta, British Columbia, Manitoba, and Saskatchewan, Canada West actively engages key stakeholders to advance its mission. In addition to participating in workshops and conferences, researchers at Canada West interact regularly with the media. In 2013, twenty-three of their commentaries were referenced in over forty media outlets.[26]

References to the Canada West Foundation in Selected Canadian Newspapers

CALGARY HERALD

Breakenridge, Rob. "We Need Pipelines, Not Pipe Dreams." 12 February 2013, A16.

Brookman, George, and Brian Felesky. "Sustainable Funding Could Transform Calgary." 22 June 2012, A15.

Coad, Len. "Premiers Should Focus on Labour, Transportation." 25 July 2013, A13.

Corbella, Licia. "BC Residents Vote for the NDP at Their Peril." 11 May 2013, A15.

Cryderman, Kelly. "Harper Will Be among Mourners at Lougheed Memorial in Calgary; Public Invited to Line Up for Seating Starting at 10 AM." 21 September 2012, A4.

– "No Pipeline Resolution after Clark, Redford Have 'Frosty' Meeting; No Agreement Reached in Calgary Talks." 2 October 2012, A4.

Ewart, Stephen. "Feared Pipeline Bottleneck Has Arrived." 2 March 2013, C1.

– "Pipeline Would Benefit Saint John." 8 February 2013, D1.

Gibbins, Roger. "Securing Alberta's Respected Place in the World." 8 June 2012, A15.

Gray, Jim. "Be Bold, and Aim for Singles, Not Home Runs." 8 December 2012, A15.

Henton, Darcy, and Chris Varcoe. "Redford TV Address to Detail Fiscal Woes." 24 January 2013, A1.

Hussain, Yadullah. "Does Canada Need an Energy Champion?" 3 August 2012, E.6.

Legge, Adam. "It's Time for the 'Alberta Advantage' Plan B."
28 December 2012, A15.

Lynch, Kevin, and Pau Woo Yuen. "Canada Must Act Before Asia Finds
Energy Supply." 20 March 2013, A11.

O'Donnell, Sarah. "Province's Promise to 'Save' at Odds with Budget
Woes; Albertans Want Savings, Insists Horner." 4 February 2013, A4.

O'Neil, Peter. "Equalization Could Kill Unity: Dodge; Former Bank
Boss Warns of East-West Divide." 1 August 2012, A4.

Parker, David. "Colliers Tests Waters for New Tower." 26 October
2012, C2.

– "Foundation's Head Finds His Way Home." 29 November 2012, C2.

Roach, Robert. "Even an Imperfect Energy Strategy Is Worth Pursuing."
27 September 2012, A13.

Varcoe, Chris, Wood, James. "Dark Clouds Starting to Lift from
Alberta's Economic Outlook." 3 June 2013, A1.

Vineberg, Robert. "Importing Tradespeople Is Just Part of the Solution."
12 December 2012, A15.

Volmers, Eric. "How the West Became 'Home'; Foundation Book Offers
Some Fresh Points of View." 14 December 2012, D5.

Wood, James. "BC Election May Not Decide Alberta Pipeline Projects;
Redford Intent Oil Will Get to West Coast." 11 May 2013, A4.

– "Horner Warns Budget Debate Is 'Going to Get Hairy'; Unions Warn
of Cuts to Public Services." 5 March 2013, A4.

– "Meaningful Senate Reform Still Moving at Snail's Pace; Alberta
Votes Considered an 'Anomaly.'" 29 December 2012, A4.

– "Province's Savings Strategy Not 'Best Solution,' Says Economist;
Plan to Be Introduced Next Month." 12 February 2013, A8.

Yaffe, Barbara. "Ambivalence Could Be BC's Missed Opportunity."
13 March 2013, A10.

– "BC Urged to Mix Its 'Pinot Noir with a Bit of Coal Dust.'" 8 March
2013, A14.

Yedlin, Deborah. "Access to Asia Requires National Strategy." 9 June
2012, D1.

– "Prentice Grows into a New Role; Former Minister Emerges as
Passionate Voice." 28 September 2012, D1.

Zickefoose, Sherri. "Report Underlines Importance of Infrastructure to
Prosperity." 7 February 2013, B1.

GAZETTE
De Souza, Mike. "Report Delivers Infrastructure Warning." 7 February
2013, A11.

Jones, Dylan. "The Challenge in Railway Safety; Canadians Have a
 Right to Expect Their Government to Regulate and Enforce
 Appropriate Safeguards." 18 July 2013, A19.

GLOBE AND MAIL
Curry, Bill. "Ottawa Looks to Boost Spending." 5 February 2013, A1.
Curry, Bill, and Shawn McCarthy. "Ottawa Feels the Oil-Price Pinch."
 7 February 2013, A1.
Hume, Mark. "Canada Warned to Improve Energy Discussion."
 10 October 2012, S1.
Ibbitson, John. "Why Is Senate Reform Stalled? Ask the PM." 11 August
 2012, F9.
Trichur, Rita. "New Boss, New Way: Jean-Pierre Blais's Mission to
 Wake Up a Sleepy Watchdog." 3 November 2012, B1.
Wingrove, Josh. "It's Not Just about BC Any More." 11 May 2013, A4.

NATIONAL POST
Berkow, Jameson. "National Interest Comes First, Report Says Selling
 Resources." 6 June 2012, FP2.
Corcoran, Terence. "The Price for Keystone." 12 February 2013, FP11.
Gerson, Jen. "Harper Names Businessman to Senate; Albertan Appointed;
 Scott Tannas Advocates Term Limits, Reform." 26 March 2013, A8.
Hussain, Yadullah. "Alberta Takes New Direction on Pipeline; This
 Time It's North." 26 April 2013, A1.
– "Big Problem, Small-Scale Solutions; Saskatchewan Deals with
 Pipeline Constraints." 24 May 2013, FP6.
Lynch, Kevin, and Kathy Sendall. "A Path to a Richer Canada; We Must
 Work Quickly to Establish the Policies and Infrastructure Necessary
 to Ship Canadian Energy Products to Asian Markets." 6 June 2012,
 A12.
O'Neil, Peter. "Plans Tied to West's Growing Clout; National Battle
 Could Be Brewing if Oilsands Ownership Is Any Indication of What
 Is to Come." 29 May 2013, SR.2.
– "Wealth Gap Risks Unity, Dodge Says; Provincial Tension; Growing
 Disparity Could Cause Trouble." 1 August 2012, A4.

OTTAWA CITIZEN
De Souza, Mike. "Failing Infrastructure Hurts Growth: Report."
 7 February 2013, A3.
Taylor, Louisa. "Immigrant Conference Saved from Cutbacks; Think-
 Tank Sponsors Metropolis Meeting." 15 March 2013, C1.

Henton, Darcy. "Alberta Debates Sales Tax Again." 4 March 2013, A2.

TORONTO STAR
Brennan, Richard J., and Petti Fong. "'A Real Man of the People': Despite
    Faults, Voters Loved the Populist Politician." 30 March 2013, IN1.
"Budget Basics; Alberta Can Start Saving Once the Red Ink Stops
    Flowing." 12 September 2012, A12.
Ewart, Stephen. "Politics at Play in the Oilpatch; Environment,
    Economics at Centre of Debate." 1 September 2012, A3.
Hébert, Chantal. "Harper Poised to Put Senate Reform on Ice."
    18 September 2012, A6.
Steward, Gillian. "Western Cities Paint Themselves Green." 23 October
    2012, A19.
Stirrett, Shawna. "Innovation's the Thing." 22 December 2012, IN6.

VANCOUVER SUN
Bodkin, Jill. "Women of a Certain Age Wield Influence." 25 April 2013, A13.
Cayo, Don. "Worry Less about How Energy Is Produced, More How
    It's Wasted; Much Power Is Lost between Source and Fixture, No
    Matter How It's Generated." 27 May 2013, C6.
Coad, Len. "The North Needs a Coherent Energy Development Plan."
    15 June 2013, C4.
Gibbins, Roger. "Competing Interests Have Value in Northern Gateway
    Debate." 15 July 2013, A7.
Holden, Michael. "Western Premiers Need to Pitch Coordinated
    Infrastructure." 20 June 2013, A15.
O'Neil, Peter. "Provincial Wealth Disparity Could Destroy Federation;
    Fiscal Transfers Can Breed Disrespect, Resentment and Distrust,
    Essay Warns." 1 August 2012, B2.
Yaffe, Barbara. "Ambivalence to Canada Could Be Missed Opportu-
    nity for BC; Academic Says the Province Should Start Assuming a
    Leadership Role." 7 March 2013, B2
– "The West Presents Trudeau with His Greatest Challenge." 24 April
    2013, B2.
Yedlin, Deborah. "Canada Must 'Think Big' on Energy Strategy to Tap
    Asian Markets." 16 June 2012, C4.

Selected Publications of the Canada West Foundation

Bandali, Farahnaz. "Shedding Light on the TFW Program." *Canada
West Foundation*. December 2014.

- "Work Interrupted: How Federal Foreign Worker Rule Changes Hurt the West." *Canada West Foundation*. March 2015.
Cleland, Michael. "From the Ground Up: Earning Public Support for Resource Development." *Canada West Foundation*. May 2014.
Dade, Carlo. "The Business Case for Alberta to Provide International Aid." *Canada West Foundation*. December 2014.
Harder, Catherine, Geoff Jackson, and Janet Lane. "Talent Is Not Enough: Closing the Skills Gap." *Canada West Foundation*. September 2014.
Lane, Janet, and Naomi Christensen. "Competence Is the Best Credential." *Canada West Foundation*. April 2015.
Law, John, and Carlo Dade. "Construire sur notre avantage: Améliorer l'infrastructure commerciale du Canada." *Canada West Foundation*. November 2014.
McLeod, Trevor. "Walkin' the Walk: Five Steps to Efficient Cities." *Canada West Foundation*. March 2015.
Sajid, Shafak. "Restoring Trust: The Road to Public Support for Resource Industries." *Canada West Foundation*. July 2014.
Stirrett, Shawna. "The Missing Link: Constructive Ideas for Improving Urban Environmental Outcomes." *Canada West Foundation*. December 2013.

CANADIAN CENTRE FOR POLICY ALTERNATIVES (CCPA)

Tank Facts

Established:	1980
Location:	Ottawa (National Office)
Budget:	$5.5 million
Staff:	>40
President/Director:	Bruce Campbell
Website:	www.policyalternatives.ca

The Canadian Centre for Policy Alternatives was founded by a group of academic and labour economists, including Steven Langdon, Peter Findlay, and Robert Clarke, who, along with a cross-section of representatives from labour unions and left-leaning political organizations, "saw the need for an independent progressive research agency to counterbalance the right-wing Fraser and C.D. Howe Institutes."[27] Unlike the free-market-oriented C.D. Howe and Fraser Institutes, the CCPA believes that "social and economic issues ... are not something to be left to the marketplace or for governments acting alone to decide." The centre "is committed to putting forward research that reflects the concerns of women as well as men, labour as well as business, churches, cooperatives and voluntary agencies as well as governments, minorities and disadvantaged people as well as fortunate individuals."[28]

Since its inception, the CCPA has published hundreds of peer-reviewed reports, studies, and books on a wide range of social, political, and economic policy issues. Among the many topics it has examined are sexism and gender inequality, trade, poverty, and human rights. In 1994, it also launched a monthly journal, *The Monitor*, which may undergo significant change as the new editorial team looks to expand the journal's reach, and since 1995, has released the *Alternative Federal Budget*, an edited collection of articles that, as the book's title implies, suggests different ways the government could spend its revenue. In addition to conveying its ideas through its many publications, the CCPA often works closely with policy-makers and representatives from unions and other non-governmental organizations to advance its agenda. It also recognizes the importance of maintaining strong ties to the media and, according to its own findings, ranks among the most widely cited think tanks in the country.[29] CCPA closely tracks the exposure it generates in newspapers, on radio and television, and in social media.[30]

The CCPA's budget of slightly over \$5.5 million is generated primarily from the contributions of its over 12,000 organizational and individual donors.[31] Nearly half of its resources are allocated for research.[32] The institute performs contract work for various governmental and nongovernmental organizations as well. The CCPA's national headquarters is based in Ottawa, where it has more than a dozen staff members. In 1997, it expanded its operations beyond the nation's capital by opening branch offices in Manitoba, British Columbia, Nova Scotia, and Saskatchewan. The CCPA also has a regional office in Toronto.

References to the Canadian Centre for Policy Alternatives
in Selected Canadian Newspapers

THE CALGARY HERALD
Breakenridge, Rob. "Beer and Wine Should Be Sold in Grocery Stores."
   6 November 2012, A 14.
– "Federal Belt-Tightening Must Be Shared." 12 June 2013, A 14.
Fekete, Jason. "Cries Growing Louder for Federal Tax Reform."
   12 March 2013, A 4.
Gudowska, Malwina. "The Space between Us: A Letter from London."
   22 February 2013, Sw 24.

Harding, Brent. "Ample Supply." 8 November 2012, A13.

Healing, Dan. "Executive Pay 'a Bit of a Mess'." 28 June 2013, E6.

May, Kathryn, and Derek Spalding. "Report Says 29,000 Federal Jobs Face Axe." 8 April 2013, A9.

Middlemiss, Jim. "P3 Advocates Targeting City Hall." 2 May 2013, D8.

Oakey, Terrance. "It's Time for Unions to Become More Transparent." 3 August 2012, A11.

Stephenson, Amanda. "Shaw Execs Earn $30M." 8 January 2013, D1.

Van Loon, Jeremy, and Andrew Mayeda. "PM, Industry at Odds on Tax; Oilsand Firms Say Carbon Levy May Help." 2 February 2013, C4.

GLOBE AND MAIL

"Accountability Is Key." 20 June 2013, A14.

Anderssen, Erin. "The Learning Curve/Reinventing Higher Education." 6 October 2012, F1.

Bradshaw, James. "The Formula: More Graduates – and More Paths to Good Jobs." 13 April 2013, M1.

Bula, Frances. "Mayors Seek Share of Carbon-Tax Cash from Province." 12 September 2012, S1.

Carmichael, Kevin. "As Strong Loonie Pinches Manufacturing, Carney Faces Auto Workers." 20 August 2012, B1.

Eichler, Leah. "The High Cost of Violence against Women." 20 July 2013, B17.

"Forecast Deficits Lead to Austerity Push in Newfoundland." 25 March 2013, A4.

Freeland, Chrystia. "The Simmering Stew of Income Inequality." 17 May 2013, B2.

Hume, Mark. "BC's Push for Carbon Neutrality Falters." 27 March 2013, S1.

– "Groups Unite to Make Climate Change an Election Issue." 6 February 2013, S3.

– "Huge Markup on Carbon Offsets." 14 February 2013, S1.

Graham, Jennifer. "Saskatchewan Adds Private Liquor Stores to Retail Mix." 6 November 2012, A11.

McCarthy, Shawn. "Economists Warn of Canada's 'Bitumen Cliff.'" 21 February 2013, B5.

Robinson, Matthew, and Josh O'Kane. "Corporate 'Dead Money' Rises to Buoy GDP." 1 September 2012, B6.

Serson, Scott. "Indian Act Shackles." 21 June 2013, A12.

Simpson, Jeffrey. "We've Made a Choice: Health, Not Education." 12 September 2012, A17.

Stanford, Jim. "The Tax Cycle Is Turning, for the Better." 7 June 2013, A15.

Stueck, Wendy. "BC Introduces Carbon Program for Private Sector." 2 July 2013, S1.

Yakabuski, Konrad. "Inequality, Yes, but Canada's in a Sweet Spot." 18 March 2013, A11.

Yalnizyan, Armine. "Welcome to Canada's Wageless Recovery." 3 November 2012, B7.

NATIONAL POST

Blaze, Kathryn. "Thinking Outside the Tank; The Fraser Institute's Success Has Inspired the Growth of Other Public Policy Think-Tanks, and Rather Than Worry, It Embraces the Competition." 5 May 2012, A10.

Byers, Michael, and Stewart Webb. "Start from Scratch." 25 June 2013, A8.

Coyne, Andrew. "Why We Need Investments Alberta-Style; Gains Will Pay Dividends for Generations." 6 April 2013, A4.

Cross, Philip. "The Logic Cliff; 'Bitumen Cliff' Report Demonizes Canada's Resource Boom." 26 February 2013, FP11.

Foster, Peter. "Going for the Capitalist Jugular." 16 November 2012, FP11.

Isfeld, Gordon. "Jobs, Jobs, Jobs, Jobs, Jobs, Jobs; Part-time Gains Reverse July's Losses as 34,300 Find Work in August." 8 September 2012, FP1.

Lewis, Jeff. "Alberta Must Avoid 'Staples Trap': Report." 22 February 2013, FP4.

– "A New Model for Social Services." 12 November 2012, A10.

– "A New Way of Giving." 2 June 2012, FP20.

Ryan, Sid. "The Case for Zero Tuition." 1 June 2012, A16.

Stanford, Jim. "Manufacturing Success." 7 August 2012, FP6.

Yalnizyan, Armine. "Sorry, Andrew Coyne, But Income Inequality is a Real Problem." 21 December 2012, A14.

OTTAWA CITIZEN

Butler, Don. "Charity Sues 'Workspace Collective' over Trademark Dispute; Organization Serving Developmentally Disabled Says It Has Used Under One Roof Name Since 1995." 28 November 2012, D5.

Culpeper, Roy, and John Jacobs. "CETA Undermines Canada's Ability to Benefit from Increased Trade." 8 March 2013, A11.

Fekete, Jason. "Government Earmarks $850M for Public-Service Severance." 18 May 2012, A3.

Heartfield, Kate. "Ontario Can Sell the LCBO without Losing Money; The Strongest Defence of the Status Quo for Booze Sales Is That It Will Cost the Province Vital Revenue." 28 February 2013, A12.

May, Kathryn. "29,600 PS Jobs to Be Lost by 2015." 17 May 2012, A1.

– "National; Aboriginal Children Living in Poverty." 19 June 2013, A5.

Pugliese, David. "Sub Damage Still Being Assessed Two Years Later; Delay on Repairs for HMCS Corner Brook Just the Latest Snag for Canadian Fleet." 24 July 2013, A1.

Smith, Teresa. "Lectures at the Laf? Don't Laugh, It's True; The ByWard Market Pub is to Host a Debate on Public Education." 4 March 2013, C3.

Taylor, Louisa. "Head to FEMICON, Where All Women Are Superwomen; Accent on Humour at Women's Day Event." 8 March 2013, C3.

Yalnizyan, Armine. "Does Wealth Have Too Much Power in Canada?; YES." 10 May 2013, A11.

TORONTO STAR

Alamenciak, Tim. "What We Can Learn from the West: Liquor Prices in Privatized Provinces Generally More Expensive, but Bargains Can Be Found." 5 December 2012, A6.

– "Alternatives Dwindling in Province: Austerity Measures Not Helping Ontarians." 22 March 2013, A22.

Aulakh, Raveena. "Fretting about Fracking: Regina-based Filmmaker Studies Effect on Air, Water and Our Health." 7 February 2013, A15.

Benzie, Robert. "Austerity Measures Not Helping Ontarians." 18 March 2013, A1.

Brennan, Jordan, and Jim Stanford. "Inequality's Exorbitant Price: The Growing Income Gap Is Not Just a Problem for the Poor, but Hurts All of Us – Economically, Fiscally and Socially." 28 December 2012, A19.

Campion-Smith, Bruce. "Arctic Patrol Ships Will Be White Elephants, Report Warns." 12 April 2013, A3.

Daubs, Katie. "Rogers CEO Plans to Retire." 15 February 2013, A2.

Flavelle, Dana. "After the Apology: Royal Bank CEO Gord Nixon Did the Right Thing in Saying Sorry, Experts Say. But the RBC Outsourcing Controversy Has Stoked Fears about the Future of Canada's Middle Class." 13 April 2013, B1.

– "Give Students a Tuition Break." 5 March 2013, A14.

- "High-Flying Loonie Looms over Auto Talks: CAW Says It Is Being Unfairly Blamed for High Production Costs." 22 August 2012, B1.
- "Nearly Six Jobless for Every Vacancy, StatsCan Reports: Skills Training Plan Not Enough, Critics Say." 21 March 2013, B1.
- "Outsourcing to India Has Become a Booming Business: Company at the Heart of Current Outsourcing Controversy is Growing Exponentially." 10 April 2013, B1.
- "The Rising Tide of Household Debt: Despite the Warnings, Canadians Just Keep Borrowing More Money." 27 October 2012, S13.
- "Some Executives Earn Their Money: Top 100 Chief Executives in Canada Earned $7.7 million on Average." 5 January 2013, IN7.
- "Squeeze Signals End of the American Dream." 28 July 2012, B3.
- "Why Companies Sit on Their Cash: Bank of Canada Is Pushing Firms to Re-Invest in Themselves or Pay Big Dividends to Shareholders." 17 September 2012, A6.
Goar, Carol. "Flaherty Set to Tighten Screws." 20 March 2013, A21.
- "Jobless Youth Will Carry Lasting Scars." 12 October 2012, A23.
Harper, Tim. "Watchdog Would Have Welcomed Firing." 18 May 2012, A9.
Hennessy, Trish. "Hudak's LCBO Plan Fails Breathalyzer Test: With the Province Struggling to Trim Its $14-Billion Deficit, It Makes No Sense to Pour $1.66 Billion in Annual Liquor Revenues Down the Drain." 5 December 2012, A27.
Kalinowski, Tess. "Finding the Transit Tax 'Sweet Spot': Lower-Income Citizens Have a Lot to Lose from Transit Taxes – but Even More to Gain." 23 May 2013, GT.2.
Kenyon, Wallace. "Undergrad Tuition up 5 per Cent in Canada: New StatsCan Figures Show Ontario Still Has Country's Highest Fees." 13 September 2012, A6.
- "Let's Put the Kids First." 31 May 2012, A22.
Lu, Vanessa. "Free Trade Divide, 25 Years after Deal: Economists Split on Whether Agreement with US Was Good for Canada." 4 October 2012, B1.
Lu, Vanessa, Michael Lewis, and John Spears. "Surprise 'Outsider' Praised: Economists Welcome New Governor's Skills in Trade and Communication." 3 May 2013, B1.
Mackenzie, Hugh. "Inequality Frays the Ties That Bind." 31 December 2012, A13.
Mackenzie, Hugh, and Trish Hennessy. "Tight-Fisted Ontario Going Nowhere Fast." 20 March 2013, A21.

Monsebraaten, Laurie. "Report Finds Little Progress in Creating Gender Equality." 24 April 2013, A8.

– "Strategy Urged for Domestic Violence." 11 July 2013, A2.

Nino Gheciu, Alex, and Laurie Monsebraaten. "Rise in Retail Jobs Raises Red Flags: Unstable, Low-Paying Sector Now Largest Percentage of Workforce in Canada, StatsCan Survey Finds." 27 June 2013, A1.

Olive, David. "Canada Day Biz Quiz: Test Your Mettle on Facts, Stats and Other Trivia about the Nation." 1 July 2012, A13.

Parsons, Margaret, and Moya Teklu. "Money Does Indeed Talk: And Most of It since the Scarborough Shootings Has Gone toward Policing." 27 July 2012, A19.

Siddiqui, Haroon. "Linc Alexander's Unfinished Business." 25 October 2012, A21.

– "Thanks to Our Partners and Sources." 2 October 2012, V3.

– "Think-Tank Numbers Disputed: Rethinking Maritime Union." 4 December 2012, A22.

Walkom, Thomas. "Canada's Latest Commodity Trap." 21 February 2013, A12.

– "EU Free Trade Deal Bad for Ontario." 20 September 2012, A17.

Ward, Olivia. "Revisiting the Price of Cheap: Workers' Rights in Spotlight as Death Toll Continues to Rise." 5 May 2013, A6.

Watson, Paul. "Canada Takes Helm of Arctic Forum: Safe Shipping, Economic Development Named as Priorities as Two-Year Term Begins Wednesday." 13 May 2013, A4.

Whittington, Les. "Ottawa Eyes Controversial Way to Fund Social Services: Social Impact Bonds Are Used in US and Britain, but Private Sector Influence Worries Some." 9 November 2012, A6.

– "Can Unions Save Middle Class?: When Union Membership Thrives, so Does the Middle Class, Studies Show. But Lately, in an Everybody-For-Themselves Age of Globalization and Anti-Labour Legislation, Both Have Been Suffering." 1 September 2012, IN1.

Zerbisias, Antonia. "Generation NOW: Four Young Activists Speak about Their Work to Shape Canada's Political Future." 5 October 2012, A4.

VANCOUVER SUN

Anderson, Fiona. "Hungry for Power; BC Hydro Expects Demand for Electricity to Soar Over the Next 20 Years – But How to Best Address the Need Is a Subject of Much Debate." 23 June 2012, D2.

– "BC Should Axe the MSP 'Tax.'" 2 February 2013, D3.

Boyko, Ian. "Low Taxes Far from Top Concern for Young, Skilled Workers." 8 February 2013, A10.

Bramham, Daphne. "BC Is the Worst Place in Canada to Be a Kid; Victoria and Ottawa Share the Blame for Not Doing Enough to Eliminate Child Poverty at Time When Money Was Spent on Other 'Priorities.'" 9 July 2013, A9.

Calvert, John, and Marc Lee. "Clark Government Brews Recipe for Rate Hikes; Subsidizing Dirty Industries with Expensive Clean Electricity Will Raise Cost of Power for Consumers." 20 June 2012, A11.

Cayo, Don. "BC's Tax Well Not Yet Dry: Left-Leaning Analyst." 24 April 2013, C3.

– "For Better or Worse, Referendums Give Power to People; British Columbia Leads Canada in Giving Voters a First-Hand Voice on Matters." 30 March 2013, D1.

– "How Far and How Fast Should We Go With Referendums?; Even the Most Populist Leaders Know the Masses Can't Decide Every Issue." 2 April 2013, C1.

– "The Next Government Must Start to Tackle Problems with Long-Term Financial Implications; Your Decision 2013." 23 April 2013, C5.

– "A Vancouver Family's 'Living Wage' Is More Than What Most Earn." 3 May 2013, C2.

Coleman, Rich. "Keeping Hydro Rates Affordable for BC Families." 22 June 2012, A11.

Culbert, Lori. "Despite Gains, People Still Sleep on the Streets; Shawna Taylor Travelled a Long Road to Find a Small Apartment and Safety." 11 May 2013, A6.

Daub, Shannon, Seth Klein, and Randy Galawan. "British Columbians Are Ready for a Thoughtful Talk about Taxes." 4 December 2012, A14.

Erkiletian, Jim. "Let the Chinese Buy Up Canada, They Might Run It Better." 28 August 2012, A10.

Finlayson, Jock. "What Is the Right Size for the Public Sector?" 30 May 2012, A11.

Fowlie, Jonathan. "Coalition Champions Rainforest Protection; Push for BC to Complete Great Bear Agreements Competes in Crowded Election Agenda." 7 February 2013, A2.

Griffin, Kevin. "Hydrochloric Acid, Antifreeze among Chemicals Used in Fracking; Environment Canada Wants Industry to Disclose More on Manufacturing Process." 4 May 2013, E10.

Griffin Cohen, Marjorie. "BC Grapples with Forest Health, Harvests after Pine Beetle Damage; Opening Up Reserves, Finding Uses for Dead Wood and Taking Inventory of Timber Are Key Issues." 3 November 2012, H3.

– "Women Bear Brunt of Poor Policy; In British Columbia, Public Policy Changes Have Resulted in Smaller Paycheques for Female Workers." 17 December 2012, A9.

Hamilton, Gordon. "Counting Province's Trees Tops To-Do Lists; But Parties Differ on How to Manage Forests in the Post-Mountain Pine Beetle Era." 16 April 2013, C2.

Hoekstra, Gordon. "Great Bear Rainforest's Green Gold; Critics Say Conservancy Project Does Not Meet a Key Credibility Test for Carbon Credits." 19 January 2013, A11.

Hughes, Dave, and Ben Parfitt. Depleting Natural Gas Reserves Makes No Sense for the Province." 15 November 2012, A17.

Klein, Seth, and Iglika Ivanova. "The Case for Higher Taxes; It's Time for BC to Raise and Reform Taxes." 29 January 2013, A11.

Lee, Marc. "Natural Gas Strategy Nothing More Than a Fairy Tale." 20 October 2012, C4.

– "What's Next for BC's Carbon Tax?; In 2013 Budget, Government Will Face Key Decision on the Future of the Tax." 14 January 2013, A9.

May, Kathryn, and Derek Spalding. "More Front-Line Jobs to Be Cut." 8 April 2013, B3.

McInnes, Craig. "Alberta Faces Tough Tax Choices as Tide Goes Out on Oil Revenue." 2 February 2013, D4.

– "Bloated Bills Prompt Review of Pacific Carbon Trust; The 'Next Administration' Likely Will Be Taxed with Taking Action." 15 February 2013, A3.

– "Clark's Jobs Plan Goes Head to Head with Campbell's Climate Action Plan; Liquefied Natural Gas Bonanza Won't Fit Under Emissions Cap." 12 October 2012, A3.

– "Shrinking Government Trend Started under NDP." 15 April 2013, A11.

– "Numbers +6.2%." 12 September 2012, C1.

O'Neil, Peter. "Tories Signal Opposition to New Democracy Tool; NDP MP Kennedy Stewart's E-petition Proposal Has Support across the Political Spectrum, but Not in the Prime Minister's Office." 14 June 2013, B2.

Palmer, Vaughn. "Distrust Is Green Scheme's Fatal Flaw; Independent MLA Bob Simpson Wants Ouster of Pacific Carbon Trust Board, to Start." 3 April 2013, A3.

- "When It Comes to Taxes, Even the NDP Doesn't Want to Be the NDP of Yore; Dix Rejects Significant Tax Increases If His Party Forms the Next Government." 1 December 2012, A3.

Parfitt, Ben. "Lift on Logging Restraints Would Be Ill-Advised." 7 August 2012, A11.

- "LNG Projects Make No Sense; Aside from Adding to BC's CO$_2$ Emissions, the Plants May Not Be Built before the Market Is Flooded." 17 July 2012, A9.

- "Water Withdrawal Stats Run Dry; Nestle Will Voluntarily Disclose Such Vital Information, but BC Government Doesn't Seem Interested in Asking." 30 July 2013, A11.

Rowswell, Sheila. "Higher Income Taxes Pay for a More Civil Society." 2 February 2013, D3.

Saxifrage, Carrie. "Give Trees (and Frogs) a Break; Provincial Forestry Policies Neither Protect the Environment nor Provide Jobs in Exchange for Favourable Tax Rates." 26 December 2012, A19.

Sherlock, Tracy. "Living Wage Gives Boost to Staff Struggling to Make a Living; More Employers Committing to Pay Workers Enough to Meet Basic Needs." 29 June 2012, C2.

Simpson, Scott. "BC Needs Greater Scrutiny of Industrial Water Use, Report Says; Province Should Be Tracking Consumption, Making Data Available to Public." 15 November 2012, D1.

Stevens, Clare M. "Readers Answer Call for a Talk about Taxes." 11 December 2012, A15.

Veldhuis, Niels, and Jason Clemens. "Inequality Debate Full of Bluster; Myopic Arguments about Income Disparities Lead to Misunderstandings and Eventually Bad Public Policy." 3 January 2013, A15.

Weiler, Anelyse, and Gerardo Otero. "Reforms Needed to Grant Temporary Workers More Protection." 16 March 2013, C4.

Wilkinson, Andrew. "Wave Goodbye to Skilled Labourers; Long-Term Consequences of Higher Taxes Include Young Graduates Leaving for Greener, Lower-Taxed Pastures." 4 February 2013, A9.

WINNIPEG FREE PRESS

Bernas, Kirsten. "City Cuts Impede Fight Against Poverty." 22 January 2013, A7.

Black, Errol. "Workers under Threat by Right-to-Work Movement." 1 September 2012, J.6.

Fernandez, Lynne. "Don't Cut Taxes of Wealthy Manitobans." 20 April 2013, A17.

Finlayson, Jock. "Cost of the Public Sector in Canada." 29 May 2012, A10.

Flavelle, Dana. "CPP Could Fix Pension Crisis, Says Dodge: Former Bank Governor Disagrees with Ottawa on Merits of 'Pooled' Plans." 28 November 2012, B1.

Harper, Tim. "Rethinking Maritime Union." 30 November 2012, A16.

Hudson, Peter. "Taxes Reduce Inequality, Provide Vital Public Services." 11 July 2013, A15.

Kusch, Larry. "Group Pleads for More Welfare Rental Aid." 15 February 2013, A14.

– "Make Corporations Pay: MFL." 18 April 2013, A4.

McCraken, Molly. "Premiers' Focus on Transfers." 24 July 2013, A9.

Rabson, Mia. "Richest Manitobans See Biggest Growth." 9 February 2013, A4.

Rappaport, Lissie. "Sherbrook Pool – Worth Every Cent." 24 June 2013, A9.

Reimer, Brendan. "Cuts to Co-Ops Costly." 14 June 2012, A15.

Sanders, Carol. "Rally Prompts Province to Cover Health Benefits." 16 May 2013, A8.

Silver, Jim. "Errol Black: 'Manitoba's Best Trade Unionist.'" 12 November 2012, A11.

Walkom, Thomas. "Hockey, NAFTA and Why the 1% Has It All." 17 November 2012, A8.

– "Ontario Helps Kill Green Plan." 22 November 2012, A8.

Welch, Mary Agnes. "Tempers Still Hot at PST Hearing." 5 July 2013, A8.

Selected Publications of the Canadian Centre
for Policy Alternatives

Behrens, Matthew. "FINTRAC: Canada's Invasive 'Financial War against Terror.'" *The Monitor*. April 2015.

Findlay, Tammy, and Stella Lord. "A New Economy Needs Child Care." *Canadian Centre for Policy Alternatives*. 28 April 2015.

Forsey, Helen. "Excerpt: Envisaging a People's Senate, by Helen Forsey." *The Monitor*. April 2015.

Fuller, Colleen. "Cambie Corp. Goes to Court: The Legal Assault on Universal Health Care." *Canadian Centre for Policy Alternatives*. 27 April 2015.

Ismi, Asad. "Canada and the US Go Digging for Regime Change in Venezuela." *The Monitor*. April 2015.

Ivanova, Iglika, and Seth Klein. "Working for a Living Wage 2015: Making Paid Work Meet Basic Family Needs in Metro Vancouver." *Canadian Centre for Policy Alternatives.* 29 April 2015.

Khoo, Cynthia, and Steve Anderson. "How Small Towns Are Driving Canada's Digital Future." *The Monitor.* March 2015.

Mason, Peggy. "Countering Islamic State: A Failing Strategy." *The Monitor.* April 2015.

Ruby, Clayton, and Nader R. Hasan. "Bill C-51: A Legal Primer." *The Monitor.* March 2015.

Sali, Meghan, and Steve Anderson. "How the Digital Privacy Act Could Attract Copyright Trolls to Canada." *The Monitor.* April 2015.

CANADIAN COUNCIL ON SOCIAL DEVELOPMENT

Tank Facts

Established:	1920
Location:	Ottawa
Budget:	$1.5–$2 million
Staff:	4
Director/President	Peggy Taillon
Website:	www.ccsd.ca

The Canadian Council on Social Development (CCSD), Canada's oldest social policy research institute, has a succinct and unambiguous mandate: to contribute "to building stronger, more caring communities in Canada, through evidence, collaboration and design."[33] This three-pronged approach to addressing complex social problems and suggesting possible solutions has become the cornerstone of the organization. Building on the evidence it has accumulated, the CCSD then relies on the partnerships and networks it has formed with philanthropists, not-for-profit organizations, representatives from various government departments and agencies, and individuals and corporations in the private sector to discuss how best to bring key stakeholders aboard in an effort to gain policy traction. Once this has been accomplished, the CCSD turns its attention to how to frame and promote its recommendations strategically to policy-makers and the public. Over the course of its long and distinguished history, the CCSD has attempted to leave an indelible mark on several key initiatives undertaken by both the federal government and the provinces. On its website, the CCSD highlights four of what it considers its many accomplishments:

- In the 1920s, CCSD helped shape the first Old Age Pension.
- In the 1930s, CCSD promoted the concept of Employment Insurance.
- In the 1980s, CCSD put the spotlight on the plight of Aboriginal children.
- In [the last few decades], CCSD demonstrated why the National Child Benefit was a wise investment and advocated for the introduction of tax credits to assist working poor families.[34]

Led by Peggy Taillon, a former senior vice-president at the Ottawa Hospital, the CCSD relies on the support of its seven-member board and the generosity of individual contributors to keep its vision at the forefront of debates on social policy in Canada.

References to the Canadian Council on Social Development in Selected Canadian Newspapers

TORONTO STAR
Delacourt, Susan. "Never Mind How Many Wise Men There Were." 20 December 2010.
Kidd, Kenneth. "Coming Soon: Good Life Index." 10 June 2009.
Ogilvie, Megan. "Health at Risk If Long-Form Census Scrapped: Experts." 3 September 2010.
Scallan, Niamh. "Did Mariam Struggle to Fit into Her New Life?" 17 March 2012, GT1.
Steenberg, Pat. "Our Budget Woes Are Self-Inflicted." 21 May 2013, A15.

GLOBE AND MAIL
Ewing-Weisz, Chris. "Trailblazing Saskatchewan Judge Fought against Poverty and Social Injustice." 3 November 2011, S7.
Ibbitson, John. "The Aboriginal Population: Younger and More Troubled." 9 May 2013, A16.

OTTAWA CITIZEN
Taillon, Peggy. "Not Enough Support." 6 May 2013, A10.
– "Occupy Challenges All of Us." 19 November 2011, B5.

VANCOUVER SUN
McMartin, Pete. "A Tribute to the Vancouver Housewife Who Housed Thousands." 21 February 2012, A4.

*Selected Publications of the Canadian Council
on Social Development*

*Growing Up in North America: Children's Health & Safety in Canada,
US & Mexico.* 2006.
*Growing Up in North America: The Economic Well-Being of Children
in Canada, the United States, and Mexico.* 2008.
Plett, Lynette. *Programs in the Workplace: Executive Summary.* 2007.
– *Programs in the Workplace: How to Increase Employer Support.*
2007.
Roberts, Paul, and Anna Torgeson. *Overview of Selected International
Literacy Programs.* 2007.
Roberts, Paul, Louise Hanvey, and Judi Varga-Toth. *Canadian's
Children Exposure to Violence: What It Means for Parents.* 2003.
Roberts, Paul, and Rebecca Gowan. *Canadian Literacy Literature &
Bibliography Review.* 2007.
Tsoukalas, Spyridoula, and Andrew Mackenzie. *Personal Security
Index: A Reflection of How Canadians Feel Five Years Later.* 2003.
Wasserman, Miriam. *The Impact of North American Economic Inte-
gration of Children.* 2006.
Watkins, Emily. *Overview of Provincial & Territorial Policies.* 2007.

CANADIAN DEFENCE AND FOREIGN AFFAIRS INSTITUTE (CDFAI)
/ CANADIAN GLOBAL AFFAIRS INSTITUTE (CGAI)

Tank Facts

Established: 2001; renamed the Canadian Global Affairs
                     Institute in 2015
Location: Calgary, Ottawa
Budget: $500,000–$1 million
Staff: ~5; plus over two dozen fellows
President/Director: R.S. (Bob) Millar
Website: www.cdfai.org
With "a mission to be a catalyst for innovative Canadian global engage-
ment,"[35] the Canadian Defence and Foreign Affairs Institute (CDFAI),
renamed the Canadian Global Affairs Institute (CGAI) in 2015, has
made its presence felt on the country's think tank landscape. Headquar-
tered in Calgary with a branch office in Ottawa, the CGAI/CDFAI has

recruited some of Canada's most distinguished military historians and political scientists with expertise in defence, security, and foreign policy studies to write research papers and provide commentaries on a wide range of international issues. In addition to its director of research programs, David Bercuson, a prominent historian of the Canadian military, several prominent experts can be found on its roster of research fellows, including: Jack Granatstein, the well-known historian and author of numerous works pertaining to Canada's role in global affairs; Colin Robertson, a former Canadian diplomat; and former Conservative senator Hugh Segal.

Since it opened its doors, the CDFAI/CGAI has recognized the importance of engaging both the public and policy makers in discussions about Canada's role on the world stage. Through its many research papers, polls, and commentaries on topics ranging from border security to Canada's efforts in Afghanistan, the CGAI/CDFAI has established a strong and respected voice in the policy-making community. In a relatively short period of time, the institute has also become increasingly media savvy. Not only does it track its exposure in the print and broadcast media, but it keeps a close watch on its competitors, including CIGI, the CIC, and the Macdonald-Laurier Institute.[36] The CGAI/CDFAI is well aware of the recognition it has received from the *Global Go To Think Tank Index Report,* and remains committed to enhancing its stature in the national and international think tank community.

References to the CDFAI in Selected Canadian Newspapers

NATIONAL POST
Granatstein, Jack. "The World According to Harper; Thanks to the Prime Minister's Realistic Foreign and Defence Policies, Canada Can Be a Principled, Responsible Ally." 30 January 2012, A14.
Hopper, Tristin. "Shoot First, Ask Questions Later; Extra-Judicial Killings Became a Public Darling 2011." 31 December 2011, A7.
Huebert, Rob. "It's Time to Talk about Arctic Militarization." 6 May 2013, A12.
Wallace, Ron. "A Proud Moment for Canada." 10 May 2013, A14.

OTTAWA CITIZEN
Granatstein, J.L. "Canada Always Was a Warrior Nation." 3 September 2012, A9.

Pratt, David. "Eurogeddon and the Stresses on European Unity."
    1 December 2012, B7.
Sibley, Robert. "Great Game Moves to Arctic; China's Interest Proves
    Need for Canada to Assert Its Sovereignty, Observers Say." 29 October
    2011, A1.
Stairs, Denis. "The Era of Drones Is Here. Is Canada Ready?" 18 May
    2012, A13.

TORONTO STAR
Brewster, Murray. "Cost of Canada's Mission in Iraq, Syria Will Hit
    $528 Million in Coming Year." 1 April 2015.
– "Tories Won't Say How Much Mission in Syria, Iraq Will Cost."
    31 March 2015.
Copeland, Daryl. "Canada Faltered on World Stage in 2014."
– "Five Reasons Ottawa Shouldn't Extend Iraq Mission." 23 March 2015.

WINNIPEG FREE PRESS
Cash, Martin. "Canadian Company Seeks US Address." 23 November
    2011, B5.

Selected Publications of Canadian Defence
and Foreign Affairs Institute

Brodie, Ian. *After America, Canada's Moment?* February 2015.
Carment, David, and Yiagadeesen Samy. *Canada, Fragile States and the
    New Deal: Looking Beyond 2015.* August 2014.
Cooper, Barry. *Letter from Constantinople.* August 2014.
Copeland, Daryl. *Humanity's Best Hope: Increasing Diplomatic
    Capacity in Ten (Uneasy) Steps.* September 2014.
Ferris, John. *Personal Privacy and Communications Security from the
    Telegraph to the Internet.* July 2014.
Horn, Bernd. *No, but Yes. Military Intervention in the New Era:
    Implications for the Canadian Armed Forces.* March 2015.
Huebert, Rob. *Canada, the Arctic Council, Greenpeace, and Arctic Oil
    Drilling: Complicating an Already Complicated Picture.* January
    2014.
James, Patrick. *Grand, Bland or Somewhat Planned? Toward a
    Canadian Strategy for the Indo-Pacific Region.* August 2014.
Macdonald, George. *A New Way to Fly: Major Challenges Facing Air
    Force Planners over the Next 20 Years.* October 2014.

Zekulin, Michael G. *Canada's New Challenges Facing Terrorism at Home*. December 2014.

CANADIAN INTERNATIONAL COUNCIL

Tank Facts

Established: 2008 (formerly the Canadian Institute
                         of International Affairs)
Location: Toronto
Budget: ~$1.5 million
Staff: 11
President/Director   Jo-Ann Davis
Website: www.opencanada.org

Housed at the University of Toronto's Trinity College, the Canadian International Council (CIC) is "an independent, member-based council established to strengthen Canada's role in global affairs."[37] At the urging of Jim Balsillie, co-founder of Research in Motion (RIM),[38] the members of the Canadian Institute of International Affairs (CIIA)[39] voted in November 2007 to rename and reinvent the CIIA as the CIC. The Canadian Institute of Strategic Studies,[40] an independent think tank established in Toronto in 1976, folded its operations into the CIC in 2008. Balsillie would go on to serve as chair of the CIC's board from 2008, its first full year of operations, until 2012. In 2013, he was succeeded by the Hon. Bill Graham, chancellor of Trinity College and former federal Liberal cabinet minister, who held several portfolios, including defence and foreign affairs.

The CIC markets itself as Canada's hub for international affairs and relies on its digital platform, OpenCanada.org, to foster discussion about key issues and concerns in the international community. The CIC has maintained the CIIA's long-standing tradition of encouraging its member branches, now totalling fifteen, to sponsor events throughout the year. In addition to releasing a steady stream of reports and inviting high-profile speakers to address critically important challenges facing world leaders, the CIC publishes *International Journal*, Canada's premier academic journal in the field of foreign affairs. The CIC oversees several research projects, many of which draw upon the expertise of faculty at the University of Toronto and other Canadian and international universities. Among its many projects are those that focus on: natural resources and foreign policy; international intellectual property; Arctic sovereignty and security;

China; border issues; and Canada and the Americas. According to its website, the CIC receives funding from several corporate and individual donors, including RBC Financial, Scotiabank, BMO Financial Group, Power Corporation of Canada, the Hon. Bill Graham, and Tom Kierans.

*References to the Canadian International Council
in Selected Canadian Newspapers*

CALGARY HERALD

Garneau, Marc. "Resource Royalties Must Be Saved." 20 October 2012, A15.

Mundy, John. "War with Iran Would Be Colossal Mistake." 18 January 2013, A11.

Yedlin, Deborah. "It's Time We Get Serious about Saving." 9 February 2013, C1.

GLOBE AND MAIL

Decloet, Derek. "The 'Dire' Fallout of Political Inaction." 26 October 2012, A1.

Jeffs, Jennifer. "Canada Should Embrace Mexico's New Leader Now." 4 July 2012, A11.

– "Toward a More Brazilian Canada." 7 August 2013, A13.

McCarthy, Shawn, and Pav Jordan. "China's Bid to Fit In." 28 July 2012, B1.

McKenna, Barrie. "A Nine-Step Plan to Fix Canada's Resource Economy." 6 October 2012, B7.

Perkins, Tara. "Ottawa Weighs Reciprocity with China for Miners." 25 October 2012, B11.

– "Preparing for When the Oil Runs Out." 11 October 2012, A20.

NATIONAL POST

Caron, Joseph. "Rejecting Asia." 24 October 2012, FP11.

Coyne, Andrew. "Why We Need Investments Alberta-Style; Gains Will Pay Dividends for Generations." 6 April 2013, A4.

Delaney, Douglas E. "The Chalkboard Battlefield; In an Essay Series Commissioned by the Strategic Studies Working Group – a Partnership Between the Canadian International Council and the Canadian Defence and Foreign Affairs Institute – Five Expert Authors Opine on the Challenges Facing the Canadian Forces." 5 February 2013, A12.

Fergusson, James. "Up in the Air, North of 60." 7 February 2013, A15.

Girouard, Roger. "A Navy for Rough Waters." 6 February 2013, A12.
Godefroy, Andrew. "Space: An Expensive Frontier." 8 February 2013, A12.
Knight, Scott. "Preparing for Cyber-War." 9 February 2013, A20.
MacNamara, Don, and Hugh Segal. "Canada's Worth Defending." 24 December 2012, A12.
Mazurkewich, Karen. "The Funding Problem; Governments Must Refocus Distribution of Funding Dollars on Start-ups." 30 October 2012, FE.4.

OTTAWA CITIZEN
Campbell, Jennifer. "North Must Be Developed Sustainably; Sweden's Foreign Minister Outlines Arctic Strategy." 30 May 2012, C4.
Desaulniers, Darren. "The Fix Is In and We Must Stop It, Author Says; Corruption in Sports on the Move and Canada Is at Risk." 25 April 2012, B5.
Jeffery, Mike. "The Future of Foreign Military Training." 29 March 2013, A11.
Lagassé, Philippe. "Defence Procurement Problems Run Deeper Than the F-35." 7 December 2012, A12.

TORONTO STAR
Acharya Tom-Yew, Madhavi. "Q&A: The Case for Sovereign Wealth Funds in Canada." 9 January 2013, B2.
– "Brazil's Aspirations." 16 November 2012, A16.
Maharaj, Sachin. "Can China Teach Us a Lesson?" 8 April 2013, A15.
Siddiqui, Haroon. "Netanyahu Overplays His Hand with Obama." 27 September 2012, A23.
Talaga, Tanya. "Ball in Canada's Court after US Takes Stand." 28 June 2013, A1.

Selected Publications of the Canadian International Council

Cornish, Margaret. *Behaviour of Chinese SOEs: Implications for Investment and Cooperation in Canada.* February 2012.
Drohan, Madelaine. *The 9 Habits of Highly Effective Resource Economies: Lessons for Canada.* November 2012.
Greenspon, Edward. *Open Canada: A Global Positioning Strategy for a Networked Age.* May 2011.

Huntley, Wade L. *Canada-China Space Engagement: Opportunities and Prospects*. February 2011.

Keenan, Thomas. *Strategic Studies Working Group Papers*. November 2012.

Mazurkewich, Karen. *Rights and Rents: Why Canada Must Harness Its Intellectual Property Resources*. October 2011.

Potter, Pitman. *Issues in Canada-China Relations*. November 2011.

Pratt, David. *Canada's Citizen Soldiers: A Discussion Paper*. March 2011.

Robertson, Colin. *"Now for the Hard Part": A User's Guide to Renewing the Canadian-American Partnership*. February 2011.

Simon, Bernard. *Time for a Fresh Curriculum: Canada's International Education Strategy*. June 2014.

CENTRE FOR INTERNATIONAL GOVERNANCE INNOVATION (CIGI)

Tank Facts

Established:	2001
Location:	Waterloo
Budget:	>$25 million
Staff:	~80 researchers, fellows, and staff
President/Director:	Rohinton Medhora
Website:	www.cigionline.org

With a budget and endowmenт[41] that most think tanks in North America and Europe could only dream of, CIGI is, in many respects, in a class by itself. Founded by Jim Balsillie and Mike Lazaridis of the Waterloo-based telecommunications firm Research in Motion (RIM), the manufacturers of BlackBerry, with a $30 million endowment ($20 million from Balsillie and $10 million from Lazaridis), and "with more or less matching grants from the Canadian and Ontario governments,"[42] CIGI was created as "an independent, non-partisan think tank on international governance."[43] In addition to CIGI, which Michael Valpy of *The Globe and Mail* describes as "the jewel of [Balsillie's] global endeavour,"[44] the Waterloo-based entrepreneur has invested millions of dollars to build the Balsillie School of International Affairs, the Balsillie Centre for Excellence, the Canadian International Council, and the International Governance Leaders and Organizations Online (IGLOO). All told, Balsillie has spent over $100 million to secure a foothold in the international relations community. Allegations surrounding Balsillie's involvement in the academic affairs of CIGI and the Balsillie School of International Affairs, and his efforts to create programs jointly supported by CIGI and other universities in Canada have not been without controversy. Indeed, in 2012, York University was facing a rare censure from the Canadian Association of University teachers (CAUT) for considering establishing a school in international law with CIGI.[45]

According to its website, "CIGI supports research, forms networks, advances policy debate and generates ideas for multilateral governance improvements. Conducting an active agenda of research, events and publications, CIGI's interdisciplinary work includes collaboration with policy, business and academic communities around the world."[46] Since 2001, CIGI has made a concerted effort to recruit many of the top international affairs scholars around the globe. Its extensive listing of research fellows, which currently exceeds eighty, boasts several distinguished experts, including David Welch, Thomas Homer-Dixon, Fen Osler Hampson, Simon Dalby, and James Blight. With considerable expertise upon which to draw and the financial resources to sustain its work, CIGI has established a number of important research programs. These include: global economy, global security, environment and energy and global development. Many of these initiatives are supported by municipal, federal, and provincial government departments, ministries, and agencies. CIGI also receives funding from some international government agencies, such as the Geneva Centre for the Public Control of Armed Forces and the United Kingdom Department for International Development.[47]

CIGI's research output in terms of books, policy papers, briefs, and other publications has been impressive. Indeed, by 2010, the institute was generating over one hundred publications annually. CIGI is conscious of raising its public profile; however, being situated in Waterloo, Ontario instead of in a major urban centre has limited the amount of national exposure it generates (see Appendix 1).

References to the Centre for International Governance Innovation in Selected Canadian Newspapers

CALGARY HERALD

Boswell, Randy. "Report Laments Inadequate Planning for 'Great Melt.'" 27 November 2012, A9.

Yedlin, Deborah. "Keystone Critic Rather Selective in His Arguments." 4 April 2013, D1.

– "Tech Opens Doors to Academic World." 20 July 2012, D 1.

GAZETTE

Berthiaume, Lee. "Experts Puzzled over Claim of Iranian Link."
    23 April 2013, A 2.
Cohen, Tobi. "Canada Urged to Mitigate Immigrant 'Brain Drain';
    Movement of Skilled, Educated Workers Hurts Their Home
    Countries, Study Says." 29 May 2013, A 14.

GLOBE AND MAIL

Blanchfield, Mike. "Ottawa Wary of Border Tie-ups in Wake of US
    Budget Impasse." 28 February 2013, A 10.
Blustein, Paul. "The Inefficiency of International Financial Institutions."
    12 November 2012, B 4.
Bradshaw, James. "Ontario Universities Promise Funding Guide amid
    Carleton Donor Backlash." 14 July 2012, A 12.
Burney, Derek, and Fen Osler Hampson. "Dramatic Bid, Strategic
    Reply." 27 July 2012, A 15.
– "Five Reasons to Stay out of Syria." 19 June 2013, A 15.
– "Harper's Measured Verdict." 11 December 2012, A 13.
– "Let's Boldly Embrace Emerging Markets." 25 September 2012, A 17.
– "Let's Put Missile Defence Back in Our Arsenal." 21 May 2013, A 13.
– "Ticket to North American Energy Independence." 22 February
    2013, A 11.
Campbell, Clark. "Advice for Fantino on His New Beat: Keep It
    Simple." 5 July 2012, A 13.
– "Baird Visits Syria's Neighbours to Ease Tension." 11 August 2012,
    A 12.
– "Canada's New Jordan Envoy Headed Up Harper's Security Detail."
    19 April 2013, A 4.
– "Crafting Takeover Policy to Leverage Trade." 1 November 2012,
    A 15.
– "Ottawa Reaching beyond Israel-Palestinian Issues." 29 March 2013,
    A 4.
– "What the World Can – and Can't – Do." 16 August 2013, A 6.
– "Why Obama Didn't Come out Swinging." 4 July 2013, A 8.
Carmichael, Kevin. "'Austerians' Are Reeling as G 20 Avoids Fiscal
    Targets." 22 April 2013, B 1.
– "Canada Backs US Pick for World Bank." 14 April 2012, B 4.

– "China Unleashes the New Yuan." 16 April 2012, A1.
– "Economy's Foggy Future Poses Challenge for Carney." 3 September 2012, B1.
– "G7 Currency Stand Sparks Turmoil." 13 February 2013, B1.
Cheadle, Bruce. "Donors, Schools, Profs Seek Peace after Turmoil." 31 December 2012, A8.
Curry, Bill. "Canada Dives into Pacific Talks." 20 June 2012, A1.
Curry, Bill, and Sean Silcoff. "G20: Greek Election Result Spares Leaders Real-Time Fiscal Firefighting." 18 June 2012, A9.
Heinbecker, Paul. "Every Day, the Costs of Inaction Grow." 18 June 2013, A15.
– "Heed the Lessons of Iraq." 15 March 2013, A15.
Ibbitson, John. "Canada's Cold Shoulder to the UN." 2 October 2012, A3.
– "A New Model on Foreign Investment." 10 December 2012, A4.
Koring, Paul. "Why This Expert Says We Should Be Worried." 13 February 2013, A11.
Mackrael, Kim. "Canada Has Lost Stature, Chretien Says." 13 March 2013, A1.
Marlow, Iain. "In Motion: Balsillie's Life after RIM." 15 February 2013, B1.
Martin, Patrick. "Pragmatic New Finance Minister Ventures into 'A Moment of Great Risk.'" 17 July 2013, A12.
McKenna, Barrie. "BRICs Wobble, World Watches." 20 April 2012, B1.
Momani, Bessma. "'Deep State' vs. 'Brotherhoodization.'" 21 August 2013, A13.
Morgan, Gwyn. "Questions Arise from the World of University Research." 16 April 2012, B11.
Rotberg, Robert I. "A Democratic Mali Is Worth Saving." 5 February 2013, A21.
Tieku, Thomas Kwasi. "Cutting Those Shameless Perks." 1 May 2012, A13.

NATIONAL POST
Hopper, Tristin. "Canada Makes Iran's 'Demonology Charts'; Kidnapped Children, Protest Crackdowns, and 'Skeletons in the Closet.'" 19 January 2013, A8.
Jenkins, Paul. "Limits to Monetary Policy; Global Economy Needs a Lot More Than Unconventional Monetary Policy to Secure Recovery and Growth." 19 July 2013, FP9.

Siklos, Pierre. "The 6.5% Non-solution; Fed's Unemployment Target
    Stretches Bounds of Policy." 21 June 2013, FP11.

OTTAWA CITIZEN
Berthiaume, Lee. "Iran, al-Qaida Seen as Unlikely Allies; Experts
    Puzzled over Group's Link to Railway Plot." 23 April 2013, A3.
Berthiaume, Lee, and Mike Blanchfield. "France Asks for Help;
    Ambassador Seeks Canadian Assistance to Pay for Fight against
    Islamists in Mali." 17 January 2013, A4.
Burney, Derek, and Fen Osler Hampson. "Canada Should Borrow
    Australia's Asian Plan." 9 November 2012, A13.
Campbell, Jennifer. "Canada Urged to Expand Trade with Middle
    East." 1 May 2013, C4.
– "Effective Work by Canada Kept ICAO Here; Qatari Embassy Has
    No Comment." 29 May 2013, D4.
– "Japanese Ambassador Bids Fond Farewell; Kaoru Ishikawa Notes
    Continuing Progress in Mutual Interests." 17 April 2013, C4.
– "US Envoy Outlines Next Four Years; Says Economic Issues Top
    Obama's Agenda." 20 February 2013, C4.
Hampson, Fen Osler. "Discordant Canada and the Cuban Missile
    Crisis; If the Crisis Had Happened Today, Writes Fen Osler
    Hampson, There Probably Would Have Been War." 22 October
    2012, A9.
Heinbecker, Paul. "In Defence of Diplomats and Diplomacy."
    17 September 2012, A9.
– "UN is the Forum for Peace and Prosperity." 3 December 2012, A10.
Quan, Douglas, and Mark Kennedy. "Al-Qaida Said to Be behind Plot;
    'Direction and Guidance' Given for Plan to Derail Train." 23 April
    2013, A1.
Rotberg, Robert I. "Can South Africa Recapture the Hope of the
    Mandela Years?" 24 June 2013, A11.
Tunney, Catharine. "Carleton Professor Lands Prestigious Gig: Global
    Security Work at Waterloo Think-Tank." 28 April 2012, E2.

TORONTO STAR
Brown, Louise. "Waterloo Schools Face Boycott over CIGI Ties."
    28 April 2012, A2.
Campion-Smith, Bruce. "Harper Makes His Bodyguard an
    Ambassador." 19 April 2013, A8.

– "'Nickel and Diming' on Diplomacy: Canada-UK Agreement to Share Embassies Sends 'Mixed or Muddled Message' Abroad, Critics Say." 25 September 2012, A6.

Cooper, Andrew. "Why Did Carney Cross the Ocean?" 27 November 2012, A19.

Goar, Carol. "What Is It about Balsillie's Money?" 4 May 2012, A19.

Gormley, Shannon, and Drew Gough. "Building in the Boom: Architecture in Kitchener-Waterloo Mirrors the Region's Innovation and New-Found Wealth." 13 October 2012, N6.

Hampson, Fen Osler. "Israel and Iran on the Brink: An Israeli Attack on Iran's Nuclear Facilities, Possibly Months or Only Weeks Away, and the Inevitable Retaliation Would Unleash a Crisis That Could Quickly Escalate beyond the Two Countries." 19 August 2012, A13.

Momani, Bessma. "Warm Greetings, Icy Relationship." 7 February 2013, A23.

Shephard, Michelle, and Andrew Livingstone. "Terror Plot Derailed: RCMP Charge Pair in Connection with Al Qaeda–Sponsored Scheme to Wreck VIA Train." 23 April 2013, A1.

Ward, Olivia. "Don't Worry about WWIII (Just Everything Else): Existential Threats on the Decline, but the Trends Point to a Turbulent Year." 5 January 2013, IN1.

– "Kim's Rhetorical Rampage Raises Threat of War." 9 March 2013, A14.

Whittington, Les. "PM Walking a Tightrope with Beijing: China's Role in Canadian Economy Still Unclear after Controversial Nexen Sale." 9 December 2012, A1.

VANCOUVER SUN

Berthiaume, Lee. "Al-Qaida's Links to Train Plot Unclear." 23 April 2013, B2.

– "Ottawa Holds Back on Action in Mali; 'War Weariness' and Belt-Tightening Mean Canada Is Unlikely to Ramp Up Its Role, Insiders Say." 17 January 2013, B1.

Cayo, Don. "African Economy Takes Flight at Last, but Canada Hardly Notices." 25 June 2013, C3.

Edwards, Len. "Free Trade Deal Will Help Chart Future of Canada-Korea Relations; A Free Trade Agreement Would Be a Critical Sign That Each Country Believes the Other Should Be One of Its Key International Partners." 15 August 2013, B7.

Selected Publications of the Centre for International
Governance Innovation

Blustein, Paul. "Laid Low: The IMF, the Euro Zone and the First
Rescue of Greece." *CIGI Paper* no. 61 (April 2015).
Boughton, James M. "The IMF as Just One Creditor: Who's in Charge
When a Country Can't Pay?" *CIGI Paper* no. 66 (April 2015).
Caucutt, Elizabeth, Lance Lochner, and Youngmin Park. *Why Do Poor
Children Perform So Poorly?* April 2015.
Crocker, Chester A., Fen Osler Hampson, and Pamela Aall, eds.
Managing Conflict in a World Adrift. January 2015.
Hinton, James W., and Kent Howe. *The New Innovator's Commercial-
ization Dilemma: A Report on the CIGI International Intellectual
Property Law Clinic.* April 2015.
Jepsen, Henrik. "Policy Options Could Increase Ambition in the 2015
Climate Agreement." *Fixing Climate Governance Series.* April 2015.
Medhora, Rohinton P. *Managing Coexistence in Global Trade
Agreements.* April 2015.
Oyegunle, Adeboye, and Olaf Weber. "Development of Sustainability
and Green Banking Regulations – Existing Codes and Practices."
CIGI Paper no. 65 (April 2015).
Wan Hongying. "The Asian Infrastructure Development Bank: A New
Bretton Woods Moment? A Total Chinese Triumph?" *CIGI Policy
Brief* no. 59 (April 2015).
Rotberg, Robert I., ed. *On Governance: What It Is, What It Measures
and Its Policy Uses.* April 2015.

CONFERENCE BOARD OF CANADA

Tank Facts

Established: 1954
Location: Ottawa
Budget: ~$40 million
Staff: ~200
President/Director   Daniel Muzyka
Website: www.conferenceboard.ca

The Conference Board of Canada is the largest policy research institution
in Canada, but despite its visibility, the board's origins can be traced to
the United States. In 1916, the Conference Board was established in New

York to "facilitate a cross-fertilization of facts and ideas in industry as a way of identifying and solving its problems and enhancing the public's understanding of these problems."[48] Like many other think tanks created during the progressive era, the founder of the Conference Board insisted that the organization engage in "unbiased fact finding" and "refrain from all political activity."[49]

During the decades following its founding, the Conference Board established itself as a highly credible and competent research organization that proved capable of addressing the needs of both American and Canadian companies. Indeed, as Lindquist points out, "With 40 large Canadian companies alone participating in the US-based organization, the creation of a Canadian office seemed a natural step."[50] In 1954, the Conference Board opened a small office in Montreal to respond to an expanding number of Canadian companies, Canadian-based US subsidiaries, and US companies interested in obtaining more information about Canada.[51]

The Conference Board of Canada has created a well-defined niche in the policy-making community. Unlike many smaller think tanks that attempt to influence public debates through their various publications and exchanges with policy-makers and journalists, the Conference Board specializes in providing knowledge in key areas to its members in the public and private sectors. In exchange for a membership fee, the Conference Board "[helps its] members anticipate and respond to the increasingly changing global economy ... through the exchange of knowledge about organizational strategies and practices, emerging economic and social trends and key public policy issues."[52] Its primary goal is to help its members become better prepared to adapt to changes in the marketplace.

As well as providing members with access to its publications and conferences, the Conference Board undertakes contract research. Known for its expertise in economic forecasting and analysis, the board also specializes in several other areas, including corporate social responsibility, human resource management, public sector management, and information and innovation and technology.[53]

Given its size and the breadth of its research expertise, it is not surprising that the Conference Board attracts more media attention than any other policy institute in Canada, a finding that the organization showcases in its annual reports.[54] To better assess its reach and impact, it also monitors, among other things, the hundreds of research reports it has published, the number of tweets it has posted, how many followers it has on Twitter, and the frequency with which it issues news releases and advisories.[55] When it comes to determining which performance indicators to consider in evaluating their impact, the Conference Board leaves few stones unturned.

*References to the Conference Board of Canada
in Selected Canadian Newspapers*

GAZETTE
"Cure the Health System without Sacrificing the Patient." 28 October
    2014.
"Economy Slowing, but Jobs Still Growing." 21 July 2011.
Hadekel, Peter. "Montreal's Economic Woes Reflect Conflicting
    Ambitions." 12 November 2014.
– "Stagnation City: Exploring Montreal's Economic Decline."
    31 January 2015.

NATIONAL POST
Antunes, Pedro. "With Little Wriggle Room, Hard Work Begins for Joe
    Oliver on Long-Delayed Budget." 2 April 2015, FP.
Gault, Cody. "5 Things You Should Know before You Start Your Work
    Today." 26 March 2015. FP.
Hodgson, Glen. "Leave Carbon Pricing to the Provinces." 7 April 2015.
    NP.
Isfeld, Gordon. "Why Canadians Should Stop Stressing about an
    Economy That Is Stuck in Second Gear." 10 March 2015. FP.
Hussain, Yadullah. "Canadian Gas Producers Face Another Down
    Year." 17 March 2015. NP.
Kabilan, Satyamoorthy. "Hack Attacks Hit Home: The Kind of Thing
    That CEOs Get Fired For." 2 February 2015. FP.
Morgan, Geoffrey. "Oilpatch Recovery a Long Way Out, Conference
    Board Report Says." 25 March 2015. FP.
Wein, Michelle. "Canada's False Patent Promise." 17 March 2015. NP.

OTTAWA CITIZEN
Ashby, Madeline. "An Economy That Lacks Imagination." 27 January
    2015.
Bagnall, James. "How Ottawa-Gatineau Rank among Canada's Cities."
    18 September 2014.

- "Ottawa-Gatineau Economy Is Ready to Rebound: Study."
  20 October 2014.
Chapin, Angelina. "The School System Can't Solve Child Poverty."
  5 September 2014.
Fekete, Jason. "Back to Parliament: Several Prickly Issues Face Federal
  Parties." 24 January 2015.
Fekete, Jason, and Jordan Press. "Harper Says Bank of Canada's Rate
  Cut 'Appropriate,' No New Stimulus Needed." 23 January 2015.
Goldfarb, Danielle. "Five Trade Trends for 2015 and How Canada Can
  Take Advantage of Them." 1 January 2015.
Jeffrey, Anja, and Satyamoorthy Kabilan. "Economic Development Key
  to Northern Security." 24 August 2014.

TORONTO STAR
Curran, Peggy. "From the Archive: Breaking the Poverty Cycle."
  14 December 2014.
De Silva, Jan, and Carol Wilding. "Now Is the Time for Toronto to Go
  Global." 4 April 2015.
Flavelle, Dana. "Falling Oil Prices Could Cut $10 Billion from
  Government Revenues: Conference Board." 20 January 2015.
- "Toronto's Economy Gets Boost, Says Conference Board of Canada."
  19 March 2015.
Harper, Tim. "The Three Pillars of Stephen Harper's Re-election
  Hopes." 25 January 2015.
Krugel, Lauren. "Conference Board of Canada: No Quick Bounce Back
  From Crude Downturn." 25 March 2015.

Selected Publications of the Conference Board of Canada

Aguilar Melissa, Jason D. Schloetzer, and Matteo Tonello. CEO
  Succession Practices: 2015 Edition. April 2015.
Behan, Beverly. *Board and Director Evaluations in the 21st Century*.
  April 2015.
Beckman, Kip. *World Outlook: Spring 2015*. April 2015.
Brender, Natalie, Adam Fiser, Anja Jeffrey, and Brent Dowdall. *Building
  a Resilient and Prosperous North: Centre for the North Five-Year
  Compendium Report*. April 2015.
Chenier, Louise. *Waking Up: The Real Risks of Fatigue in the
  Workplace*. June 2015.

Grant, Michael. *The Economic Impact of Post-Secondary Education.*
  May 2015.
Howard, Alison. *Corporate Community Investment Webinar: Emerging
  Trends and Measuring Impact in Canada.* June 2015.
Overmeer, Willem, and Bart van Ark. *Getting a Handle on Energy:
  Global Growth Scenarios in Times of Changing Oil Prices.* April
  2015.
Palladini, Jacqueline. *Spotlight on High-Value Services: Canada's
  Hidden Export Strength.* May 2015.
Vachon, Donna Burnett. *Developing Your Future Leaders: The
  Leadership Development Outlook.* September 2015.

FRASER INSTITUTE

Tank Facts

Established:	1974
Location:	Vancouver
Budget:	~$8.5 million
Staff:	~60
President/Director	Niels Veldhuis
Website:	www.fraserinstitute.org

Well before Prime Minister Trudeau announced in his 1974 Christmas message that "the marketplace was not a reliable economic institution and would increasingly have to be replaced by government action in order to sustain the economic well-being of Canadians," the idea for creating the Vancouver-based Fraser Institute had already been cultivated.[56] Increasingly concerned by the federal government's Keynesian economic policies and the election of the first NDP government in British Columbia in 1972, T. Patrick Boyle, a senior industrial executive and then vice-president of planning at MacMillan Bloedel, began considering how best to inform Canadians about the crucial role that markets play in economic development. After meetings with several business leaders and economists, including Csaba Hajdu and Michael Walker, Boyle "conceived the establishment of an economic and social research institution which he felt had to be unlike any other in existence in Canada."[57]

In early 1974, Boyle enlisted the support of the Honourable J.V. Clyne to raise money for the institute and managed to generate $75,000. Boyle

also began working closely with Walker, Hajdu, and several other individuals, including John Raybould and Sally Pipes, to draft the institute's
mission statement and operating plan. On 21 October 1974, the charter
of the Fraser Institute, "so named for the mighty Fraser River, thereby
giving this new institute a geographical, rather than ideological reference
point," was granted by the Canadian government.[58]

The Fraser Institute experienced little difficulty locating its geographical or its ideological reference point when it opened its doors, but it
became preoccupied with staying afloat. With meagre resources during
its first year of operation, fundraising became the greatest challenge confronting the newly created organization. Sir Antony Fisher, Fraser's acting director and founder of several other policy institutes, including the
Institute of Economic Affairs in London, coordinated Fraser's fundraising efforts in 1975. A year later, Fisher left the staff of the Fraser Institute,
and Sally Pipes, who had worked in the British Columbia government's
statistical agency and for the Council of Forest Industries in the province,
assumed fundraising and membership responsibilities. Michael Walker,
who had worked in the Department of Finance and at the Bank of
Canada before joining Fraser, became the Institute's research and editorial director, a position he held until the fall of 2005, when he was
replaced by Mark Mullins.[59] The current president of the Fraser Institute
is Niels Velhuis, an economist. The institute's operating revenue and
media profile steadily increased in the last quarter of the twentieth century and continues to grow in the new millennium. With a full-time staff
of over sixty and a budget in the $8–9 million range, Fraser has become
one of Canada's most talked about and written about think tanks. Indeed,
in its annual reports, it goes to great lengths to provide detailed statistics
on its media exposure and ranking in the *Global Go To Think Tanks
Index Report*.[60] Fraser also oversees an active research program that has
resulted in the publication of a monthly opinion journal, *The Fraser
Forum*, and dozens of books, conference reports, and bulletins. Because
it also recognizes the importance of encouraging and training future generations of conservative thinkers, the institute sponsors a university student internship program and an annual student essay competition.

As a free-market think tank, Fraser has cultivated a reputation, and
deservedly so, as a conservative advocacy-oriented institute that places
considerable emphasis on shaping public opinion and public policy.
Indeed, its propensity to propose market solutions to economic problems has often made it an easy target for critics.

References to the Fraser Institute
in Selected Canadian Newspapers

CALGARY HERALD

Buchanan, Fiona. "Report Finds Canada First in Education." 25 June 2013, A20.

Milke, Mark. "BC Homeowners Learn a Heritage Lesson the Hard Way." 15 June 2013, A11.

– "Canada's Founding Fathers Had the Right Idea." 29 June 2013, A17.

– "The Harper Tories' Multibillion-Dollar Transparency Problem." 22 June 2013, A15.

– "What Governments Did While You Were on Holiday." 6 July 2013, A15.

NATIONAL POST

Bourdais, Michaelle, and Ravina Bains. "Let First Nations Thrive." 21 June 2013, A10.

Dowd, Alan. "Why Canada Needs Missile Defences." 9 July 2013, A12.

Foster, Peter. "Ding! Get Your Carbon $." 14 June 2013, FP11.

Gerson, Jen. "Owning Homes a Benefit to Native Well-Being: Study; Fraser Institute Extols Private Ownership." 20 June 2013, A6.

Kesselman, Rhys. "What Caused RRSP Dip?" 12 July 2013, FP11.

Kheiriddin, Tasha. "Tony Clement's $3 Suitcase." 18 July 2013, A10.

Kline, Jesse. "Let Interns Work for Free." 19 June 2013, A10.

VANCOUVER SUN

Andrews, Chris. "Progressive Income Taxes Cut While Regressive Taxes Climb." 12 July 2013, 14.

Beardsley, Richard. "Public School Students Receive Quality Education." 20 June 2013, A15.

Esmail, Nadeem. "'Fat Tax' is Bad Public Policy; No Single Food or Beverage is Responsible for Obesity." 16 July 2013, A11.

Keeselman, Rhys. "CPP Expansion Not Hindered by RRSP Responses." 16 July 2013, A11.

Milke, Mark. "Canada as Seen through the Eyes of Our Founding Fathers." 29 June 2013, D5.

Mulgrew, Ian. "Victoria's Approach on Heritage Property Dispute Is Draconian." 2 July 2013, A4.

Sherlock, Tracy. "Controversial Report Card Ranks Private Schools High." 18 June 2013, A5.

WINNIPEG FREE PRESS
Cash, Martin. "Eviction Notice Adds to Gloom in Mining Sector."
4 July 2013, A14.

GLOBE AND MAIL
McFarland, Janet. "Expanding CPP Could Reduce Voluntary Saving,
Study Warns." 26 June 2013, B3.
Moist, Paul. "Grow the CPP." 1 July 2013, A8.
Yakabuski, Konrad. "McGuinty's Green Energy 'Vision' Starts to Fade."
27 June 2013, A13.

TORONTO STAR
Acharya-Tom Yew, Madhavi. "Better Late Than Never for Tax Freedom
Day." 17 June 2013, B2.

Selected Publications of the Fraser Institute

Bacchus, Barua, and Nadeem Esmail. "Regulation Review: Giving
Canadians Faster Access to New Medicines." *Fraser Forum.*
November/ December 2013.
Boudreaux, Donald, eds. *What America's Decline in Economic
Freedom Means for Entrepreneurship and Prosperity.* April 2015.
Clemens, Jason, Milagros Palacios, and Niels Veldhuis. "Reforming Old
Age Security: A Good Start but Incomplete." *Fraser Forum.*
November/ December 2013.
Clemens, Jason, Milagros Palacios, Niels Veldhuis, and Robert
P. Murphy. *Economic Principles for Prosperity.* December 2014.
Clemens, Jason, and Niels Veldhuis. "Should Right-to-Work Come to
Canada?" *Fraser Forum.* November/December 2013.
Di Matteo, Livio. *Measuring Government in the 21st Century.* January
2014.
Green, Kenneth P. "Pensions and Government Both Hurting from
Canada's Inability to Ship Oil to Market." *Fraser Forum.* November/
December 2013.
Milke, Mark. "Controlling Soaring Public Sector Pension Costs: Lessons
from the Saskatchewan NDP." *Fraser Forum.* November/December
2013.
Williams, Walter. "Honesty & Trust." *Fraser Forum.* November/
December 2013.

FRONTIER CENTRE FOR PUBLIC POLICY

Tank Facts

Established: 1997
Location: Winnipeg, Calgary, Regina
Budget: ~$1 million
Staff: 8 staff; 15 research fellows
President/Director: Peter Holle
Website: www.fcpp.org

Founded in Winnipeg, the Frontier Centre for Public Policy (FCPP) also has offices in two other Prairie cities: Calgary and Regina. Relying on a "core group of staff and policy analysts who work with outside experts to conduct research on a wide variety of issues at the federal, provincial, and municipal levels," the goal of the free market "libertarian" think tank is "to develop effective and meaningful ideas for good governance and reform."[61] As its name implies, the Frontier Centre is concerned primarily with initiating conversations that focus on the political, social, and economic challenges confronting the Prairies, although it also addresses several national concerns. To this end, it publishes over two dozen policy papers each year on topics ranging from the feasibility of constructing two new hydroelectric dams in Manitoba to restructuring transportation subsidies in Saskatchewan to assessing the state of environmental sustainability in Canada.

In addition to producing policy papers and holding workshops and seminars around various themes, the Frontier Centre makes its views known through the dozens of media commentaries it publishes each year and by updating many of its followers through Twitter and Facebook. It also conveys its ideas through a weekly radio program that is broadcast in seventeen cities across the Prairies.[62] Despite modest resources, the western-based think tank has made its presence felt in Western Canada and throughout the country.

References to the Frontier Centre for Public Policy
in Selected Canadian Newspapers

CALGARY HERALD
Corbella, Licia. "Jack and Gilles Take Over Parliament Hill."
3 December 2008.

Moore, Patrick. "Better to Have Global Warming Than Global Cooling."
24 September 2014.

LEADER-POST
Chabun, Will. "Think Tank Pushes Service Reduction." 13 February
2015.
– "Trim Down Civil Service, Think Tank Suggests." 12 February 2015.
Niebergall, Stu. "Economic Gains Offset by Housing Costs."
9 December 2013.

TORONTO STAR
Ferguson, Rob. "Medicare Takes a Back Seat." 28 September 2008.
Goar, Carol. "PM's Friends Are His Biggest Mistake." 19 July 2010.
Gorrie, Peter. "Another Earth Hour Ignored: Too Bad, It's the Right
Idea." 3 April 2010.
Lafleur, Steve. "The Roots of Toronto's Budget Crisis." 17 August
2011.
MacKinnon, David. "Ontario: Cash Cow for the Rest of Canada."
25 February 2011.
Pentland, Ralph, and Jim Bruce. "How Much Longer Can We Go
without Leadership on Water?" 11 September 2008.
Tuckey, Bruce. "Need for GTA Development Competing with Greenbelt
Act." 15 December 2014.

WINNIPEG FREE PRESS (ONLINE EDITION)
"The Dangers of Hog Expansion Moratorium." 18 September 2011.
"Focus on the Child, Not Region." 19 January 2010.
"Frontier Centre Touts Water Export." 24 June 2008.
"Manitoba Movers." 12 January 2009.
"Per Student-Costs in Manitoba Rising: Think-Tank." 6 January 2015.
"The Rights Thing." 24 January 2011.
"Winnipeg's Housing Affordability Erodes." 25 January 2010.
"Winnipeg Ranks Low on Government Transparency: Think-Tank."
4 February 2014.

Selected Publications of the Frontier Centre for Public Policy

Atkins, Frank. "Issues Concerning Heritage Preservation." 10 November
2015.

Enright, Jane, Halina Sapeha, and Conrad Winn. "Self-Governance
for First Nations." 17 November 2015.
Flanagan, Tom, and Laura Johnson. "Towards a First Nations
Governance Index." 2 December 2015.
Moore, Patrick. "Alarmism in Perspective." 24 November 2015.
Shimuzu, Hiroko, and Pierre Desrochers. "Speed or Greed: Does
Automated Traffic Enforcement Improve Safety or Generate
Revenue?" 8 December 2015.

INSTITUTE FOR RESEARCH ON PUBLIC POLICY

Tank Facts

Established:	1972
Location:	Montreal
Budget:	$2–$2.5 million
Staff:	15
President / Director:	Graham Fox
Website:	www.irpp.org

The Institute for Research on Public Policy (IRPP) is unique among Canadian think tanks. To begin with, with the exception of CIGI and a handful
of other think tanks, it is one of the few policy institutes in the country
whose financial security has been guaranteed by a sizeable endowment.
With a current market value of close to $40 million, IRPP's "endowment
fund was built up in the 1970s and 1980s by $10 million from the private
sector and provincial governments, matched by $10 million from the fed-
eral government."[63] Since the interest earned from the endowment covers
most of IRPP's operating expenses, the IRPP, unlike other think tanks in
Canada, does not have to mount annual fundraising campaigns. IRPP is
also unique because it is among the few independent English-language
public-policy research institutes in Quebec. After IRPP opened its doors in
Montreal in 1972, its head office moved to several cities, including Ottawa,
Halifax, and Victoria, before relocating to Montreal in 1991.

The IRPP's creation was inspired by the eminent Canadian economist
Ronald Ritchie, who was commissioned by Prime Minister Trudeau in
1968 to examine the feasibility of creating an independent multidisci-
plinary research institute in Canada. After surveying the think tank landscape in several countries, including the United States, and after
interviewing dozens of think tank directors and policy-makers, Ritchie
recommended that an institute similar to the Brookings Institution be

established in Canada to provide long-term strategic analysis. Although Ritchie's report did not result in the creation of a think tank on the scale of the Brookings Institution, it did lead to the founding of the IRPP and several other policy research institutes.

Remaining loyal to Ritchie's vision of an institute conducting independent policy analysis, IRPP has undertaken a "measured approach to public policy, which revolves around informing policy debates rather than advancing a particular ideological position."[64] It seeks to inform and educate policy-makers and the public, primarily through its magazine *Policy Options* and through its book-length studies. While staff members from the institute have also testified before parliamentary committees and submitted op-ed articles to Canadian newspapers, IRPP has claimed in the past that enhancing its media profile is not a priority. However, this position appears to have changed as the institute, mirroring other think tanks, pays close attention to its "impact" in the public arena. Indeed, on the first page of its *2014 Annual Report*, IRPP summarizes its impact by highlighting in bold blue that in the past year, it recorded: 370,322 website page views, 111,280 website visitors, 2,440 Twitter Followers, 332 Facebook Followers, 615 stories in the media, 17 publications, 16 events, and published 6 issues of *Policy Options*.[65]

Despite allocating the bulk of its $2–$2.5 million budget to research, the IRPP has not developed significant in-house expertise. Indeed, rather than hiring several researchers, the institute, like C.D. Howe, relies on its small staff to coordinate research projects that are undertaken largely by academics at various universities. IRPP's current research activity focuses on several areas, including: skills and labour market policy, international trade and global commerce, faces of aging, income inequality, and health and public policy.

References to the Institute for Research on Public Policy in Selected Canadian Newspapers

NATIONAL POST
Cross, Philip. "The Idea Marketers: Canada Should Cull Proliferation of Think Tanks, Let Market Do the Funding." 24 September 2014, FP.
Reevely, David. "Seniors' Discounts for Public Services a Worsening Drain on Cities' Finances, Report Warns." 28 February 2015, NP.
Watson, William. "Ideas Market Works Fine." 26 August 2014, FP.

OTTAWA CITIZEN

Butler, Don. "Trudeau Plants Seeds of 'Revolution' by Expelling Liberal Senators from Caucus." 30 January 2014.

May, Kathryn. "Fixing the Public Service: Groom Stronger, Specialized Managers for Public Service." 3 September 2014.

Winter, Jesse. "Indian Prime Minister Modi Will Face Mixed Reception in Ottawa Tuesday." 13 April 2015.

TORONTO STAR

Bernier, Nicole F. "Drugs Are No Solution to Nursing Home Underfunding." 21 May 2014.

Flavelle, Dana. "CAW Steers Auto Debate." 16 April 2012.

Goar, Carol. "Canada Can Be Green without Sacrificing Growth." 11 November 2014.

– "Provinces Push Pharmacare out of Reach." 3 March 2015.

– "Time to Pull the Plug on Auto Subsidies." 24 February 2014.

Lang, Eugene. "Industrial Policy Is Back – Except in Ontario." 14 July 2013.

Regg Cohn, Martin. "Why Ontario's Economy Is Running Out of Energy." 7 December 2013.

Tam, Vivian. "It's Time for a Universal Pharmacare System." 11 December 2014.

Selected Publications of the Institute for Research on Public Policy

Assaf, Dany H., and Rory A. McGillis. *Foreign Direct Investment and the National Interest: A Way Forward.* 18 April 2013.

"Building a Brighter Future." *Policy Options.* March–April 2015.

Drummond, Don. *Wanted: Good Canadian Labour Market Information.* 11 June 2014.

– "Environmental Faith." *Policy Options.* January–February 2015.

Finnie, Ross, and David Gray. *Labour-Force Participation of Older Displaced Workers in Canada: Should I Stay or Should I Go?* 24 February 2011.

Halliwell, Cliff. *No Shortage of Opportunity: Policy Ideas to Strengthen Canada's Labour Market in the Coming Decade Focus on Skills, Not the Number of Workers, as Workforce Ages.* 8 November 2013.

Hicks, Peter. *The Enabling Society.* 9 April 2015.

Morgan, Steven G., Jamie R. Daw, and Michael R. Law. *Are Income-Based Public Drug Benefit Programs Fit for an Aging Population?* 3 December 2014.
- "Policyflix." *Policy Options.* November–December 2014.
Van Assche, Ari. *Global Value Chains and the Rise of a Supply Chain Mindset.* 28 April 2015.

INSTITUTE ON GOVERNANCE

Tank Facts

Established: 1990
Location: Ottawa
Budget: $1.5–$2 million
Staff: 23
President/Director: Maryanntonett Flumian
Website: www.iog.ca

Located in the heart of Ottawa's historic Byward Market,[66] the Institute on Governance (IOG) has as its mission to advance "better governance in the public interest, which the institute accomplishes by exploring, developing and promoting the principles, standards and practices which underlie good governance in the public sphere."[67] With expertise rooted in "innovative leadership practices, ongoing and applied research and practice-based insights," the IOG works with governments, local communities, and the voluntary and private sectors to establish and promote more effective institution building.

According to its website, the IOG offers its clients:

1) A systems approach taking into account the interaction of complex systems and decision-making;

2) A neutral, impartial, independent and confidential working environment for clients addressing real-time governance challenges;

3) Access to a network of leading thinkers on governance, with domestic and global expertise in the government, private and non-profit sectors, as well as Indigenous and other governance areas;

4) A documentation centre and access to research and development resources to enable clients to apply leading-edge practices.[68]

Although much of the research the IOG conducts is commissioned by various organizations, it has maintained core expertise in five principal areas: public governance exchange, digital governance applied research, talent management exchange, indigenous research agenda, and board and organizational governance.[69] The IOG does not provide its annual reports online.

References to the Institute on Governance
in Selected Canadian Newspapers

NATIONAL POST

May, Kathryn. "Canadians Harsh on Governments in New Survey: Only 22% Believe Federal Level Is Working." 29 December 2014, NP.
Quesnel, Joseph. "Demand Accountability for Taxpayer-Funded Native Groups." 28 June 2010.

OTTAWA CITIZEN

May, Kathryn. "Canadians Satisfied with Life – If They Have Enough Money." 30 December 2014.
– "Harper Gets New Security Adviser amid Major Shuffle of Senior Public Service." 6 January 2015.
– "Local Government Gets Better Marks Than Other Levels." 28 December 2014.
– "Mistrust between Bureaucrats and Politicians Bad for Canada: Survey." 27 December 2014.
– "Reforms to Bring Neutrality to Public Service Could Lead to 'Government by the Unelected': Think Tank." 27 June 2014.

TORONTO STAR

Delacourt, Susan. "Canadians' Trust in Elections Low before 2015 Federal Vote." 2 January 2015.
Editorial. "Stephen Harper Is Wrong on Murdered Aboriginal Women." 22 August 2014.

Selected Publications of the Institute on Governance

Cain, Todd, Laura Edgar, and Dustin Munroe. *The Not for Profit Board's Role in Stakeholder Relations: Survey Results and Analysis.* 11 July 2014.
The Environs Institute. *2014 Survey of Public Opinion on Public Governance in Canada.* 6 January 2015.

Nason, Eddy. *The Return on Investment in Team: Return on Investment Analysis Framework, Indicators and Data for Interprofessional Care and Interprofessional Education in Health.* 24 May 2013.

Nickerson, Marcia. *Closing the Gap – Beyond Section 35 BC Symposium Summary.* 25 April 2013.

– *Public Service Transformation: Public Sector Human Resources and Talent Management.* 1 September 2014.

– *Report from Our July 22 Event on 'Nudges' and Behavioural Economics.* 8 August 2014.

– *Revisiting RCAP – Towards Reconciliation: The Future of Indigenous Governance.* 14 January 2015.

– *Revisiting the Royal Commission on Aboriginal Peoples.* 30 October 2014.

Salgo, Karl. *A Risk Lens on Governance – A Public Governance Exchange Discussion Paper.* 4 July 2013.

Salgo, Karl, and Tim Gauthier. *Case Study: The Governance Continuum and the Canadian Wheat Board: 1965–2017.* 19 December 2012.

INTERNATIONAL INSTITUTE FOR SUSTAINABLE DEVELOPMENT

Tank Facts

Established:	1990
Location:	Winnipeg (with branch offices in Ottawa, New York, Geneva, and Beijing)
Budget:	~$17 million
Staff:	~200
President/Director:	Scott Vaughan
Website:	www.iisd.org

Headquartered in Winnipeg, the International Institute for Sustainable Development (IISD) operates in over thirty countries. The origin of the IISD can be traced to Prime Minister Brian Mulroney's decision in 1988 "to establish an international institute dedicated to advancing sustainable development at the United Nations."[70] As the IISD recalls, "the idea for the institute was rooted in recommendations by a National Task Force on Environment and Economy ... also known as the Brundtland Report ... published in 1987."[71] Three years later, at the Globe Conference in Vancouver, Manitoba's Premier Gary Filmon and Canada's Environment Minister Lucien Bouchard signed the agreement that officially created IISD.[72]

With a mandate "to help improve the well-being of the world's environment, economy and society ... the institute champions global sustainable development through innovation, research and relationships that span the entire world."[73] The IISD works closely with decision-makers in government, non-governmental organizations, and other sectors to advance its core mission. As a charitable organization that received core funding from CIDA, an organization cut by the Harper government, the International Development Research Centre (IDRC), and the Province of Manitoba, and project funding from various foreign governments, United Nations agencies, foundations, and private individuals, IISD carries out research in the fields of economic law and policy, and energy and water. Much of its work is coordinated through its branch offices in the United States, Switzerland, and China.

References to the International Institute for Sustainable Development in Selected Canadian Newspapers

TORONTO STAR
Aulakh, Raveena. "Experimental Lakes Saved but Faces Uncertain Future." 2 April 2014.
Cheadle, Bruce. "Feds Spend $40 Million to Pitch Natural Resources." 28 November 2013.
MacCharles, Tonda. "G8 Leaders Set Sights on Economic Fix." 6 July 2009.
Watson, Paul. "Norway Has a Nest Egg. Should We? Is Norway's Nest Egg a Lesson for Canada?" 23 August 2014.
Woods, Allan. "Canada's Climate Change Plans to Fall Short, New Study Says." 7 November 2011.
– "Tories Feel the Heat over Climate." 15 January 2009.
– "US Green Scheme Beats Canada's." 1 December 2009.

WINNIPEG FREE PRESS
"Agreement Finalized on Transfer of Experimental Lakes Area." 1 April 2014.
Paul, Alexandra. "Manitobans Deeply in Touch with Their Green Sides: Poll." 13 February 2015.
– "Pellets of Power." 25 April 2014.
– "10 Successes since Rio." 29 August 2002.
Turner, James. "'Enormous Benefits,' in ELA Research as Manitoba, Ontario Commit Interim Funding." 2 September 2013.

Wazny, Adam. "Winnipeggers Feel Better about Their City Than They Realize, Study Indicates." 20 March 2015.
– "The World Summit: 10 Failures since Rio." 1 September 2002.

*Selected Publications of the International Institute
for Sustainable Development*

Brooks, David B. *Prioritizing 'No Significant Harm' over 'Reasonable and Equitable' in Governance of Aquifers.* 20 March 2015.
Chenghui, Zhang, Simon Zadek, Chen Ning, and Mark Halle. *Greening China's Financial System: Synthesis Report.* 16 March 2015.
Denjean, Benjamin, Jason Dion, Lei Huo, and Tilmann Liebert. *Green Public Procurement in China: Quantifying the Benefits.* 16 April 2015.
Harris, Melissa, Philip Gass, Anne Hammill, Jo-Ellen Parry, Jason Dion, Robert Repetto, and Yanick Touchette. *Towards a Low Carbon, Climate Resilient Ontario: IISD Input to MOECC's Climate Change.* 13 April 2015.
Kidney, Sean, Beate Sonerud, and Padraig Oliver. *Growing a Green Bonds Market in China.* 1 March 2015.
Pan, Tao, Yu Geng, and David Sawyer. *Business Sentiments Survey of China's Low-Carbon and Energy Policies.* 6 March 2015.
Sawyer, David, and Hubert Thieriot. *Policy Trends and Drivers of Low-Carbon Development in China's Industrial Zones.* 6 March 2015.
Silva, Mariana Hug, and George Scott. *Empowering Small and Medium-Sized Enterprises (SMEs) by Leveraging Public Procurement: Eight Big Ideas From Mexico.* 23 March 2015.
Stiebert, Seton. *Implementing Greenhouse Gas Inventory Management Systems for Economic Zones in China.* 6 March 2015.
Thieriot, Hubert, and Carlos Dominguez. *Public-Private Partnerships in China: On 2014 as a Landmark Year, with Past and Future Challenges.* 16 April 2015.

MACDONALD-LAURIER INSTITUTE FOR PUBLIC POLICY

Tank Facts

Established: 2010
Location: Ottawa
Budget: ~$1 million
Staff: 5 staff; 11 research fellows

President/Director: Brian Lee Crowley
Website: www.macdonaldlaurier.ca

Named in honour of two of Canada's most beloved prime ministers (a diehard conservative and a passionate liberal) the Macdonald-Laurier Institute (MLI) burst onto the think tank scene with a mission to "make poor quality public policy unacceptable in Ottawa."[74] To achieve this, the MLI is committed to "proposing thoughtful alternatives to Canadians and their political and opinion leaders through non-partisan and independent research and commentary."[75] Founded by Brian Lee Crowley, founding president of the Atlantic Institute for Market Studies (AIMS), the small but dynamic institute, with markedly conservative leanings, has made its presence felt in key policy-making circles. No stranger to the world of think tanks, Crowley has assembled an impressive cohort of research fellows to weigh in on several formidable policy challenges in several policy areas, including national defence and security, foreign affairs, Aboriginal issues, energy, justice, and immigration. He has also paid close attention to the many channels upon which the MLI can rely to convey its ideas to key stakeholders. In addition to showcasing several books and studies authored by scholars affiliated with the MLI, the institute publishes a magazine, *Inside Policy*, published six times a year. It also releases a steady stream of policy commentaries and a report entitled *The MLI Leading Indicator* which tracks recent trends in the economy. To further enhance its presence in the nation's capital and around the country and to highlight the importance of the domestic and foreign policy challenges confronting Canadians, the Institute sponsors several conferences, seminars, and debates that have featured many prominent policy-makers, journalists, and academics.

Well aware of the difficulty think tanks have in measuring their impact, the MLI, like many of its competitors, relies on several performance indicators and rankings from the *Global Go To Think Tanks Index Report* to assess its standing. In its *2013 Annual Report,* the MLI points out that, according to the 2013 edition of the think tank index, "it ranked third in the world in the category of best young institute," and indeed with "great policy products, it also managed to rank ahead of other older think tanks."[76] The MLI also keeps tabs of how often it is referenced by the national media and how many followers it has on Twitter and Facebook. In its annual report, it also references the number of visitors annually that access its website. However, unlike most think tanks that offer little more than statistics to convince readers how much influence they ostensibly wield, the MLI provides information about how and why it believes it was able to help shape policy discussions. Indeed, in the section devoted to "Impact and Public Policy" in its annual report, the MLI makes a concerted effort to demonstrate the similarities between its policy recommendations and legislation adopted by policy-makers.[77] Although far more research must be undertaken to confirm their findings, the MLI at least recognizes the importance of offering more than mere statistics about the influence it exercises.

References to the Macdonald-Laurier Institute in Selected Canadian Newspapers

NATIONAL POST

Buckley, F.H. "Yes, Incomes Are Less Equal. But There Isn't Much We Can Do about It." 30 March 2015, FP.

Cross, Philip. "Why the Provinces Are Mired in Debt, While the Federal Government Is Just Fine." 15 April 2015, FP.

Freeland, Chrystia. "The Erosion of Middle-Class Jobs in Canada Is Finally Being Exposed." 30 March 2015, FP.

Ivison, John. "Rejection of Mandatory Minimum for Gun Crimes Confirms Supremes' Politicization." 14 April 2015, NP.

Kay, Barbara. "Universities Are Teaching Students What to Think, Not How to Think." 11 March 2015, NP.

Newman, Dwight. "A Court Gone Astray on the Right to Strike." 26 February 2015, NP.

OTTAWA CITIZEN

Brewster, Murray. "Brain Drain, Staff Cuts and Red Tape Blamed for Dysfunctional DND Purchasing." 14 January 2015.

Crowley, Brian Lee. "Japan, Not China, Key to Canada's Asia-Pacific Aspirations." 27 March 2015.

– "The Power of Money in Politics." 30 January 2015.

MacLeod, Ian. "Liberals Ignored Science-Based Evidence, Too." 27 February 2015.

– "Supreme Court Strikes at Mandatory-Minimum Sentences." 14 April 2015.

Perry, David. "How to Fix Defence Procurement." 21 January 2015.

– "Photos: Around Town at Macdonald-Laurier Dinner." 19 February 2015.

TORONTO STAR

Ali Khan, Mohammed Azhar. "Islamaphobia Raises Its Head in
Immigration Debate." 4 March 2014.
Goar, Carol. "New Safety Nets Needed for Era of Chronic Inequality."
14 April 2015.
Harper, Tim. "Conservatives Hold Their Breath as US Election Day
Looms." 9 October 2012.
Levitz, Stephanie. "Right-Leaning Charities Escape Tax Audits, Broad-
bent Institute Says." 21 October 2014.
Morton, Peter. "Trans-Pacific Partnership: How Canada's Inclusion
Changes Dynamic at the Table." 21 June 2012.

*Selected Publications of the Macdonald-Laurier Institute
for Public Policy*

Auld, Douglas, and Ross McKitrick. *Money to Burn: Assessing the
Costs and Benefits of Canada's Strategy for Vehicle Biofuels.*
26 June 2014.
Cairns, Malcolm. *Staying on the Right Track: A Review of Canadian
Freight Rail Policy.* 20 February 2015.
Coates, Ken. *Sharing the Wealth: How Resource Revenue Agreements
Can Honour Treaties, Improve Communities, and Facilitate
Canadian Development.* 27 January 2015.
Cross, Philip. *Giving and Taking Away: How Taxes and Transfers
Address Inequality in Canada.* 16 April 2015.
Hage, Robert. *Risk, Prevention and Opportunity: Northern Gateway
and the Marine Environment.* 13 March 2015.
Murphy, Robert P. *The Carbon Tax Win-Win: Too Good to Be True?*
30 October 2014.
Perrin, Benjamin. *The Supreme Court of Canada: Policy-Maker of the
Year (2014).* 27 November 2014.
Perry, David. *Putting the 'Armed' Back into the Canadian Armed Forces:
Improving Defence Procurement in Canada.* 14 January 2015.
Sheikh, Munir. *Great Gatsby v. Zero Dollar Linda: Assessing the
Relationship Between Income Inequality, Social Mobility and the Tax
Transfer System.* 9 April 2015.
Singleton, Solveig. *Finding the Balance on Digital Privacy: Toward
a New Canadian Model for Data Protection in the 21st Century.*
10 June 2014.

MONTREAL ECONOMIC INSTITUTE (MEI)

Tank Facts

Established: 1999
Location: Montreal
Budget: $2.25 million
Staff: 13
President/Director: Michel Kelly-Gagnon
Website: www.iedm.org

"When he launched the MEI's operations in 1999, our current President and CEO Michel Kelly-Gagnon, had at his disposal a staggering budget of $15,000, and his office equipment consisted of a telephone and a fax machine set up in one corner of his apartment," recalls Hélène Desmarais, chairman of MEI's board in the organization's *2014 Annual Report*.[78] But a year later, with the backing of a small group of supporters, the free-market-oriented MEI was able to escape obscurity in its journey toward occupying a visible presence on Quebec's public policy landscape. Its goal is clear: "to stimulate debate on public policies in Quebec and across Canada by proposing wealth-creating reforms based on market mechanisms."[79] With a budget of little more than $2 million, raised primarily from individual donors, businesses, and foundations (no government money is accepted), the MEI has established itself as a strong and assertive voice on provincial and federal policy initiatives. Critical to MEI's success has been its ability to engage the media and other key stakeholders. As Michel Kelly-Gagnon acknowledges, "The evolution of the MEI's status to that of a privileged media partner was confirmed in 2014. Never worried about stirring things up and ruffling a few feathers, the MEI's researchers are still ready and willing to challenge preconceptions. But they are now increasingly cited for their original research, referenced as representative of one of the main positions in a debate, and invited to clarify a complex policy issue."[80]

MEI's research focus is wide-ranging and includes studies on agriculture, energy, health care, housing, labour, and taxation. In addition to the many studies and policy briefs it has published, the institute encourages its scholars to interact with the media. According to its findings in 2013–2014, the MEI was referenced by the media over 4,387 times, had 2,307 followers on Facebook, 3,590 followers on Twitter, and 24,401 views on YouTube.[81] And like the Macdonald-Laurier Institute, the MEI has taken steps to explain how it has made a difference in various public policy debates. There is little doubt that it has made great strides since its humble beginnings.

References to the Montreal Economic Institute
in Selected Canadian Newspapers

MONTREAL GAZETTE

Canadian Press. "Fourth Wireless Carrier Could Result in $1 Billion Savings: Competition Bureau." 15 May 2014.

Derfel, Aaron. "Number of Quebec Doctors Opting out of Medicare Up Sharply." 9 June 2014.

Magder, Jason. "Are Tolls on the New Champlain Bridge Inevitable?" 17 December 2014.

– "Surprise! Canada's Cell Phone Rates Are Competitive." 13 September 2012.

Mennie, James. "Cocaine, Protests and Debt?" 7 Match 2013.

News Desk. "Could Cannabis Regulation Eliminate Quebec's Deficit?" 12 March 2014.

NATIONAL POST

Corcoran, Terrence. "Billions Lost, but Ottawa Keeps Purchasing Wireless Carrier." FP. 17 September 2014.

Foster, Peter. "The Carbon in the Climate Talks." FP. 12 December 2014.

Kheiriddin, Tasha. "Another 'Maple Spring' Likely Not." NP. 25 March 2015.

Kline, Jesse. "Homeowners Should Have Choice." NP. 20 November 2013.

McParland, Kelly. "Blame Alberta: Death Comes to 'No New Taxes' as 'Tax and Spend' Rises from the Grave." NP. 31 March 2015.

Solomon, Lawrence. "When Quebec Will Leave." 13 March 2014, FP.

TORONTO STAR

Chung, Andrew. "Disorder Descends to New Level as Some Bombs Shut Down Montreal Subway." 10 May 2012.

MacCharles, Tonda. "Think-Tank Says It Was Targeted with Tax Audit Because of Its Politics." 5 September 2014.

Opinion. "Rotating Strikes: Canada Post's Death March." 6 June 2011.

Shalom, Francois. "Direct Flights Will Fuel Montreal's Development."

Woods, Allan. "Quebec Weighs Mandatory Prices for New Books."
9 August 2013.

Wright, Lisa. "Think Tank Urges Canada to Flow towards Water
Exporting." 27 August 2008.

Selected Publications of the Montreal Economic Institute

Bédard, Mathieu, and Jasmin Guénette. *Private Reinforcements for
Public Police Forces?* 29 January 2015.

Chassin, Youri, and Alexandre Moreau. *Viewpoint – Public Sector Pay
Grades.* 12 March 2015.

– *Viewpoint – The Tax Burden and Disposable Income of Quebecers.*
14 April 2015.

Chassin, Youri, and Bradley Doucet. *Viewpoint – Quebec's Energy
Choices: For Richer or Poorer?* 23 April 2015.

Descôteaux, David. *The Cree and the Development of Natural
Resources.* 19 March 2015.

Labrie, Yanick. *Improving Access to Care by Expanding the Role of
Pharmacists.* 30 April 2015.

– *The Other Health Care System: Four Areas Where the Private Sector
Answers Patients' Needs.* 31 March 2015.

Labrie, Yanick, and Bradley Doucet. *Economic Freedom Improves
Human Well-Being.* 12 February 2015.

Dumais, Mario. *The Negative Consequences of Agricultural Marketing.*
September 2012.

– *Viewpoint on the Shortcomings of Agricultural Policies.* 15 December
2010.

MOWAT CENTRE

Tank Facts

Established:	2009
Location:	Toronto
Budget:	~$2.5 million
Staff:	18
President/Director:	Matthew Mendelsohn
Website:	http://mowatcentre.ca

Housed in the School of Public Policy & Governance at the University of
Toronto, the Mowat Centre, named for Sir Oliver Mowat (1820–1903),

Ontario's third and longest-serving premier (1872–96), has as its mission to "provide an independent Ontario voice on public policy by conducting and communicating analytically-rigorous, evidence-based public policy research that has meaningful impact, actionable recommendations and strengthens Ontario in a rapidly changing world."[82] With a grant of $900,000 from the Government of Ontario, the Mowat Centre conducts research in four main areas: intergovernmental economic and social policy, government transformation, the not-for-profit sector, and energy. In carrying out its research, the Centre sees itself as performing three roles: as an idea generator capable of identifying and disseminating information on key policy issues; as a convenor that holds seminars, workshops, and conferences, and engages in informal conversations with various target audiences; and as a communicator who, through its research and gatherings, is constantly "developing and leveraging relationships among stakeholders, influencers [a term you won't find in the *Oxford Dictionary*], leaders and decision-makers."[83]

Unlike many think tanks that take for granted that their ideas permeate key decision-making circles, the Mowat Centre pays close attention to the "impact" its research has on constituent groups. In its *2014 Annual Report*, the Centre provides an "Impact-Performance Indicators Legend" that outlines the different kinds of impact and reach it could achieve. These include: references/citations in official government reports and documents and legislative debates; media mentions; published op-eds; references in research studies; and website activity. Alongside each publication listed in its annual reports, the Centre references these and other indicators to highlight the study's impact. Although keeping track of how often the Centre was cited in research studies or in the Ontario legislature may speak to how engaged Mowat researchers are in various public debates, and may go a long way in impressing potential donors, outputs are not outcomes. As noted, visibility does not guarantee policy influence, an observation not highlighted in the Centre's annual reports. Aware that these and similar indicators may not go far enough in documenting how much of an impact it has, the Centre goes one step further by tracking the level and frequency of access its staff have secured to policy-makers at different levels and branches of municipal, provincial, federal, and foreign governments.[84] While the nature and result of its interactions with policy-makers is difficult to quantify, the Mowat Centre is clearly aware of the importance of portraying itself as an active participant in the policy research community.

How much of an impact the organization has had is debatable. Still, there is little doubt that in a short period of time, it has filled an important niche in the Canadian think tank community by becoming a leading voice on critical issues facing the province of Ontario.

*References to the Mowat Centre
in Selected Canadian Newspapers*

NATIONAL POST
Coyne, Andrew. "If We Really Want to Soak the Rich, We Should Abolish Corporate Income Tax." 8 July 2014.
– "Federal Transfer System Not to Blame for Ontario's Fiscal Shortfall." 19 July 2014.
– "Returning to the Fairness of the 'A Buck Is a Buck' Principle of Taxation." 27 November 2014.
Falk, Will, and Dylan Marando. "Dawn of the 'Smartphone Doctor.'" 20 February 2015.
Hanniman, Kyle. "What If a Province Goes the Way of Greece?" 29 February 2015.
Keller, Tony. "The Winners and Losers in the New NHL Deal." 8 January 2013.
McGregor, Glen. "Inside the Secret Planning for Justin Trudeau's Senate Bombshell – and How a Senator's Trip Nearly Derailed It." 30 January 2014.
McParland, Kelly. "Report Says Ontario Is Big Loser in Broken Equalization Program." 21 December 2012.
Mendelsohn, Matthew. "Oliver's Flawed Facts: Ontario a Net Contributor to Canada, Ottawa's Assertion Notwithstanding." 8 July 2014.
Selley, Chris. "EI Needs Reinventing, Not Tweaking." 23 May 2012.

TORONTO STAR
Goar, Carol. "Canada's Top Energy Regulator Unfazed by Controversy." 16 April 2015.
Goodman, Lee-Anne. "How the Toronto Factor Exposes EI's Outdated System." 4 September 2014.
Hepburn, Bob. "Trudeau at Crossroads on Two-Year Anniversary." 4 April 2015.

Keenan, Edward. "Catching Up to the Post-Jobs Economy."
20 February 2015.
Levitz, Stephanie. "Income Splitting Tax Measure Would Pinch
Provincial Pockets Too, Report Says." 18 September 2014.
Lu, Vanessa. "Do Companies like Uber, Handy Fuel Underground
Economy?" 23 February 2015.
– "Dropping Water Levels Could Lead to Economic Blues." 26 June
2014.
– "Uber, Airbnb Highlight Need for Regulation." 17 February 2015.
Mendelsohn, Matthew. "Ontario Is Being Cheated by the Federal
Government." 15 June 2014.
Talaga, Tanya. "Oil Price Plunge Would Be Felt Throughout Canadian
Economy." 10 December 2014.

Selected Publications of the Mowat Centre

Carlson, Richard, and Eric Martin. *Re-energizing the Conversation:
Engaging the Ontario Public on Energy Issues.* 17 October 2014.
Carlson, Richard, Rob Dorling, Peter S. Spiro, and Mike Moffatt.
A Review of the Economic Impact of Energy East on Ontario.
30 March 2015.
Galley, Andrew, and Jill Shirey. *Brokering Success: Improving Skilled
Immigrant Employment Outcomes through Strengthened
Government-Employer Engagement.* 3 December 2014.
Gold, Jennifer. *International Delivery: Centres of Government and the
Drive for Better Policy Implementation.* 22 September 2014.
Hanniman, Kyle. *Calm Counsel: Fiscal Federalism and Provincial
Credit Risk.* 6 February 2015.
Johal, Sunil. *Income Splitting or Trojan Horse?: The Federal Government's
Proposal and Its Impact on Provincial Budgets.* 18 September 2014.
Johal, Sunil, and Noah Zon. *Policymaking for the Sharing Economy:
Beyond Whack-A-Mole.* 16 February 2015.
The Ontario Chamber of Commerce. *Emerging Stronger 2015: A
Transformative Agenda for Ontario's Economic Future.* 4 February
2015.
Van Ymeren, Jamie. *An Open Future: Data Priorities for the Not-for-
Profit Sector.* 20 February 2015.
Zon, Noah, Matthias Oschinski, and Melissa Molson. *Building Blocks:
The Case for Federal Investment in Social and Affordable Housing in
Ontario.* 22 September 2014.

PARKLAND INSTITUTE

Tank Facts

Established: 1996
Location: Edmonton
Budget: ~$500,000
Staff: 6
President/Director: Trevor Harrison
Website: www.parklandinstitute.ca

Located in the Faculty of Arts at the University of Alberta, with a second office in Calgary, "Alberta's left-leaning" Parkland Institute, as its critics often label it, "studies economic, social, cultural and political issues facing Albertans and Canadians using the perspective of political economy."[85] According to its 2008 "Self-Study," Parkland's values "include being open, critical, innovative, transformative, and solutions oriented."[86] Its mission rests on five pillars:

- To [provide] top quality policy research focussing on Canadian energy security and environmental sustainability, social justice, and social equity;
- To lead and expand the policy and political debate through research and outreach programming that changes the framing of issues in Alberta and Canada;
- To [provide] policy research that is transformative, proposing positive policy solutions that lead to systematic and structural changes that improve the quality of life and social justice;
- To help inform an engaged public by publishing our research in accessible language, disseminating our work widely, and by creating spaces (colloquia, conferences, symposia, web dialogues) where academics and citizens can actively engage with each other on current issues; and
- To foster provincial, national, and international research networks and synergies.[87]

The Parkland Institute began its life with "three years of seed funding from the Faculty of Arts"[88] and, despite its small staff and modest resources, has been able to establish a strong foothold in Western Canada. Its stature has been enhanced in recent years by the launch of an endowment program propelled by a million dollar donation. In addition to its many research studies on health care, environmental sustainability, and energy, the Parkland Institute has relied on several other channels to communicate its findings and policy recommendations to multiple audiences. The Institute hosts several workshops and conferences throughout the year and its staff and research fellows regularly interact with the media. Parkland is well aware of the importance of demonstrating to potential donors how much of an impact its work has on shaping public opinion and public policy. It also recognizes that it may have a greater impact at some stages of the policy cycle than others. To this end, it has compiled a body of data to assess its reach and impact relative to some of its competitors.[89] Although the Parkland Institute may not enjoy the same level of public visibility and notoriety as the Fraser Institute, the C.D. Howe Institute, and other public policy research organizations, it occupies an important position on the Canadian think tank landscape.

References to the Parkland Institute
in Selected Canadian Newspapers

CALGARY HERALD

Acuna, Ricardo. "Klein's Policies Got Us into This Mess." 24 February 2015.

Breakenridge, Rob. "Fears over Alberta's Gender-Pay Gap Are Overstated." 10 March 2105.

Editorial. "Oil and Gas Fuelled Calgary's Wealth." 14 May 2014.

Klassen, Karin. "Why I Have a Poor Opinion of Polls." 9 March 2015.

Lakritz, Naomi. "Tradition No Reason to Leave Far Workers Unprotected." 17 January 2015.

Markusoff, Jason. "The Budget Public Hearing, As It Happened." 29 November 2010.

– "Parkland Institute on Muni Taxes and Fees. At Least, Some Taxes and Fees." 15 January 2010.

EDMONTON JOURNAL

Annable, Kristin, and Bill Mah. "Liquor Privatization: Did Albertans Get What Was Promised?" 23 August 2013.

Harrison, Trevor. "The Realities of Alberta Conservatism." 9 January 2015.

Ibrahim, Mariam. "Liberals Push to Close Pay Gap between Men and Women." 8 April 2015.

Kleiss, Karen. "Report Urges Injury, Death Coverage for Far Workers."
15 Janury 2015.
Lahey, Kathleen A. "For Women, It's the Alberta Disadvantage."
9 March 2015.
Mah, Bill, and Kristin Annable. "We Put Every Bootlegger Out of
Business: Steve West." 26 August 2013.
Pratt, Sheila. "Alberta Women Losing Ground in Economic Equality."
4 March 2015.
Weber, Barret. "Post-secondary Education Not Premier's Priority."
19 March 2015.

NATIONAL POST
Braid, Don. "Welcome to Alberta, Canada's Tax Haven." 2 December 2014.

TORONTO STAR
Hall, Ashley, and Jessica Nelson. "Selling Beer and Wine in Grocery
Stores Carries Serious Risks." 13 April 2015.
Laxer, Gordon. "Quebec 'Non' Looms over West-to-East Pipeline
Gambit." 13 October 2012.
– "What in Tar-Nation." 26 July 2011.
McQuaig, Linda. "Go Ahead and Reopen NAFTA." 3 June 2008.
Olive, David. "Alberta's Inconvenient Truths." 14 October 2007.
– "Solutions for Alberta's Petro-Budget Woes." 3 April 2015.
Steward, Gillian. "Alberta Premier Alison Redford Flip-Flops on Budget
Promises." 28 January 2013.
Walkom, Thomas. "Canadian Left Split over Alberta's Oilsands."
10 January 2014.

Selected Publications of the Parkland Institute

Barnetson, Bob. *A Dirty Business: The Exclusion of Alberta Farm
Workers from Injury Compensation.* 15 January 2015.
Campanella, David. *A Profitable Brew: A Financial Analysis of the
SLGA and Its Potential Privatization.* 3 December 2014.
Campanella, David, Bob Barnetson, and Angella MacEwen. *On the Job:
Why Unions Matter in Alberta.* 21 May 2014.
Flanagan, Greg. *From Gap to Chasm: Alberta's Increasing Income
Inequality.* 20 April 2015.
– *Looking in the Mirror: Provincial Comparisons of Public Spending.*
19 March 2015.

Harrison, Trevor, and Harvey Krahn. *Less Exclusion, More Engagement: Addressing Declining Voter Turnout in Alberta.* 23 April 2014.

Hudson, Mark, and Evan Bowness. *Directly and Adversely Affected: Public Participation in Tar Sands Development 2005–2014.* 29 October 2014.

Krahn, Harvey, Trevor Harrison, and Katherine Hancock. *A Monochrome Political Culture?: Examining the Range of Albertans' Values and Beliefs.* 9 April 2015.

Lahey, Kathleen. *The Alberta Disadvantage: Gender, Taxation, and Income Inequality.* 4 March 2015.

Roy, Jim. *Billions Forgone: The Decline in Alberta Oil and Gas Royalties.* 23 April 2015.

PEMBINA INSTITUTE

Tank Facts

Established:	1985
Location:	Calgary (with branch offices in Edmonton, Toronto, Vancouver, and Yellowknife)
Budget:	$4–$5 million
Staff:	~50
President/Director:	Ed Whittingham
Website:	www.pembina.org

The Pembina Institute for Appropriate Development was incorporated in 1985 in response to a "major sour gas well" blowout near Lodgepole, Alberta on 17 October 1982. For nearly two months, the Amoco Canada well "spewed 200 million cubic feet per day of deadly hydrogen sulfide gas – or poisonous sulphur dioxide when it was on fire – along with toxic condensates."[90] According to the Pembina Institute, "the emergency response by the company and government was completely inadequate, characterized by the denial of responsibility, downplaying of human health and environmental impacts, and failure to protect the community. As a result, more than 200 residents joined together to form the Pembina Area Sour Gas Exposures Committee."[91]

With intense media exposure and growing public concern, the group was able to help launch a public inquiry into the Lodgepole blowout. The result was that many of the recommendations made by the group to prevent similar catastrophes were adopted. It was from this experience that a handful of individuals, including Rob Macintosh and Wally Heinrichs, decided to establish and incorporate the Pembina Institute.[92] The mission of the institute is "to advance clean energy solutions through innovative research, education, consulting and advocacy." To this end, "it envisions a world in which our immediate and future needs are met in a manner that protects the earth's living systems; ensures clean air, land and water; prevents dangerous climate change; and provides for a safe and just global community."[93]

Headquartered in Calgary, with four branch offices, the Pembina Institute focuses on six main policy areas, including energy efficiency, liquefied natural gas, and the oil sands. Since its creation, it has released an impressive array of publications and media commentaries. Many of its experts write op-eds for several Canadian newspapers, and through Pembina's Speakers' Bureau, address various audiences on a range of issues pertaining to the organization's mandate.

References to the Pembina Institute
in Selected Canadian Newspapers

CALGARY HERALD
"Alberta Expected to Unveil Updated Climate Change Strategy by
    Month's End." 15 December 2014.
Derworiz, Colette. "Environment Department Sees Cut in Alberta
    Budget." 26 March 2015.
– "Experts Weigh In on the Best Ways for Alberta to Address Climate
    Change." 18 April 2015.
Ewart, Stephen. "Alberta's New Climate Change Minister Carries Great
    Expectations." 24 March 2014.
– "Alberta Oil Hits a Hurdle En Route to World Markets in Quebec
    City." 15 April 2015.
Healing, Dan. "Crude Oil Emissions Variability Surprises Researchers."
    14 April 2015.
McClure, Matt. "Alberta's Claims of Greenhouse Gas Success Don't
    Measure Up, Experts Say." 22 March 2015.
Stark, Erika. "McQueen Insists Province Will Meet 2020 Emissions
    Reduction Target, Despite Past Misses." 20 March 2015.
Whittingham, Ed. "Prentice's Budget Is about 'Setting Things Right.'"
    4 April 2015.

Van Loon, Jeremy. "Spotlight Shifts to Alberta as Quebec Phases Out
    Coal Power Plants." 14 April 2015.

EDMONTON JOURNAL

Garner, Ryan. "Alberta Green Condo Guide Offers Tips for Energy,
    Cost Savings." 27 March 2015.
Howell, David. "Alberta Economy Benefits from Investment in
    Technology to Reduce Greenhouse Gas Emissions, Study Finds."
    5 March 2015.
– "New Rules for Oilsands Fluid Tailings, River Water Management."
    13 March 2015.
– "Play-Based Regulation Could Benefit Energy Industry: Report."
    13 January 2015.
Pratt, Sheila. "Edmonton Air Pollution Must Be Reduced, Provincial
    Report Says." 3 February 2015.
– "Edmonton's Bad Air Is Dirtier Than Toronto's, Which Has Five
    Times the People." 15 April 2015.
    "Ground Breaking Technology Stores Wind Power in Salt Caverns."
    7 December 2014.

TORONTO STAR

Aulakh, Raveena. "Include Climate Change When Assessing Pipeline
    Projects, Groups Urge." 11 December 2014.
De Souza, Mike. "An Inside Look at US Think Tank's Plan to Undo
    Environmental Legislation." 24 August 2014.
Flanagan, Erin. "On Climate Change, Provinces Are Doing What
    Ottawa Won't." 13 April 2015.
Kalinowski, Tess. "GTA Home Buyers Prefer Walkable
    Neighbourhoods, Study Says." 24 September 2014.
– "Toronto Lags Other Canadian Cities in Holiday Transit: Pembina
    Report." 5 September 2014.
Keesmaat, Jennifer, and Cherise Burda. "Greenbelt Makes GTA More,
    Not Less, Visible." 17 March 2015.
Pigg, Susan. "Ontario Farmland under Threat as Demand for Housing
    Grows." 27 February 2015.
Potter, Mitch. "US-China Climate Deal Reverberates North and South."
    12 November 2014.
Walkom, Thomas. "Don't Expect Kathleen Wynne to Block Energy East
    Pipeline." 5 December 2014.

Watson, Paul. "For Oil-Rich Norway, It's Not Easy Being Green."
14 September 2014.

Selected Publications of the Pembina Institute

Burda, Cherise, and Geoffrey Singer. *Location Matters Factoring
Location Costs Into Homebuying Decisions.* 21 January 2015.
Comette, Penelope, Steven Cretney, Maximilian Kniewasser, and
Kevin Sauve. *The British Columbia Clean Energy Jobs Map.*
24 April 2015.
Flanagan, Erin. *Crafting an Effective Canadian Energy Strategy: How
Energy East and the Oilsands Affect Climate and Energy Objectives.*
14 April 2015.
– *Oilsands Expansion, Emissions and the Energy East Pipeline.*
3 December 2014.
Horne, Matt, and Josha MacNab. *Liquefied Natural Gas and Climate
Change: The Global Context.* 27 October 2014.
Horne, Matt, and Kevin Sauve. *The B C Carbon Tax: A Backgrounder.*
5 November 2014.
Pembina Institute. *Background on Alberta's Climate Strategy.*
16 December 2014.
Row, Jesse. *Alberta Green Condo Guide.* 26 March 2015.
Sauve, Kevin, Josha MacNab, Steven Cretney, and Matt Horne. *Is B C
LNG Really a Climate Change Solution? An Infographic.* 23
December 2014.
Thibault, Benjamin. *How Solar and Wind Lower Your Power Bill:
Understanding Renewable Energy Prices in Alberta.* 12 November
2014.

PUBLIC POLICY FORUM

Tank Facts

Established: 1987
Location: Ottawa
Budget: $3.5–$4 million
Staff: 22
President/Director: Larry Murray (acting president)
Website: www.ppforum.ca

Located a few blocks from Parliament Hill, the roots of the Public
Policy Forum (PPF) can be traced to "a formative meeting in Calgary
[in 1987] with federal deputy ministers and private sector leaders."[94]
At that meeting, "a strong consensus emerged regarding the need to
create an independent space where leaders from the private and public
sectors could meet regularly to discuss governance and public policy."[95] As the Public Policy Forum points out in its brief history of the
organization, "Since that time, the Forum's membership has grown to
include more than 180 leading organizations from business, federal,
provincial and territorial governments, academic institutions, unions,
and the voluntary and not-for-profit sectors."[96] The PPF does not
regard itself as an advocacy think tank that seeks to impose its agenda
on policy-makers. Indeed, in its promotional literature, the institute
emphasizes that it does not take positions on any policy issues. As
noted, it was founded not to advance a particular set of ideological
goals, but "to provide a neutral venue where the private sector and the
public sector could meet to learn from one another."[97] According to
the PPF, "In the 1980s, it became clear that, in the global arena where
the quality of government directly affected the competitiveness of the
nation, Canada suffered from the isolation of government from the
private sector."[98] To remedy this problem, the PPF's former president
David Zussman noted, "We help to bridge the gap between the two
solitudes – government and the private sector – in order to deal more
effectively with issues of common concern."[99] For many years, the
organization has also included representatives from the voluntary, or
"third," sector in its policy forums.

The PPF's emphasis on organizing conferences and workshops for
policy-makers and representatives from the private and non-profit
sectors is reflected in the allocation of its resources. Approximately
sixty percent of the institute's operating budget of $3.5–$4 million,
raised almost entirely from membership donations, is set aside for
this purpose. Among its more than one hundred members are the
Bank of Montreal, Bell Canada, Canada Post Corporation, and several provincial governments. Only 20–25 percent of its budget is
allocated for research, a function to which the PPF has begun to
devote more attention. The forum, which has done considerable
work in economic, social, and trade policy, has identified three themes
in its 2013–16 *Strategic Plan* that fall under the broad categories of
public service and governance, economy and competitiveness, and
human capital.

References to the Public Policy Forum
in Selected Canadian Newspapers

NATIONAL POST
Editorial Board: "Restore Decorum to the House." 8 October 2010.
Kheiriddin, Tasha. "A Step Toward a Cleaner QP – Minus the Bloc."
    7 October 2010.
Libin, Kevin. "Bringing Civility to Question Period." 8 October 2010.
Martin, Don. "Tories Need Manning's Touch of Class." 3 May 2010.
Selley, Chris. "Live from St John's, It's the Canadian Parliament."
    11 February 2011.
– "On the Long-Gun Registry, the Conservatives Always Win."
    15 September 2010, NP.
Solomon, Lawrence. "Don't Bother to Vote." 30 April 2011.
– "New Parliament Younger, More Diverse: Study." 30 June 2011.
Special to Financial Post. "Oil and Gas Partnerships Drive Efficiency
    through Technological Innovation." 23 July 2013.
– "Transcript: Allow Voluntary CPP Contributions." 21 February
    2013.
Stinson, Scott. "Our Houses No Longer Homes for Democracy."
    17 October 2011.

OTTAWA CITIZEN
Macleod, Ian. "World's Oldest Operating Reactor, in Chalk River, to
    Close in 2018." 16 March 2015.
May, Kathryn. "Mistrust between Bureaucrats and Politicians Bad for
    Canada: Survey." 27 December 2014.
– "New Plan for the PS of the Future." 11 May 2014.
May, Kathryn, and Jason Fekete. "Wayne Wouters: Retiring Clerk
    Sparked Controversy and Compliments." 24 August 2014.
Mitchell, David, and Sara Caverley. "The Year's Top Policy Stories."
    28 December 2014.
Pugliese, David. "Canada's Members of Parliament Lack Experience
    Says New Report." 4 May 2009.
Sibley, Robert. "Essay: Never Mind the Economy, It's the 'Trade
    Deficit.'" 11 April 2009.

TORONTO STAR
Brender, Natalie. "Canada's Diverted Public Service Poses a Threat to
    Our Future." 15 April 2013.

Delacourt, Susan. "Canadians Weary of Antics in the Commons: Poll."
15 September 2010.
– "Tory MP Takes a Crack at Restoring Civility in Ottawa."
16 September 2010.
Editorial. "We Need to Protect Canada's Public Service." 15 April
2013.
Flavelle, Dana. "Ontario's Pension Timeline 'Ambitious' Minister Says."
8 October 2014.
– "'Self-Control Problems' Plague Canadian Retirement Savings,
Economist Warns." 9 October 2014.
Goar, Carol. "How Canadian Voters Became Election Pawns."
28 March 2011.
Hébert, Chantal. "Nursing Medicare Back to Health Carries Political
Risk." 3 May 2010.
Hepburn, Bob. "Whose Job Is It to Boost Voter Turnout?" 31 August
2011.
Mayers, Adam. "A Closer Look at Our Public Sector Pension Envy."
16 October 2014.

Selected Publications of the Public Policy Forum

Agile Government: Responding to Citizens' Changing Needs. 30 March
2015.
Atlantic Summit on Healthcare and Drug Cost Sustainability. 9 January
2015.
Building Sustainable Value: A Canada-US Energy Roundtable.
19 December 2014.
Canada's Airports – Advancing Our Prosperity and Trade Agenda.
28 January 2015.
Changing the Game: Public Sector Productivity in Canada. 7 January
2015.
Connecting Communities Initiative. 25 March 2015.
Reducing Transportation GHG Emissions in Canada (Final Report).
5 December 2013.
Regulatory Diplomacy Report. 19 December 2014.
Retirement Security for Everyone: Enhancing Canada's Pension System.
3 February 2015.
Social Finance in Canada 2013. 23 May 2013.

VANIER INSTITUTE OF THE FAMILY

Tank Facts

Established: 1965
Location: Ottawa
Budget: ~$1.3 million
Staff: 8
President/Director: Nora Spinks
Website: www.vanierinstitute.ca

Established under the patronage of Their Excellencies Canada's Governor General Georges P. Vanier (1959–1967) and Madame Pauline Vanier, the "Vanier Institute of the Family began its work in 1965 immediately following the Canadian Conference on the Family the two patrons convened at Government House."[100] As the Vanier Institute observes in its brief history of the organization, "That founding conference brought together distinguished men and women from all walks of life, each of whom knew that the contribution of families is vitally important and ultimately shapes the world in which we live."[101] Governor General Vanier's "vision to create an enduring organization dedicated to the cause of our society through the family was supported by the leadership of renowned Canadian neuroscientist, Dr. Wilder Penfield."[102]

The Vanier Institute's vision to promote "the well-being of Canadian families" is anchored by a four-pronged strategy to:

- Build public understanding of important issues and trends affecting the healthy functioning of Canadian families;
- Foster a society that identifies and provides for the needs and aspirations of families;
- Encourage a family perspective among policy-makers, service providers, employers, educators and others whose work affects the lives of families; and
- Promote the inherent capacity of families to help themselves.[103]

To convey its ideas to multiple stakeholders, the Vanier Institute relies on its robust research program, its commitment to public education and traditional family values and its willingness to form "strategic partnerships with public and private institutions, corporations, the media and the non-profit sector."[104] The Vanier Institute pays close attention to its public profile. In its annual reports, figures can be found on how often its publications, including its magazine, *Transition*, have been downloaded, the various media outlets with which its researchers have interacted, and the number of people who have attended the many conferences, seminars, and workshops it has organized.[105] With investments greater than $16 million, the Vanier Institute is well-positioned to continue the mandate it carved out over fifty years ago with the assistance of one of English Canada's most popular governor generals.

References to the Vanier Institute of the Family in Selected Canadian Newspapers

NATIONAL POST
Boesveld, Sarah. "The Rise of the Single Dad and 10 Other Takeaways from the Census' Family and Household Figures." 19 September 2012.
– "State of the Unions: How a New Generation Is Redefining What Marriage Looks Like." 9 February 2015.
– "Though the Number of Adult Children Moving Back Home Is Holding Steady, Number of Couples Moving Back Is on the Rise." 19 September 2012.
Kirkey, Sharon. "Global Recession Linked to 10,000 'Economic Suicides' across North America and Europe: Study." 12 June 2014.
Leong, Melissa. "The Cost of Infertility." FP. 28 September 2013.
Macdougall, Jane. "Step Off the Evil Stepmother Wagon for a History Lesson on the World's Toughest Job." 10 May 2014.
Marr, Gary. "What to Do When There's More Value in Your House Than Your Marriage." 11 October 2014, FP.
Martin, Sandra E. "The Skyrocketing Cost of Raising Kids." 15 December 2012, FP.
McDowell, Adam. "State of the Unions: Why Marriage May Be Better the Second, or Third, Time Around." 13 February 2015.
Quinn, Greg. "Decline in Working Women Could Stagnate Economic Growth." 5 June 2014, FP.

OTTAWA SUN
Dube, Dani-Elle. "Contract Marriages Might Be Better for True Love." 9 August 2014.
Robson, John. "Canada No Better Than Their Government When It Comes to Spending."

TORONTO STAR

Editorial. "The Daycare Disconnect." 12 February 2011.

Flavelle, Dana. "Why Canadians Have Record-High Debt." 27 October 2012.

Griffiths, Alison. "6 Ways to Help Juggle Kids and Elder Care." 6 November 2011.

Olive, David. "The Danger in Our Savings Shortfall." 18 February 2011.

Purdy, Chris. "Three Children? Canadian Families Growing Say Some Experts." 23 August 2012.

Roseman, Ellen. "Seniors Burdened by Rising Debt." 8 June 2014.

Rubin, Josh. "Average Household Debt Tops $100,000." 17 February 2011.

Ubelacker, Sheryl. "Canada's Typical Family Shows Married Couples with Kids in the Minority: Report." 4 October 2010.

USA Today and Star Staff. "Remarrying in Retirement Can Be Complicated Financially." 13 June 2014.

Weikle, Brandie. "School's Out but Work Is Not." 24 June 2011.

Selected Publications of the Vanier Institute of the Family

Battams, Nathan. "No Longer Just 'Child's Play': Electronic Gaming in Canada." *Transition* 45, no. 1 (2015).

Cayley, Paula. "Caring Canines: Therapy Dogs and Well-Being." *Transition* 44, no. 1 (2014).

Fieldhouse, Paul. "(Still) Eating Together: The Culture of the Family Meal." *Transition* 45, no. 1 (2015).

Johnson, Matthew. "To Share or Not to Share: Online Privacy and Publicity among Canadian Youth." *Transition* 44, no. 1 (2014).

Kennedy, Nicole. "Marking a Moment in Time." *Transition* 44, no. 1 (2014).

MacNaull, Sara. "Off the Vanier Bookshelf – Family Futures by the United Nations Department of Economic and Social Affairs Division for Social Policy and Development." *Transition* 45, no. 1 (2015).

Posen, Dr David B. "Sleep and Families." *Transition* 45, no. 1 (2015).

Spinks, Nora. "50 Years of Understanding Families in Canada." *Transition* 45, no. 1 (2015).

– "Strong Families, Healthy Communities." *Transition* 44, no. 1 (2014).

Thompson, Craig. "Putting the 'F' in EFAP: The Evolution of Workplace Mental Health Supports." *Transition* 44, no. 1 (2014).

WELLESLEY INSTITUTE

Tank Facts

Established: 2006
Location: Toronto
Budget: ~$1.5–$2 million
Staff: 8
President/Director: Kwame McKenzie
Website: www.wellesleyinstitute.com

Several think tanks in Canada study health care and make various recommendations on how to improve the mental and physical well-being of
Canadians, but few owe their existence to a hospital, the central pillar of
the health care system. When the Wellesley Central Hospital in southeast
Toronto closed its doors in 1998, "a group of former board members
and community activists remained determined to protect the legacy of
the hospital."[106] As a result of their efforts, the Wellesley Central Health
Corporation (WCHC) was formed." In 2006, the WCHC changed its
name to the Wellesley Institute "reflecting its evolution from developer
to think tank. Today, the Wellesley Institute is a non-profit and non-
partisan research and policy institute focused on finding solutions to
problems of population health."[107]

In addition to its sustained commitment to advancing urban health,
the Wellesley Institute was formed "to reduce health inequities by driving change on the social determinants of health through applied research,
effective policy solutions, knowledge mobilization, and innovation."[108]
In carrying out its mission, the institute focuses on four priorities:

- shaping policy and program change that will reduce the depth and
  severity of economic inequality, precarious work and poverty, and
  their adverse health impacts;
- improving access to affordable housing and reducing the adverse
  health impacts of homelessness and inadequate housing;
- ensuring more equitable access to high-quality health care for all;
- working on interconnected issues that cross social determinants,
  such as identifying the foundations of healthier and more equitable communities.[109]

Although the Wellesley Institute is relatively new to the Canadian think
tank scene, it clearly understands what it takes to have an impact. Indeed,

by its own admission, high-quality research alone is not sufficient to attract the attention of policy-makers and other key stakeholders. What is also required is a strategic communications and knowledge mobilization plan, effective and innovative partnerships, and a willingness to establish proper performance indicators to assess their impact and reach in the policy-making community.[110] At the Wellesley Institute, research focuses on four main areas: building healthy communities, economic inequality, health equity, and housing.

References to the Wellesley Institute
in Selected Canadian Newspapers

NATIONAL POST

Alcoba, Natalie. "City Searches for Affordable-Housing Solution." 18 December 2010.

– "Housing Board Controversy Opening Doors for Ford." 5 March 2011.

– "TCHC Could Net $13M from 22-House Sale." 5 April 2011.

Hopper, Tristin. "Restauranteur Pitches Plan to Chase Away Montreal's Summertime 'Squeegee Punks.'" 8 August 2012.

Leslie, Keith. "Ontario Will Hike $10.25 Minimum Wage Retroactively to 2010, When It Was Frozen." 27 January 2014.

Marr, Gary. "For Mike Harris's Forgotten Legacy, Look Up." 23 November 2012, FP.

Special to the National Post. "The Calmest Revolution: Making Alternative Medicine More Affordable." 17 March 2012.

Wong-Tam. "Why Undocumented Workers Should Have Access to Critical City Services." 4 March 2013.

OTTAWA CITIZEN

Mills, Carys. "How Can Ottawa Tackle Affordable Housing and Homelessness." 14 September 2014.

Ottawa Citizen. "Housing Consultations to Begin." 5 June 2009.

– "Ontario Set to Retroactively Raise Minimum Wage." 30 June 2014.

TORONTO STAR

Boyle, Theresa. "Doctor Tends to Toronto's 'Urban Health' in New Role." 25 March 2014.

Editorial. "Pharmacare Should Be a Federal Election Issue." 17 February 2015.

Goar, Carol. "City Hall Fails Toronto's Vulnerable Residents."
    16 October 2014.
Kane, Laura. "Is This the End of the Urban Trailer Park in Ontario?"
    12 April 2014.
Keenan, Edward. "Catching Up to the Post-Jobs Economy."
    20 February 2015.
Keung, Nicholas. "Co-ordinated Services Urged to Help Young
    Homeless Immigrants." 25 November 2014.
Mojtehedzadeh, Sara. "After Cancer Diagnosis Those in Precarious
    Work Suffer More." 18 March 2015.
– "One-Third of Ontario Workers Lack Medical/Dental Benefits,
    Study Says." 17 February 2015.
– "Reversing Income Inequality in the City Possible, Experts Say."
    27 February 2015.
Monsebraaten, Laurie, and Richard J. Brennan. "Social Groups
    Applaud Plan to End Homelessness in Ontario, But Urge Deadline."
    3 September 2014.

TORONTO SUN
Agar, Jerry. "Too Many White People on City Council?" 22 March 2011.
Filey, Mike. "Toronto Hospitals Have Fascinating History: The Way
    We Were." 22 March 2014.
Jeffords, Shawn, and Don Peat. "John Tory Slammed for Skipping
    Housing Debate." 17 October 2014.
Kinsella, Warren. "What Gives with Charity Crackdown?"
    24 September 2011.
Levy, Sue-Ann. "Housing's Unusual Suspects Show Up at Council
    Executive Meeting." 10 October 2012.
Peat, Don. "Deputy Mayor Norm Kelly Adds Personal Touch to City
    Hall." 2 December 2013.
– "Women's Groups Slam Ford Budget." 11 January 2012.
Yuen, Jenny. "Wanted: Fake Homeless." 23 March 2009.

Selected Publications of the Wellesley Institute

Abban, Vanessa. *Getting It Right: What Does the Right to Health
    Mean for Canadians?* 19 March 2015.
Allan, Dr Billie, and Dr Janet Smylie. *First Peoples, Second Class
    Treatment.* 3 February 2015.

Barnes, Steve. *Dealing with Urban Health Crises: Responses to Cuts to the Interim Federal Health Program.* 21 March 2014.
– *Healthy Policy for a Healthy Toronto.* 31 October 2014.
– *Low Wages, No Benefits.* 17 February 2015.
Block, Sheila. *The Colour Coded Labour Market by the Numbers.* 16 September 2014.
Freeman, Lisa. *Toronto Suburban Rooming Houses: Just a Spin on a Downtown "Problem"?* 15 October 2014.
Mahamoud, Aziza. *Breast Cancer Screening in Racialized Women.* 21 March 2014.
Marwah, Sonal. *Refugee Health Care Cuts in Canada: System Level Costs, Risks and Responses.* 25 February 2014.
Roche, Brenda, Sheila Block, and Vanessa Abban. *The Health Impacts of Contracting Out.* 9 April 2015.

APPENDICES

References to Selected Canadian Think Tanks in the National Media, 2000–2015

Table A.1 References to selected Canadian think tanks in the national media, 2000–2015

Institute	Radio and television transcripts*	Newspapers	Total	% of total
Conference Board of Canada	649	24,429	25,078	22
Fraser Institute	194	22,225	22,888	20
C.D. Howe Institute	152	11,292	11,444	10
Pembina Institute	212	8,560	8,772	7
Canadian Centre for Policy Alternatives	214	6,982	7,196	6
Canada West Foundation	122	4,454	4,576	4
Montreal Economic Institute	54	3,083	3,137	2
Centre for International Governance Innovation (CIGI)	146	2,752	2,898	2
Asia Pacific Foundation of Canada (APFC)	241	2,577	2,818	2
Public Policy Forum	323	2,292	2,615	2
Institute for Research on Public Policy	86	2,415	2,501	2
Macdonald-Laurier Institute	11	2,444	2,455	2
Frontier Centre for Public Policy	41	2,200	2,241	1
Atlantic Institute for Market Studies (AIMS)	8	1,436	1,448	1
Canadian Defence and Foreign Affairs Institute (CDFAI)	129	1,317	1,446	1
Vanier Institute of the Family	21	1,284	1,305	1
International Institute for Sustainable Development	22	1,262	1,284	1
Mackenzie Institute	127	868	995	<1
Parkland Institute	23	944	967	<1
Canadian Urban Institute	13	874	887	<1
Mowat Centre	8	877	885	<1
Saskatchewan Institute of Public Policy	12	842	854	<1
Canadian Institute of Strategic Studies / Canadian International Council	74	642	716	<1
Canadian Council on Social Development	14	672	686	<1
Canadian Institute for Advanced Research	18	652	670	<1

Table A.1 References to selected Canadian think tanks in the national media, 2000–2015 (*continued*)

Institute	Radio and television transcripts*	Newspapers	Total	% of total
Canadian Tax Foundation	15	596	611	<1
Canadian Policy Research Networks (closed)	38	521	559	<1
Wellesley Institute	0	426	426	<1
Caledon Institute of Social Policy	14	399	413	<1
The North-South Institute	19	379	398	<1
Canadian Institute of International Affairs	17	319	336	<1
Economic Council of Canada	23	241	264	<1
Parliamentary Centre	66	307	373	<1
Couchiching Institute on Public Affairs	4	105	109	<1
National Council on Welfare	5	98	103	<1
Science Council of Canada	5	88	93	<1
Canadian Institute for Int's Peace and Security	0	15	15	<1
Pearson-Shoyama Institute	0	13	13·	<1
Quebec Institute of Advanced Int'l Studies	0	0	0	0
Total	3,120	110,882	114,475	100

Note: "Radio" refers to public/commercial radio broadcasting; internet broadcasting; satellite broadcasting. "Television" refers to public/commercial subscriber-based telecommunications; internet recorded/streaming telecommunications.

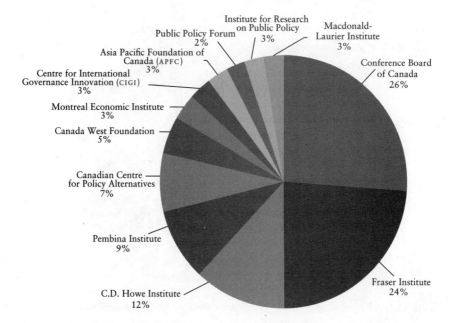

Figure A1.1 References to selected Canadian think tanks in the national media, 2000–2015

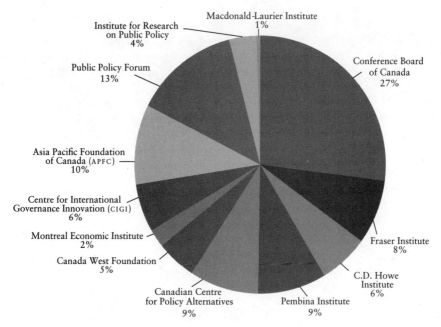

Figure A1.2 References to selected Canadian think tanks in the national media (radio and television), 2000–2015

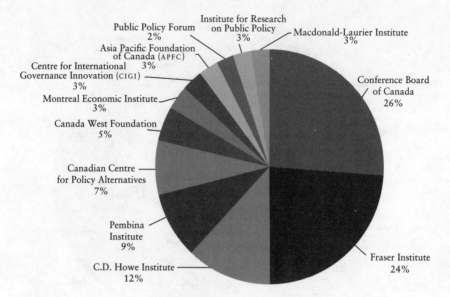

Figure A1.3 References to selected Canadian think tanks in the national media (newspapers), 2000–2015

Table A1.2 References to selected Canadian think tanks in national newspapers, 2000–2015

Institute	Globe & Mail	Toronto Star	National Post	Toronto Sun	Montreal Gazette	Vancouver Sun	Edmonton Journal	Ottawa Citizen	Halifax Daily News	Charlottetown Guardian	Total
Fraser Institute	652	533	1,382	391	772	1,314	779	962	130	999	7,914
Conference Board of Canada	1,482	1,079	903	196	754	909	757	871	197	623	7,771
C.D. Howe Institute	1,101	556	1,624	69	316	461	312	476	58	234	5,207
Pembina Institute	468	351	217	36	141	279	957	171	31	515	3,166
Canada West Foundation	284	89	220	14	81	218	515	127	17	839	2,404
Canadian Centre for Policy Alternatives	286	585	180	43	131	540	153	260	93	90	2,361
Institute for Research on Public Policy	222	170	364	15	138	122	95	196	28	70	1,420
Asia Pacific Foundation of Canada (APFC)	258	68	0	8	44	300	56	77	0	0	811
Macdonald-Laurier Institute	134	34	187	18	41	97	40	210	0	0	761
Montreal Economic Institute	64	23	222	23	290	17	19	41	3	10	712
Public Policy Forum	105	102	90	6	42	40	45	240	2	17	689
Vanier Institute of the Family	103	106	111	3	75	84	73	119	0	0	674
Canadian Institute of Strategic Studies/ Canadian International Council	149	55	101	16	36	28	51	124	15	33	608

Table A1.2 References to selected Canadian think tanks in national newspapers, 2000–2015 (continued)

Institute	Globe & Mail	Toronto Star	National Post	Toronto Sun	Montreal Gazette	Vancouver Sun	Edmonton Journal	Ottawa Citizen	Halifax Daily News	Charlottetown Guardian	Total
Canadian Defence and Foreign Affairs Institute (CDFAI)	122	55	91	30	42	30	55	140	N/A	0	565
Mackenzie Institute	55	35	130	43	22	46	38	120	14	43	546
Parkland Institute	25	16	22	3	11	9	318	10	2	92	508
Canadian Policy Research Networks (closed)	105	76	49	21	25	35	49	96	14	34	504
Frontier Centre for Public Policy	37	20	203	13	38	67	47	31	2	45	503
Canadian Council on Social Development	50	85	44	13	33	26	32	70	23	30	406
Canadian Tax Foundation	81	42	74	12	27	32	28	54	15	32	397
Atlantic Institute for Market Studies (AIMS)	98	26	136	1	26	29	25	12	N/A	0	353
Canadian Urban Institute	86	169	43	12	6	6	6	13	2	4	347
Caledon Institute of Social Policy	91	108	32	1	11	27	17	35	5	7	334
Canadian Institute for Advanced Research	88	59	58	29	13	31	16	17	2	7	320
Mowat Centre	73	105	54	5	14	19	19	28	N/A	N/A	317

The North-South Institute	78	45	9	2	10	6	14	42	1	2	209
Wellesley Institute	28	135	12	3	1	6	9	8	N/A	N/A	202
Canadian Institute of International Affairs	44	18	46	3	17	17	10	35	1	11	202
Centre for International Governance Innovation (CIGI)	75	46	31	0	4	5	10	29	N/A	N/A	200
International Institute for Sustainable Development	66	49	19	0	17	12	17	19	N/A	N/A	199
Economic Council of Canada	72	13	29	0	10	7	6	9	5	10	161
Parliamentary Centre	15	5	22	4	0	2	5	26	0	1	80
Saskatchewan Institute of Public Policy	34	3	3	0	5	8	7	10	1	2	73
Couchiching Institute on Public Affairs	10	21	7	2	7	2	2	7	0	0	58
National Council of Welfare	6	17	5	2	4	5	5	1	5	6	56
Science Council of Canada	8	7	9	0	1	3	5	6	0	1	40
Canadian Institute for International Peace and Security	3	3	1	0	1	1	2	3	0	1	15

Table A1.2 References to selected Canadian think tanks in national newspapers, 2000–2015 (*continued*)

Institute	Globe & Mail	Toronto Star	National Post	Toronto Sun	Montreal Gazette	Vancouver Sun	Edmonton Journal	Ottawa Citizen	Halifax Daily News	Charlottetown Guardian	Total
Pearson-Shoyama Institute	0	1	2	0	1	1	0	7	2	0	14
Canadian Council for International Peace and Security	2	0	0	0	0	0	0	1	0	0	3
Quebec Institute of Advanced International Studies	0	0	0	0	0	0	0	0	0	0	0
Total	6,562	4,884	6,596	1,036	3,181	4,312	4,569	4,691	668	3,758	41,110

Note: Herald records not accessible through UWO resources. No records available for Charlottetown-based newspapers after 2007, and *Halifax Daily News* no longer indexed by Factiva or LexisNexis.

Source: LexisNexis, Factiva (database has amalgamated television and radio transcripts; LexisNexis did the same; difference between radio and television transcripts not discernible/accessible). Search parameters: 1 January 2000–8 May 2015.

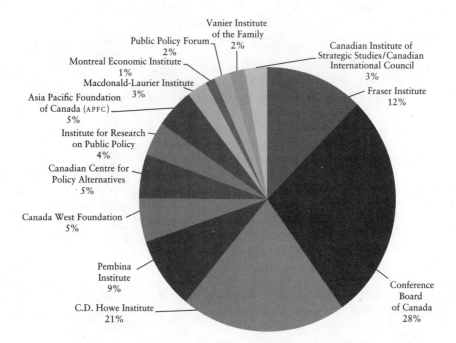

Figure A1.4 References to selected Canadian think tanks in the *Globe and Mail*, 2000–2015

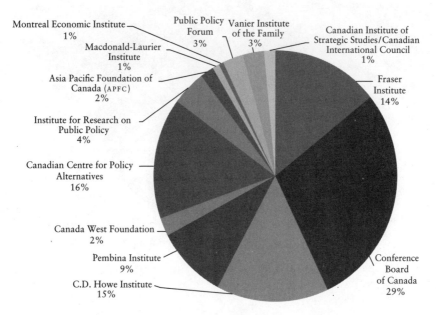

Figure A1.5 References to selected Canadian think tanks in the *Toronto Star*, 2000–2015

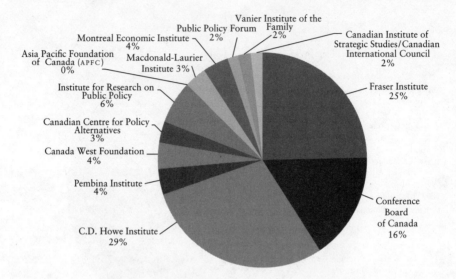

Figure A1.6 References to selected Canadian think tanks in the *National Post*, 2000–2015

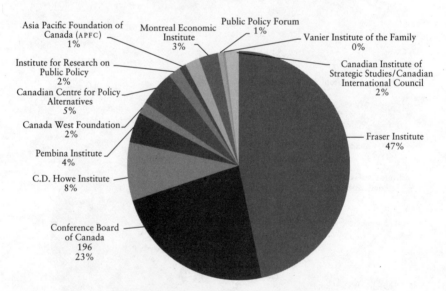

Figure A1.7 References to selected Canadian think tanks in the *Toronto Sun*, 2000–2015

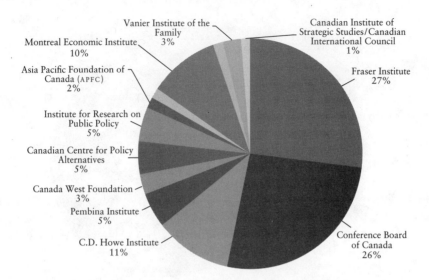

Figure A 1.8 References to selected Canadian think tanks in the *Montreal Gazette*, 2000–2015

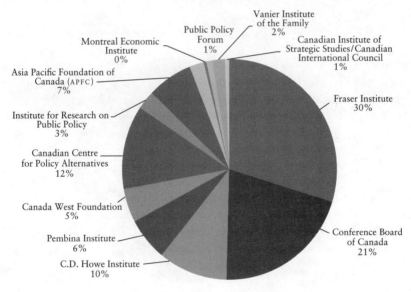

Figure A 1.9 References to selected Canadian think tanks in the *Vancouver Sun*, 2000–2015

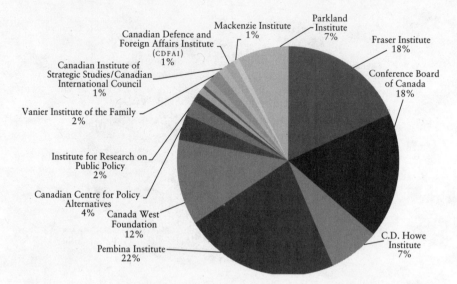

Figure A1.10 References to selected Canadian think tanks in the *Edmonton Journal*, 2000–2015

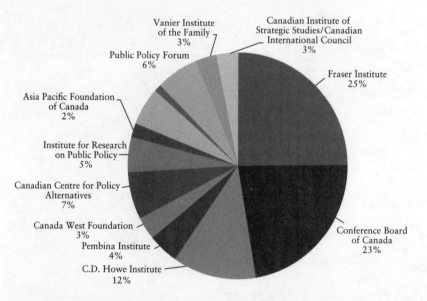

Figure A1.11 References to selected Canadian think tanks in the *Ottawa Citizen*, 2000–2015

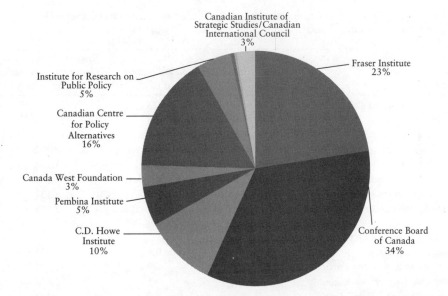

Canadian Institute of
Strategic Studies/Canadian
International Council
3%

Fraser Institute
23%

Institute for Research on
Public Policy
5%

Canadian Centre
for Policy
Alternatives
16%

Canada West Foundation
3%

Pembina Institute
5%

C.D. Howe
Institute
10%

Conference Board
of Canada
34%

Figure A1.12 References to selected Canadian think tanks in the *Halifax Daily News*,
2000–2015

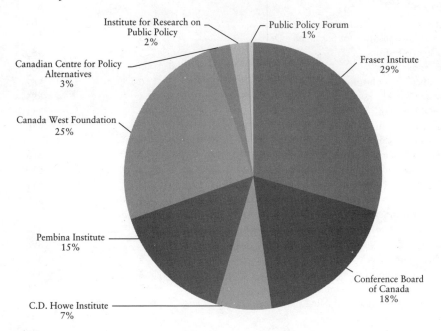

Institute for Research on
Public Policy
2%

Public Policy Forum
1%

Canadian Centre for Policy
Alternatives
3%

Fraser Institute
29%

Canada West Foundation
25%

Pembina Institute
15%

Conference Board
of Canada
18%

C.D. Howe Institute
7%

Figure A1.13 References to selected Canadian think tanks in the *Charlottetown
Guardian*, 2000–2015

Table A1.3 Comparison of annual budget to number of media appearances for selected Canadian think tanks, 2000–2015

Institute	Annual budget (millions of dollars)	Number of television, newspaper, and radio references
Conference Board of Canada	25	25,078
The Fraser Institute	4,5	22,888
C.D. Howe Institute	9	11,444
Pembina Institute	9	8,772
Canadian Centre for Policy Alternatives	5	7,196
Canada West Foundation	8,9	4,576
Montreal Economic Institute	2,25	3,137
Centre for International Governance Innovation (CIGI)	42	2,898
Asia Pacific Foundation of Canada (APFC)	2	2,818
Public Policy Forum	0,8	2,615
Institute for Research on Public Policy	39	2,501
Macdonald-Laurier Institute	1	2,455
Frontier Centre for Public Policy	0	2,241
Atlantic Institute for Market Studies (AIMS)	0,6	1,448
Canadian Defence and Foreign Affairs Institute (CDFAI)	0,7	1,446
Vanier Institute of the Family	16,8	1,305
International Institute for Sustainable Development	16,5	1,284
Mackenzie Institute	0	995
Parkland Institute	0	967
Canadian Urban Institute	0	887
Mowat Centre	2,4	885
Saskatchewan Institute of Public Policy	0	854
Canadian Institute of Strategic Studies/Canadian International Council	1,3	716
Canadian Council on Social Development	2	686
Canadian Institute for Advanced Research	21,8	670
Canadian Tax Foundation	5	611
Canadian Policy Research Networks, Inc. (closed)	5	559
Wellesley Institute	(not disclosed)	426
Caledon Institute for Social Policy	2	413
The North-South Institute	2	398
Parliamentary Centre	9	373
Canadian Institute for International Affairs	2	336
Canadian Centre for Philanthropy*	12	131
Couchiching Institute on Public Affairs	0	109
National Council of Welfare	0	103
Atlantic Provinces Economic Council*	2	97
Institute on Governance*	2	17
Canadian Centre for Foreign Policy Development*	5	3

*Source: LexisNexis.

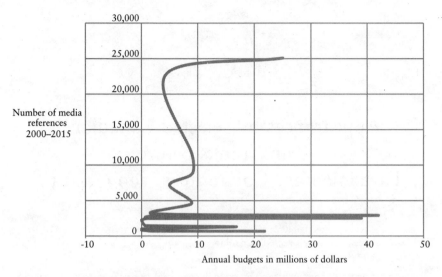

Figure A1.14 Comparison of annual budget (millions of dollars) to number of media references for selected Canadian think tanks, 2000–2015

APPENDIX TWO

Appearances by Selected Canadian Think Tanks before Parliamentary Committees, 1999–2015

Table A2.1 Appearances by selected Canadian think tanks before parliamentary committees, 1999–2008

Institute	Number of appearances
Conference Board of Canada	143
C.D. Howe Institute	98
Fraser Institute	73
Canadian Council on Social Development	47
Canadian Centre for Policy Alternatives	46
Caledon Institute of Social Policy	35
North-South Institute	33
National Council on Welfare	31
Public Policy Forum	28
Parliamentary Centre	26
Canada West Foundation	26
Canadian Policy Research Networks	22
Institute for Research on Public Policy	17
Canadian Institute for Strategic Studies	11
Canadian Institute for International Affairs	8
Mackenzie Institute	4
Canadian Tax Foundation	2
Canadian Council for International Peace and Security	1
Pearson-Shoyama Institute	0

Source: Library of Parliament, http://www.parl.gc.ca/common/Library.asp.

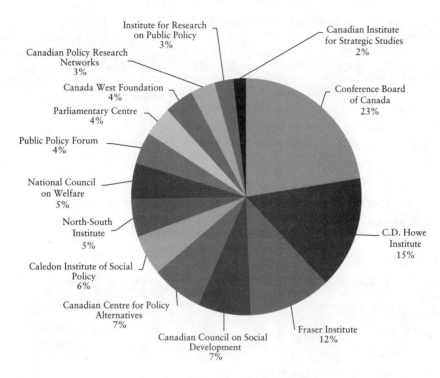

Institute for Research
on Public Policy
3%

Canadian Policy Research
Networks
3%

Canada West Foundation
4%

Parliamentary Centre
4%

Public Policy Forum
4%

National Council
on Welfare
5%

North-South
Institute
5%

Caledon Institute of Social
Policy
6%

Canadian Centre for Policy
Alternatives
7%

Canadian Council on Social
Development
7%

Canadian Institute
for Strategic Studies
2%

Conference Board
of Canada
23%

C.D. Howe
Institute
15%

Fraser Institute
12%

Figure A 2.1 Appearances by selected Canadian think tanks before parliamentary committees, 1999–2008

Table A2.2 Appearances by selected Canadian think tanks before parliamentary committees, 2008–2015

Institute	Number of appearances
Conference Board of Canada	27
Canadian Centre for Policy Alternatives	19
C.D. Howe Institute	14
Canadian Policy Research Networks	13
Fraser Institute	8
Canadian Defence and Foreign Affairs Institute (CDFAI)	8
Canadian Council on Social Development	6
Macdonald-Laurier Institute	6
Mowat Centre	6
Wellesley Institute	5
Canadian Institute of Strategic Studies/Canadian International Council	4
Parliamentary Centre	4
International Institute for Sustainable Development	4
North-South Institute	4
Caledon Institute of Social Policy	3
Institute for Research on Public Policy	3
Asia Pacific Foundation of Canada (APFC)	3
Mackenzie Institute	3
National Council of Welfare	2
Canada West Foundation	2
Vanier Institute of the Family	2
Atlantic Institute for Market Studies (AIMS)	2
Centre for International Governance Innovation (CIGI)	2
Public Policy Forum	1
Canadian Tax Foundation	1
Canadian Institute for International Affairs	0
Canadian Council for International Peace and Study	0
Pearson-Shoyama Institute	0
Total	152

Note: 35th Parliament data are not available.
Source: http://www.parl.gc.ca/parliamentarians/en/publicationsearch?PubType=40017.

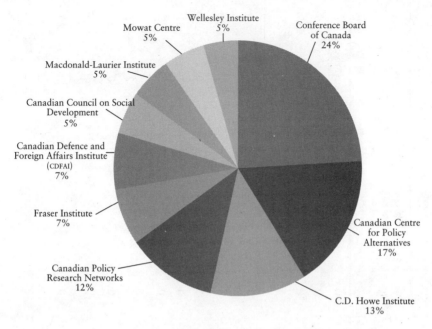

Figure A2.2 Appearances by selected Canadian think tanks before parliamentary committees, 2008–2015

Table A2.3 Appearances by selected Canadian think tanks before House of Commons committees, 1999–2008

Institute	36th Parliament 2nd Session 04/99–10/00 Liberal	37th Parliament 1st Session 01/01–09/02 Liberal	37th Parliament 2nd Session 09/02–11/03 Liberal	37th Parliament 3rd Session 02/04–05/04 Liberal	38th Parliament 1st Session 10/04–11/05 Liberal	39th Parliament 1st Session 04/06–09/07 Conservative	39th Parliament 2nd Session 10/07–09/08 Conservative	Totals
Conference Board of Canada	18	22	25	0	30	21	10	126
C.D. Howe Institute	12	18	15	0	18	15	7	85
Fraser Institute	6	18	7	5	12	8	4	60
Canadian Council on Social Development	7	11	11	0	13	2	1	45
Canadian Centre for Policy Alternatives	7	4	3	0	10	7	6	37
North-South Institute	5	13	4	3	5	2	0	32
National Council on Welfare	5	6	7	0	5	7	1	31
Public Policy Forum	4	15	5	0	4	0	0	28
Caledon Institute of Social Policy	10	5	2	0	5	3	2	27
Parliamentary Centre	3	7	2	0	3	10	0	25
Canada West Foundation	5	7	2	0	7	0	1	22
Canadian Policy Research Networks	6	0	7	0	2	5	0	20
Institute for Research on Public Policy	0	3	2	0	4	2	0	11

Canadian Institute for Strategic Studies	0	6	3	0	2	0	11
Canadian Institute for International Affairs	0	5	2	0	1	0	8
Mackenzie Institute	1	1	0	0	1	0	3
Canadian Tax Foundation	0	0	0	0	2	0	2
Canadian Council for International Peace and Security	0	0	0	0	0	0	0
Pearson-Shoyama Institute	0	0	0	0	0	0	0
	89	141	97	8	124	82	573

Source: Library of Parliament, http://www.parl.gc.ca/common/Library.asp.

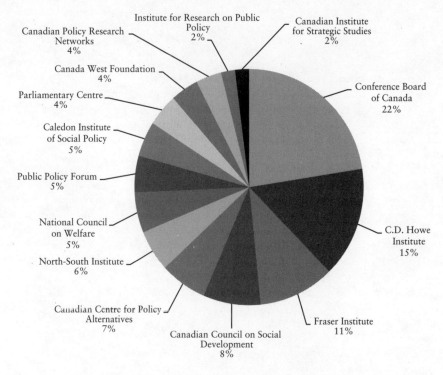

Institute for Research on Public Policy
2%

Canadian Policy Research Networks
4%

Canada West Foundation
4%

Parliamentary Centre
4%

Caledon Institute of Social Policy
5%

Public Policy Forum
5%

National Council on Welfare
5%

North-South Institute
6%

Canadian Centre for Policy Alternatives
7%

Canadian Institute for Strategic Studies
2%

Conference Board of Canada
22%

C.D. Howe Institute
15%

Fraser Institute
11%

Canadian Council on Social Development
8%

Figure A2.3 Appearances by selected Canadian think tanks before House of Commons committees, 1999–2008

Table A2.4 Appearances of selected Canadian think tanks before House of Commons committees, 2008–2015

Institute	40th Parliament 1st Session 11/08–12/08 Conservative	40th Parliament 2nd Session 01/09–12/09 Conservative	40th Parliament 3rd Session 03/10–03/11 Conservative	41st Parliament 1st Session 06/11–09/13 Conservative	41st Parliament 2nd Session 10/13–08/15 Conservative	Total
Conference Board of Canada	0	9	5	8	5	27
Canadian Centre for Policy Alternatives	0	5	3	5	6	19
Canadian Policy Research Networks (closed)	0	3	0	0	0	13
C.D. Howe Institute	0	3	1	4	4	12
Fraser Institute	0	0	4	3	1	8
Canadian Council on Social Development	0	2	3	1	0	6
Wellesley Institute	0	3	1	0	1	5
Macdonald-Laurier Institute	0	0	2	2	1	5
The North-South Institute	0	1	0	2	1	4
Parliamentary Centre	0	3	0	1	0	4
International Institute for Sustainable Development	0	1	0	1	2	4
Canadian Defence and Foreign Affairs Institute (CDFAI)	0	0	0	1	3	4
Caledon Institute of Social Policy	0	2	0	0	1	3
Asia Pacific Foundation of Canada (APFC)	0	0	0	2	1	3
Mackenzie Institute	0	1	0	0	2	3
Institute for Research on Public Policy	0	0	1	0	2	3
Mowat Centre	0	0	0	0	3	3

Table A2.4 Appearances of Selected Canadian think tanks before House of Commons committees, 2008–2015 (*continued*)

Institute	40th Parliament 1st Session 11/08–12/08 Conservative	40th Parliament 2nd Session 01/09–12/09 Conservative	40th Parliament 3rd Session 03/10–03/11 Conservative	41st Parliament 1st Session 06/11–09/13 Conservative	41st Parliament 2nd Session 10/13–08/15 Conservative	Total
Atlantic Institute for Market Studies (AIMS)	0	0	1	1	0	2
Canada West Foundation	0	0	1	1	0	2
Centre for International Governance Innovation (CIGI)	0	1	0	1	0	2
Canadian Institute of Strategic Studies/Canadian International Council	0	0	0	2	0	2
Vanier Institute of the Family	0	2	0	0	0	2
Public Policy Forum	0	0	0	1	0	1
Canadian Tax Foundation	0	0	0	1	0	1
Canadian Institute for International Affairs	0	0	0	0	0	0
Canadian Council for International Peace and Security	0	0	0	0	0	0
Pearson-Shoyama Institute	0	0	0	0	0	0
Total		38	22	37	33	130

Source: http://www.parl.gc.ca/ParlBusiness/Senate/Debates/Calendar.asp?Language=E&Parl=41&Ses=2.

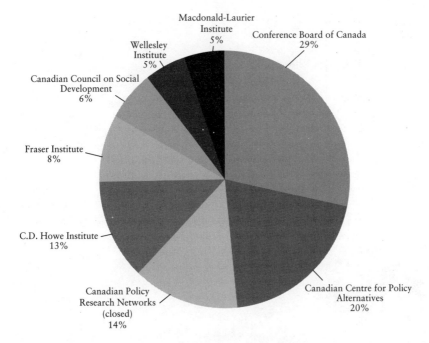

Figure A 2.4 Appearances by selected Canadian think tanks before House of Commons committees, 2008–2015

Table A2.5 Appearances of selected Canadian think tanks before Senate committees, 1999–2008

Institute	36th Parliament 2nd Session 04/99–10/00 Liberal	37th Parliament 1st Session 01/01–09/02 Liberal	37th Parliament 2nd Session 09/02–11/03 Liberal	37th Parliament 3rd Session 02/04–05/04 Liberal	38th Parliament 1st Session 10/04–11/05 Liberal	39th Parliament 1st Session 04/06–09/07 Conservative	39th Parliament 2nd Session 10/07–09/08 Conservative	Totals
Conference Board of Canada	0	3	0	0	4	7	3	17
Fraser Institute	0	1	3	1	3	5	0	13
C.D. Howe Institute	2	1	0	0	4	5	1	13
Canadian Centre for Policy Alternatives	0	0	1	0	1	3	4	9
Caledon Institute of Social Policy	0	0	0	0	0	2	6	8
Institute for Research on Public Policy	0	0	0	1	0	4	1	6
Canada West Foundation	0	0	1	0	1	2	0	4
Canadian Council on Social Development	0	0	0	0	0	1	1	2
Canadian Policy Research Networks	0	0	0	0	1	1	1	2
North-South Institute	0	1	0	0	2	0	0	1
Parliamentary Centre	0	0	0	0	0	1	0	1
Canadian Council for International Peace and Security	1	0	0	0	0	0	0	1

Mackenzie Institute	0	0	0	0	1	0	0	1
National Council on Welfare	0	0	0	0	0	0	0	0
Canadian Institute for Strategic Studies	0	0	0	0	0	0	0	0
Canadian Institute for International Affairs	0	0	0	0	0	0	0	0
Canadian Tax Foundation	0	0	0	0	0	0	0	0
Public Policy Forum	0	0	0	0	0	0	0	0
Pearson-Shoyama Institute	0	0	0	0	0	0	0	0
Total	3	6	5	2	17	31	16	80

Source: Library of Parliament, http://www.parl.gc.ca/common/Library.asp.

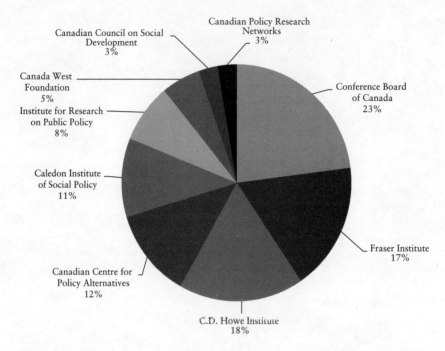

Figure A2.5 Appearances by selected Canadian think tanks before Senate committees, 1999–2008

Table A2.6 Appearances by selected Canadian think tanks before Senate committees, 2008–2015

Institute	40th Parliament 1st Session 11/08–12/08 Conservative	40th Parliament 2nd Session 11/09–12/09 Conservative	40th Parliament 3rd Session 03/10–03/11 Conservative	41st Parliament 1st Session 06/11–09/13 Conservative	41st Parliament 2nd Session 10/13–08/15 Conservative	Total
Canadian Institute of Strategic Studies/Canadian International Council	0	0	2	0	0	2
Mowat Centre	0	0	0	3	0	3
Canadian Defence and Foreign Affairs Institute (CDFAI)	0	0	1	2	1	4
C.D. Howe Institute	0	0	0	0	2	2
Fraser Institute	0	0	0	0	0	0
Canadian Policy Research Networks (closed)	0	0	0	0	0	0
Macdonald-Laurier Institute	0	0	1	0	0	1
Conference Board of Canada	0	0	0	0	0	0
Canadian Centre for Policy Alternatives	0	0	0	0	0	0
National Council of Welfare	0	0	0	0	0	0
Canadian Council on Social Development	0	0	0	0	0	0
The North-South Institute	0	0	0	0	0	0
Parliamentary Centre	0	0	0	0	0	0
International Institute for Sustainable Development	0	0	0	0	0	0
Atlantic Institute for Market Studies (AIMS)	0	0	0	0	0	0
Caledon Institute of Social Policy	0	0	0	0	0	0

Table A2.6 Appearances by selected Canadian think tanks before Senate committees, 2008–2015 (continued)

Institute	40th Parliament 1st Session 11/08–12/08 Conservative	40th Parliament 2nd Session 11/09–12/09 Conservative	40th Parliament 3rd Session 03/10–03/11 Conservative	41st Parliament 1st Session 06/11–09/13 Conservative	41st Parliament 2nd Session 10/13–08/15 Conservative	Total
Asia Pacific Foundation of Canada (APFC)	0	0	0	0	0	0
Canadian Institute for International Affairs	0	0	0	0	0	0
Public Policy Forum	0	0	0	0	0	0
Canada West Foundation	0	0	0	0	0	0
Centre for International Governance Innovation (CIGI)	0	0	0	0	0	0
Wellesley Institute	0	0	0	0	0	0
Mackenzie Institute	0	0	0	0	0	0
Institute for Research on Public Policy	0	0	0	0	0	0
Canadian Tax Foundation	0	0	0	0	0	0
Vanier Institute of the Family	0	0	0	0	0	0
Canadian Council for International Peace and Security	0	0	0	0	0	0
Pearson-Shoyama Institute	0	0	0	0	0	0
Total	0	0	4	5	3	12

Source: http://www.parl.gc.ca/SenCommitteeBusiness/AllMeetings.aspx?parl=35&ses=1&Language=E&searchMeetings=1.

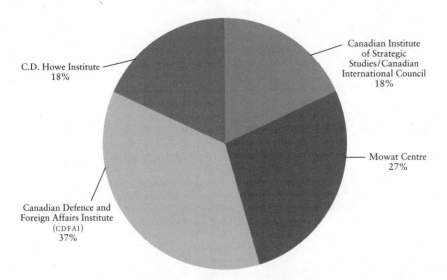

Figure A2.6 Appearances by selected Canadian think tanks before Senate committees, 2008–2015

References to Selected Canadian Think Tanks in Parliament, 1994–2015

Table A3.1 References to selected Canadian think tanks in the House of Commons, 1994–2008

Institute	35th Parliament 1st Session 01/94–02/96	35th Parliament 2nd Session 02/96–04/97	36th Parliament 1st Session 09/97–09/99	36th Parliament 2nd Session 04/99–10/00	37th Parliament 1st Session 01/01–09/02	37th Parliament 2nd Session 09/02–11/03	37th Parliament 3rd Session 02/04–05/04	38th Parliament 1st Session 10/04–11/05	39th Parliament 1st Session 04/06–09/07	39th Parliament 2nd Session 10/07–09/08	Totals
	Liberal	Liberal	Liberal	Liberal	Liberal	Liberal	Liberal	Liberal	Conservative	Conservative	
Conference Board of Canada	35	6	52	32	34	14	6	40	26	21	266
Fraser Institute	55	60	40	14	18	19	4	21	15	13	259
C.D. Howe Institute	25	12	33	7	8	6	4	11	14	16	136
National Council on Welfare	13	12	20	15	6	6	2	5	4	9	92
Canadian Centre for Policy Alternatives	4	0	5	0	4	6	1	15	19	11	65
Canadian Council on Social Development	8	4	13	2	4	9	4	6	3	2	55

Table A3.1 References to selected Canadian think tanks in the House of Commons, 1994–2008 (continued)

Institute	35th Parliament 1st Session 01/94–02/96 Liberal	35th Parliament 2nd Session 02/96–04/97 Liberal	36th Parliament 1st Session 09/97–09/99 Liberal	36th Parliament 2nd Session 04/99–10/00 Liberal	37th Parliament 1st Session 01/01–09/02 Liberal	37th Parliament 2nd Session 09/02–11/03 Liberal	37th Parliament 3rd Session 02/04–05/04 Liberal	38th Parliament 1st Session 10/04–11/05 Liberal	39th Parliament 1st Session 04/06–09/07 Conservative	39th Parliament 2nd Session 10/07–09/08 Conservative	Totals
Public Policy Forum	7	4	6	4	5	2	1	5	3	0	37
Canada West Foundation	10	4	4	0	4	1	2	0	2	2	29
Canadian Tax Foundation	3	3	6	0	1	0	0	1	8	1	23
Caledon Institute of Social Policy	4	2	7	0	2	0	0	0	4	3	22
Mackenzie Institute	9	4	0	0	7	0	0	0	0	0	20
Institute for Research on Public Policy	1	2	0	2	2	2	1	0	4	0	14
Canadian Institute for Strategic Studies	1	0	0	0	4	0	0	0	2	0	7

North-South Institute	2	0	0	0	0	0	0	0	0	0	5
Canadian Policy Research Networks	0	0	0	0	1	0	0	2	1	0	5
Parliamentary Centre	1	0	0	0	1	1	0	1	0	0	3
Canadian Council for International Peace and Security	0	0	0	0	0	0	0	0	0	0	0
Canadian Institute for International Affairs	0	0	0	0	0	0	0	0	0	0	0
Pearson-Shoyama Institute	0	0	0	0	0	0	0	0	0	0	0
Total	178	113	186	76	103	67	25	107	105	78	1,038

Source: Library of Parliament, http://www.parl.gc.ca/common/Library.asp.

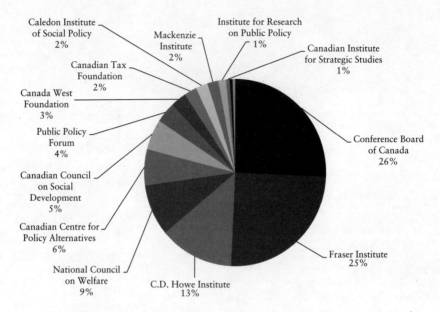

Figure A3.1 References to selected Canadian think tanks in the House of Commons, 1994–2008

Table A3.2 References to selected Canadian think tanks in the House of Commons, 2008–2015

Institute	40th Parliament 3rd Session 03/10–03/11 Conservative	40th Parliament 2nd Session 01/09–12/09 Conservative	40th Parliament 3rd Session 03/10–03/11 Conservative	41st Parliament 1st Session 06/11–09/13 Conservative	41st Parliament 2nd Session 10/13–08/15 Conservative	Totals
Conference Board of Canada	10	21	40	121	88	280
Canadian Centre for Policy Alternatives	0	26	19	44	44	133
C.D. Howe Institute	0	31	15	20	65	131
Fraser Institute	0	4	17	28	23	72
National Council of Welfare	0	2	1	59	4	66
International Institute for Sustainable Development	0	0	2	18	9	29
Wellesley Institute	1	4	5	6	6	22
Canada West Foundation	0	3	4	7	3	17
Caledon Institute of Social Policy	1	6	4	4	0	15
Mowat Centre	0	0	3	7	4	14
Macdonald-Laurier Institute	0	0	0	11	2	13
Canadian Tax Foundation	0	0	0	10	0	10
Institute for Research on Public Policy	0	2	1	6	0	9
Canadian Council on Social Development	0	1	3	2	2	8
The North-South Institute	0	1	0	0	6	7
Asia Pacific Foundation of Canada (APFC)	0	0	1	1	4	6
Atlantic Institute for Market Studies (AIMS)	0	0	0	0	3	3
Canadian Defence and Foreign Affairs Institute (CDFAI)	0	0	0	0	3	3

Table A3.2 References to selected Canadian think tanks in the House of Commons, 2008–2015 (continued)

Institute	40th Parliament 3rd Session 03/10–03/11 Conservative	40th Parliament 2nd Session 01/09–12/09 Conservative	40th Parliament 3rd Session 03/10–03/11 Conservative	41st Parliament 1st Session 06/11–09/13 Conservative	41st Parliament 2nd Session 10/13–08/15 Conservative	Totals
Public Policy Forum	0	0	1	0	1	2
Centre for International Governance Innovation (CIGI)	0	1	0	1	0	2
Parliamentary Centre	0	0	1	0	1	2
Canadian Institute of Strategic Studies/	0	0	0	1	0	1
Vanier Institute of the Family	0	0	0	0	0	0
Canadian Policy Research Networks (closed)	0	0	0	0	0	0
Mackenzie Institute	0	0	0	0	0	0
Canadian Institute for International Affairs	0	0	0	0	0	0
Canadian Council for International Peace and Security	0	0	0	0	0	0
Pearson-Shoyama Institute	0	0	0	0	0	0
Canadian International Council						
Total	12	102	117	346	268	845

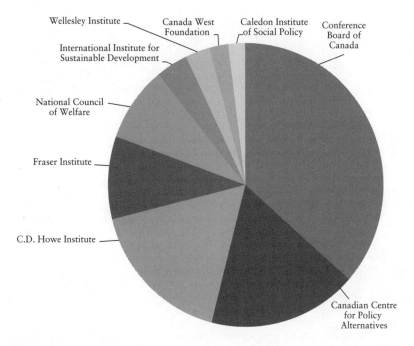

Figure A3.2 References to selected Canadian think tanks in the House of Commons, 2008–2015

Table A3.3 References to selected Canadian think tanks in the Senate, 1994–2008

Institute	35th Parliament 1st Session 01/94–02/96	35th Parliament 2nd Session 02/96–04/97	36th Parliament 1st Session 09/97–09/99	36th Parliament 2nd Session 04/99–10/00	37th Parliament 1st Session 01/01–09/02	37th Parliament 2nd Session 09/02–11/03	37th Parliament 3rd Session 02/04–05/04	38th Parliament 1st Session 10/04–11/05	39th Parliament 1st Session 04/06–09/07	39th Parliament 2nd Session 10/07–09/08	Totals
	Liberal	Liberal	Liberal	Liberal	Liberal	Liberal	Liberal	Liberal	Conservative	Conservative	
Conference Board of Canada	0	4	18	10	8	16	8	24	18	9	115
C.D. Howe Institute	0	5	4	5	4	2	0	8	12	8	48
Fraser Institute	0	0	3	1	1	0	0	6	16	6	33
Canada West Foundation	0	0	0	6	0	2	2	0	12	2	24
Institute for Research on Public Policy	0	0	0	3	2	1	1	4	8	0	19
National Council on Welfare	0	2	11	2	1	0	0	1	0	0	17
Caledon Institute of Social Policy	0	2	2	0	1	0	0	0	10	0	15
Canadian Tax Foundation	0	0	4	0	1	0	0	2	2	1	10
Canadian Council on Social Development	0	2	1	0	2	0	0	1	2	1	9

Institution										Total
Parliamentary Centre	0	0	1	1	2	1	0	2	1	0	8
Canadian Policy Research Networks	0	2	0	1	0	1	0	0	4	0	8
Public Policy Forum	0	0	1	1	3	1	0	1	0	0	7
Canadian Centre for Policy Alternatives	0	1	0	1	0	0	0	0	2	2	6
Canadian Institute for International Affairs	0	0	0	1	0	3	1	0	0	0	5
Canadian Institute for Strategic Studies	0	1	0	1	2	0	0	0	0	0	4
North-South Institute	0	0	0	0	0	1	0	1	0	0	2
Mackenzie Institute	0	0	0	0	0	2	0	0	0	0	2
Canadian Council for International Peace and Security											0
Pearson-Shoyama Institute	0	0	0	0	0	0	0	0	0	0	0
Total	0	19	45	33	27	30	12	50	87	29	332

Source: Library of Parliament, http://www.parl.gc.ca/common/Library.asp.

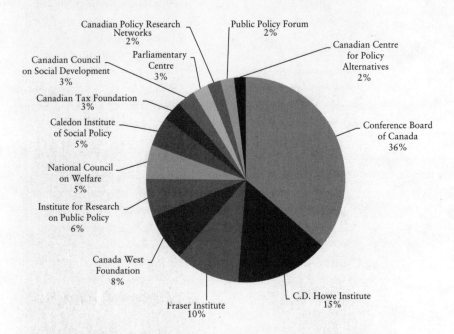

Canadian Policy Research
Networks
2%

Public Policy Forum
2%

Canadian Centre
for Policy
Alternatives
2%

Canadian Council
on Social Development
3%

Parliamentary
Centre
3%

Canadian Tax Foundation
3%

Caledon Institute
of Social Policy
5%

National Council
on Welfare
5%

Institute for Research
on Public Policy
6%

Canada West
Foundation
8%

Conference Board
of Canada
36%

C.D. Howe Institute
15%

Fraser Institute
10%

Figure A3.3 References to selected Canadian think tanks in the senate, 1994–2008

Table A3.4 References to selected Canadian think tanks in the Senate, 2008–2015

Institute	40th Parliament 3rd Session 03/10–03/11 Conservative	41st Parliament 1st Session 06/11–09/13 Conservative	41st Parliament 2nd Session 10/13–08/15 Conservative	Total
Canadian Institute of Strategic Studies/ Canadian International Council	83	131	90	304
Parliamentary Centre	27	66	56	149
Canadian Council on Social Development	33	55	32	120
Conference Board of Canada	29	53	20	102
Canadian Tax Foundation	20	61	20	101
Public Policy Forum	24	37	28	89
Institute for Research on Public Policy	25	38	18	81
Fraser Institute	20	35	25	80
Canadian Policy Research Networks (closed)	14	37	18	69
Canada West Foundation	13	34	17	64
Canadian Centre for Policy Alternatives	9	36	16	61
Canadian Institute for International Affairs	11	30	14	55
Canadian Council for International Peace and Security	9	31	9	49
National Council of Welfare	5	19	9	33
Canadian Defence and Foreign Affairs Institute (CDFAI)	2	15	5	22
International Institute for Sustainable Development	6	13	3	22
The North-South Institute	5	8	5	18
Atlantic Institute for Market Studies (AIMS)	3	10	2	15
Centre for International Governance Innovation (CIGI)	2	10	3	15
C.D. Howe Institute	1	5	4	10
Macdonald-Laurier Institute	1	6	3	10
Asia Pacific Foundation of Canada (APFC)	1	5	4	10
Mackenzie Institute	2	2	0	4
Caledon Institute of Social Policy	0	1	3	4
Mowat Centre	0	1	1	2
Wellesley Institute	0	1	1	2
Vanier Institute of the Family	0	1	0	1
Pearson-Shoyama Institute	0	0	0	0
Total	345	741	406	1,492

Note: Data on think tank references in the Senate are not available between the 35th and 41st Parliaments [NB: Thank you to Catherine Piccinin, treasurer and deputy principal clerk of the Canadian Study of Parliament Group, Committees Directorate, of the Senate of Canada, for her assistance in locating and navigating the data gap.]

Source: http://www.parl.gc.ca/ParlBusiness/Senate/Debates/Calendar.asp?Language=E&Parl=41&Ses=2.

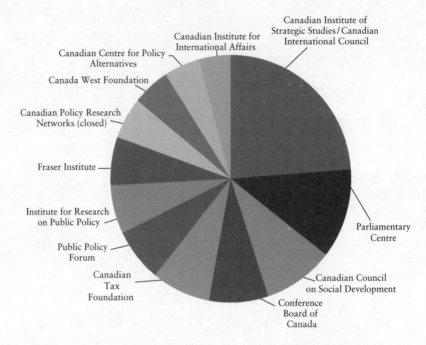

Figure A 3.4 References to selected Canadian think tanks in the Senate, 2008–2015

Notes

INTRODUCTION

1 See Smith, *The Idea Brokers.*
2 See Smith, *The Brookings Institution at Seventy-Five* and *Strategic Calling.*
3 This question has been explored by Abelson in "National Interest or Self-Interest?"
4 The closure of the North-South Institute (NSI) generated considerable media attention. See, for instance, Crawford, "North-South Institute, Ottawa-Based Think Tank, to Close"; cbcnews.ca, "North-South Institute to Close"; Goar, "Another Canadian Window on the World Closes," and Martin et al., "North-South Institute: We've Lost a Canadian Asset."
5 The Canadian federal government's audit of the Canadian Centre for Policy Alternatives (CCPA) and several other high-profile charitable organizations is discussed in McQuaig, "Harper Ramps Up His War"; Daifallah, "Unmuzzle the Charities"; Keenan, "Why Haven't Any Harper-Friendly Charities Been Scrutinized?"; Beeby, "CRA to Oxfam"; Cheadle, "After CRA Audit"; Levitz, "Right-Leaning Charities Escape Tax Audits"; Canadian Press, "CRA Audits CCPA" and Crowe, "PM's Charity Audits." Although the CCPA and its supporters claim that the CRA has targeted mostly left-leaning think tanks, the Fraser Institute, according to its president Niels Veldhuis, has been audited three times in its forty-year history. See MacCharles, "Think-Tank Says It Was Targeted."
6 See Gutstein, *Harperism;* Harris, *Party of One,* 37–9; Flanagan, *Harper's Team,* 72, 79; and Bourrie, *Kill the Messengers,* 306–7.
7 See Lipton, Williams, and Confessore, "Foreign Powers Buy Influence at Think Tanks." For reactions to the allegations made in this article, see Bruckner, "Fund a Think Tank, Buy a Lobbyist?"; Drezner, "Why I'm Not

Freaking Out"; Lipton, "Proposal Would Require Think Tanks to
Disclose"; Halper, "Stop Foreign Governments from Buying"; Yakabuski,
"Think Tanks Need to Show Us the Money"; and *Think Tank Watch*,
"Think Tanks Rush to Defend Funding" and "New House Rules."

8 In recent years, a growing number of articles, book chapters, and books
have profiled think tanks in several different countries. See, for example,
Medvetz, *Think Tanks in America*; Pautz, *Think Tanks, Social Democracy
and Social Policy*; Pirie, *Think Tank: The Story of the Adam Smith
Institute*; and Abelson, "Think Tanks and US Diplomatic and Military
Affairs."

9 Several studies have helped lay the foundations for a closer examination of
think tanks. See, for example, Dickson, *Think Tanks*; Peschek, *Policy-
Planning Organizations*; Orlans, *The Nonprofit Research Institute*; Ricci,
The Transformation of American Politics; Stone, *Capturing the Political
Imagination*; Smith, *The Idea Brokers*; Abelson, *American Think Tanks*;
McGann, *The Competition for Dollars;* and Weaver, "The Changing World
of Think Tanks."

10 On the relationship between think tanks and the government of Margaret
Thatcher, see Cockett, *Thinking the Unthinkable*; Denham, *Think Tanks of
the New Right;* Pirie, *Think Tank;* and Stone, *Capturing the Political
Imagination.* For a discussion of the role played by conservative think
tanks in spearheading the Reagan revolution, see Edwards, *The Power of
Ideas*, and Anderson, *Revolution.* And on the efforts of a handful of well-
placed think tanks to influence US foreign and defence policy in the post-
9/11 era, see Frum and Perle, *An End to Evil*, and Abelson, *A Capitol Idea.*

11 See Medvetz, *Think Tanks in America*; Abelson, "Think Tanks and US
Diplomatic and Military Affairs"; Pautz, *Think Tanks, Social Democracy
and Social Policy;* and Pirie, *Think Tanks: The Story of the Adam Smith
Institute.*

12 See Stone, "Banking on Knowledge."

13 McGann, *2006 Global Go To Think Tanks Index Report.*

14 McGann, *2014 Global Go To Think Tanks Index Report.*

15 Muggah and Owen examine the closure of several foreign affairs think
tanks in Canada in "Decline in Canadian Think Tanks." For more on the
history of think tanks in Canada, see Lindquist, "A Quarter-Century of
Think Tanks in Canada"; Dobuzinsis, "Trends and Fashions in the
Marketplace of Ideas"; Mackinnon, "The Canadian Think Tank Scene";
and Abelson, "Surveying the Think Tank Landscape in Canada," and "Any
Ideas?"

16 For a history of these and other US think tanks, see Abelson, *American Think Tanks;* Critchlow, *The Brookings Institution;* Smith, *The Idea Brokers;* Schulzinger, *The Wise Men of Foreign Affairs;* Edwards, *The Power of Ideas;* Abella, *Soldiers of Reason;* and Kaplan, *The Wizards of Armageddon.*

17 Abelson, *A Capitol Idea,* 167.

CHAPTER ONE

1 Soanes and Hawker (eds), *Compact Oxford English Dictionary,* s.v. "Think Tank."

2 Guralnik, *Webster's New World Dictionary,* s.v. "Think Tank."

3 See, for instance, two encyclopaedic entries by Abelson, "Think Tanks and US Military and Diplomatic Affairs" and "Think Tanks"; and one by Weaver, "Think Tanks." Also see the Fraser Institute, "What is a Think Tank?" at fraserinstitute.org.

4 Gerson, "Your Think-Tank Lineup Card." Also included in this list is the C.D. Howe Institute, the Fraser Institute, the Canadian Centre for Policy Alternatives, and the Broadbent Institute, which, unlike the other three think tanks, is not a registered charity, a feature it shares with the Manning Centre.

5 McGann, *Competition for Dollars,* 9.

6 McGann, *2012 Global Go To Think Tanks Index Report.*

7 See, for instance, Abelson, *Do Think Tanks Matter?;* McGann and Weaver, *Think Tanks & Civil Societies;* and Stone, *Capturing the Political Imagination.*

8 Abelson, "Think Tanks and US Military and Diplomatic Affairs," 354–5.

9 Several studies have been written on the history of the RAND Corporation. See Kaplan, *The Wizards of Armageddon;* Samaan, *The Rand Corporation;* Abella, *Soldiers of Reason;* and Smith, *The Rand Corporation.*

10 My thanks to Professor Monda Halpern for making the connection between the functions performed by settlement houses and those carried out by think tanks.

11 For an overview of these and other think tanks, see Abelson, "Old World, New World."

12 The Fraser Institute is just one of many think tanks in Canada that derives significant benefits from maintaining its status as a charitable organization. See Hong, "Charitable Fraser Institute Received $4.3 Million in Foreign Funding Since 2000."

13 The requirements for charitable organizations under the Income Tax Act
    can be viewed at http://www.cra-arc.gc.ca/chrts-gvng/chrts/menu-eng.html.
14 It is important to note that both non-profit organizations (also referred to
    as non-profit corporations) and charitable organizations are tax-exempt.
    Non-profit organizations receive tax exemptions provided by the Income
    Tax Act as long as they satisfy eligibility requirements. Nonetheless, both
    charitable organizations and non-profit organizations may be required to
    pay taxes on the building space they occupy and on some related costs.
    Unlike charitable organizations, non-profit organizations that are not
    designated as charities are not permitted to issue tax receipts for charitable
    donations. See http://pattersonlaw.ca/NewsArticleView/tabid/179/ArticleId/
    136/Charitable-and-Non-Profit-Organizations-and-Canada-s-Income-Tax-
    Act.aspx, and Boutis and Ali, "How Changes to the Income Tax Act," at
    http://rabble.ca/columnists/2012/09/
    changes-income-tax-act-will-restrict-charities-political-activities.
15 The requirements for charitable organizations under Section 501(c)(3) of
    the Internal Revenue Code can be viewed at http://www.irs.gov/Charities-
    & Non-Profits/Charitable-Organizations/Exemption-Requirements-
    Section-501(c)(3)-Organizations.
16 On the relationship between donors and for-profit think tanks, see
    Mendizabal, "For-Profit Think Tanks."
17 Daifallah, "Unmuzzle the Charities."
18 See Troy, "Devaluing the Think Tank," and Bender, "Many DC Think
    Tanks." Also view http://www.irs.gov/Charities-%26-Non-Profits/Other-
    Non-Profits/Types-of-Organizations-Exempt-under-Section-501(c)(4).
19 Periodically, think tanks in the United States prefer to describe themselves
    as bipartisan rather than as non-partisan. This allows them to create the
    impression that they do not embrace the political agenda of either the
    Democrats or Republicans, but are available to lend their expertise to
    elected officials from any political party.
20 The distinction between being non-partisan and non-ideological is often
    blurred. See Badger, "Think Tanks Are Nonpartisan? Think Again."
21 For more on the relationship between think tanks and Canadian political
    parties, see Gailus, "Mind Games," and Baier and Bakvis, "Think Tanks
    and Political Parties."
22 For an examination of how think tanks in Canada are funded, see
    McLevey, "Think Tanks, Funding, and the Politics of Policy Knowledge."
23 http://www.cra-arc.gc.ca/chrts-gvng/chrts/plcy/cps/cps-022-eng.html#
    N101D6.
24 Ibid.

25 Ibid.
26 Ibid.
27 See Thunert, "Expert Policy Advice in Germany," and Braml, "Determinants of German Think Tanks." For more information about think tanks in Germany, see Pautz, *Think-Tanks, Social Democracy and Social Policy.* In a recent study, *Harperism,* Donald Gutstein reveals the intimate ties between the Harper government and several conservative think tanks, and refutes the notion that the latter are concerned about sacrificing their autonomy by aligning themselves with political parties. Also see McQuaig, "Harper Ramps Up His War," and Goar, "Another Canadian Window on the World Closes."
28 http://www.irs.gov/Charities-&-Non-Profits/Charitable-Organizations/Exemption-Requirements-Section-501(c)(3)-Organizations.
29 Ibid.
30 Ibid.
31 Think tanks in Canada are also well aware of the consequences of having their charitable status revoked. Depending on the actual violation think tanks have committed, penalties could range from a reprimand, or fine, to losing their designation as a registered charity. This is what happened to the organization Dying with Dignity in early 2015. See Kelly Crowe, "PM's Charity Audits." According to several news reports that surfaced in the summer of 2014, the Canada Revenue Agency was investigating whether a handful of other charitable organizations, including the Canadian Centre for Policy Alternatives (CCPA), engaged in inappropriate political activities. Approximately sixty charitable organizations were being audited at the time. Several critics claimed that the Harper government was using the CRA to stifle political debate. See Beeby, "CRA Audited Left-Wing Think Tanks"; "NDP calls For Independent Probe"; "CRA Audits CCPA Think-Tank"; and "CRA to Oxfam." In response to the CRA audit of the CCPA, an open letter to the Minister of National Revenue, along with a petition, was posted on the Progressive Economics Forum, urging "the CRA to put a moratorium on its audits of think tanks, until such time as a truly neutral criteria and auditing process are implemented." To date, over 400 researchers from across Canada have signed the petition, "Academics against the CCPA audit." See Seccareccia and Rochon, "Update: A Petition of Academics," at http://www.progressive-economics.ca/2014/09/11/a--petition-of-academics-against-the-ccpa-audit/. What appears to be at issue is whether some of the activities conducted by think tanks are political in nature, or are pursued for educational purposes. According to a 1999 Supreme Court of Canada ruling, "so long as useful information or

training was provided in a structured manner and for a genuine educational purpose – that is to advance the knowledge or abilities of the recipients – and not solely to promote a particular point of view or political orientation it might properly be regarded as for the advancement of education." For more on this, see Mendizabal and Beeby, "CRA Audited Left-Wing Think Tanks."

32 Abelson, *American Think Tanks,* 16–18.
33 Selee addresses this topic in his study, *What Should Think Tanks Do?*
34 Abelson, "Old World, New World," 130–4.
35 Research was not always carried out for altruistic purposes. For more on this, see Parmar, *Foundations of the American Century.*
36 Muggah and Owen, "Decline in Canadian Think-Tanks."
37 See, for instance, Abelson, "It Seemed Like a Good Idea."
38 Weaver, "The Changing World of Think Tanks," 567.
39 Knickerbocker, "Heritage Foundation's Ideas." For a detailed history of the Heritage Foundation, see Edwards, *The Power of Ideas* and *Leading the Way.*
40 See Troy, "Devaluing the Think Tank."
41 For an interesting history of the Adam Smith Institute, see Pirie, *Think Tank.* On the Fraser Institute, see Abelson, *Do Think Tanks Matter?*, 45–7.
42 On the extent to which the success of think tanks has contributed to the further marginalization of social science research, see Medvetz, *Think Tanks in America.*
43 Data on think tank expenditures can be found in their annual reports, usually available on their websites.
44 See Smith, *The Idea Brokers.*
45 See Selee, *What Should Think Tanks Do?*
46 Abelson, "Environmental Lobbying or Political Posturing?"
47 This is one of the many strategies employed by the Heritage Foundation to keep a close watch on congressional activity. See Abelson, *American Think Tanks,* 55–9.
48 See Government of Canada, "Justice Laws," at http://laws-lois.justice.gc.ca/eng/acts/L-12.4/.
49 See US House of Representatives, Office of the Clerk, "Lobbying Disclosure," at http://lobbyingdisclosure.house.gov/lda.html.
50 Williams and Silverstein, "Meet the Think Tank Scholars."
51 See Lipton, Williams, and Confessore, "Foreign Powers Buy Influence at Think Tanks," and Williams, Lipton, and Parlapiano, "Foreign Government Contributions to Nine Think Tanks." For more on the role of think tanks as lobbyists, see Williams and Silverstein, "Meet the Think Tank Scholars."

Candid responses to these articles can be found in Mendizabal, "Think Tank Accountability"; Bruckner, "Fund a Think Tank, Buy a Lobbyist?"; Drezner, "Why I'm Not Freaking Out"; Talbott, "A Message from Strobe Talbott, President of the Brookings Institution," and "Brookings Statement on *New York Times* Article." For a more detailed discussion about the relationship between donors and think tanks, see Silverstein, *Pay to Play*, and Yakabuski, "Think Tanks Need to Show Us the Money."

52 See House Resolution 5, 114th Congress, 1st Session, 5 January 2015. Also see Lipton, "Proposal Would Require Think Tanks"; Halper, "Stop Foreign Governments from Buying American Think Tanks"; and *Think Tank Watch*, "New House Rules."

CHAPTER TWO

1 For more on how think tanks are managed, see Selee, *What Think Tanks Should Do?*, and Struyk, *Managing Think Tanks*.

2 McGann, *2008 Global Go To Think Tanks Index Report*, 12.

3 McGann, *2014 Global Go To Think Tanks Index Report*, 52.

4 The total number of think tanks included in this report could be exaggerated since several of the organizations surveyed may not qualify as think tanks. Professional academic associations such as the Canadian Economics Association is but one example of an organization that should not be part of the *Global Go To Think Tanks Index Report* database.

5 Several scholars have developed typologies of think tanks. See, for instance, Stone, *Capturing the Political Imagination*; McGann, "Academics to Ideologues"; Weaver, "Changing World of Think Tanks"; McGann and Weaver, *Think Tanks & Civil Societies*; and Abelson, *Do Think Tanks Matter?*

6 See Avins, "In-Depth: The New Think-and-Do Tank."

7 Weaver, "Changing World of Think Tanks."

8 McGann, "Academics to Ideologues."

9 For more on the role played by these and other philanthropists in creating think tanks during the progressive era, see Abelson, "Think Tanks and US Diplomatic and Military Affairs"; and Parmar, *Foundations of the American Century*.

10 Weaver, 564.

11 On the evolution of think tanks from institutions engaged primarily in policy research to those invested in political advocacy, see Smith, *The Idea Brokers*; Critchlow, *The Brookings Institution*; Abelson, "From Policy Research to Political Advocacy"; and Medvetz, *Think Tanks in America*.

12 For more on the history and evolution of IRPP, see Dobell, *IRPP*.

13 Several studies have been written about the RAND Corporation, including
    Abella, *Soldiers of Reason*; Kaplan, *The Wizards of Armageddon*; Smith,
    The Rand Corporation; Samaan, *The Rand Corporation (1989–2009)*; and
    Ghamari-Tabrizi, *The Worlds of Herman Kahn*. For background informa-
    tion on the Urban Institute, see Abelson, *Do Think Tanks Matter?*, 187.
14 Abelson, *Do Think Tanks Matter?*, 69.
15 Weaver, 567.
16 Lindquist, "Think Tanks?," 576.
17 See Smith, *The Idea Brokers* and Critchlow, *The Brookings Institution*.
18 Several scholars have argued that philanthropists and philanthropic foun-
    dations often support research institutions to advance their own ideologi-
    cal and political interests. See, for example, Parmar, *Foundations of the
    American Century*; Sealander, *Private Wealth*; Culleton Colwell, *Private
    Foundations*; Berman, *The Influence of the Carnegie*; Stefancic and
    Delgado, *No Mercy*; Bellant, *The Coors Connection*; Freund, *Narcissism
    and Philanthropy*; and Schulman, *Sons of Wichita*.
19 For a more complete chronological listing of think tanks created during
    this period, see McGann, "Academics to Ideologues."
20 See Abelson, "From Policy Research to Political Advocacy," and Freund,
    Narcissism and Philanthropy.
21 Lipton, Williams, and Confessore, "Foreign Powers Buy Influence at Think
    Tanks."
22 Talbott, "A Message from Strobe Talbott."
23 Abelson, *American Think Tanks*, 35.
24 See, for example, Pollack, *The Threatening Storm*.
25 Among the many factors that could account for the fact that Canada,
    unlike the United States, did not develop several prominent research insti-
    tutions during the early 1900s is the absence of large-scale philanthropic
    foundations dedicated to social science research. For more on this, see
    Richardson and Fisher, *The Development of the Social Sciences*, especially
    the introduction.
26 Several Canadian representatives attended the first gathering of the
    Institute of Pacific Relations (IPR) in Honolulu, which took place in June
    and July of 1925. Among those representing Canada were: John Nelson
    (chairman), Stanley Brent (secretary), Mary Bollert of the University of
    British Columbia, Kate Foster, field secretary of the YWCA, and George
    Cowan, KC, ex-MP, Vancouver. Canadian representation at the second
    conference of the IPR in July 1927 was even stronger, with 18 represen-
    tatives. In attendance were: General Sir Arthur Currie, Professor
    W.W. Goforth of McGill University, and NS Professor T.F. McIlwraith of

the University of Toronto. For more on the early history of the IPR and Canada's role in helping to establish it, see the Canadian Institute of International Affairs, *Its Organization*.

27 Despite concerns about how the rankings of the *Global Go To Think Tanks Index Report* are determined, Chatham House consistently ranks among the top foreign policy think tanks in the world. For a summary of some of the objections raised about the global think tank rankings, see Mendizabal, "The Go to Think Tank Index: Two Critiques" and "Think Tank Rankings and Awards"; Taylor, "Think Tank Rankings"; Duggal, "Tanks for the Rankings"; *Think Tank Watch*, "Think Tank Awards & Rankings"; and Abelson, "Think Tanks by the Numbers." Chatham House's stately headquarters on London's St James Square was a gift, made possible by a Canadian soldier, Colonel R.W. Leonard.

28 See Lindquist, "Think Tanks?"

29 For more on the early history of the CIIA, see Manny, "The Canadian Institute of International Affairs; Osendarp, "A Decade of Transition"; Holmes, "The CIIA," 9–10; Demson, "Canadian Institute of International Affairs"; Greathead, "Antecedents and Origins"; Boulden, "Independent Policy Research"; and the Canadian Institute of International Affairs, *Its Organization*.

30 Canadian International Council, *2008–2009 Annual Report*, 5. For more on Balsillie's involvement with the CIC, see "Jim Balsillie Leads in the Creation of the New Canadian International Council," and Church, "RIM's Balsillie Seeds Major Foreign Policy Think Tank."

31 The history of the CCSD is examined in Splane, *75 Years of Community Service*.

32 The RAND Corporation, often referred to simply as RAND, is a leading defence contractor in the US. Along with other institutes, including the Center for Naval Analyses and the Institute for Defense Analyses, RAND advises the US government on a host of defence issues. In recent years, RAND has expended its research program to focus on key domestic policy issues, including health care reform, population and aging, energy and the environment, and children and families. It also participates in several research initiatives with the University of California at Los Angeles. In addition to its headquarters in Santa Monica, California, RAND maintains smaller offices in four other US cities, in Australia, and in Europe.

33 The Urban Institute was created in 1968 at the request of President Lyndon B. Johnson and his domestic policy advisers and was originally conceived as the domestic policy equivalent of RAND. For more on the Urban Institute see Abelson, *Do Think Tanks Matter?*, 187.

34 Lipton, Williams, and Confessore, "Foreign Powers Buying Influence at Think Tanks." For more on CSIS, see Smith, *Strategic Calling*.

35 See Powell, *Covert Cadre*.

36 Abelson and Carberry, "Following Suit?," 534.

37 C.D. Howe Institute, www.cdhowe.org, "A History of the Institute."

38 Abelson and Lindquist, "Think Tanks in North America," 41.

39 Vanier Institute of the Family, www.familyforum.com.

40 For a discussion of how task forces and royal commissions have been used as sources of expertise for the Canadian government, see Bradford, *Commissioning Ideas*, and Jenson, "Commissioning Ideas."

41 Abelson and Lindquist, "Think Tanks in North America," 42.

42 Ibid.

43 For more on the PRI, see Anderson, "The New Focus."

44 For a rich history of the Heritage Foundation, see Edwards, *The Power of Ideas* and *Leading the Way*.

45 Abelson, *American Think Tanks*.

46 Abelson and Lindquist, "Think Tanks in North America." For more on the IRPP, see Dobell, *IRPP*, and Ritchie, *An Institute for Research on Public Policy*.

47 Ibid.

48 Canadian Centre for Philanthropy, www.ccp.ca. The Canadian Centre for Philanthropy is now called Imagine Canada, www.imaginecanada.ca.

49 See Gellner, "Political Think-Tanks."

50 See Melton, "Closing of Dole's Think Tank."

51 Abelson, "Changing Minds, Changing Course."

52 On the closure of the National Council of Welfare, see Goar, "Harper Throws."

53 Abelson and Lindquist, "Who's Thinking about International Affairs?"

54 See Gutstein, *Harperism* and Harris, *Party of One*.

CHAPTER THREE

1 Mills, *The Power Elite*.

2 Much has been written about President Eisenhower's farewell address and his concerns about the military–industrial complex. For a recent examination of this address in the broader context of his presidency, see Smith, *Eisenhower*.

3 Altman, "Is Syria a Pay-to-Play Conflict?"

4 See Abelson, *Do Think Tanks Matter?*, especially chap. 2.

5 See Bentley, *The Process of Government* and Truman, *The Governmental Process*.

6   Skocpol, *Bringing the State Back In* and Krasner, *Defending the National Interest.*

7   For example, see Kingdon, *Agendas, Alternatives,* and Stairs, "Public Opinion."

8   See Peschek, *Policy Planning Organizations*; Dye, *Who's Running America?*; Domhoff and Dye, *Power Elites and Organizations*; Saloma, *Ominous Politics*; and Shoup, *Wall Street's Think Tank.*

9   See Lipton, Williams, and Confessore, "Foreign Powers Buy Influence at Think Tanks"; and Williams, Lipton, and Parlapiano, "Foreign Government Contributions to Nine Think Tanks." For a response to the findings presented in these articles, see Bruckner, "Fund a Think Tank," and Mendizabal, "Think Tank Accountability."

10 A Gramscian approach to the study of think tanks is provided by Gill in *American Hegemony and the Trilateral Commission.* On the various streams of Marxism, see Kolakowski, *Main Currrents of Marxism.*

11 Quoted in Lipton, Williams, and Confessore, "Foreign Powers Buy Influence at Think Tanks."

12 Mendizabal, "Think Tank Accountability."

13 Quoted in Lipton, Williams, and Confessore, "Foreign Powers Buy Influence at Think Tanks."

14 Domhoff, *The Power Elite and the State.*

15 Newsom, *The Public Dimension of Foreign Policy,* 141–62.

16 The American pluralist tradition is strongly rooted in the belief that society is composed of individual groups that compete for power and status in the policy-making community. Two studies in particular have had a major impact on shaping this perspective: Bentley, *The Process of Government*; and Truman, *The Governmental Process.*

17 Pal and Weaver (eds), *The Government Taketh Away.*

18 See Davidson, *Foreign Policy Inc.,* and Walt and Mearsheimer, *The Israel Lobby.*

19 See Skocpol, *Bringing the State Back In,* and Krasner, *Defending the National Interest.*

20 Steelman, review of *Do Think Tanks Matter?*

21 Krasner, *Defending the National Interest,* 11.

22 Steelman, 165.

23 For more on the relationship between Richard Nixon and the US Congress, see Schlessinger, *The Imperial Presidency.*

24 See Smith, *George Bush's War.*

25 On the relationship between the Executive and Congress in US foreign policy, see Hinckley, *Less Than Meets the Eye.*

26 See Maraniss, *First in His Class*, and Abelson, "Changing Minds."
27 See Critchlow, *The Brookings Institution*; Edwards, *The Power of Ideas*; Abella, *Soldiers of Reason*; and Schulzinger, *The Wise Men of Foreign Affairs*.
28 On the rise of think tanks in the United States and around the globe, see McGann and Weaver (eds), *Think Tanks & Civil Societies*; and Stone and Denham (eds), *Think Tank Traditions*.
29 For example, see Haas (ed), *Knowledge, Power*.
30 See Heclo, "Issue Networks"; Lindquist, "Think Tanks?"; and Stone, *Capturing the Political Imagination*.
31 Kingdon, *Agendas, Alternatives*, and Stairs, "Public Opinion."

CHAPTER FOUR

1 Abelson, "Think Tanks Must Think."
2 Troy, "Devaluing the Think Tank."
3 On the management of think tanks, see Selee, *What Should Think Tanks Do?*, and Struyk, *Managing Think Tanks*.
4 Dobell, *IRPP*.
5 Comments made on *The Agenda with Steve Paikin*.
6 Edwards, *Leading the Way*.
7 On the role of public intellectuals, see Wiseman, *The Public Intellectual in Canada*; Posner, *Public Intellectuals*; Misztal, "Public Intellectuals and Think Tanks"; and Sowell, *Intellectuals and Society*.
8 For background information on the Security and Defence Forum, go to the Department of National Defence home page at http://www.forces.gc.ca/en/news/article.page?doc=the-security-and-defence-forum/hnmx190r.
9 On the role of policy entrepreneurs, see Phillipe-David, "Policy Entrepreneurs."
10 Information on the Canada Institute can be found at http://www.wilson center.org/program/canada-institute
11 See Troy, "Devaluing the Think Tank."
12 For an interesting examination of how think tank activity on the Internet might be used to measure their visibility and influence, see McNutt and Marchildon, "Think Tanks and the Web."
13 See Abelson, "It Seemed Like a Good Idea."
14 Comments made by Fraser Institute president Niels Veldhuis at the 2014 Manning Networking Conference's panel entitled "Who Generates Ideas – Think Tanks or Government?"

15 Doctorow, "Conference Board of Canada Admits."
16 Several former staffers from Canadian think tanks have informed me that they were often asked to falsify data in their reports to appease donors. Unfortunately, the author is unable to substantiate their allegations.
17 AEI is currently building its new $50 million headquarters next to the Carnegie Endowment for International Peace and the Brookings Institution. Among other things, it will contain showers for those who prefer to bike to work. The renovated building located at 1785 Massachusetts Ave, NW, is scheduled for completion in May 2016. See *Think Tank Watch*, "AEI's New Headquarters."
18 Ross Joynt, "One of Washington's."
19 Private communication with a congressional staffer, who confirmed that policy-makers often rely on satellite reconnaissance photos provided by CSIS to help them in their deliberations in Congress.
20 Information about Heritage's 2013 revenues and expenses can be found at http://www.heritage.org/about/financials.
21 Edwards, *Leading the Way.*
22 Ibid.
23 See Lipton, Williams, and Confessore, "Foreign Powers Buying Influence at Think Tanks," and Talbott, "A Message from Strobe Talbott."
24 For more on this matter, see Crovitz, "Don't Cross Elizabeth Warren"; Hamburger, "How Elizabeth Warren Picked a Fight with Brookings"; and Cirilli, "Top Brookings Economist Fired."
25 *The Agenda with Steve Paikin.* For more on the support the Fraser Institute receives from foreign donors, see Hong, "Charitable Fraser Institute Received $4.3 million in Foreign Funding Since 2000"; Harris, *Party of One*, 37–9; and Gutstein, *Harperism.*
26 Ibid. For more on Medhora's insights about the contribution of CIGI and other Canadian think tanks to foreign policy, see https://www.opencanada.org/features/rise-and-influence-foreign-policy-think-tank/.
27 Bender, "CIGI Receives Highest Rating."
28 On the reaction to the CCPA audit by the CRA, see Beeby, "More Than 400 Academics," and "CRA Denies Agency Audits"; Keenan, "Why Haven't Any Harper-Friendly"; McQuaig, "Harper Ramps Up His War"; and Daifallah, "Unmuzzle the Charities."
29 On the closure of the NSI, see Goar, "Another Canadian Window on the World Closes"; McLeod Group, "North-South Institute Ends"; Martin et al., "North-South Institute."
30 Young and Everitt (eds), *Advocacy Groups.*

31 Smith, *The Idea Brokers.*
32 These and other observations about the annual Manning Networking
   Conference can be found at http://www.pressprogress.ca/en/post/
   video-highlights-years-biggest-conservative-gathering.
33 Davidson, *Foreign Policy, Inc.*
34 See Abelson, "Theoretical Models and Approaches."
35 Abelson, *A Capitol Idea*, especially chap. 9.
36 Gutstein, *Harperism.*
37 Abelson, "Theoretical Models and Approaches."

CHAPTER FIVE

1 For a detailed examination of how different political systems influence the
   behaviour of think tanks, see Abelson, *Do Think Tanks Matter?*; McGann
   and Weaver (eds), *Think Tanks and Civil Societies*; and Stone and Denham
   (eds), *Think Tank Traditions.*
2 See Edwards, *The Power of Ideas* and *Leading the Way.*
3 For example, the Canadian Centre for Policy Alternatives (CCPA) has
   maintained close ties to the NDP, whereas the Fraser Institute is often portrayed as a staunch ally of the Conservative Party and conservative ideology, a label to which the Fraser Institute's president, Niels Veldhuis,
   objects. He maintains that the institute's work is "not value-based, it's
   driven by data." See his comments in MacCharles, "Think-Tank Says It
   Was Targeted." Notwithstanding Veldhuis's remarks, Stephen Tapp of the
   Institute for Research on Public Policy (IRPP) has used data from Twitter
   to make a series of assumptions about the ideological orientation of several Canadian think tanks. See his blog, "What Can a Little Birdie
   (Twitter) Tell Us?"
4 On the role of think tanks in Germany, see Thunert, "Expert Policy
   Advice"; Braml, "Determinants of German Think Tanks"; and Pautz,
   Think-Tanks, Social Democracy.
5 For more on how the Ontario NDP government of Bob Rae relied on think
   tanks and other NGOs to mobilize opposition to NAFTA, see Abelson,
   "Environmental Lobbying or Political Posturing?," and Abelson and
   Lusztig, "The Consistency of Inconsistency."
6 The relationship between think tanks and several US presidential candi-
   dates is explored by Abelson in "Changing Minds"; "What Were They
   Thinking?"; *A Capitol Idea*; and *American Think Tanks.*
7 On the role of American think tanks during the progressive era, see Smith,
   The Idea Brokers, and Weiss, *Organizations for Policy Analysis.*

8 Alter, "Voter Turnout in Midterm Elections."
9 Rogers, "Only about 52 per cent." For a detailed examination of elections in Ontario, see Cross et al., *Fighting for Votes*.
10 The phenomenon of growing apathy among voters in the United States is examined by Davidson in *Foreign Policy, Inc.* and by Putnam in *Bowling Alone*.
11 For a thorough discussion on the Patriot Act, see Crotty, *The Politics of Terror*; Brookings Institution, *Protecting the American Homeland: A Preliminary Analysis* and *Protecting the American Homeland: One Year On*; and Bremer and Meese, *Defending the American Homeland*. Many of the concerns raised by Americans about the extent to which the Patriot Act would encroach on civil liberties are similar to those being flagged by Canadians in reaction to the Harper government's efforts to pass Bill C-51, commonly known as the "Anti-Terrorism Act." See an article by the Canadian Association of University Teachers (CAUT), entitled, "Critics Fear Bill C-51." For a thoughtful exploration of the tension between national security and civil liberties, see Roach, *September 11: Consequences for Canada*.
12 See Abelson, *A Capitol Idea*, chapter 9.
13 See Edwards, *Leading the Way*.
14 Abelson, "Thinking Out Loud."
15 The Brookings Institution, the Heritage Foundation, and CSIS are among the handful of think tanks inside the Washington Beltway that have their own television and radio facilities.
16 Abelson, "Thinking Out Loud."
17 Abelson, "It Seemed Like a Good Idea."
18 According to the *Global Go To Think Tanks Index Report*, Chatham House consistently ranks among the world's top think tanks.
19 Personal correspondence with media relations personnel at Chatham House.
20 Comments made by Niels Veldhuis, president of the Fraser Institute, at the 2014 Manning Networking Conference.
21 On the evolution of IRPP, see Ritchie, *An Institute for Research on Public Policy*, and Dobell, *IRPP*. For a history of the Brookings Institution, see Critchlow, *The Brookings Institution*.
22 Parmar, *Foundations of the American Century*.
23 Lipton, Williams, and Confessore, "Foreign Powers Buy Influence at Think Tanks."
24 Talbott, "A Message from Strobe Talbott."
25 Abelson, *American Think Tanks*, 52–5.

26 McGann, *The Competition for Scholars.*
27 See Stone, *Banking on Knowledge.*

CHAPTER SIX

1 Dozens of books and hundreds of articles focus on the similarities and differences between the United States and Canada. Among the many titles that should be consulted are: Clarkson, *Canada and the Reagan Challenge*; Doran, *Forgotten Partnership*; Thompson and Randall, *Canada and the United States*; Bothwell, *Your Country, My Country*; and Hale, *So Near Yet So Far.*
2 For example, see Wilson, *American Government*, and Dyck and Cochrane, *Canadian Politics.*
3 For an interesting examination of the PCO and PMO, see Savoie, *Breaking the Bargain.*
4 A useful place to begin an examination of this trend is Saloma, *Ominous Politics.*
5 Several studies have examined the growing influence of the National Rifle Association. See, for example, Sugarman, *National Rifle Association*; Anse Patrick, *The National Rifle Association and the Media*; and Gray Davidson, *Under Fire.*
6 On the role of the Israel and Arab lobby in shaping US foreign policy, see Mearsheimer and Walt, *The Israel Lobby*; Tivnan, *The Lobby*; Flesher, *Transforming America's Israel Lobby*; Davidson, *Foreign Policy, Inc.*; Hostettler, *Nothing for the Nation*; and Bard, *The Arab Lobby.*
7 Lipton, Williams, and Confessore, "Foreign Powers Buying Influence at Think Tanks." Also see Silverstein, *Pay to Play*; and Williams, "Meet the Think Tank Scholars."
8 For an interesting examination of the various conspiracy theories that have surfaced in the post-9/11 era, see Kay, *Among the Truthers.*
9 See Abelson, *American Think Tanks* and *A Capitol Idea.* Also see Medvetz, *Think Tanks in America.*
10 Abelson and Lindquist, "Who's Thinking About International Affairs?," and Muggah and Owen, "Decline in Canadian Think Tanks."
11 For more on this, see Weiss, *Organizations for Policy Analysis*; Stone, *Capturing the Political Imagination*, especially chap. 3; and Weaver, "The Changing World."
12 Interview with David Zussman, 14 September 1999.
13 Stone, *Capturing the Political Imagination.*

14 For an interesting examination of the involvement of think tanks in various government departments and agencies, see Burch, *Research in Political Economy*.

15 Ibid.

16 Several articles have examined think tanks that specialize in local politics. See, for instance, Scott, "Intellectuals Who Became Influential," and Moore, "Local Right Thinkers."

17 Weiss, *Organizations for Policy Analysis*.

18 In addition to 100 senators and 435 members of the US House of Representatives, there are three non-voting members representing the District of Columbia who sit in the House.

19 Weaver, "Changing World."

20 See Gellner, "Think Tanks in Germany."

21 On the role of these and other public think tanks, see Robinson, "Public Think Tanks in the US."

22 See Abelson, *A Capitol Idea*.

23 See Abelson, "What Were They Thinking?," and "Changing Minds."

24 On the role of advisers in the Bush campaign, see Abelson, "What Were· They Thinking?"; Van Slambrouck, "California Think Tank"; Hager, "Bush Shops for Advice"; Swanson, "Brain Power"; and Schmitt, "Foreign Policy Experts."

25 Abelson, "Changing Minds."

26 Abelson, *American Think Tanks*.

27 With the Canada Elections Act of 1996, the minimum election period was shortened from forty-seven to thirty-six days. A sitting government may run a longer election period, but politically it has rarely been in its interest to do so. A longer election period provides opposition parties with more time to criticize government policies.

28 Amy Minsky, "What Does the Fixed-Election Law Really Mean Anyway," *National Post*, 19 May 2011.

29 For more on this, see Baier and Bakvis, "Think Tanks and Political Parties."

30 Guy, *People, Politics and Government*, 215.

31 For more on the use of royal commissions and commissions of inquiry, see Bradford, *Commissioning Ideas*, and Jenson, "Commissioning Ideas."

32 See the discussion on restrictions placed on the partisan activities of think tanks in chap. 1.

33 Steve Paikin, the host of TVO's *The Agenda with Steve Paikin*, repeatedly asked Jason Clemens of the Fraser Institute to acknowledge the

conservative leanings of the Fraser Institute during a show devoted to Canadian think tanks in the fall of 2014. Clemens was reluctant to do so.

34 Interview with author, 15 December 1998.
35 Interview with author, 17 December 1998.
36 Interview with author, 14 September 1999.
37 This point is reinforced by Lindquist in "Transition Teams and Government Succession."
38 Guy, *People, Politics and Government*, 215.
39 Interview with author, 16 December 1998. For more on Battle's influence in key Liberal policy circles, see Greenspon and Wilson-Smith, *Double Vision*, especially chap. 9.
40 Ibid.
41 Interview with author, 16 December 1998.
42 Ibid.
43 See Lindquist, *Behind the Myth*.
44 For data on PhDs awarded in Canada, go to http://www.statcan.gc.ca/pub/81-004-x/2008002/article/10645-eng.htm.
45 *2013–14 IRPP Annual Report*.
46 For more on the role of foundations in the United States, see Berman, *Influence*; Sealander, *Private Wealth*; and Parmar, *Foundations of the American Century*.
47 Abelson, *American Think Tanks*, 53–4.
48 See Schulman, *Sons of Wichita*; Mayer, "The Kochs v. CATO"; and Antle, "The Kochs and the CATO Institute."
49 For more on the relationship between think tanks and corporate donors, see Stefancic and Delgado, *No Mercy*.
50 Abelson and Carberry, "Following Suit?," 546–7.
51 Kingdon, *Agendas, Alternatives*, 129.
52 Ibid., 130.
53 See Phillipe-David, "Policy Entrepreneurs."
54 Harrison and Hoberg, "Setting the Environmental Agenda."
55 Abelson and Carberry, "Following Suit?," 547. For more on theories of entrepreneurship, see Schneider and Teske, "Political Entrepreneur"; and Checkel, *Ideas*.
56 Ibid., 548.
57 For more on the origins of the Fraser Institute, see Lindquist, *Behind the Myth*, 377–80.
58 Abelson, *Do Think Tanks Matter?*, 290, n. 51.
59 Abelson and Carberry, "Following Suit?," 548.
60 Gray, "Think Tanks."

61 Lipset, "Canada and the US," 110. For other treatments of US-Canadian comparisons, see Presthus, *Cross-National Perspectives*, and Merelman, *Partial Visions*.

62 Lipset, *Continental Divide*, 13.

63 See Abelson, *American Think Tanks*, "What Were They Thinking?," and "Changing Course."

64 Information on the educational backgrounds of experts can be found on the websites of policy institutes.

65 Abelson, *Do Think Tanks Matter?*, 291, n. 63.

66 Lindquist, *Behind the Myth*.

67 Quoted in Stone, *Capturing the Political Imagination*, 43.

CHAPTER SEVEN

1 Interview with author, 17 April 2014.

2 The CDFAI was renamed the Canadian Global Affairs Institute (CGAI) in the summer of 2015. Bercuson is currently its director of programs.

3 *2012 Global Go To Think Tanks Index Report*.

4 CDFAI, *Press Release*, 23 January 2013.

5 Ibid.

6 *2012 Global Go To Think Tanks Index Report*, 61.

7 *2011 Global Go To Think Tanks Index Report*, 44.

8 *2012 Global Go To Think Tanks Index Report*, 61.

9 The methodology employed in the *Global Go To Think Tanks Index Report* is discussed at the beginning of each year's report.

10 *2012 Global Go To Think Tanks Index Report*, 61.

11 Ibid., 66–7.

12 Ibid.

13 Ibid., 88–95.

14 See *2013 Global Go To Think Tanks Index Report*, 36; and the *2014 Global Go To Think Tanks Index Report*, 71.

15 Canadian Defence and Foreign Affairs Institute, *Press Release*, 5 February 2015.

16 Ibid.

17 McCoy, "Centre's Director Dr. David Bercuson Honoured."

18 Fraser Institute, *Press Release*, 22 January 2015.

19 Ibid.

20 Ibid.

21 Remarks made by Niels Veldhuis on a panel devoted to think tanks at the 2014 Manning Networking Conference, held in Ottawa, 28 February 2014.

22 Ibid.
23 See Abelson, "Ideas, Influence and Public Policy."
24 The Center for Global Development has offices in London, England and Washington, DC. See a report by Gelb et al., entitled, "Measuring Think Tank Performance."
25 See, for example, *Prospect Magazine*, "Think Tank Awards 2014." Also see Chafuen, "The Top Free-Market Institutes."
26 See the home page of Transparify at http://www.transparify.org/.
27 Bender, "CIGI Receives Highest Rating."
28 *The Agenda with Steve Paikin*, 17 November 2014.
29 CIGI, "Can Think Tanks Make a Difference?" Also see Kuntz, "Communications and Impact Metrics for Think Tanks."
30 Ibid., 3.
31 Personal correspondence with staff at Chatham House.
32 See http://tvnews.vanderbilt.edu/.
33 Abelson, *A Capitol Idea*, especially the appendices.
34 Abelson, *Do Think Tanks Matter?*, especially chap. 4.
35 Abelson, *American Think Tanks*, 16–17.
36 See Selee, *What Should Think Tanks Do?*, and Struyk, *Managing Think Tanks*.
37 See McNutt and Marchildon, "Think Tanks and the Web."
38 For this and related information, access the following websites: http://www.archives.gov/congress/hearings.html; http://www.parl.gc.ca/CommitteeBusiness/WitnessInformation.aspx?Language=E&Mode=1.
39 See Rich and Weaver, "Think Tanks, the Media."
40 Abelson, *Do Think Tanks Matter?*, especially chap. 5.
41 Abelson, *A Capitol Idea*, 167.
42 Ibid. Also see Pautz, *Think Tanks, Social Democracy*.

CHAPTER NINE

1 Asia-Pacific Foundation of Canada Act, R.S.C., 1985, C.A. 13.
2 Asia-Pacific Foundation of Canada Home Page, www.asiapacific.ca. Also see the *2014 Annual Report*.
3 Atlantic Institute for Market Studies, "Introduction," *1995–1996 Annual Report*.
4 Atlantic Institute for Market Studies, "President's Message," *1995–1996 Annual Report*.
5 C.D. Howe Home Page, www.cdhowe.org.

6 Ibid.
7 Ibid. For a detailed discussion of the C.D. Howe Institute and its various incarnations, see Ernst, "From Liberal Continentalism."
8 C.D. Howe Institute, *2013 Annual Report*, 1.
9 In its *2013 Annual Report*, 33, C.D. Howe lists 7 fellows-in-residence; 49 senior fellows; 11 research fellows; and 12 international fellows.
10 Ibid.
11 C.D. Howe Institute, *2007 Annual Report*.
12 Ibid.
13 C.D. Howe Institute, *2013 Annual Report*, 5.
14 On the closing of the National Council of Welfare, see Goar, "Harper Throws National Council of Welfare."
15 Interview with Ken Battle, 16 December 1998.
16 Ibid.
17 Abelson, *Do Think Tanks Matter?*, 47.
18 See "About Us" on the Caledon Institute's website, www.caledoninst.org.
19 Interview with Ken Battle, 16 December 1998.
20 Abelson, "Public Visibility and Policy Relevance."
21 Canada West Foundation, *1997 Annual Report*, 1.
22 Canada West Foundation, *2013 Annual Report*, 25.
23 Canada West Foundation, *1997 Annual Report*, 1.
24 Ibid.
25 Canada West Foundation, *2013 Annual Report*, 7.
26 Ibid., 8.
27 Abelson, *Do Think Tanks Matter?*, 196.
28 Ibid.
29 Canadian Centre for Policy Alternatives, *Annual Report* 2014, 26.
30 Ibid.
31 Ibid., 42.
32 Ibid.
33 Canadian Council on Social Development, website (ccsd.ca). See "About Us."
34 Ibid.
35 Canadian Defence & Foreign Affairs Institute, *2013 Annual Report*, 1.
36 Ibid.
37 Canadian International Council website, www.opencanada.org.
38 For more on Balsillie's role in creating the CIC, see Valpy, "Balsillie's Disappointing Foray into Global Affairs."
39 For a profile of the CIIA, see Abelson, *Do Think Tanks Matter?*, 43–4.
40 Ibid., 195.

41 According to its 2014 *Financial Statements*, CIGI had revenues in excess of $27 million and a long-term endowment valued over $55 million. See CIGI, 2014 *Financial Statements* and its 2014 *Annual Report*.

42 Valpy, "Balsillie's Disappointing Foray into Global Affairs."

43 CIGI website (www.cigionline.org).

44 Valpy, "Balsillie's Disappointing Foray into Global Affairs."

45 For more on this, see Hopper, "York University Rejects RIM Co-founder." Additional information on Balsillie's involvement in CIGI and the Balsillie School of International Affairs can be found in the Canadian Association of University Teachers, *Open For Business: On What Terms?*

46 Ibid.

47 Ibid.

48 Lindquist, "Behind the Myth," 347.

49 Ibid.

50 Ibid.

51 Ibid.

52 Conference Board of Canada, "About Us," home page, www.conferenceboard.ca.

53 Ibid.

54 Conference Board of Canada, 2014 *Annual Report*, 4.

55 Ibid., 4–5.

56 The Fraser Institute, *Challenging Perceptions*, 2.

57 Ibid., 3.

58 Ibid., 4.

59 Ibid., 8.

60 The Fraser Institute, 2013 *Annual Report*, 48–9.

61 Frontier Centre for Public Policy, 2013 *Annual Report*, 1.

62 Ibid., 17.

63 Jérôme-Forget, "Institute for Research on Public Policy," 92. For more on the IRPP, see Dobell, *IRPP*, and Mackinnon, "The Canadian Think Tank Scene."

64 Ibid., 87.

65 Institute for Research on Public Policy, 2014 *Annual Report*, 1.

66 The Institute on Governance also maintains a second office in Toronto.

67 The Institute on Governance, "About Us," homepage, www.iog.ca.

68 Ibid.

69 Ibid.

70 The International Institute for Sustainable Development, "Our History" homepage, www.iisd.org.

71 Ibid.

72 Ibid.
73 Ibid.
74 Macdonald-Laurier Institute for Public Policy, "Who We Are," homepage, www.macdonaldlaurier.ca.
75 Ibid.
76 Macdonald-Laurier Institute for Public Policy, *2013 Annual Report*, 1.
77 Ibid., 10–11.
78 Montreal Economic Institute, *2014 Annual Report*, 3.
79 Montreal Economic Institute, "About – Who We Are," homepage, www.iedm.org.
80 Ibid., 4.
81 Ibid., 5.
82 Mowat Centre, *2014 Annual Report*, 1.
83 Ibid.
84 Ibid., 17.
85 Parkland Institute, home page, "About the Parkland Institute," www.parklandinstitute.ca.
86 Parkland Institute, "Self-Study," www.parklandinstitute.ca.
87 Ibid., 4.
88 Ibid., 2.
89 Ibid., 15–17.
90 Pembina Institute, "About – Institute Story," www.pembina.org.
91 Ibid.
92 Ibid.
93 Ibid.
94 Public Policy Forum, "About" home page, www.ppforum.ca. The PPF has a second office in Toronto.
95 Ibid.
96 Ibid.
97 Abelson, *Do Think Tanks Matter?*, 197.
98 Ibid.
99 Ibid.
100 Vanier Institute of the Family, "About Us – Our History," www.vanier institute.ca.
101 Ibid.
102 Ibid.
103 Vanier Institute of the Family, *2013 Annual Report*, 1
104 Ibid.
105 Ibid., 16.
106 Wellesley Institute, "About – History," www.wellesleyinstitute.org.

107 Wellesley Institute, "Our History Flip Sheet," 2. www.wellesleyinstitute. org.

108 Wellesley Institute, *Strategic Plan: FY14–FY18*, 1.

109 Ibid., 2.

110 Ibid., 7.

Bibliography

Abella, Alex. *Soldiers of Reason: The Rand Corporation and the Rise of the American Empire*. New York: Harcourt, Inc., 2008.

Abelson, Donald E. "It Seemed Like a Good Idea at the Time: Reflections on the Evolution of American Think Tanks." *Canadian Review of American Studies*, 46(1), 2016: 139–57.

– "National Interest or Self-Interest? Advocacy Think Tanks, 9/11, and the Future of North American Security." In *Game Changer: The Impact of 9/11 on North American Security*, edited by Jonathan Paquin and Patrick James, 175–92. Vancouver: UBC Press, 2014.

– "Think Tanks by the Numbers." *Transparify*, 16 June 2014.

– "Ideas, Influence and Public Policy: Think Tanks in Canada and the United States." Presentation given at the 2014 Manning Networking Conference, Ottawa, Ontario, 28 February 2014.

– "Old World, New World: The Evolution and Influence of Foreign Affairs Think-Tanks." *International Affairs* (UK) 90 (1), 2014: 125–42.

– "Changing Minds, Changing Course: Obama, Think Tanks and American Foreign Policy." In *Obama and the World: New Directions in US Foreign Policy*, 2nd ed., edited by Inderjeet Parmar, Linda B. Miller, and Mark Ledwidge, 107–19. London: Routledge, 2014.

– "Think Tanks and US Diplomatic and Military Affairs." In *The Oxford Encyclopedia of American Military & Diplomatic History*, edited by Timothy J. Lynch, 354–63. New York: Oxford University Press, 2013.

– "Theoretical Models and Approaches to Understanding the Role of Lobbies and Think Tanks in US Foreign Policy," in *Policy Expertise in Contemporary Democracies*, edited by Stephen Brooks, Dorota Stasiak, and Tomasz Zyro, 9–30. London: Ashgate, 2012.

– "Think Tanks." In *Encyclopedia of Global Studies*, edited by Helmut K. Anheier and Mark Juergensmeyer, 1645–7. Los Angeles: Sage, 2012.
– "Thinking Out Loud." Research Paper no. 2. The Canada-US Institute, the University of Western Ontario, July 2012.
– "Think Tanks Must Think More about Issues of National Interest, Not Self-Interest." London School of Economics – Blog – Impact of Social Sciences: Maximizing the Impact of Academic Research. http://blogs.lse.ac.uk/impactofsocialsciences2011/10/11/think-tanks-national-interest/.
– "What Were They Thinking? Think Tanks, the Bush Administration and US Foreign Policy," in *New Directions in US Foreign Policy*, edited by Inderjeet Parmar, Linda B. Miller, and Mark Ledwidge, 92–105. London: Routledge, 2009.
– *Do Think Tanks Matter? Assessing the Impact of Public Policy Institutes.* 2nd ed. Montreal & Kingston: McGill-Queen's University Press, 2009.
– *A Capitol Idea: Think Tanks & US Foreign Policy.* Montreal & Kingston: McGill-Queen's University Press, 2006.
– "Do Think Tanks Matter? Opportunities, Incentives and Constraints for Think Tanks in Canada and the United States." *Global Society* 14, no. 2 (2000): 213–36.
– "Surveying the Think Tank Landscape in Canada." In *Public Administration and Policy: Governing in Challenging Times*, edited by Martin W. Westmacott and Hugh Mellon, 91–105. Scarborough: Prentice-Hall, 1999.
– "Public Visibility and Policy Relevance: Assessing the Impact and Influence of Canadian Policy Institutes." *Canadian Public Administration* 42, no. 2, (Summer 1999): 240–70.
– "Policy Experts and Political Pundits: American Think Tanks and the News Media." *NIRA Review*, Summer 1998: 40–3.
– "In Search of Policy Influence: The Strategies of American Think Tanks." *NIRA Review*, Spring 1998: 28–32.
– "Think Tanks in the United States." In *Think Tanks Across Nations: A Comparative Approach*, edited by Diane Stone, Andrew Denham, and Mark Garnett, 107–26. Manchester: Manchester University Press, 1998.
– *American Think Tanks and Their Role in US Foreign Policy.* London and New York: Macmillan and St Martin's Press, 1996.
– "From Policy Research to Political Advocacy: The Changing Role of Think Tanks in American Politics." *Canadian Review of American Studies* 25, no. 1 (1995): 93–126.
– "Environmental Lobbying and Political Posturing: The Role of Environmental Groups in Ontario's Debate Over NAFTA." *Canadian Public Administration* 38, no. 3 (Fall 1995): 352–81.

- "A New Channel of Influence: American Think Tanks and the News Media."
  Queen's Quarterly 99, no. 4 (1992): 849–72.
Abelson, Donald E., and Christine M. Carberry. "Following Suit or Falling
  Behind? A Comparative Analysis of Think Tanks in Canada and the United
  States." *Canadian Journal of Political Science* 31, no. 3 (1998): 525–55.
- "Policy Experts in Presidential Campaigns: A Model of Think Tank Recruit-
  ment." *Presidential Studies Quarterly* 27, no. 4 (Fall 1997): 679–97.
Abelson, Donald E., and Evert A. Lindquist. "Think Tanks in North America."
  In *Think Tanks and Civil Societies: Catalyst for Ideas and Action*, edited by
  R. Kent Weaver and James G. McGann, 37–66. New Brunswick, NJ:
  Transaction Publishers, 2000.
- "Who's Thinking about International Affairs? The Evolution and Funding of
  Canada's Foreign and Defence Policy Think Tanks." Paper presented at the
  Annual Meeting of the Canadian Political Science Association, Ottawa,
  June 1998.
Abelson, Donald E., and Michael Lusztig. "The Consistency of Inconsistency:
  Tracing Ontario's Opposition to the North American Free Trade Agreement."
  Canadian Journal of Political Science 29, no. 4, (December 1996): 681–98.
Alter, Charlotte. "Voter Turnout in Midterm Elections Hits 72-Year Low."
  Time, 10 November 2014.
Altman, Daniel. "Is Syria a Pay-to-Play Conflict?" *Foreign Policy*, 25
  September 2014.
Anderson, George. "The New Focus on the Policy Capacity of the Federal
  Government." *Canadian Public Administration* 39, no. 4 (Winter 1996):
  469–88.
Anderson, Martin. *Revolution*. New York: Harcourt Brace Jovanovich, 1988.
Anse Patrick, Brian. *The National Rifle Association and the Media: The
  Motivating Force of Negative Coverage*. Palmyra, MI: Goatpower
  Publishing, 2012.
Antle, James. "The Kochs and the Cato Institute: A Hostile Takeover?" *The
  Guardian*, 2 April 2012.
Asia Pacific Foundation of Canada. *2014 Annual Report*. Vancouver: Asia
  Pacific Foundation of Canada, 2014.
Atlantic Institute for Market Studies. *1995–1996 Annual Report*. Halifax:
  Atlantic Institute for Market Studies, 1996.
Avins, Jeremy. "In-Depth: The New Think-and-Do Tank: Rigorous,
  Independent, and Strategic." Published by the Redstone Strategy Group.
  www.redstonestrategy.com.
Badger, Emily. "Think Tanks Are Nonpartisan? Think Again." *Pacific Standard
  Magazine*, 17 February 2012.

Baier, Gerald, and Herman Bakvis. "Think Tanks and Political Parties: Competitors or Collaborators?" *Isuma: Canadian Journal of Policy Research* 2, no. 1 (Spring 2001): 107–13.

Balsillie, Jim. "Why We're Creating the Canadian International Council." *National Post*, 18 October 2007.

Bard, Mitchell. *The Arab Lobby: The Invisible Alliance That Undermines America's Interests in the Middle East*. New York: Harper, 2010.

Beeby, Dean. "More Than 400 Academics Demand CRA Cancel 'Politically Motivated' Audit of Left-Leaning Think Tank." *National Post*, 14 September 2014.

– "CRA Denies Agency Audits Target Charities with Anti-Government Political Leanings." *National Post*, 3 August 2014.

– "CRA to Oxfam: 'Preventing Poverty' Not a Charitable Goal When It Comes to Taxes." *National Post*, 25 July 2014.

– "NDP Calls for Independent Probe into CRA's Targeting of Charities." *National Post*, 16 July 2014.

– "CRA Audited Left-Wing Think Tank Because Its Research Shows 'Bias.'" *The Canadian Press*, 1 September 2014.

Beers, David. "Buttoned-Down Bohemians." *San Francisco Chronicle*, 3 August 1986.

Beigie, C.E. "Economic Policy Analysis: The Role of the C.D. Howe Research Institute." *Canadian Business Review* 39 (Summer 1974): 39–42.

Bellant, Russ. *The Coors Connection: How Coors Family Philanthropy Undermines Democratic Pluralism*. Boston: South End Press, 1999.

Bender, Bryan. "Many DC Think Tanks Now Players in Partisan Wars." *Boston Globe*, 11 August 2013.

Bender, Tammy. "CIGI Receives Highest Rating Among Think Tanks Globally for Financial Transparency." *CIGI News Release*, 17 February 2015.

Bentley, Arthur F. *The Process of Government*. Chicago: University of Chicago Press, 1908.

Berman, Edward H. *The Influence of the Carnegie, Ford and Rockefeller Foundations on American Foreign Policy: The Ideology of Philanthropy*. New York: State University of New York Press, 1983.

Bindman, Stephen. "Loss of a Legal Think-Tank." *Ottawa Citizen*, 11 March 1992.

Bothwell, Robert. *Your Country, My Country: A Unified History of the United States and Canada*. New York: Oxford University Press, 2015.

Boulden, Jane. "Independent Policy Research and the Canadian Foreign Policy Community." *International Journal*, Autumn 1999: 625–47.

Bourrie, Mark. *Kill the Messengers: Stephen Harper's Assault on Your Right to Know.* Toronto: Patrick Crean Editions, 2015.

Boutis, Paula, and Shelina Ali. "How Changes to the Income Tax Act Will Restrict Charities' Political Activities." *rabble.ca,* 13 September 2012.

Bradford, Neil. *Commissioning Ideas: Canadian National Policy Innovation in Comparative Perspective.* Toronto: Oxford University Press, 1998.

Bradshaw, James. "York Profs Revolt Against Pact with Balsillie Think Tank." *The Globe and Mail,* 21 March 2012.

– "York University, Balsillie Think Tank Near $60-Million Deal on Partnership." *The Globe and Mail,* 23 February 2012.

Braml, Josef. "Determinants of German Think Tanks' Public Policy Roles." In *Policy Expertise in Contemporary Democracies,* edited by Stephen Brooks, Dorota Stasiak, and Thomas Zyro. Aldershot: Ashgate, 2012.

Bremer, L. Paul, III, and Edwin Meese III. *Defending the American Homeland.* Washington, DC: The Heritage Foundation, 2002.

Bremner, Robert H. *American Philanthropy.* Chicago: University of Chicago Press, 1988.

Brodie, Janine M., and Jane Jenson. *Crisis, Challenge, and Change: Party and Class in Canada.* Toronto: Methuen, 1980.

Brookings Institution. "Brookings Statement on *New York Times* Article Examining Foreign Government Funding of US Think Tanks." *Brookings Institution News Release,* 6 September 2014.

– *Protecting the American Homeland: A Preliminary Analysis.* Washington, DC: The Brookings Institution, 2002.

– *Protecting the American Homeland: One Year On.* Washington, DC: The Brookings Institution, 2003.

Bruckner, Till. "Fund a Think Tank, Buy a Lobbyist?" *Huffington Post,* 10 September 2014.

Burch, Philip H. *Research in Political Economy.* Supplement 1, *Reagan, Bush and Right-Wing Politics: Elites, Think Tanks, Power and Policy.* Greenwich, CT: JAI Press, 1997.

Caledon Institute. http://www.caledoninst.org.

Campbell, Colin. *Managing the Presidency: Carter, Reagan, and the Search for Executive Harmony.* Pittsburgh, PA: University of Pittsburgh Press, 1986.

Campbell, John L. "Institutional Analysis and the Role of Ideas in Political Economy." *Theory and Society* 27 (1998): 377–409.

Canada Institute. www.wilsoncenter.org/program/canada-institute.

Canada Revenue Agency. "Income Tax Act – Requirements for Charitable Organizations." http://www.cra-arc.gc.ca.

Canada West Foundation. *Annual Report 1997: 25 Years of Commitment to the West within a Strong Canada*. Calgary, AB: Canada West Foundation, 1997.

– *2013 Annual Report*. Calgary, AB: Canada West Foundation, 2013.

Canadian Association of University Teachers (CAUT). "Critics Fear Bill C-51 Could Limit Freedom of Speech on Campus." *CAUT Bulletin* 62, no. 3 (March 2015), 1.

– *Open for Business – On What Terms? An Analysis of 12 Collaborations between Canadian Universities and Corporations, Donors and Governments*. Ottawa: Canadian Association of University Teachers, 2013.

Canadian Centre for Philanthropy. www.ccp.ca.

Canadian Centre for Policy Alternatives. www.policyalternatives.ca.

– *2014 Annual Report*. Ottawa: Canadian Centre for Policy Alternatives, 2014.

Canadian Council on Social Development. www.ccsd.ca.

Canadian Defence and Foreign Affairs Institute, *Press Release*, 5 February 2015

– *News Release*, 23 January 2013.

– *2013 Annual Report*. Calgary: Canadian Defence and Foreign Affairs Institute, 2013.

Canadian Institute of International Affairs. *The Canadian Institute of International Affairs – Its Organization, Objects, and Constitution*. Montreal: Southam Press, 1929.

Canadian International Council. www.opencanada.org.

– *2008–2009 Annual Report*. Toronto: Canadian International Council, 2009.

Canadian Press. "CRA Audits CCPA Think-Tank Due to Alleged Bias." 2 September 2014.

CBC. "North-South Institute to Close After Federal Funding Cut." *CBCnews.ca*, 11 September 2014.

C.D. Howe Institute. "A History of the Institute." C.D. Howe Institute homepage. www.cdhowe.org.

– *2013 Annual Report*. Toronto: C.D. Howe Institute, 2013.

– *2007 Annual Report*. Toronto: C.D. Howe Institute, 2007.

Centre for International Governance Innovation. "Can Think Tanks Make a Difference?" *Conference Report*, 20 September 2011.

– *2014 Financial Statements*. Waterloo: Centre for International Governance Innovation, 2014.

– *2014 Annual Report*. Waterloo: Centre for International Governance Innovation, 2014.

CIGI. "Jim Balsillie Leads in the Creation of the New Canadian International Council." *CIGI online*, 6 September 2007. https://www.cigionline.org/articles/2007/09/jim-balsillie-leads-creation-new-canadian-international-council.

Chafuen, Alejandro. "The Top Free-Market Institutes: 2014 Rankings." *Forbes*, 22 January 2015.

Cheadle, Bruce. "After CRA Audit, Dying with Dignity Group Stripped of Charitable Tax Status." *The Canadian Press*, 20 January 2015.

Checkel, Jeffrey T. *Ideas and International Political Change*. New Haven, CT: Yale University Press, 1997.

Church, Elizabeth. "RIM's Balsillie Seeds Major Foreign Policy Think Tank." *The Globe and Mail*, 5 September 2007.

Cirilli, Kevin. "Top Brookings Economist Forced Out Over Biz-Backed Study," *The Hill*, 29 September 2015.

Clarkson, Stephen. *Canada and the Reagan Challenge: Crisis in the Canadian-American Relationship*. Toronto: Lorimer, 1982.

Cockett, Richard. *Thinking the Unthinkable: Think-Tanks and the Economic Counter-Revolution, 1931–1983*. London: HarperCollins, 1994.

Coleman, William D., and Grace Skogstad, eds. *Public Policy and Policy Communities in Canada: A Structural Approach*. Toronto: Copp Clark Pitman, 1990.

Conference Board of Canada. www.conferenceboard.ca.

– *2014 Annual Report*. Ottawa: Conference Board of Canada, 2014.

Covington, Sally. *Moving a Public Policy: The Strategic Philanthropy of Conservative Foundations*. Washington, DC: National Committee for Responsive Philanthropy.

Crawford, Blair. "North-South Institute, Ottawa-Based Think Tank, to Close." *Ottawa Citizen*, 10 September 2014.

Critchlow, Donald T. *The Brookings Institution, 1916–52: Expertise and the Public Interest in a Democratic Society*. DeKalb, IL: Northern Illinois University Press, 1985.

Cross, William P., Jonathan Malloy, Tamara A. Small, and Laura B. Stephenson. *Fighting for Votes: Parties, the Media, and Voters in an Ontario Election*. Vancouver: UBC Press, 2015.

Crotty, William J. *The Politics of Terror: The US Response to 9/11*. Boston: Northeastern University Press, 2004.

Crovitz, Gordon L. "Don't Cross Elizabeth Warren." *Wall Street Journal*, 4 October 2015.

Crowe, Kelly. "PM's Charity Audits Look for 'Bias, One-Sidedness.'" *CBC.ca*, 4 February 2015.

Crowley, Brian Lee. "How Can Think Tanks Win Friends and Influence People in the Media?" *Insider* no. 264 (October 1999).

Culleton Colwell, Mary Anna. *Private Foundations and Public Policy: The Political Role of Philanthropy*. New York: Garland, 1993.

Daifallah, Adam. "Unmuzzle the Charities." *National Post*, 13 August 2014.

David, Charles-Phillipe. "Policy Entrepreneurs and the Reorientation of National Security Policy Under the G.W. Bush Administration (2001–04)." *Politics & Policy* 43, no. 1 (2015): 163–95.

Davidson, Lawrence. *Foreign Policy, Inc.: Privatizing America's National Interest*. Lexington: The University Press of Kentucky, 2009.

Demson, Sandra. *A Brief History of the Canadian Institute of International Affairs*. Toronto: Canadian Institute of International Affairs, 1995.

Denham, Andrew. *Think Tanks of the New Right*. Aldershot: Dartmouth, 1996.

Denham, Andrew, and Mark Garnett. *British Think-Tanks and the Climate of Opinion*. London: UCL Press, 1998.

Department of National Defence. www.forces.gc.ca.

Dickson, Paul. *Think Tanks*. New York: Atheneum, 1972.

Dobell, Peter. *IRPP: The First 30 Years*. Montreal: Institute for Research on Public Policy, 2002.

Dobuzinskis, Laurent. "Trends and Fashion in the Marketplace of Ideas." In *Policy Studies in Canada: The State of the Art*, edited by Laurent Dobuzinskis, Michael Howlett, and David Laycock, 91–124. Toronto: University of Toronto Press, 1996.

Doctorow, Cory. "Conference Board of Canada Admits That Its Publicly Funded, Plagiarized, Biased Copyright 'Research' Is Junk." *BoingBoing*, 28 May 2009. http://boingboing.net/2009/05/28/conference-board-of.html.

Domhoff, William G. *The Power Elite and the State: How Policy Is Made in America*. New York: Aldine de Gruyter, 1990.

Domhoff, William G., and Thomas R. Dye. *Power Elites and Organizations*. London: Sage, 1987.

Doran, Charles F. *Forgotten Partnership: US-Canada Relations Today*. Baltimore: Johns Hopkins University Press, 1985.

Drezner, Daniel W. "Why I'm Not Freaking Out Too Much about the Foreign Funding of American Think Tanks." *Washington Post*, 8 September 2014.

Duggal, Sneh. "Tanks for the Rankings." *Embassy*, 5 February 2014.

Dyck, Rand, and Christopher Cochrane. *Canadian Politics: Critical Approaches*, 7th ed. Toronto: Nelson, 2013.

Dye, Thomas R. *Who's Running America? The Conservative Years*. Englewood Cliffs, NJ: Prentice-Hall, 1986.

Edwards, Lee. *Leading the Way: The Story of Ed Feulner and the Heritage Foundation.* New York: Crown Forum, 2013.
– *The Power of Ideas: The Heritage Foundation at 25 Years.* Ottawa, IL: Jameson Books, 1997.
Ernst, A. "From Liberal Continentalism to Neoconservatism: North American Free Trade and the Politics of the C.D. Howe Institute." *Studies in Political Economy* 39 (1992): 109–40.
Evans, Peter B., Dietrich Rueschemeyer, and Theda Skocpol. *Bringing the State Back In.* Cambridge, MA: Cambridge University Press, 1985.
Flanagan, Tom. *Harper's Team: Behind the Scenes in the Conservative Rise to Power.* Montreal & Kingston: McGill-Queen's University Press, 2009.
Fleshler, Dan. *Transforming America's Israel Lobby: The Limits of Its Power and the Potential for Change.* Herndon, VA: Potomac Books, 2009.
Fraser Institute. "Fraser Institute Top Think Tank in Canada and Now Among Top 20 Worldwide: Annual Global Survey." *Press Release,* 22 January 2015.
– *2013 Annual Report.* Vancouver: The Fraser Institute, 2013.
– *Challenging Perceptions: Twenty-Five Years of Influential Ideas: A Retrospective, 1974–1999.* Vancouver: The Fraser Institute, 1999.
– "What Is a Think Tank?" www.fraserinstitute.org.
Freund, Gerald. *Narcissism and Philanthropy: Ideas and Talent Denied.* New York: Viking, 1996.
Frontier Centre for Public Policy. *2013 Annual Report.* Winnipeg: Frontier Centre for Public Policy, 2013.
Frum, David, and Richard Perle. *An End to Evil: How to Win the War on Terror.* New York: Random House, 2004.
Gailus, Jeff. "Mind Games: Think Tanks Compete for Hearts and Minds – and Influence How Government Acts." *Alberta Views,* March 2009.
Gelb, Alan, Anna Dofasi, Nabil Hashmi, and Lauren Post. "Measuring Think Tank Performance: Updated with 2014 Data." *Center for Global Development Essays,* 17 March 2015. http://www.cgdev.org/publication/measuring-think-tank-performance-updated-2014-data.
Gellner, Winand. "Think Tanks in Germany." In *Think Tanks across Nations,* edited by Diane Stone, Andrew Denham, and Mark Garnett, 82–106. Manchester: Manchester University Press, 1998.
– "Political Think-Tanks and Their Markets in the US: Institutional Setting." *Presidential Studies Quarterly* 25, no. 3 (Summer 1995): 497–510.
Gerson, Jen. "Your Think-Tank Lineup Card: Who Are These Groups That Hold So Much Sway Over Policy?" *National Post,* 22 September 2014.

Ghamari-Tabrizi, Sharon. *The Worlds of Herman Kahn: The Intuitive Science of Thermonuclear War.* Cambridge: Harvard University Press, 2005.

Gill, Stephen. *American Hegemony and the Trilateral Commission.* New York: Cambridge University Press, 1990.

Goar, Carol. "Another Canadian Window on the World Closes." *Toronto Star,* 23 September 2014.

– "Harper Throws National Council of Welfare on the Scrap Heap." *Toronto Star,* 12 April 2012.

Government of Canada. Justice Laws website. http://laws-lois.justice.ca.

– Statistics Canada website. http://www.statscan.gc.ca.

Gray, Colin S. "Think Tanks and Public Policy." *International Journal* 33, no. 1 (Winter 1977–78): 177–94.

Gray Davidson, Osha. *Under Fire: The NRA and the Battle for Gun Control.* New York: Henry Holt, 1993.

Greathead, E.D. "The Antecedents and Origins of the Canadian Institute of International Affairs." In *Empire and Nations: Essays in Honour of Frederic H. Soward,* edited by Harvey L. Dyck and Peter Krosby. Toronto and Vancouver: University of Toronto Press and University of British Columbia Press, 1969.

Greenspan, Edward, and Anthony Wilson-Smith. *Double-Vision: The Inside Story of the Liberals in Power.* Toronto: Doubleday, 1996.

Grose, Peter. *The Inquiry: The Council on Foreign Relations from 1921 to 1996.* New York: Council on Foreign Relations, 1996.

Guralnik, David B. *Webster's New World Dictionary of the American Language,* 2nd college ed. New York: The World Publishing Company, 1970.

Gutstein, Donald. *Harperism: How Stephen Harper and His Think Tank Colleagues Have Transformed Canada.* Toronto: James Lorimer & Company, 2014.

Guy, John James. *People, Politics and Government,* 3rd ed. Scarborough, ON: Prentice-Hall, 1995.

Haas, Peter M., ed. *Knowledge, Power and International Policy Coordination.* Columbia, SC: University of South Carolina Press, 1997.

Hagedorn, Hermann. *Brookings: A Biography.* New York: Macmillan, 1936.

Hager, George. "Bush Shops for Advice at California Think Tank: Ex-White House Stars Fill." *Washington Post,* 8 June 1999.

Hale, Geoffrey. *So Near Yet So Far: The Public and Hidden Worlds of Canada-US Relations.* Vancouver: UBC Press, 2012.

Halper, Daniel. "Stop Foreign Governments from Buying American Think Tanks." *The Weekly Standard,* 21 September 2014.

Hamburger, Tom. "How Elizabeth Warren Picked Fight with Brookings and Won." *The Washington Post*, 29 September 2015.

Harris, Michael. *Party of One: Stephen Harper and Canada's Radical Makeover*. Toronto: Viking Canada, 2014.

Harrison, Kathryn, and George Hoberg. "Setting the Environmental Agenda in Canada and the United States: The Cases of Dioxin and Radon." *Canadian Journal of Political Science* 24, no. 1 (1991): 3–27.

Heclo, Hugh. "Issue Networks and the Executive Establishment." In *The New American Political System*, edited by Anthony King. Washington, DC: The American Enterprise Institute, 1978.

Hellebust, Lynn, ed. *Think Tank Directory: A Guide to Nonprofit Public Policy Research Organizations*. Topeka, KS: Government Research Service, 1996.

Heritage Foundation. *2013 Financial Statements*. Washington, DC: The Heritage Foundation, 2013.

‒ *1998 Annual Report*. Washington, DC: The Heritage Foundation, 1998.

Hess, Stephen. *Organizing the Presidency*. Washington, DC: Brookings Institution, 1988.

Hinckley, Barbara. *Less Than Meets the Eye: Foreign Policy Making and the Myth of the Assertive Congress*. Chicago: University of Chicago Press, 1994.

Holmes, John. "The CIIA: A Canadian Institution." *Bout de Papier* 7, no. 4 (1990): 9–10.

‒ "Letter to the Rt. Hon. Kenneth Younger, 29 July 1966." Archival File: Canadian Institute of International Affairs 3/6/Can C, Chatham House Archives, London, UK.

Hong, Beth. "Charitable Fraser Institute Received $4.3 Million in Foreign Funding since 2000." *Vancouver Observer*, 30 August 2012.

Hostettler, John N. *Nothing for the Nation: Who Got What out of Iraq*. Evansville, IN: Publius House, 2008.

Institute for Research on Public Policy (IRPP). *2013–2014 Annual Report*. Montreal: IRPP, 2014.

Institute on Governance. www.iog.ca.

Internal Revenue Service. "Requirements for Charities and Non-Profits." www.irs.gov.

International Institute for Sustainable Development. www.iisd.org.

Jenson, Jane. "Commissioning Ideas: Representation and Royal Commissions." In *How Ottawa Spends: Making Change*, edited by Susan D. Phillips, 39–71. Ottawa: Carleton University Press, 1994.

Jérôme-Forget, Monique. "Institute for Research on Public Policy." In *Think Tanks and Civil Societies: Catalysts for Ideas and Actions*, edited by R. Kent

Weaver and James McGann, 87–102. New Brunswick, NJ: Transaction Publishers, 2000.

Kaiser, Robert G., and Ira Chinoy. "How Scaife's Money Powered a Movement." *Washington Post,* 2 May 1999.

Kaplan, Fred. *The Wizards of Armageddon.* New York: Simon and Schuster, 1985.

Kay, Jonathan. *Among the Truthers: North America's Growing Conspiracist Underground.* Toronto: Harper Collins, 2012.

Keenan, Edward. "Why Haven't Any Harper-Friendly Charities Been Scrutinized." *Toronto Star,* 23 January 2015.

Kingdon, John W. *Agendas, Alternatives, and Public Policies.* New York: Harper Collins, 1984.

Kitschelt, Herbert P. "Political Opportunity Structures and Political Protest: Anti-Nuclear Movements in Four Democracies." *British Journal of Political Science* 16 (1986): 57–85.

Knickerbocker, Brad. "Heritage Foundation's Ideas Permeate Reagan Administration." *Christian Science Monitor,* 7 December 1984.

Kolakowski, Leszek. *Main Currents of Marxism: The Founders – The Breakdown – The Golden Age.* New York: W.W. Norton, 2007.

Krasner, Stephen D. *Defending the National Interest: Raw Material Investment and US Foreign Policy.* Princeton: Princeton University Press, 1978.

Kuntz, Fred. "Communications and Impact Metrics for Think Tanks." *CIGI Blog,* 11 July 2013. www.cigionline.org.

Levitz, Stephanie. "Right-Leaning Charities Escape Tax Audits, Broadbent Institute Says." *The Canadian Press,* 21 October 2014.

Lindquist, Evert A. "A Quarter-Century of Think Tanks in Canada." In *Think Tanks Across Nations: A Comparative Approach,* edited by Diane Stone, Andrew Denham, and Mark Garnett, 127–44. Manchester: Manchester University Press, 1998.

– "Citizens, Experts and Budgets: Evaluating Ottawa's Emerging Budget Process." In *How Ottawa Spends 1994–95,* edited by Susan D. Phillips, 91–128. Ottawa: Carleton University Press, 1994.

– "Think Tanks or Clubs? Assessing the Influence and Roles of Canadian Policy Institutes." *Canadian Public Administration* 36, no. 4 (1993): 547–79.

– "Transition Teams and Government Succession: Focusing on the Essentials." In *Taking Power: Managing Government Transitions,* edited by Donald J. Savoie. Toronto: Institute of Public Administration of Canada, 1993.

– "Behind the Myth of Think-Tanks: The Organization and Relevance of Canadian Policy Institutes." PhD dissertation, University of California at Berkeley, 1989.

Lipset, Seymour Martin. *Continental Divide.* New York: Routledge, 1990.

- "Canada and the US: The Cultural Dimension." In *Canada and the United States,* edited by Charles F. Doran and John H. Sigler. Englewood Cliffs, NJ: Prentice-Hall, 1985.

Lipton, Eric. "Proposal Would Require Think Tanks to Disclose Funding by Foreign Governments." *New York Times,* 17 September 2014.

Lipton, Eric, Brooke Williams, and Nicholas Confessore. "Foreign Powers Buy Influence at Think Tanks." *New York Times,* 6 September 2014.

MacCharles, Tonda. "Think-Tank Says It Was Targeted with Tax Audit Because of Its Politics." *Toronto Star,* 5 September 2014.

Macdonald-Laurier Institute. www.macdonaldlaurier.ca.

- *2013 Annual Report.* Ottawa: Macdonald-Laurier Institute, 2013.

Manning Networking Conference 2104. *Next Steps.* Panel entitled "Who Generates Ideas – Think Tanks or Government?" 28 February 2014.

Manny, Carter. "The CIIA, 1928–1939." BA thesis, Harvard University, 1971.

Maraniss, David. *First in His Class: A Biography of Bill Clinton.* New York: Simon and Schuster, 1995.

Martin, Paul, Joe Clark, Ed Broadbent, and Joseph Ingram. "North-South Institute: We've Lost a Canadian Asset." *The Globe and Mail,* 22 September 2014.

Mayer, Jane. "The Kochs v. Cato: Winners and Losers." *The New Yorker,* 27 June 2012.

- *Dark Money: The Hidden History of the Billionaires Behind the Rise of the Radical Right.* New York: Doubleday, 2016.

McCoy, Heath. "Centre's Director Dr David Bercuson Honoured." *University of Calgary Press Release,* 27 November 2014.

McGann, James G. *2014 Global Go To Think Tanks Index Report.* Philadelphia: Think Tanks and Civil Societies Program, University of Pennsylvania, 2015.

- *2013 Global Go To Think Tanks Index Report.* Philadelphia: Think Tanks and Civil Societies Program, University of Pennsylvania, 2014.

- *2012 Global Go To Think Tanks Index Report.* Philadelphia: Think Tanks and Civil Societies Program, University of Pennsylvania, 2013.

- *2011 Global Go To Think Tanks Index Report.* Philadelphia: Think Tanks and Civil Societies Program, University of Pennsylvania, 2012.

- *2010 Global Go To Think Tanks Index Report.* Philadelphia: Think Tanks and Civil Societies Program, University of Pennsylvania, 2011.

- *2009 Global Go To Think Tanks Index Report.* Philadelphia: Think Tanks and Civil Societies Program, University of Pennsylvania, 2010.

- *2008 Global Go To Think Tanks Index Report*. Philadelphia: Think Tanks and Civil Societies Program, University of Pennsylvania, 2009.
- *2007 Global Go To Think Tanks Index Report*. Philadelphia: Think Tanks and Civil Societies Program, University of Pennsylvania, 2008.
- *2006 Global Go To Think Tanks Index Report*. Philadelphia: Think Tanks and Civil Societies Program, University of Pennsylvania, 2007.
- "The Think Tank Index." *Foreign Policy,* January/February 2009.
- *Think Tanks and Policy Advice in the United States*. London: Routledge, 2007.
- *Think Tanks, Catalysts for Ideas in Action: An International Survey*. Tokyo: National Institute for Research Advancement, 1999.
- *The Competition for Dollars, Scholars and Influence in the Public Policy Research Industry*. Lanham, MD: University Press of America, 1995.
- "Academics to Ideologues: A Brief History of the Public Policy Research Industry." *PS: Political Science and Politics* 24, no. 4 (December 1992): 739–40.
McGann, James G., and R. Kent Weaver. *Think Tanks and Civil Societies: Catalysts for Ideas and Action*. New Brunswick, NJ: Transaction Publishers, 2000.
McLeod Group. "North-South Institute Ends with a Whimper." *McLeod Group Blog,* 11 September 2014. www.mcleodgroup.ca.
McLevey, John. "Think Tanks, Funding, and the Politics of Policy Knowledge in Canada." *Canadian Review of Sociology* 51, no. 1 (2014): 54–75.
McNutt, Kathleen, and Gregory Marchildon. "Think Tanks and the Web: Measuring Visibility and Influence." *Canadian Public Policy* 35, no. 2 (2009): 219–36.
McQuaig, Linda. "Harper Ramps Up His War on Independent Thought." *iPolitics,* 17 September 2014.
Mearsheimer, John J., and Stephen M. Walt. *The Israel Lobby and US Foreign Policy*. New York: Farrar, Straus and Giroux, 2007.
Medhora, Rohinton P., and John de Boer. "The Rise and Influence of the Foreign Policy Think Tank." https://www.opencanada.org/features/rise-and-influence-foreign-policy-think-tank/.
Medvetz, Tom. *Think Tanks in America*. Chicago: University of Chicago Press, 2012.
Melton, R.H. "Closing of Dole's Think Tank Raises Questions about Fundraising." *Washington Post,* 18 June 1995.
Mendizabal, Enrique. "Think Tank Accountability: Are They Really Just Hired Guns?" *On Think Tanks,* 10 September 2014. http://onthinktanks.org.
- "Think Tank Rankings and Awards: Rigged, Futile, or Useful?" *On Think Tanks,* 28 July 2014. http://onthinktanks.org.

– "For Profit Think Tanks and Implications for Funders." *On Think Tanks*.
  23 October 2013. https://onthinktanks.org/articles/for-profit-think-tanks-
  and-implications-for-funders/.
– "The Go To Think Tank Index: Two Critiques." *On Think Tanks*, 14 March
  2012. http://onthinktanks.org.
Merelman, R.M. *Partial Visions*. Madison, WI: University of Wisconsin Press,
  1991.
Mills, C. Wright. *The Power Elite*. New York: Oxford University Press,
  1959.
Minsky, Amy. "What Does the Fixed-Election Law Really Mean Anyway?"
  National Post, 19 May 2011.
Misztal, Barbara A. "Public Intellectuals and Think Tanks: A Free Market in
  Ideas." *International Journal of Politics, Culture, and Society* 25, no. 4
  (2012): 127–41.
Montreal Economic Institute. www.iedm.org.
– *2014 Annual Report*. Montreal: Montreal Economic Institute, 2014.
Moore, W. John. "Local Right Thinkers." *National Journal*, 1 October 1988.
Mowat Centre. *2014 Annual Report*. Toronto: Mowat Centre, 2014.
Muggah, Robert, and Taylor Owen. "Decline in Canadian Think Tanks
  Couldn't Come at a Worse Time." *Toronto Star*, 9 October 2013.
Newsom, David D. *The Public Dimension of Foreign Policy*. Bloomington, IN:
  Indiana University Press, 1996.
Orlans, Harold. *The Nonprofit Research Institute: Its Origin, Operation,
  Problems and Prospects*. New York: McGraw-Hill, 1972.
Osendarp, J.E. "A Decade of Transition: The Canadian Institute of
  International Affairs, 1928–1939." MA thesis, York University, 1983.
Paikin, Steve. "Think Tanks and Policy Planks." *The Agenda with Steve Paikin*.
  Aired on TVO, 17 November 2014.
Pal, Leslie A., and R. Kent Weaver, eds. *The Government Taketh Away: The
  Politics of Pain in the United States and Canada*. Washington, DC:
  Georgetown University Press, 2003.
Parkland Institute. www.parklandinstitute.ca.
Parmar, Inderjeet. *Foundations of the American Century: The Ford, Carnegie,
  and Rockefeller Foundations in the Rise of American Power*. New York:
  Columbia University Press, 2012.
Patterson Law. "Charitable and Non-Profit Organizations and Canada's
  Income Tax Act." www.pattersonlaw.ca.
Pautz, Hartwig. *Think Tanks, Social Democracy and Social Policy*. Basingstoke:
  Palgrave Macmillan, 2012.
Pembina Institute. www.pembina.org.

Perloff, James. *The Shadows of Power: The Council on Foreign Relations and the American Decline.* Appleton, WI: Western Islands, 1988.

Peschek, Joseph G. *Policy Planning Organizations: Elite Agendas and America's Rightward Turn.* Philadelphia, PA: Temple University Press, 1987.

Pirie, Madsen. *Think Tank: The Story of the Adam Smith Institute.* London: Biteback Publishing, 2012.

Pollack, Kenneth. *The Threatening Storm: What Every American Needs to Know before an Invasion in Iraq.* New York: Random House, 2003.

Posner, Richard A. *Public Intellectuals: A Study of Decline.* Cambridge: Harvard University Press, 2009.

Powell, S. Steven. *Covert Cadre: Inside the Institute for Policy Studies.* Ottawa, IL: Green Hill Publishers, 1988.

Presthus, Robert A. *Cross-National Perspectives.* Leiden: E.J. Brill, 1977.

Prospect. "Think Tank Awards 2014: The Results." *Prospect,* 17 July 2014.

Public Policy Forum. www.ppforum.com.

Putnam, Robert D. *Bowling Alone: The Collapse and Revival of American Community.* New York: Simon and Schuster, 2001.

RAND. *An Introduction to RAND: The Reach of Reason.* Santa Monica, CA: RAND, 1999.

Rich, Andrew. "Think Tanks as Sources of Expertise for Congress and the Media." Paper presented at the annual meetings of the American Political Science Association, Boston, September 1998.

– "Perceptions of Think Tanks in American Politics: A Survey of Congressional Staff and Journalists." *Burson-Marstellar Worldwide Report,* December 1997.

Rich, Andrew, and R. Kent Weaver. "Advocates and Analysts: Think Tanks and the Politicization of Expertise." In *The Development of the Social Sciences in the United States and Canada: The Role of Philanthropy,* edited by Theresa Richardson and Donald Fisher. Stanford, CA: Ablex Publishing Corporation, 1999.

– "Think Tanks, the Media and the Policy Process." Paper presented at the 1997 annual meetings of the American Political Science Association, Washington, DC, August 1997.

Richardson, Theresa, and Donald Fisher, eds. *The Development of the Social Sciences in the United States and Canada: The Role of Philanthropy.* Stanford, CA: Ablex Publishing Corporation, 1999.

Ritchie, R.S. *An Institute for Research on Public Policy: A Study of Recommendations.* Ottawa: Information Canada, 1971.

Roach, Kent. *September 11: Consequences for Canada.* Montreal & Kingston: McGill-Queen's University Press, 2003.

Robinson, William H. "Public Think Tanks in the United States: The Special
Case of Legislative Support Agencies." Paper presented at the conference
"Think Tanks in the USA and Germany," University of Pennsylvania,
Philadelphia, 1993.

Rogers, Kaleigh. "Only About 52 per Cent of Electorate Cast Ballots in
Ontario Election." *The Globe and Mail*, 13 June 2014.

Ross Joynt, Carol. "One of Washington's Oldest Think Tanks Celebrates a
$100 Million New Building." *Washingtonian*, 22 October 2013.

Saloma, John S. *Ominous Politics: The New Conservative Labyrinth*.
New York: Hill and Wang, 1984.

Samaan, Jean-Loup. *The Rand Corporation (1989–2009): The Reconfiguration
of Strategic Studies in the United States*. Basingstoke: Palgrave Macmillan,
2012.

Saunders, Charles B. *The Brookings Institution: A Fifty Year History*.
Washington, DC: Brookings Institution, 1966.

Savoie, Donald J. *Breaking the Bargain: Public Servants, Ministers, and
Parliament*. Toronto: University of Toronto Press, 2003.

Schlesinger, Arthur Meier. *The Imperial Presidency*. Boston: Houghton Mifflin,
1989.

Schmidt, Eric. "A Cadre of Familiar Foreign Policy Experts Is Putting Its
Imprint on Bush." *New York Times*, 23 December 1999.

Schneider, Mark, and Paul Teske. "Toward a Theory of the Political Entrepreneur: Evidence from Local Government." *American Political Science Review*
86 (1992): 737–47.

Schulman, Daniel. *Sons of Wichita: How the Koch Brothers Became America's
Most Powerful and Private Dynasty*. New York: Grand Central Publishing,
2014.

Schulzinger, Robert D. *The Wise Men of Foreign Affairs: The History of the
Council on Foreign Relations*. New York: Columbia University Press,
1984.

Scott, Janny. "Intellectuals Who Became Influential: The Manhattan Institute
Has Nudged New York to the Right." *New York Times*, 12 May 1997.

Sealander, Judith. *Private Wealth and Public Life: Foundation Philanthropy
and the Reshaping of American Social Policy from the Progressive Era to the
New Deal*. Baltimore, MD: Johns Hopkins University Press, 1997.

Seccareccia, Mario, and Louis-Phillipe Rochon. "Update: A Petition of
Academics against the CCPA Audit." *The Progressive Economics Forum*.
11 September 2014.

Selee, Andrew. *What Should Think Tanks Do? A Strategic Guide to Policy
Impact*. Stanford, CA: Stanford University Press, 2013.

Shoup, Laurence H. *Wall Street's Think Tank: The Council on Foreign Relations and the Empire of Neoliberal Geopolitics, 1976–2014*. New York: Monthly Review Press, 2015.

Shoup, Laurence H., and William Minter. *Imperial Brain Trust: The Council of Foreign Relations and the United States Foreign Policy*. New York: Monthly Review Press, 1977.

Silk, Leonard, and Mark Silk. *The American Establishment*. New York: Basic Books, 1980.

Silverstein, Ken. "Pay to Play Think Tanks: Institutional Corruption and the Industry of Ideas." 15 June 2014. www.ethics.harvard.edu.

Smith, Bruce L.R. *The Rand Corporation: Case Study of a Nonprofit Advisory Corporation*. Cambridge, MA: Harvard University Press, 1966.

Smith, James A. *Strategic Calling: The Center for Strategic and International Studies 1962–92*. Washington, DC: Center for Strategic and International Studies, 1993.

– *Brookings at Seventy-Five*. Washington, DC: The Brookings Institution, 1991.

– *The Idea Brokers: Think Tanks and the Rise of the New Policy Elite*. New York: The Free Press, 1991.

Smith, Jean Edward. *Eisenhower in War and Peace*. New York: Random House, 2012.

– *George Bush's War*. New York: Henry Holt & Co., 1992.

Soanes, Catherine, and Sara Hawker, eds. *Compact Oxford English Dictionary of Current English*, 3rd rev. ed. Oxford: Oxford University Press, 2008.

Sowell, Thomas. *Intellectuals and Society*, rev. ed. New York: Basic Books, 2012.

Splane, Richard. *75 Years of Community Service to Canada: Canadian Council on Social Development, 1920–1995*. Ottawa: Canadian Council on Social Development, 1996.

Stairs, Denis. "Public Opinion and External Affairs: Reflections on the Domestication of Canadian Foreign Policy." *International Journal* 33, no. 1 (Winter 1977–78): 128–49.

Statistics Canada. "Earned Doctorates, by Field of Study and Sex, Canada, 2005." In *Education in Canada, 1997*. Ottawa: Supply and Services, 2005.

Steelman, Aaron. "Review of *Do Think Tanks Matter? Assessing the Impact of Public Policy Institutes*." *Cato Journal* 23, no. 1 (Spring/Summer 2003).

Stefancic, Jean, and Richard Delgado. *No Mercy: How Conservative Think Tanks Changed America's Social Agenda*. Philadelphia: Temple University Press, 1966.

Stone, Diane. *Banking on Knowledge: The Genesis of the Global Development Network*. London: Routledge, 2003.

 – *Capturing the Political Imagination: Think Tanks and the Policy Process.*
London: Frank Cass, 1996.

Stone, Diane, Andrew Denham, and Mark Garnett, eds. *Think Tanks across
Nations: A Comparative Approach.* Manchester: Manchester University
Press, 1998.

Struyk, Raymond J. *Managing Think Tanks: Practical Guidance for Managing
Organizations.* Budapest: Central European University Press, 2005.

Swanson, J. "Brain Power: Bush Aligns with Hoover Think Tank." *Dallas
Morning News,* 11 August 1999.

Talbott, Strobe. "A Message from Strobe Talbott, President of the Brookings
Institution." *Brookings Institution News Release,* 7 September 2014.

Tapp, Stephen. "What Can a Little Birdie (Twitter) Tell Us about Think Tank
Ideology?" *Blog Post–IRPP,* 19 November 2014.

Taylor, Peter Shawn. "Think Tank Rankings Prove to Be Controversial."
Maclean's, 29 March 2011.

Think Tank Watch. "AEI's New Headquarters to Cost $50 Million."
4 February 2014.

 – "Think Tank Awards & Rankings: A Futile Exercise?" 22 July 2014.

 – "Think Tanks Rush to Defend Funding Policies Amid NYT Report." 7 September 2014.

 – "New House Rules Go after Think Tank Funding." 6 January 2015.

Thompson, John Herd, and Stephen J. Randall. *Canada and the United States:
Ambivalent Allies.* Montreal & Kingston: McGill-Queen's University Press,
2008.

Thunert, Martin W. "Expert Policy Advice in Germany." In *Policy Expertise in
Contemporary Democracies,* edited by Stephen Brooks, Dorota Stasiak, and
Tomasz Zyro. Aldershot: Ashgate, 2012.

Tivnan, Edward: *The Lobby: Jewish Political Power and American Foreign
Policy.* New York: Simon and Schuster, 1987.

Transparify. http://www.transparify.org/.

Troy, Tevi. "Devaluing the Think Tank." *National Affairs* no. 10 (Winter 2012):
75–90.

Truman, David B. *The Governmental Process: Political Interests and Public
Opinion.* New York: Alfred A. Knopf, 1951.

US House of Representatives, Office of the Clerk. "Lobbying Disclosure."
http://www.lobbyingdisclosure.house.gov.

 – House Resolution 5, 114th Congress, 1st Session, 5 January 2015.

Valpy, Michael. "Balsillie's Disappointing Foray into Global Affairs." *The
Globe and Mail,* 16 December 2009.

Vanderbilt Television and News Archive. http://tvnews.vanderbilt.edu.

Vanier Institute of the Family. www.familyforum.com.
– 2013 Annual Report. Ottawa: Vanier Institute of the Family, 2013.
Van Slambrouck, Paul. "California Think Tank Acts as Bush 'Brain Trust.'"
    Christian Science Monitor, 2 July 1999.
Wallace, William. "Between Two Worlds: Think-Tanks and Foreign Policy." In
    Two Worlds of International Relations: Academics, Practitioners and the
    Trade in Ideas, edited by Christopher Hill and Pamela Beshoff, 139–63.
    London: Routledge, 1994.
Weaver, R. Kent. "Think Tanks." In Encyclopedia of US Foreign Relations,
    edited by Bruce W. Jentleson and Thomas G. Paterson, 194–5. New York:
    Oxford University Press, 1997.
– "The Changing World of Think Tanks." PS: Political Science and Politics 22,
    no. 2 (September 1989): 563–78.
Weiss, Carol H. Organizations for Policy Analysis: Helping Government
    Think. Newbury Park, CA: Sage Publications, 1992.
Wellesley Institute. www.wellesleyinstitute.org.
– Strategic Plan FY14–FY18. Toronto: Wellesley Institute, 2014.
Williams, Brooke, Eric Lipton, and Alicia Parlapiano. "Foreign Government
    Contributions to Nine Think Tanks." New York Times, 7 September 2014.
Williams, Brooke, and Ken Silverstein. "Meet the Think Tank Scholars Who
    Are Also Beltway Lobbyists." New Republic, 10 May 2013.
Wiseman, Nelson. The Public Intellectual in Canada. Toronto: University of
    Toronto Press, 2013.
Wilson, James Q. American Government: Brief Version, 13th ed. New Jersey:
    Wadsworth, 2011.
Yakabuski, Konrad. "Think Tanks Need to Show Us the Money." The Globe
    and Mail, 9 February 2015.
Young, Lisa, and Joanna Everitt, eds. Advocacy Groups. Vancouver: UBC
    Press, 2005.

Index

The letter *f* or *t* following a page number denotes a figure or a table.

advocacy, think tanks and, 12, 15, 28–30, 36, 40, 53, 60–1, 66, 83, 92, 159, 161, 163. *See also* political advocacy, think tanks and

advocacy think tanks, 38–9, 42–4, 56, 58, 87, 97, 137, 164–5, 233, 262

AEI (American Enterprise Institute for Public Policy Research), 8, 18, 58, 71, 95, 110, 117, 126, 132, 137, 331n17

AIMS (Atlantic Institute for Market Studies), 46, 49, 63–4, 131, 141, 165, 167, 175–6, 179–81, 246, 275t, 280t, 288t, 292t, 298t, 303t, 311t, 317t; *Beacon*, 175; and Marco Navarro-Génie, 49t, 131, 174, 176. *See also* Crowley, Brian Lee

APEC (Atlantic Provinces Economic Council), 46t, 49t, 56, 175, 288t

APFC (Asia Pacific Foundation of Canada), 46t, 167–70, 173, 275t, 277f, 279t, 283–5f, 288t, 292t, 297t, 304t, 311t, 317t; and Stewart Beck, 49t, 168–69

Balsillie, Jim, 54, 64, 219, 222, 225, 227; Balsillie Centre for Excellence, 222; Balsillie School of International Affairs, 54, 88, 166, 222–3, 340n45; and Mike Lazaridis, 64, 222; Research in Motion (RIM), 54, 64, 219, 222, 225. *See also* CIC; CIGI

Battle, Ken, 49, 63, 129–30, 137, 139, 194–5, 197, 336n39. *See also* Caledon Institute

Broadbent Institute, 18, 62, 101, 110, 167, 248, 321n4; and Ed Broadbent, 18

Brookings, Robert, 26, 39, 45, 84, 134

Brookings Institution, 3–4, 8, 16, 28, 34, 39–41, 44, 52, 59, 71, 77, 94, 97, 103, 107, 115, 128, 130–1, 142–3, 153, 158, 160, 163–4, 238–9, 331n17, 333n15; founding of, 26, 46, 52; Institute for Government Research, 18, 52; and

Robert Litan, 98; and Strobe
Talbott, 52, 97–8, 116–17, 136
Bush, George H.W., 76, 110
Bush, George W., 53, 76, 102, 104,
110, 126, 137, 149, 335n24

Caledon Institute, 9, 11, 46t, 49t,
63–4, 129, 131, 137, 155, 167,
194–7, 276t, 280t, 288t, 290t,
291f, 292t, 294t, 296f, 297t, 300t,
302f, 303t, 308t, 310f, 311t, 313f,
314t, 316f, 316t ; and Alan
Broadbent, 194–5. See also Battle,
Ken; Maytree Foundation
Canada Elections Act (1996), 335n27
Canada Institute, 90; and Laura
Dawson, 90
Carnegie, Andrew, 26, 39–40, 45, 84,
134
Carter, Jimmy, 56, 137; Carter Center
and Emory University, 62
Cato Institute, 59, 133
CBOC (Conference Board of
Canada), 16, 41, 44, 47t, 50t, 52,
56, 59, 85, 92, 95, 103, 131, 164,
167, 228–31, 275t, 277–8f, 279t,
283–7f, 288t, 290t, 291f, 292t,
293f, 294t, 296f, 297t, 299f, 300t,
302f, 303t, 307t, 310f, 311t, 313f,
314t, 316f, 317t, 318f; and Daniel
Muzyka, 50t, 228; plagiarism,
92–3
CCF (Canadian Constitution
Foundation), 46t, 49t
CCPA (Canadian Centre for Policy
Alternatives), 4, 20, 46t, 49t, 60,
71, 98, 108, 127, 167, 175, 203–4,
213–14, 275t, 277–8f, 279t, 283–
7f, 288t, 290t, 291f, 292t, 293f,
292t, 296f, 297t, 299f, 300t, 302f,

303t, 307t, 310f, 311t, 313f, 315t,
316f, 317t, 318f, 321n4; CRA audit
of, 319n5, 323n31, 331n28; and
Bruce Campbell, 49t, 128, 203,
211; The Monitor, 204, 213–4; and
New Democratic Party (NDP), 108,
127–8, 332n3. See also CRA
CCSD (Canadian Council on Social
Development), 18, 46t, 49t, 54, 59,
128, 167, 194, 214–6, 275t, 280t,
288t, 290t, 292t, 294t, 297t, 299f,
300t, 302f, 303t, 307t, 310f, 311t,
314t, 316f, 317t, 318f, 327n31;
and Peggy Taillon, 49t, 214–15
CDFAI (Canadian Defence and
Foreign Affairs Institute), 8, 47t,
49t, 64, 141–4, 167, 216–17, 218,
220, 275t, 280t, 286f, 288t, 292t,
293t, 297t, 303t, 305f, 311t, 317t;
and David Bercuson, 64, 141–4,
217, 337. See also CGAI
C.D. Howe Institute, 9, 18, 41, 46t,
49t, 59, 62, 71, 85, 89, 117, 129,
139, 142, 167, 175, 181–3, 189,
193, 195, 203, 239, 256, 286–7f,
288t, 290t, 291f, 292t, 293f, 294t,
296f, 297t, 299f, 300t, 302f, 303t,
305f, 307t, 310f, 311t, 313f, 314t,
316f, 317t, 321n4; and William
B.P. Robson, 49t, 181–2, 184,
186, 197
CEA (Canadian Economics
Association), 16, 166, 325n4
CEIP (Carnegie Endowment for
International Peace), 8, 26, 70, 94,
331n17; founding of, 18, 45
Center for American Progress, 19, 25,
29, 91, 131, 137
Center for Global Development, 4,
34, 65, 69, 147, 338n24

Centre for Foreign Policy Studies, 85
CFR (Council on Foreign Relations),
    8, 12, 18, 52, 77, 155
CGAI (Canadian Global Affairs
    Institute), 8, 47t, 49t, 64, 141, 167,
    216, 337n2; and R.S. Millar, 49t,
    216
Chrétien, Jean, 225; government of,
    58
CIC (Canadian International
    Council), 8, 18, 47t, 50t, 53–4, 59,
    142, 167, 217, 219–22, 275t, 279t,
    283–7f, 303t, 305f, 312t, 317t,
    318f; and Jim Balsillie, 54, 219,
    327n30, 339n38; and Jo-Ann
    Davis, 50t, 219; International
    Journal, 219; OpenCanada.org,
    50t, 219
CIDA (Canadian International
    Development Agency), 42, 193, 244
CIFAR (Canadian Institute for
    Advanced Research), 47t, 60, 275t,
    280t, 288t
CIGI (Centre for International
    Governance Innovation), 8–9, 13,
    41, 47t, 50t, 54, 64–5, 88–9, 92,
    95, 103, 115, 118, 131, 136, 142,
    148–50, 166–7, 217, 222–3, 226,
    228, 238, 275t, 277–8f, 281t, 288,
    292t, 298t, 304t, 312t, 317t; and
    Jim Balsillie, 340n45; and
    Rohinton Medhora, 50t, 98, 222,
    228, 331n26; and York University,
    possible censure of, 223
CIIA (Canadian Institute of
    International Affairs), 8, 18, 53–4,
    142, 219, 276t, 281t, 326n26,
    327n29. See also CIC; RIIA
CISS (Canadian Institute of Strategic
    Studies), 54, 59, 219, 275t, 279t,

    283–7f, 288t, 292t, 298t, 303t,
    305f, 312t, 317t, 318f. See also
    CIC
Clemens, Jason, 85, 98, 212, 235;
    and The Agenda with Steve Paikin,
    148, 335n33. See also Fraser
    Institute
Clinton, Bill, 76, 98, 137
CPRN (Canadian Policy Research
    Networks, Inc.), 63–4, 130, 276t,
    280t, 288t, 290t, 291f, 292t, 293f,
    294t, 296f, 297t, 299f, 300t, 302f,
    303t, 309t, 312t, 315t, 316f, 317t,
    318f
CRA (Canada Revenue Agency):
    Policy Statement CPS-022, 22;
    think tanks, audit of, 19, 98–9,
    151, 319n5, 323n31, 331n28;
    think tanks, charitable status, 18,
    20, 22, 25, 33, 116, 323n31; think
    tanks, permissible political activity,
    19, 21–3; think tanks, prohibited
    political activity, 22–3, 323n31
Crowley, Brian Lee, 183, 190, 192;
    and AIMS, 64, 141, 175, 246; and
    MLI, 64, 131, 140, 175, 246–7
CSE (Citizens for a Sound Economy
    Foundation), 62, 133. See also
    Empower America; FreedomWorks
CSIS (Center for Strategic and
    International Studies), 3–4, 55–6,
    94–5, 128, 142, 331n19, 333n15
CSLS (Centre for the Study of Living
    Standards), 47t, 50t, 63
CTF (Canadian Tax Foundation), 47t,
    50t, 56, 59, 276t, 280t, 288t, 290t,
    292t, 295t, 298t, 301t, 304t, 308t,
    310f, 311t, 314t, 316f, 317t
CUI (Canadian Urban Institute), 47t,
    50t, 275t, 280t, 288t

CWF (Canada West Foundation), 9,
13, 46t, 49t, 60, 85, 131, 167, 198–
9, 202–3, 275t, 277–8f, 279t, 283–
7f, 288t, 290t, 291f, 292t, 294t,
296f, 298t, 300t, 302f, 304t, 308t,
310f, 311t, 314t, 316f, 317t, 318f;
and Dylan Jones, 49t, 198, 201

Dalhousie University, 85. *See also*
Centre for Foreign Policy Studies
donations and donors, 5, 7–8, 11, 15,
19, 25, 31, 33–4, 52, 67, 69–71,
73, 92–3, 97–8, 100–1, 110, 112–
19, 122, 132–3, 140, 145, 150,
161, 164, 169, 176, 183, 195,
204, 220, 249, 252, 255–6, 262,
322n16, 324n51, 331n16, 331n25,
336n49. *See also* fundraising, think
tanks and
Donner Foundation, 174, 183
Dying with Dignity, charitable status,
loss of, 323n31

ECC (Economic Council of Canada),
41, 57–8, 63, 135, 163, 276t, 281t
Eisenhower, Dwight, 67, 328n2
elite theory, 66–7, 80, 160
Empower America, 62, 133. *See also*
Citizens for a Sound Economy
Foundation; FreedomWorks
epistemic communities, 77–8

FCPP (Frontier Centre for Public
Policy), 47t, 50t, 63, 167, 236–7,
275t, 280t, 288t; and Peter Holle,
50, 236
foreign policy, think tanks and, 5, 8,
11, 13, 17, 25, 29, 34, 40, 42,
52–4, 56–9, 73, 75–6, 80, 100–2,
105, 111, 113–14, 122, 124, 126,

132, 136, 144, 153, 155–6, 162,
164, 166, 168, 219, 246, 327n27
Fraser Institute, 9, 13, 29, 44, 47t,
50t, 60–1, 71, 85, 92, 95, 98, 114,
135, 139, 142–4, 148, 153–4, 165,
167, 175, 195, 203, 206, 232–5,
256, 275t, 277–8f, 279t, 283–7f,
288t, 290t, 291f, 292t, 293f, 294t,
296f, 297t, 299f, 300t, 302f, 303t,
307t, 310f, 311t, 313f, 314t, 316f,
317t, 318f, 321n4; as advocacy
think tank, 44; as charitable organization, 18, 321n12; and conservatism, 20, 104, 127, 146, 332n3,
335n33; CRA audit of, 319n5;
Fraser Forum, 233, 235. *See also*
Clemens, Jason; Veldhuis, Niels
FreedomWorks, 62, 133
fundraising, think tanks and, 22, 83,
138, 233, 238. *See also* donations
and donors

GDN (Global Development
Network), 6
Georgetown University, 39
government relations firms, 17–18,
36–7, 106, 152; Global Public
Affairs, 36; Hillwatch, 36; Policy
Concepts, 36

Harper government: 4, 19, 42, 64–5,
99, 102, 104, 127, 132, 242, 248;
and Bill C-51 (Anti-Terrorism Act),
110, 333n11; think tanks, relations
with, 162–3, 319n5, 323n27,
323n31
Harper, Stephen, 65, 171, 173, 183–5,
187, 196, 199, 201–2, 217, 224,
226, 231, 234, 242
Harrison, Trevor, 51t, 255–6, 258

Harvard University, 45, 52, 88, 169
Heritage Foundation, 8, 19, 25, 28, 34, 53, 71, 77, 80, 85, 95, 97, 100, 107, 110, 116, 125, 128, 131, 133, 137, 153, 158, 160, 333n15; as advocacy think tank, 44; and Edwin Feulner, 28, 96, 134, 154; founding of, 20, 58; Heritage Action for America (Heritage Action), 25; and Paul Weyrich, 28, 96
Hoover, Herbert, 26, 39, 45, 84
Hoover Institution, 18, 40, 52, 70, 115, 126, 131, 137
Hudson Institute, 55, 83

IISD (International Institute for Sustainable Development), 48t, 51t, 168, 243–5, 275t, 281t, 288t, 292t, 297t, 303t, 311t, 313f, 317t; and Scott Vaughan, 51t, 243
Imagine Canada, 46t, 49t, 59; Canadian Centre for Philanthropy, 46t, 59, 328n48
Income Tax Act (Canada), 18, 70, 98, 322n13–14; non-profit organizations, 160, 322n14
interest groups, 4, 10, 18, 20, 21, 31–2, 37, 68, 72–4, 80–2, 100–3, 105, 108, 119, 122, 152, 159–60; definition of, 33–34
IOG (Institute on Governance), 48t, 51t, 60, 167, 241–2, 288t, 340n66; and Maryantonett Flumian, 51t, 241
IPR (Institute of Pacific Relations), 18, 53; Canada and first meeting of, 326n26
IPS (Institute for Policy Studies), 56, 71

Iraq War, 53, 102, 104, 218, 225
IRPP (Institute for Research on Public Policy), 9, 13, 27, 41, 48t, 59–60, 63, 85, 89, 115, 131, 142, 163, 167, 175, 238–40, 275t, 277–8f, 279t, 283–7f, 288t, 290t, 291f, 292t, 294t, 296f, 297t, 300t, 302f, 304t, 308t, 310f, 311t, 314t, 316f, 317t, 318f, 332n3, 333n21; and Graham Fox, 51t, 238; Policy Options, 239–41
IRS (Internal Revenue Service): 19, 24–5, 35; Internal Revenue Code (US), 24, 70; Section 501(c)(3), 19, 24–5, 322n15; Section 501(c)(4), 19, 25; think tank charitable status, 19

Johns Hopkins University, 45, 94
Johnson, Lyndon B., 55, 327n33

Kingdon, John, 78–80, 134. See also Stairs, Denis
Krasner, Stephen, 74–5, 80–1

Lindquist, Evert, 43, 57, 138, 229; and epistemic communities, 77
lobbying: 5, 10, 17–18, 24, 52–3, 70, 82, 97, 101–3, 105, 116, 122, 152, 159–60, 190, 324n51, 334n6; lobby groups, organizations, 62, 92; Lobbying Act (Canada), 34; Lobbying Disclosure Act (US), 34; lobbying firms, 32, 34–5

Mackenzie Institute, 48t, 51t, 60, 275t, 280t, 286f, 288t, 290t, 292t, 295t, 297t, 301t, 304t, 308t, 310f, 312t, 315t, 317t; and Andrew Majoran, 51t

Manning Centre for Building
Democracy, 15–16, 18, 61–2, 101,
110, 167, 321n4; Manning
Foundation, 16, 61–2; Manning
Networking Conference, 61, 101,
146, 332n32
Manning, Preston, 16, 18, 61, 263
Maytree Foundation, 63, 132, 195.
See also Caledon Institute
McGann, James, 16; The Global Go
To Think Tanks Index Report, 7,
16, 38, 141, 143–4, 148, 166, 217,
233, 246, 333n18, 337n9; Think
Tanks and Civil Societies Program
(University of Pennsylvania), 7, 16;
and think tank typology, 39, 320n9
Medhora, Rohinton, 50t, 98, 222,
228, 331n26
media, think tanks and, 3, 8–9, 11,
14, 23, 33, 43–4, 58, 64, 70, 73–5,
80, 86, 92, 95–7, 99–100, 106,
111–15, 119, 121, 130–1, 133,
139–40, 142, 145, 147, 150–5,
157, 161, 165, 170, 176, 181–3,
195, 199, 204, 217, 229, 233, 236,
239, 246, 249, 252, 256, 258–9,
265–6, 275–6t, 277–8f, 288–9f,
319n4
MEI (Montreal Economic Institute),
48t, 51t, 63, 71, 168, 249–51,
275t, 277–8f, 279t, 283–5f, 288t;
and Michel Kelly-Gagnon, 51t, 249
Mendizabal, Enrique, 7, 69, 322n16,
324n51, 327n27
MLI (Macdonald-Laurier Institute),
48t, 64, 129, 131, 140, 168, 175,
217, 246–9, 277–8f, 279t, 283–4f,
288t, 292t, 293f, 297t, 299f, 303t,
311t, 317t; Inside Policy, 246; The

MLI Leading Indicator, 246. See
also Crowley, Brian Lee
Mowat Centre, 9, 41, 48t, 51t, 64,
166, 168, 251–4, 275t, 280t, 288t,
292t, 293f, 297t, 303t, 305f, 311t,
317t; and Matthew Mendelsohn,
51t, 251, 253–4
Mulroney, Brian, 64, 243; government of, 41, 58, 64, 163, 194

NAFTA (North American Free Trade
Agreement), 34, 108, 188, 213,
257, 332n5
Nanjing University, 6
Nixon, Richard, 76; (Nixon) Center
for Peace and Freedom, 62
NPA (National Planning Association),
56
NRA (National Rifle Association),
122, 334n5
NSI (North-South Institute), 60, 63,
115, 130, 142–3, 276t, 281t, 288t,
290t, 291f, 292t, 294t, 296f, 297t,
300t, 303t, 309t, 311t, 315t, 317t;
closure of, 4, 8, 42, 59, 99, 132,
319n4, 331n29; and Roy
Culpepper, 42. See also Trudeau,
Pierre Elliott

Obama, Barack, 64, 76, 80, 109, 126,
137, 184, 221, 224, 226
On Think Tanks (blog). See
Mendizabal, Enrique

Parkland Institute, 41, 48t, 51t, 64,
71, 89, 166, 168, 255–7, 275t,
280t, 286f, 288t; and Trevor
Harrison, 51t, 255–6, 258
Patriot Act, 110, 333n11

PCO (Privy Council Office), 58, 106, 122, 128, 334n3

Pearson Peacekeeping Centre, closure of, 8

Pearson-Shoyama Institute, 62, 276t, 282t, 290t, 292t, 295t, 298t, 301t, 304t, 309t, 312t, 315t, 317t

Pembina Institute, 48t, 51t, 60, 168, 258–61, 275t, 277–8f, 279t, 283–7f, 288t; and Ed Whittingham, 51t, 258–9

Persian Gulf, US invasion of, 76

philanthropic foundations, think tanks and, 5, 7–8, 44, 67, 69–71, 100, 106, 110, 115–16, 132, 326n18, 326n25. See also donations and donors

pluralism, 66–8, 72–4, 78, 80, 160; US tradition of, 329n16

PMO (Prime Minister's Office), 106, 122, 127, 211, 334n3

PNAC (Project for the New American Century), 102, 104, 110

policy clubs, 43, 61

policy-making and policy-makers, 3, 8–10, 13, 15, 18, 92, 95–7, 100, 102, 104–12, 114–16, 118–20, 122–5, 129–30, 133–4, 136–9, 146, 148, 150–9; 161–2, 165, 181–3, 194–5, 204, 214, 217, 229, 238, 246–7, 252, 262, 265, 269, 329n16, 331n19

policy networks, 5, 118, 161

policy research, think tanks and, 26–9, 36–9, 41–4, 45, 53–5, 57–8, 63–4, 86–7, 92, 94, 97, 103–4, 131, 152, 159–61, 163–5, 170, 198, 214, 228, 238–9, 252–3, 255–6, 325n11

policy research institutions, 38, 41, 43–4, 103

political action committees (PACs), 33; super PACs, 33

political advocacy, think tanks and, 5, 10, 19, 26, 28–9, 32, 34, 37, 44, 58, 92, 101–4, 109, 117, 146, 159, 161, 163, 325n11. See also advocacy, think tanks and; advocacy think tanks

PPAC (Private Planning Association of Canada), 56, 182; and C.D. Howe Institute, 59

PPF (Public Policy Forum), 48t, 51t, 60, 124, 128, 138, 168, 261–4, 275t, 277–8f, 279t, 283–7f, 288t, 290t, 291f, 292t, 294t, 296f, 298t, 301t, 304t, 308t, 310f, 312t, 315t, 316f, 317t, 341n94; and Larry Murray, 51t, 261

PRI (Policy Research Initiative), 58. See also Privy Council Office

private sector, 18–19, 34, 40, 45, 57, 59–60, 85–8, 130, 132–7, 165, 168–9, 175, 195, 214, 229, 238, 241, 262

public opinion, think tanks and, 3, 5, 10, 12, 22, 24, 31–2, 34, 37, 58, 61, 66, 70–1, 86, 89, 92, 97, 101, 111, 114, 119, 125, 138–40, 146, 149–50, 151, 153, 159, 166, 195, 229, 233, 256

public policy, think tanks and, 3, 5, 10, 12, 22, 24, 31–2, 37, 58, 69, 70–1, 72, 78–9, 86, 92, 97, 99, 101, 104–5, 111, 119, 125, 128, 138–40, 146, 149–50, 153, 159, 166, 233, 256

Queen's University, 3, 167. See also CIR

RAND Corporation, 8, 16–17, 41, 71,
      77, 103, 131, 142, 158, 160,
      326n13, 326n32, 327n33;
      founding of, 17, 54–5, 321n9
Reagan, Ronald, 5, 28–9, 58, 110,
      126, 137, 154, 320n10
Revenue Canada. *See* Canada
      Revenue Agency
RIIA (Royal Institute of International
      Affairs), 113; Chatham House, 53,
      113, 142–3, 150, 163, 327n27,
      333n18. *See also* CIIA

Sandler, Joseph: think tanks and
      influence on public, 70, 96
Saint Mary's University, 169
SCC (Science Council of Canada), 41,
      57–8, 135, 163, 276t, 281t
Smithsonian Institution, 90
social media: Facebook, 6, 96, 150,
      153, 236, 239, 246, 249; Twitter, 6,
      96, 150, 153, 230, 236, 239, 246,
      249, 332n3; YouTube, 249. *See also*
      social media, think tanks' use of
social media, think tanks' use of, 6,
      11, 33, 91, 95–6, 111, 142, 149,
      204, 330n12. *See also* social media
Stairs, Denis, 78–9, 218
state theory, 74–6, 80; statism, 66, 68,
      74

Taillon, Peggy, 49t, 214–15
Thatcher, Margaret, 5, 320n10
think-and-do tank, 38, 43–4, 61
think tanks: in Asia, 6; in Canada,
      11–13, 17–18, 22, 25–8, 37–9,
      41–5, 46–51t, 53–4, 56–66, 71,
      76–7, 79, 82–5, 89–90, 93–5,
      98–100, 102, 104, 107–8, 111,
      115, 119–20, 121, 123–4, 126–30,

131–3, 135–9, 142–4, 146, 150,
      152, 158–65, 166–7, 181, 194,
      233, 238, 246, 253, 256, 268; in
      China, 6, 166, 244; definition of,
      14–17; in Europe, 4, 6–7, 9, 19, 39,
      79, 115, 142, 150, 222, 327n32;
      for-profit, 19, 322n16; in France,
      166; in Germany, 23, 108, 125,
      323n27, 332n4; as government
      contractors, 38, 41, 54–6; influence
      of, 3, 5, 8, 11–12, 21, 26–9, 31, 35,
      37, 42, 56, 58, 61, 69, 72–3, 75,
      79–80, 84, 90, 92, 96, 99, 103–4,
      111, 113–4, 116, 122, 125–6, 129–
      30, 138–9, 140–1, 145–6, 148–50,
      152–8, 160, 165, 182, 246–7, 252;
      in Japan, 138, 166; legacy-based,
      43, 62, 135; in Mexico, 142–3;
      non-ideological, 20, 322n20; non-
      profit, 18, 24–5, 31, 59–60, 130,
      145, 160, 164, 175, 241, 262, 265,
      268, 322n14; in South Africa, 166;
      study of, 4, 6, 12, 16–17, 21, 26,
      29–30, 32, 34, 37–9, 44–5, 66–9,
      71–2, 74–81, 103–4, 113, 118,
      125, 128, 136–7, 140, 145–6, 149,
      151–6, 159–61, 320n8–9, 325n5,
      326n18, 329n10; in the United
      Kingdom, 4, 9, 166; in the United
      States, 3–4, 6–9, 12–13, 17–19,
      24–6, 29, 34–5, 37–42, 45, 52–4,
      56, 58–63, 65–6, 69–71, 77, 81–4,
      90, 93–5, 97–8, 104, 107–8, 112,
      115–16, 119–5, 127–9, 130–4,
      135–9, 144, 146, 150, 152, 158,
      160–3, 165–6, 238, 244, 322n19,
      330n28, 332n6–7; university-
      based, 16, 86–7, 89. *See also* CRA;
      Income Tax Act; IRS; *specific
      organizations and topics*

Think Tank Watch, 7, 319n7
Transparify, 7, 98, 148
Trudeau, Justin, 63, 162–3, 202, 240, 253; and Global Affairs Canada, 63
Trudeau, Pierre Elliott, 59–60, 63, 32, 162–3, 238; global peace initiative, 135. *See also* North-South Institute
TTI (Think Tank Initiative), 7

University of Alberta, 64, 71, 89, 166, 169, 255. *See also* Parkland Institute
University of British Columbia, 89, 170, 326n26; and Liu Institute for Global Studies, 89
University of Chicago, 45
University of Ottawa, 126
University of Pennsylvania, 7, 16, 144, 147–8
University of Regina, 63
University of Toronto, 54, 64, 88, 166, 192, 219, 251. *See also* CIC; Mowat Centre
University of Victoria, 43, 85; and Centre for Global Studies, 85, 167
University of Waterloo, 41, 88, 166. *See also* CIGI
Urban Institute, 41, 55, 327n33

Vanier, Governor General Georges P., 57, 265; and Madame Pauline Vanier, 57, 265
Vanier Institute of the Family, 9, 48t, 51t, 57, 168, 265–7, 275t, 279t, 283–6f, 288t, 292t, 298t, 304t, 312t, 317t; and Nora Spinks, 265
Veldhuis, Niels, 50t, 61, 144, 146, 154, 232, 319n5; Manning Networking Conference remarks, 146, 330n14, 332n3, 337n21. *See also* Fraser Institute

War on Terror, 80, 110
Weaver, Kent, 125; and think tank typology, 39, 42–3
Wellesley Institute, 48t, 51t, 64, 168, 268–70, 276t, 281t, 288t, 292t, 293f, 297t, 299f, 304t, 311t, 313f, 317t; and Kwame McKenzie, 51t, 268
Wilfrid Laurier University, 41, 88, 166. *See also* CIGI
Williams, Brooke, 52, 97, 116; and Kevin Silverstein, 35
Woodrow Wilson International Center for Scholars, 90

York University, possible censure of, 223